THE OLD FARMER'S ALMANAC

CALCULATED ON A NEW AND IMPROVED PLAN FOR THE YEAR OF OUR LORD

Being 2nd after Leap Year and (until July 4) 242nd year of American Independence

FITTED FOR BOSTON AND THE NEW ENGLAND STATES, WITH SPECIAL CORRECTIONS AND CALCULATIONS TO ANSWER FOR ALL THE UNITED STATES.

Containing, besides the large number of Astronomical Calculations and the Farmer's Calendar for every month in the year, a variety of NEW, USEFUL, & ENTERTAINING MATTER.

ESTABLISHED IN 1792
BY ROBERT B. THOMAS (1766–1846)

All sorts of things and weather / Must be taken in together,
To make up a year / And a Sphere.
–Ralph Waldo Emerson, American writer (1803–82)

Cover design registered U.S. Trademark Office

Copyright © 2017 by Yankee Publishing Incorporated
ISSN 0078-4516

Library of Congress Card No. 56-29681

Cover illustration by Steven Noble • Original wood engraving (above) by Randy Miller

THE OLD FARMER'S ALMANAC • DUBLIN, NH 03444 • 603-563-8111 • ALMANAC.COM

The Country Doctor's
Kitchen Secrets
Handbook

Did you know ... cherries will help you sleep, bananas boost your energy, and baking soda can tenderize meat and stop cancer! Your kitchen is full of proven remedies — right now — to solve countless health and household problems! Oatmeal, cinnamon, vinegar ... even plain old table salt, and so much more! See all these secrets inside *The Country Doctor's Kitchen Secrets Handbook: 1,267 Pantry Prescriptions and Refrigerator Remedies for Almost Every Health and Household Problem* ...

▶ The delicious all-purpose health food you should eat daily!
▶ Eat to beat dementia. 12 fabulous foods to protect memories!
▶ Amazing oil that causes belly fat to slide right off your middle!
▶ How to spend less on groceries — without coupons.
▶ 5 cancer-causing foods to avoid at all costs!

Here's how to order your copy...

Call Toll Free: (800)-226-8024
Use promo code: Q2-4702

Go To: AlmanacCountryDoc.com

Send a Check For:
$9.99 plus $3.00 s/h to:
FC&A, Dept. Q2-4702,
103 Clover Green,
Peachtree City, GA 30269.

All orders will receive a free gift, *THE LITTLE BOOK OF QUICK PANTRY CURES* guaranteed. Order right away!

©FC&A 2017

100% Satisfaction Guaranteed

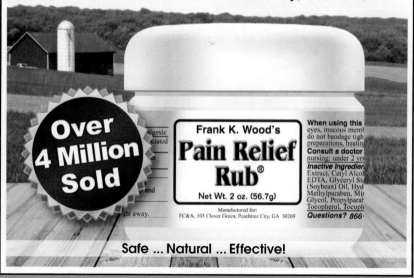

CONTENTS

20

26

42

2018 TRENDS
Forecasts, Facts, and Fascinating Ideas

192

SPECIAL REPORT

GARDENING

NATURE

HISTORY

HOME REMEDIES

WEATHER

MISCELLANY

YOUR LIFE WITH THIS ALMANAC

Last year, to celebrate this Almanac's 225th anniversary, we invited you to tell us what the Almanac means to you. Thanks to everyone who responded! We'd like to share a few of the comments:

• "My Almanac makes my life richer and my thumb greener and my decisions more thoughtful and more planned." –*Paul P.*

• "I have learned that sometimes the old ways [are] the best ways." –*Dimitri K.*

• "The Almanac means tradition, wisdom, pause, and work . . . curiosity and entertainment, information and snickers . . . and when to cut my hair. It's logic and whimsy wrapped in the tried and true." –*Meridien P.*

• "The Almanac was one of my first readers. Seventy-four years later, it is still one of my favorite readers and is my favorite reference." –*Charles R.*

• "My Uncle Stony taught me how to read the charts in the Almanac. . . . When I became a teacher, I made sure that every student knew how to read and use it." –*John J.*

• "Life may be complicated, but as long as you have the Almanac, you have the answers." –*Benita Y.*

• "It's a fantastic link to the world around us." –*Charles T.*

• "It's part of my upbringing, and to this day, I refer to it off and on." –*Lynn T.*

• "My mom and pop live miles away, but the Almanac brings us together." –*Sharon B.*

• "To live a simpler, well-balanced lifestyle, with a side order of humor." –*Grant K.*

• "It's a bit of the past, the present, and the future all rolled up into one." –*Callie S.*

Here's something else we'd like to share: Your daily Almanac is now available on the Amazon Echo and Google Home voice-operated assistants! Say "Ask Farmer's Almanac about today" and get date-specific fun facts and trivia seven times a week. Check it out! We'll be introducing other useful features, too.

And there's this: Beginning with this year, our previous Western and Southern editions will be supplanted by this new, more robust National edition that is usable throughout the United States. If you previously used our Western or Southern edition, we hope you enjoy the improvement.

Thank you for your enthusiasm for, loyalty to, and trust in this Almanac.
–J. S., June 2017

However, it is by our works and not our words that we would be judged. These, we hope, will sustain us in the humble though proud station we have so long held in the name of

Your obedient servant,

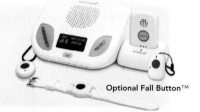

The Future of Farming

by Stacey Kusterbeck

Farming in America is changing, and so are farmers. While 90 percent of U.S. farmers are white men, there's an increasing number of ethnically, racially, and culturally diverse growers. These folks are challenging not only historic statistics but also how food is grown, bought, and sold.

"American farmers today, especially young and beginning farmers, include a growing number of women, people of color, veterans, and people in their second career," says Elanor Starmer, former administrator of the U.S. Department of Agriculture's Agricultural Marketing Service.

The future of farming is bright indeed. We are seeing more . . .

Ethnic diversity

The most recent USDA Census of Agriculture (2012) showed that while minority-owned farms were few, their numbers were growing quickly. The number of nonwhite farmers had risen 15 percent since the previous census (2007), while the population of white farmers had declined 5 percent. The fastest-growing minority farm populations were Asian-Americans (+22 percent), Hispanics (+21 percent), African-Americans (+9 percent), and American Indians or Native Alaskans (+9 percent).

(continued)

ABOUT 150,000 FARMERS AND RANCHERS NATIONWIDE SELL DIRECTLY TO CONSUMERS.

Female Farmers

Nearly 1 million women are working America's lands, generating $12.9 billion in annual agricultural sales. To put it another way, 30 percent of farmers are female. "We are seeing increased attention paid to providing resources to enable women to thrive in the agricultural sector," says Lauren L. Griffeth, extension leadership specialist at University of Georgia's College of Agricultural and Environmental Sciences.

Small and Local Farms

The vast majority of U.S. farms are small (75 percent of them gross less than $50,000 a year), and about 150,000 farmers and ranchers nationwide sell directly to consumers.

The local food movement, strong in the Northeast for years, is taking hold in other regions. "We are starting to see Midwest growers going into farmers' markets," says Jamie M. Cruz of SpringDell Farm in Littleton, Massachusetts. "The community wants to be involved in the farm. It goes beyond their CSA [community-supported agriculture] share. People want to know their farmers."

The "buy local" movement shows no sign of slowing. "There is a large push to drift away from the big box stores that have largely overrun the small local business owner in the course of the last few decades," says New Jersey tree farmer Tyler Cerbo, who recently started a CSA program for a thriving produce portion of his business.

Some farmers insist that the direct-to-consumer trend is more than just smart business. It also shortens the distance—both geographic and personal—between growers and consumers. "We are seeing a return to the farm in this way," says Kirstin Bailey, who operates a CSA at Fox Run Farms in Brainard, Nebraska.

"New" Farmers

About 20 percent of growers have farmed for fewer than 10 years; the 2012 USDA Census of Agriculture counted 40,499 young beginners. Starting out requires more than enthusiasm and determination; significant capital

A Financial Fix for Farmers?

As a means to enable young college graduates to enter the profession of farming, federal legislation has been introduced. The House bill titled The Young Farmer Success Act of 2015 (H.R. 2590) would allow new farm managers and employees to qualify for certain federal student loan forgiveness programs by being designated as "public service employees." The bill failed to reach the House floor in 2015 but was reintroduced in 2017.
–Dr. Ellen Peffley, Texas Tech University

THE "BUY LOCAL" MOVEMENT SHOWS NO SIGN OF SLOWING.

investment—or the ability to borrow money—is needed, due in part to the high cost of land.

"More people would jump into farming if they could see light at the end of the tunnel," says Cruz. "They want to do this, but the door isn't easy to open."

First-generation farmers are coming into the business with new ideas, in some cases shaking up the status quo. Adds Cruz: "Old-timers and seasoned farmers need to be open-minded and welcoming to them."

For some beginning growers, farming is a way to simplify modern life by getting their hands into the dirt and away from the corporate rat race. Raj Sinha of Liberty Farms says that farming is "the hardest and most demanding and unforgiving endeavor you may ever undertake. But if you are truly passionate about agriculture, then—as George Washington believed—farming is the most noble of professions."

Kate Bowen of Meadowdale Farm in Putney, Vermont, echoes this sentiment, calling farming "the most honest way a human being can make a living. No one in their right mind would ever get into agriculture if they saw how hard they were going to work and how much money they were going to lose."

Regardless of their background, many modern-day growers chose farming for the simplest of reasons: They like it better than any other job. ■

Young Farmers, Unite!

Farming organizations designed specifically to tackle challenges that young farmers encounter have been formed in recent years with the goal of facilitating a new generation of successful, young, independent farmers. One such group is The National Young Farmers Coalition (NYFC; youngfarmers.org). The NYFC is a nonprofit organization sponsored by The Center for Rural Affairs.

—Peffley

Stacey Kusterbeck compiles our annual Trends section of "forecasts, facts, and fascinating ideas." She lives in New York State.

RAJ SINHA

WARREN BROCKMAN

TENISIO SEANIMA

AMANDA FREUND

JAMIE CRUZ

DEAN HUTTO

Raj Sinha photo: Amy Lobban

The Faces of Farming

compiled by Stacey Kusterbeck

We reached out to some of America's farmers and growers with these questions:

1. How or why did you become a farmer?

2. What is the hardest part of your job?

3. What is the best part of your job?

4. What is your favorite farming or gardening tradition?

5. What advice would you give someone who wants to be a farmer today?

6. What, in your opinion, is the future of farming?

Their answers speak to both changes underfoot and timeless traditions. *(continued)*

KOLE NIELSEN

KEN SUZUKI

KATE BOWEN

Kirstin Bailey
Fox Run Farms
Brainard, Nebraska

1. My mom has always had a large garden. We thought that together, we could make it into a CSA farm.

2. Relying on nature. There is so much at stake.

3. Connecting directly with our customers.

4. We always plant our potatoes on Good Friday.

5. Have a strong plan and a realistic budget. Be flexible.

6. Women-led, small-scale, sustainable farms.

Kate Bowen
Meadowdale Farm
Putney, Vermont

1. I grew up in the woods just off a dirt road, where we always heated with wood and raised chickens. When I met my husband, we decided to expand from just selling forest products to raising livestock.

2. Having no money.

3. Our family working as a team.

4. My grandfather always told me to "plant peas when the daffodils bloomed."

5. Jump in and do it. Don't overanalyze.

6. Consumers are demanding fresh, local foods. Over the next decade, we farmers will find our niche and get a proper price for our food.

Warren Brockman
Hemlock Trails
Cranberry Company
Cranmoor, Wisconsin

1. After college, I took over our farm from my father, who wanted to retire.

2. Balancing the needs of the family with those of the farm. Long hours with no time off.

3. Having the chance to be around as our kids grow up.

4. We start frost-protecting when we see blooming serviceberries or ash tree leaves the size of a squirrel's ear.

5. Start small and stay out of debt.

6. Farmers will have to grow more for less and market more of their crop themselves.

Tyler Cerbo
Cerbo's North Jersey
Tree Farm
Branchville, New Jersey

1. Coming from a large family that has been in business for 103 years, I found that farming was a lifestyle that just could not be turned down.

2. Tying tomatoes.

3. Harvesting—whether it be a field of trees or a simple basket of eggplant.

4. Every spring we have a week's worth of late nights to get the new plantings in the ground on time.

5. Have a flexible schedule.

6. The bumper sticker slogan "No Farmers, No Food" sums up the future of farming. *(continued on page 198)*

Consumer Cellular

AARP | Member Advantages
Real Possibilities

CONSUMER CELLULAR HAS BEEN RECOGNIZED BY J.D. POWER
"Highest in Customer Service among Non-Contract Wireless Providers, Two Times in a Row."

LOW PRICES

Our average customer's monthly bill is just $22.57* for all the talk, text and data they need. Many pay even less, as our straightforward, no-contract plans start at just $10/month. Plus, activation is free— a $35 value!

OUTSTANDING CUSTOMER SUPPORT

Count on Consumer Cellular for service and support that's second to none! Our 100% U.S. based team is always just a call—or a click—away.

100% RISK-FREE GUARANTEE

If you're not satisfied within the first 30 days, 300 minutes, 300 text messages or 300MB of web data, whichever comes first, cancel and pay nothing—completely hassle-free.

AARP MEMBER BENEFITS

Consumer Cellular has been an approved AARP provider since 2008 because of the superior support and outstanding value we offer. AARP members receive a 5% discount on service and usage every month, plus a 30% discount on accessories.

OUR AVERAGE CUSTOMER'S MONTHLY BILL.

GREAT VARIETY OF PHONES AND DEVICES.

BRING YOUR OWN PHONE— OUR SIM CARDS ARE FREE.

CALL CONSUMER CELLULAR AT
(888) 270-8608

VISIT US ONLINE AT
ConsumerCellular.com/8608

AVAILABLE AT ◎ **TARGET**

2018 TRENDS

IN THE GARDEN

Plant identification apps are out.
Virtual reality designers are in.
In 2018, we will see the use of technology
in the garden like never before.

–Katie Dubow, Garden Media Group

PEOPLE ARE TALKING ABOUT . . .

- growing pink pumpkins to support breast cancer research: www. pinkpumpkinpatch.org

'PORCELAIN DOLL' PINK PUMPKIN

EXPERTS' IDEAS FOR MAXIMUM EFFECT

- cherry and slicer tomatoes or flowers, veggies, and herbs (e.g., petunia, peppers, and cilantro) in a single container

–Katie Rotella, Ball Horticultural

- interplanting spring greens with spring bulbs; incorporating artichokes or cardoons into annual plantings;

adding highbush blueberries to a mixed border.

–Todd Forrest, horticulturalist, The New York Botanical Garden

- unusual or gourmet varieties: 'Cucamelon' and 'Mother Mary's Pie Melon'; compact plants: 'Bush Crop' cucumbers; 'Silvery Fir Tree', 'Grushovka', and 'Russian Saskatchewan' tomatoes.

–Tanya Stefanec, Heritage Harvest Seed

BY THE NUMBERS

In United States:

$401:

average spent
by households
on backyard or
balcony gardening
in 2015

36%

of households
grew food

34%

of households
grew flowers

–National Gardening Survey

Photos, from top: VR Home&Garden.com; NE Seed

BY THE NUMBERS
In Canada:

57%
of households grew fruit, herbs, vegetables, or flowers:

4%
participated in community gardens

81%
gardened in yards

30%
gardened on balconies

22%
gardened indoors

–2013 Households and the Environment Survey, released in 2015

PROS' PICKS
• butterfly/bee attractors: 'Ice Ballet' swamp milkweed; 'Gay Butterflies' and 'Hello Yellow' butterfly weed; 'Ava' and 'Blue Boa' hyssops
–Sonia Uyterhoeven, head of horticulture, Greenwood Gardens

• shade-suited *Hydrangea arborescens* 'Haas' Halo'; 'Blushing Belle', 'Black Tulip', and 'Green Mile' late-flowering magnolia cultivars; fragrant and disease-resistant roses, e.g., 'Summer Romance'
–Todd Forrest

• 'Royal Hawaiian Maui Gold' and 'Black Magic' elephant ears
–Duane Otto, Minnesota Landscape Arboretum

OPTIONS FOR EASE
• subscription services for seeds, artisanal microgreens, heirloom bulbs, and plants

• apps that use GPS to recommend plants suited to a garden's specific terrain, trees and structures, and sun and shade

(continued)

Naturescaping: growing native plants to attract birds, insects, and other wildlife

'HAAS' HALO' HYDRANGEA

ON THE FARM

LocalHarvest.org estimates that small farms comprise 80 percent of the 2 million U.S. farms. These small, owner-operator farms . . . tend to not be included in a formal census, further exacerbating the perceived paucity of younger farmers. . . . This younger brand of farmers [is] willing to try innovative cropping systems, such as high tunnels for year-round culture systems, while using hydroponic systems and fewer natural resources.

–Dr. Ellen Peffley, professor emerita, Dept. of Plant and Soil Sciences, Texas Tech University

WHAT FARMERS ARE GROWING . . .

- peaches in translucent bags to protect against pests organically

- strawberries on raised, hydroponic beds for robot harvesters

PAIRING WITH PURPOSE

- Beekeepers are electronically providing the location of their hives to pesticide sprayers, who then avoid coming too close.

- Farmers are planting wildflowers to attract pollinators.

- Researchers are asking the public to identify invasive plants, then removing them to halt their spread.

PEOPLE ARE TALKING ABOUT . . .

- buying low-price, imperfect produce at supermarkets and through subscription services, in part to reduce food waste

(continued)

- appliances that turn food scraps into compost in a day
- groups collecting discarded food from dumpsters and turning it into liquid fertilizer

ANCIENT AG, REBORN

Scientists are cultivating nearly extinct grains and crops and distributing seed to growers, e.g., 'Purple Straw', 'White Lammas', and 'Turkey' wheats; 'Seashore', a tall-growing rye; 'Sea Island' red peas; 'Carolina African' runner peanut; and 'Purple Ribbon' sugarcane.

BY THE NUMBERS

$4 billion:
worldwide annual revenue from agricultural robotics (e.g., robotic milkers, drones, driverless tractors)

14,093:
certified organic farms in the United States

8,669:
U.S. farmers' markets

4,120:
farms in Canada with organic products for sale

TECH EFFECTS

- Drones study airborne microbes that cause plant disease.
- Apps predict extreme weather to help farmers plan when to irrigate and fertilize.

RURAL REPOPULATION

- Some rural Canadian towns are giving land to people who agree to build a house on it within a year.
- The U.S. National Park Service is leasing federal land to people who will farm it and share their agricultural knowledge.

IN THE KITCHEN

The modern era of "snackified eating" has fully emerged.
–*Laurie Demeritt, CEO, The Hartman Group*

SNACK FACTS

- Snacks are replacing meals.
- 47% of Americans can't get through a day without at least one snack.

F-A-A-AST FOOD

The time spent on or saved by a food or drink product will become a clear selling point.
–*Jenny Zegler, global food and drink analyst, Mintel*

(continued)

INCREASINGLY FAVE CRAVES

- plant-based alternatives to milk, yogurt, and cheese
- plant waters, e.g., aloe, artichoke, cactus, and maple

- vegetarian food with meat's texture and taste, such as yellow-pea burgers and shredded jackfruit "pulled pork"
- mayonnaise made from aquafaba (liquid in which chickpeas have been cooked and/ or canned)

FOR THE HEALTH OF IT

- Medical schools are offering cooking classes so that new doctors can better understand and "prescribe" healthy foods.
- Doctors' offices are including kitchens for teaching healthy cooking to patients.

DID YOU KNOW?

- Consumers want beef raised on "regenerative grazing" land (fertilized by the animals' manure).
- Mushrooms, not sugar, are being used to reduce the

BY THE NUMBERS

42%
of Americans prefer (healthier) dark chocolate to milk or white chocolate

$3.5 billion:
annual U.S. sales of plant-based alternative foods

3%
of Americans eat strictly vegan or vegetarian;
9% do so most of the time

1.7:
number of meals, on average, that Americans eat with family over the Thanksgiving holiday

32%
of Americans prefer to make holiday meals from a kit

bitterness of cacao beans in chocolate.

- Soy protein, not salt, is being used as a flavor enhancer.

PEOPLE ARE TALKING ABOUT . . .

- LED lighting in supermarket fridges
- milk in light-blocking containers to protect its flavor and nutrition

- groceries delivered by a small, self-driving, robotic vehicle

FORAGING FUN

Volunteers are creating free "food forests" in public parks, where visitors can munch on edible trees, shrubs, and flowers. (See page 80.)
(continued)

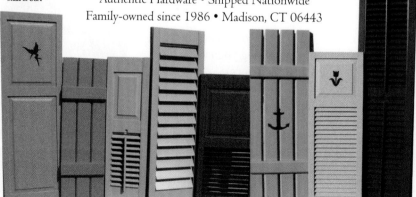

OUR ANIMAL FRIENDS

Robots will start to enter our lives as
our new "smart" furry friends.
–Daniel Levine, The Avant-Guide Institute

PEOPLE ARE TALKING ABOUT . . .

- apartment building managers offering "house dogs" for pet-less residents to play with

- pet supply companies that donate product or profits

- dog treats made with invasive Asian carp, thus helping to keep pets—and rivers—healthy

PETS RELAX WITH . . .

- pet sounds: species-specific music, in calming frequencies

- "doga" classes (dogs doing yoga with their owners)

- crates and beds that absorb vibrations from thunderstorms or fireworks

- grooming products made with chamomile and lavender

THE CANADIAN PET-SPECTIVE

- Technologies, medications, and treatments developed for people and adapted for pets, plus research into pet therapies, are resulting in healthier pets.
–David Dorman, publisher, PETS Magazine

- Owners should give pets "enrichment toys" to aid mental acuity.
–Jennifer Nosek, editor, Modern Dog/Modern Cat

(continued)

BY THE NUMBERS

1%
of dogs and cats
have health
insurance

68%
of U.S.
households have
at least one pet

$15 billion
is spent annually
on pet health
care in the U.S.

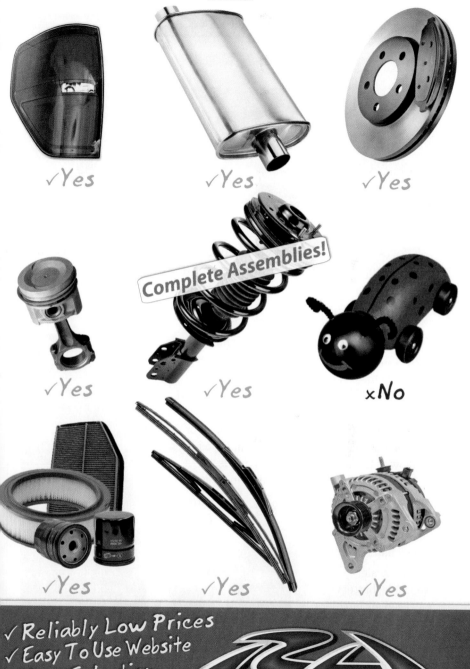

HEALTH & WELLNESS

Efforts to reduce stress will emphasize adequate nutrition and sleep, relaxation techniques, mindfulness meditation, and emotional and spiritual well-being.

–Thomas R. Milam, MD, Virginia Tech Carilion School of Medicine and Research Institute

PEOPLE ARE TALKING ABOUT . . .

- improving air quality with "living walls" of grass, ferns, or mosses

- pills with sensors that tell physicians we swallowed them

- software-enabled caps that detect brain wave activity and direct it to control wheelchairs and cars

- small-scale, wearable, battery-powered air purifiers

WALKING THE WALK

- Male commuters who cycled to work were 11 pounds lighter, on average, than car drivers; women were 9.7 pounds lighter.

- When British commuters switched from driving to walking, cycling, or public transit, each lost 2 pounds, on average, in 2 years.

(continued)

BY THE NUMBERS

$2.60: cost per day to satisfy the federal dietary guidelines for fruit and vegetables

26% of U.S. food budgets is spent on fruit and vegetables

85% of Americans fall short of recommended fruit and vegetable consumption

2,481: calories consumed by the average American daily

AROUND THE HOUSE

Small-scale, four-season spaces [outbuildings] with lots of natural light will start popping up in urban backyards as home offices, kids' hangouts, and art or yoga studios.

–Sarah Keenleyside, HGTV Canada

FOOT NOTES

Real estate agents have a new selling point: As we become more interested in getting our steps in, the "walk score" of a neighborhood is going to become more important.

–Marianne Canada, HGTV design expert

PEOPLE ARE TALKING ABOUT . . .

• in-home robots that fold laundry

• designated rooms for kids to do high-tech homework

• weeds and wildflowers from around the yard displayed in vases

• roofs that absorb carbon dioxide when rained on

• the return of dumbwaiters

BRIGHT IDEAS

• electric fireplace logs whose ultraviolet light removes air pollutants

• wall-hung fireplaces fueled by bioethanol processed from garbage

• wireless lightbulbs that float in midair

• GPS lightbulbs that light upon detecting residents' imminent arrival *(continued)*

- skylights that darken on sunny days, saving on A/C bills

MUST-HAVES FOR HOMES

- furniture made into bathroom sink cabinets and kitchen countertops of manmade quartz (in realistic marble and stone finishes), Brazilian macaubas quartzite, or glass
–HGTV's Canada

- freestanding furniture (not built-in cabinets) or "feet" on lower kitchen cabinets for a furniture-like look
–Rachel Hardage Barrett, editor in chief, Country Living

- lofts to separate family members while still in close proximity

- massive artworks leaning against walls

MONEY MATTERS

Instant payments, money movement via peer-to-peer, digital watch apps, and digital wallet technologies are becoming more mainstream.

–Kimmie Greene, spokesperson, Mint

WHERE MONEY GOES

- **22%** of Americans have contributed to an online "crowdfunded" project
- **3%** of Americans have created an online crowdfunded project

- **17.3 billion:** number of checks written by Americans in 2015 (down from 41.9 billion in 2000)

- **22%** of transactions in 2016 were cash
(continued)

Longlight
Beeswax Candles

Think *GREEN* - Think *BEESWAX*
- *Environmentally friendly*
- *No Toxins or Carcinogens*
- *Produces Negative Ions to help Purify the Air*
- *Smokeless & Dripless*

100 Hour Coiled Beeswax Candle
- Beautiful Unique Brass Base
- Self-Extinguishing Holder
- 100+ Hour Burn Time
- Refills available

100 Hour Candle — $89

30, 60 & 75 hour available

Our candles make great gifts...

place your order today!

50 Hour Decorator Candle
- Unique Cast Brass Base
- Self-Extinguishing Holder
- 50+ Hour Burn Time
- Refills Available

50 Hour Candle — $55

30, 60 & 75 hour available

Made in USA. All orders plus shipping & handling.

Longlight Candles
1-866-583-3400
longlightcandles.com

ISRAEL IN HISTORY AND PROPHECY

FREE BOOKLET

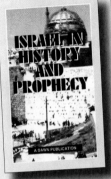

For many centuries the Jewish p e o p l e have been s c a t t e r e d throughout the earth. Now today, with Israel well established as a nation, the world witnesses what can only be seen as fulfillment of Old Testament prophecies. Read about the way God has brought His People back to their Promised Land and what his plans are for their future. Read *"Israel in History and Prophecy"* and see what the Bible says.

phone or write for your

FREE 36 page copy
1-800-234-DAWN

DAWN PUBLISHING
199 RAILROAD AVENUE
EAST RUTHERFORD NJ

Visit our website
www.dawnbible.com

- **24%** of Americans do not make any purchases with cash in a typical week

Americans who bought at least one item . . .

- online: **79%**
- via cell phone: **51%**
- from a social media site link: **15%**

OUR DIGITAL ECONOMY

Ways Americans earned money . . .

1%: renting out property on a home-sharing site

8%: doing a job or task on a digital platform

18%: selling something online

WE'RE MAKING CENTS . . .

- opening bank accounts at home, with electronically verified IDs
- planning meals with apps that alert us to

BY THE NUMBERS

10%:
the pay raise, on average, that students can expect for every extra year of math classes

64%
of Americans prefer brick-and-mortar to online stores

43%
of online shoppers have bought something while in bed

$7 per month:
how much more in taxes Floridians would be willing to pay for public tree-planting (which enhances property values)

$5.60:
return in energy savings and increased property values for every $1 spent on planting trees in New York City neighborhoods

ingredients on sale at the grocery store

PREVAILING PURCHASE INFLUENCERS

Social media phenomena [bloggers and online ratings] will change how we decide what to buy and where. . . . We'll see opportunistic small, nimble, and social retailers gain stature.

–Kit Yarrow, PhD, author, Decoding the New Consumer Mind

F-A-A-AST CASH

Time it takes when we pay by . . .

Check: **67 seconds**

Cash: **25 seconds**

Credit card: **24 seconds**

Debit card: **20 seconds**

(continued)

OUR PASSION FOR FASHION

After years of wanting the cheapest prices possible for their clothes, consumers are starting to consider how their clothes are made and their impact on the environment.

–Lorynn Divita, PhD, associate professor, apparel merchandising, Baylor University

LATEST LOOKS FOR MENSWEAR

- washable suits made of wrinkle-free nylon
- sneakers worn with pinstriped suits
- dress shirts in stretchy, moisture-wicking fabrics

LATEST LOOKS FOR LADIES

- kimono sleeves
- cropped pants with unfinished hems

- classic nylon bomber jackets
- high necklines

–Steven Faerm, associate professor of fashion, Parsons School of Design

BY THE NUMBERS

11%

of women spend over an hour getting ready each morning (compared to 2% of men)

$85

is spent by men each month, on average, on clothing and accessories (compared to $75 for women)

7.8:

pairs of shoes, on average, bought by Americans each year

67.9:

number of garments, on average, bought by Americans each year

FAUX, FISHY, AND FAKE

Alternatives to cowhide include . . .

- synthetic leather that looks, feels, and smells real
- fish skins
- leather grown from lab cells "programmed" to

Home. Cooked.
GOODNESS.
The taste of togetherness.

HEARTLAND QUALITY
OMAHA STEAKS
SINCE 1917

The Happy Family Feast

2 (5 oz.) Filet Mignons
2 (5 oz.) Top Sirloins
2 (4 oz.) Boneless Pork Chops
4 (3.5 oz.) Chicken Fried Steaks
4 (3 oz.) Kielbasa Sausages
4 (4 oz.) Omaha Steaks Burgers
12 oz. pkg. All-Beef Meatballs
4 (3 oz.) Potatoes au Gratin
4 (4 oz.) Caramel Apple Tartlets
Omaha Steaks Seasoning Packet (.33 oz.)

48269MTD

$213.91 separately **Combo Price** $49⁹⁹

ORDER NOW &
SAVE 77%*

100% GUARANTEE

Plus get 4 more
Burgers FREE

1-800-811-7832 ask for 48269MTD | www.OmahaSteaks.com/tender09

produce collagen identical to that of a cow or other animal

–Lorynn Divita

SIGNS OF THE TIMES

• selling unwanted, nearly new clothing through online consignment sites

• removing clothing's designer logos to be advertising-free

PEOPLE ARE TALKING ABOUT . . .

• stylists re-creating hairstyles of ancient Romans

• jackets embedded with speakers: Music emanates from different areas of the body.

• clothes that adjust according to your body temperature

• jeans with mini cell phone chargers in pockets

• belts that vibrate to give wearers directions

CUES TO CULTURE

Family leisure is becoming more elusive for families trapped in the hectic pace of society.

–Karen K. Melton, PhD, assistant professor, child and family studies, Baylor University

BUZZWORD

Biophilic: describing our innate instinct to connect with nature

TO INCREASE TIME TOGETHER, FAMILIES ARE . . .

• becoming acquainted with people and cultures by overnighting in private houses (not hotels) and taking cooking lessons in home kitchens (not on tours)

• going "nomadic"— selling possessions to travel the world

(continued)

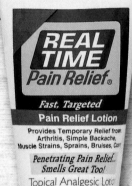

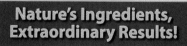

DATA ON OUR DOWNTIME

We told researchers that we're happy...

- at home
- doing unplanned activities
- outdoors, instead of indoors

We're seeking out strangers...

- in coffee shops where laptops are banned and "conversation starter" cards invite patrons to talk

BY THE NUMBERS

55%
of Americans say that they pray every day

21%
of U.S. adults were raised in a mixed-faith home

52%
of Americans do not use all of their paid vacation days

7.2:
average number of vacation days workers give up each year

- on the subway, where riders wear badges to signal that they're open to small talk
- at home, where telecommuters virtually join office parties via webcam
- in art galleries, where patrons don giant puzzle pieces and find a "piece" that fits

PEOPLE ARE TALKING ABOUT . . .

- chair bags that unfold into a small stool and bike helmets that fold
- "plyscrapers," high-rise buildings made of wood, e.g., University of British Columbia's new 18-story student residence

- sneakers with push buttons to tighten or loosen the fit
- spherical car tires for steering sideways into a parking space

LEISURE LEANINGS

- paying "bibliotherapists" to recommend books to boost our spirits
- paddling transparent canoes and kayaks while watching the water world below
- playing lawn games, e.g., bocce and shuffleboard

(continued)

Thanks to BetterWOMAN, I'm winning the battle for
Bladder Control.

All Natural
Clinically-Tested
Herbal Supplement

- Reduces Bladder Leaks
- Reduces Bathroom Trips
- Sleep Better All Night
- Safe and Effective – No Known Side Effects
- Costs Less than Traditional Bladder Control Options
- **Live Free of Worry, Embarrassment, and Inconvenience**

You don't have to let bladder control problems control you.

Call now!

Frequent nighttime trips to the bathroom, embarrassing leaks and the inconvenience of constantly searching for rest rooms in public – for years, I struggled with bladder control problems. After trying expensive medications with horrible side effects, ineffective exercises and uncomfortable liners and pads, I was ready to resign myself to a life of bladder leaks, isolation and depression. But then I tried **BetterWOMAN**.

When I first saw the ad for BetterWOMAN, I was skeptical. So many products claim they can set you free from leaks, frequency and worry, only to deliver disappointment. When I finally tried BetterWOMAN, I found that it actually works! It changed my life. Even my friends have noticed that I'm a new person. And because it's all natural, I can enjoy the results without the worry of dangerous side effects. Thanks to BetterWOMAN, I finally fought bladder control problems and I won!

Also Available: **BetterMAN**®
The 3-in-1 Formula Every Man Needs –
Better **BLADDER**, Better **PROSTATE**, and Better **STAMINA!**
Order online at **www.BetterMANnow.com.**

Limited Time Offer

Call Now & Ask How To Get A
FREE BONUS BOTTLE
CALL TOLL-FREE 1-888-475-4365
or order online: www.BetterWOMANnow.com

These statements have not been evaluated by the FDA. This product is not intended to diagnose, treat, cure or prevent any disease. *Use as directed. Individual results may vary.*
BetterMAN and BetterWOMAN are the trademarks of Interceuticals, Inc. ©2017 Interceuticals, Inc.

COLLECTORS' CORNER

Today's collectors are split evenly into two categories:
the high end and the low end.

–Eric Bradley, Heritage Auctions

COMMODITIES TO CASH IN ON NOW

- Civil War–era tax forms; Form 1040 for 1913 (the first); badges worn by IRS agents; "wanted" posters of tax criminals

- airsickness bags with whimsical designs or from obscure airlines (a 90-year-old bag from France's now-defunct Farman Airways brought $500 at auction)

STEADY STAKES

- Staffordshire pottery; art glass

paperweights and vases; inkwells and fountain pens; antique perfume bottles; brass military badges—each in the $50 to $500 price range

- playable rock and jazz vinyl records: "Memorabilia associated with The Beatles and Elvis Presley continue to top auction results."

–Antoinette Rahn, online editor, Antique Trader

ACTION AT AUCTION

$60,000: NY Yankees bobblehead ("nodder") doll

$14,640: 1902 amusement park electric shock machine

$4,750: rare hay stacker wrench from Dain Mfg. Company, in excellent condition

$450: lesser-quality version of the same Dain wrench ■

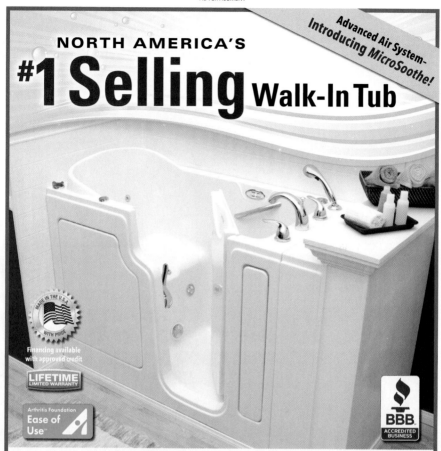

Edibles *for the* Kid in You

BY SHERYL NORMANDEAU

Got a favorite vegetable? Everybody has a few. They're the ones that we grow every year for all of the right reasons: They produce reliably, taste great, and keep or cook up wonderfully. Grow them again—but also set the seeds of a surprise or two for the kid in you (or those of any age). This season, make space for one or a few of these uncommon and uncommonly good-tasting crops!

PRECIOUS KERNELS

Every garden has hidden jewels, but none sparkles quite like 'Carl's Glass Gem' corn. Each ear fairly glows with brilliant blue, green, pink, white, yellow, or purple kernels. Named for Carl "White Eagle" Barnes, a Cherokee farmer from Oklahoma who spent decades breeding species of corn with significance to the indigenous peoples who lived in the area, glass gem corn is quick to mature and harvestable in 110 to 120 days. It is best used as a flour corn, although kernels can be popped (the kernels do not keep their amazing colors after popping, but they are tastier than other popping corns).

(continued)

45

A TOMATO LEGEND

In the fairy tale "Rapunzel," the heroine lets down her long hair so that visitors can climb up it to where she is being held captive in a tower. In the garden, 'Rapunzel' is a sweet, red, cherry-type tomato that produces trusses up to 3½ feet long. 'Rapunzel' reaches maturity in 75 days and yields up to 40 tomatoes per truss. This is an excellent container tomato. Just remember to hang it high, in full sun.

SAVOIR FARE

Have a ball—or a bunch of them—in your garden pot or plot with a quick-growing crop of French heirloom carrots. Dark orange-red, sweet, and delicious, the 'Parisian' variety dates from the 19th century and matures in only 60 days. This carrot is especially good for growing in clay soils, because it does not have an extensive root system. Provide sufficient moisture as the carrots develop; drought will yield long, thin specimens that lack this variety's round-as-a-radish shape.

MUNCHKIN PUMPKINS

'Jack Be Little' pumpkins are a handful: Each one is petite—2 to 3 inches wide—and edible. They're yummy roasted, sautéed, or even pickled. Plus, they're ideally suited as a decoration for autumn holidays. 'Jack Be Little' matures in 90 days; in most climates, there is no need to start it early indoors. Each healthy vine will produce about six pumpkins. *(continued)*

Photos, from top: SimplySeed.co.uk; www.sustainableseedco.com; W. Atlee Burpee Company

CUKIE-CUTIES

Mouse melons *(Melothria scabra)*, also known as cucamelons and Mexican sour gherkins, resemble tiny watermelons and even have the familiar flecked green skin, but they are not related to watermelons at all. Mouse melons are native to Mexico and Central America and are fairly recent arrivals to gardens in North America. In a full sun location and with sufficient moisture, these vines spread vigorously and produce several pounds of fruit during the growing season. Mouse melons have a taste similar to that of cucumbers. Chop them into fresh salads and salsas or pickle them.

SCRAMBLED EGGS

Even hens may be envious of these orbs: The ivory fruit of 'Japanese White Egg' eggplants look like large (2- to 3-inch) eggs. This plant performs best in cooler temperatures; excessive heat may actually cause the fruit to turn yellow and become bitter to the taste. Chow down on 'Japanese White Egg' eggplant grilled, in stir-fries, or in casseroles only 65 days after planting in ground or container.

BEAN STALKS

While you could allow 'Asparagus Yardlong' beans to grow up to 36 inches long, it's best to harvest them at 18 inches or less, when they are at their most tender and flavorful. Sow this vigorous heirloom climber in warm soil (the seed will not germinate well in cool temperatures) and allow 80 days to maturity. Sweet-tasting 'Asparagus Yardlong' beans are delicious sautéed, steamed, or in stir-fries. *(continued)*

Photos, from top: Tigerente/Wikimedia; My Lestary Seeds; W. Atlee Burpee Company

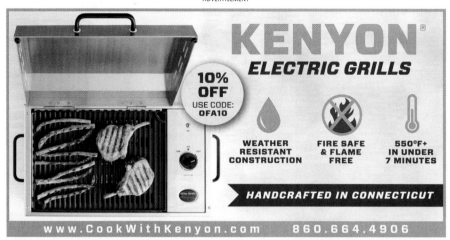
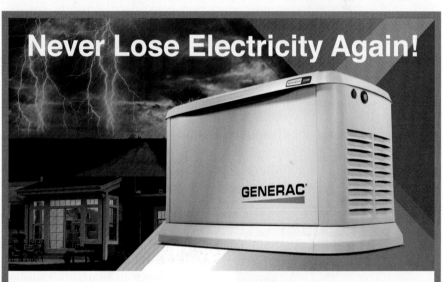

SWEET TREATS
MINTS WITH HINTS

How about a bit of chocolate in your harvest? Mint cultivar *Mentha* x *piperita* 'Chocolate' and pineapple mint (*M. suaveolens* 'Variegata') melt in your mouth (so to speak), and each has the flavor that its name suggests. Like their cousins, these mints grow quickly, with spreading root systems, so it's best to keep them confined to a container. Chocolate mint is a delicious addition to vanilla ice cream or milkshakes, and pineapple mint is refreshing in iced tea or fruit salads.

WHITE DELIGHTS

Double your pleasure with pineberries (*Fragaria chiloensis* x *virginiana*)—white strawberries that have the mild aroma and taste of pineapple. These ever-bearing beauties, a result of cross-breeding by Dutch horticulturists, produce fruit from early summer through fall. Grow them in a warm, sunny location and be aware that high temperatures will hinder fruit production. Make sure that their soil drains well and water moderately; soggy conditions will lead to crown rot. Pineberries are a perfect dessert berry—if they make it to the kitchen!

RADICAL RADISH

Light up faces with 'Starburst' radishes, first when they are pulled from the soil, revealing their white bodies and fuchsia roots, and again when slicing displays the bright pink flesh. Grow these sweet orbs in fall or early spring; they are a cool weather crop and may bolt during intense summer heat. 'Starburst' matures quickly: You'll be picking 60 days after sowing the seeds. Enjoy them fresh from the soil or preserved: They make excellent pickles. *(continued)*

 Photos, from top: Park Seed; Monrovia; Stark Bro's

STOP STRUGGLING ON THE STAIRS TODAY!

An Acorn Stairlift can prevent you from falling on the stairs. We are the perfect solution for:

- Arthritis/COPD sufferers
- Those with mobility issues
- Anyone with stair struggle

$250* OFF!

CALL TODAY TO SAVE $250*

AND RECEIVE YOUR *FREE* INFORMATION KIT WITH DVD!

1-866-235-3235

ACORN STAIRLIFTS

*Not valid on previous purchases. Not valid with any other offers or discounts. Not valid on refurbished models. Only valid towards purchase of a NEW Acorn Stairlift directly from the manufacturer. $250 discount will be applied to new orders. Please mention this ad when calling. AZ ROC 278722, CA 942619, MN LC670698, OK 50110, OR CCB 198506, RI 88, WA ACORNSI8940B, WV WV049654, MA HIC169936, NJ 13VH07752300, PA PA101967, CT ELV 0425003-R5.

BBB ACCREDITED BUSINESS

Arthritis Foundation Ease of Use

HAIL THE KALE

Walking stick kale, aka Jersey cabbage (*Brassica olera-cea* var. *longata*), with its stems reaching 7 to 10 feet tall and often much higher, tends to leave even the experienced gardener in awe. This member of the cabbage family will reach this astonishing height in one growing season and produce a mound of edible foliage on top. In Zones 7 and higher, it acts as a perennial, living for 2 or 3 years and producing a new top each year. A native of the Channel Islands (UK), it has been historically harvested for both its leaves and its stem, which—true to its name—can be cut, dried, and varnished for use as a walking stick. Due to its extreme height, walking stick kale may, ironically, need a cane—er, stake—to keep it from blowing over in high winds.

HORNS OF PLENTY

No musicality is required for success with a *Cucurbita moschata* squash called "tromboncino." Its sprawling vines can grow 5 or more feet long and produce slender fruit that twist and curl ahead of a bulbous seed head (it's oddly more like a tuba than its Italian namesake, the trombone) and await discovery under large, dense foliage. (For straight squash, trellis the vine.) Harvest pale green fruit at 10 to 12 inches to slice or spiralize and sauté, or pick when tan and doubled (or tripled) in size to roast like butternut squashes.

ROYAL SPUDS

Potatoes are fun. Digging for them is like a hunt for hidden treasure, and with 'Purple Majesty' potatoes, the search is even more rewarding: These spuds are purple on both the outside and inside, and they keep both their regal color and nutritional value when cooked. They are cited as a super food for being high in antioxidants. 'Purple Majesty' makes potato salads pretty and fries more fun. ■

Sheryl Normandeau is an avid gardener, writer, and blogger in Calgary, Alberta.

 Photos, from top: Center of the Webb; Nadia Talent/Wikimedia; W. Atlee Burpee Company

Pick Parsley!

TO SWEETEN
THE MOUTH AND SAUCE
THE STEAK

By SUSAN PEERY

Parsley. It's the world's most popular
(and ubiquitous) herb, and you probably are
thinking, Ho-hum, I already know
about parsley. It's that curly green sprig
I push to the side of the plate in restaurants,
that herb-garden staple that bolts
when it gets hot, that decorative sprinkle of
green on a mound of mashed potatoes.
Perhaps a few of these parsley
(Petroselinum crispum) facts will
surprise you . . .
(continued)

Parsley is gharsley.
–Ogden Nash, American poet (1902–71)

⚘ In Health ⚘

• A hot poultice of parsley leaves (made by tying the leaves in muslin and soaking briefly in hot water) can relieve the pain and itching of insect stings. Parsley tea is thought to strengthen the teeth, improve skin tone, and aid indigestion.

• Parsley is considered a sweet herb. Wrote Thomas Hill (English astrologer and author of *The Gardener's Labyrinth*) in 1577, "There is nothing that doth like sweeten the mouth, as the freshe and greene Parselie eaten." The plant's high chlorophyll content helps to absorb odors, disguising even garlic on the breath (within reason).

• To stimulate the scalp and reduce hair loss, massage with an infusion of parsley in olive oil.

• To condition dry hair, make an infusion of fresh or dried parsley, strain, and pour through the hair.

• Folklore suggests treating bruises with a plaster of chopped parsley mixed with butter.

• Parsley is rich in folate, iron, and vitamins A, C, and K. *(continued)*

CHESAPEAKE CRAB CAKES

Never Frozen
Never Pasteurized
Nationwide Shipping

We pride ourselves on using only the freshest (non-pasteurized) crab meat blended with the finest ingredients. You will not be disappointed.

Order Online Today & Save!
10% ON YOUR ORDER with ALMANAC code

www.**ChesapeakeCrabCakes**.com
443.956.9800

DROLL YANKEES®
The World's Best Bird Feeders®

JFB-S80

JFB-S8B

For people who are new to birding or for those who simply love nature, these songbird feeders help in making a world difference.

It might be hard to believe that one person feeding birds in their yard can help restore the balance of nature. ***But it's true.*** Because in nature, everything is connected. And everything matters.

So, Just Feed Birds and Make a World of Difference®

These colorful feeders come equipped with a FREE colorful pocket sized "Birds at the Feeder Identification Guide" featuring birds that are likely to be seen feeding at backyard bird feeders.

Find a store or shop online at drollyankees.com
Droll Yankees Inc. | www.drollyankees.com
Phone: (860) 779-8980
email: drollbird@drollyankees.com

When sowing parsley, patience is the gardener's best companion.

–John Randolph, U.S. congressman (1773–1833)

🌿 IN THE GARDEN 🌿

• Of the three main types of parsley (flat-leaf, or Italian; curly; Hamburg, or turnip-rooted), flat-leaf is thought to have the most flavor, while curly was more of a curiosity until modern times, although rabbits have always loved it the best. Hamburg is prized for its hardiness and is widely eaten as a root crop.

• Parsley should be sown early in the spring in northern zones for use all summer and fall or in late summer in warmer zones for peak flavor in late fall and winter.

• All types of parsley have a long taproot and dislike being transplanted. Because the roots can penetrate to 4 feet, parsley can be grown as a cover crop to improve and aerate soil.

• Consider growing parsley in deep pots in order to move it into shade in the heat of summer. Hot weather can make it bolt and become bitter.

• The caterpillar of the swallowtail butterfly *(above)* is one of parsley's few pests. The black-and-green–stripe caterpillars with yellow dots can strip parsley plants. The best way to control them is to pick and remove them from the plants.

• Parsley is a biennial, so those who want to save seeds can enjoy the leaves of new plants in the first season, winter over the plants (in a cold frame or well mulched, parsley can take outside temperatures down to 10°F), and let them flower and go to seed in the second year. *(continued)*

🌿 In Lore 🌿

- In the Victorian language of flowers, parsley stood for festivity.
- Ancient Greeks and Romans fed parsley to their horses to make them run faster.
- Parsley is one of the first herbs to green up in the spring; it symbolizes renewal of life in a Passover seder.
- In medieval Europe, parsley was traditionally planted on Good Friday. The seeds take up to 6 weeks to germinate, and common wisdom held that parsley seed goes "nine times to the devil before coming up." Good Friday was chosen because it was believed to be the only day that the devil was powerless. To deter the devil, some people poured boiling water over the soil; curiously, it may have aided germination, as the seeds prefer warm soil. (But note: Do not pour boiling water on seeds.)

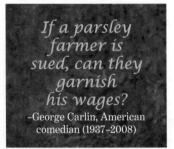

If a parsley farmer is sued, can they garnish his wages?

–George Carlin, American comedian (1937–2008)

The cook can never be without it, there being nothing more proper for stuffing and other sauces.

–*The Practical Kitchen Gardiner,* by Stephen Switzer, garden designer (1682–1745)

🌿 In the Kitchen 🌿

- Parsley stays tender and sweet with frequent harvest of its rosettes of leaves, taking the outside stems first.
- To preserve parsley, chop large quantities, add enough water or olive oil to make a thick slurry, and freeze in ice cube trays for use in soups, stews, and other dishes. Pop the frozen cubes *(above)* into plastic bags for easier storage in the freezer.

For some saucy recipes using parsley, see page 253. ∎

Susan Peery lives in Nelson, New Hampshire (Zone 5, with luck), where she keeps parsley and other herbs close at hand in her kitchen garden.

Had I but 4 square feet of ground at my disposal,
I would plant a peony in the corner and proceed to worship.

–*The Book of Peony (1917),* by Alice Harding (c. 1846–1948)

PEONIES PROMISE

POP!

AS A FOCAL POINT OR BORDER, PEONIES PUT ON A SHOW.

A VISION IN A VASE

Peonies make wonderful cut flowers, sometimes lasting more than a week. For best results, cut long stems when the buds are still fairly tight. Every day thereafter, snip off the bottoms of the stems to allow them to sip fresh water. (If a few ants come in on the buds, leave them alone.)

BY CYNTHIA VAN HAZINGA

Most gardeners agree: Peonies are outrageously beautiful in bloom! They're lusciously large and delicately dramatic in exquisite pastel colors, always eliciting ooh-ahhs and awe from onlookers. What's more, after the pom-pom flowers fade, their lush foliage lasts long into summer.

Named for Paeon, physician to the Greek gods, peonies (*Paeonia* spp.) have been valued for magical and medicinal properties for centuries. Legend has it that a peony poultice cured Pluto of a wound inflicted by Hercules.

When you plant peonies, you and they make a commitment. The plants will provide beautiful borders and sumptuous bouquets for years. (They have been known to thrive in the same spot for over a century!) You need only to give them a good start.   *(continued)*

'Julia Rose' peony

63

WHEN THE SHOW DOES NOT GO ON . . .

Sometimes peonies just don't bloom. Weather can be a cause, such as an excessively hot spell; a severe late frost can kill buds. Sometimes the problem is close at hand:

• Does the peony get too much shade? Peonies love full sun (except in southern gardens, where they need some shade). Although they can manage with a half-day's sunlight, they bloom best out of the shadows. If necessary, prune the tree or move the peony.

• Is the peony too close to nearby trees or shrubs? Peonies do not like competition for food or moisture. For good air circulation, make sure that there are 3 to 4 feet between individual peonies and 3 to 4 feet between peonies and the nearest trees and shrubs.
(continued)

Set the Stage

Fall is the best time to plant peonies—in late September and October in most of the United States and Canada and later in the U.S. South. (They're hardy to Zone 3 and grow well as far south as Zone 7 and into Zone 8. Some folks claim success in Zone 9, too.) Peonies should be settled into place before the first hard frost. They relish cold winters because they need low temperatures for bud formation. How low? A minimum of 30 days of below-freezing temperatures.

Autumn is also the time to divide and move established plants. If you decide to lift and pot peonies in fall for planting in spring, protect the potted plants from severe freezes (extended periods below 10°F) by storing them in a garage or shed.

Potted, overwintered peonies can be planted in spring, but, generally speaking, spring-planted peonies lag behind those planted in fall by about

Misaka peony

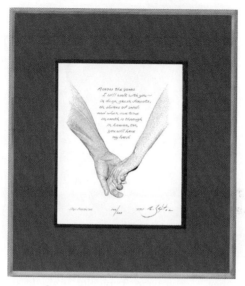

'Lady Orchid' peony

• Is the peony root tuber buried? The eyes on a peony root tuber should be no deeper than 1½ to 2 inches below the soil line (or 1 inch in the South). If, as years slip past, soil builds up on and around the tubers, brush it away to retain the desired depth.

• Did you fertilize the peony? Overfertilizing can prevent bloom. If your soil is poor, apply fertilizer—preferably bonemeal, compost, or well-rotted manure—in early summer, after the peony has bloomed and you've deadheaded spent blossoms. Do not fertilize more than every few years.

a year. Typically, a single shoot or two or three will emerge; about 25 percent of the time, spring-planted peonies bloom in the first year. Full maturity, however, could take 5 to 6 years.

Plot the Scene

In most of the United States and southern Canada, peonies need only full sun and well-drained soil.

Prepare the area for planting by digging a hole about 2 feet deep and 2 feet square. The soil should drain well; if it is heavy or sandy, enrich it with compost or aged manure. Mix in about 1 cup of bonemeal and tamp the soil firmly.

Set the root tuber on top of the firmed soil so that the eyes face upward. Press it no more than 2 inches below the soil surface. In southern gardens, plant tubers of early-blooming varieties about 1 inch deep. Then backfill the hole, taking care that you do not bury the tuber more than 2 inches. Water thoroughly.

Mulch lightly with pine needles or shredded bark, especially in the first winter after planting.

(continued)

Photo: Doreen Wynja for Monrovia

IN MEMORIAM

Peonies, or "pineys," were carried to the New World by the earliest settlers from England. On May 5, 1868, 3 years after the Civil War had ended, a U.S. military general order from Washington, D.C., established May 30 as the date on which to honor the graves of the war dead with flowers. The flowers of choice were what we now call Memorial Day peonies, *P. officinalis,* so named because they bloom in late May.

The memorial day and date have changed—in 1971, Decoration Day was renamed Memorial Day and established as the last Monday in May—but in many parts of the United States, the May 30 tradition continues. *P. officinalis* 'Rubra Plena' is the red variety cherished by the pioneers, but this old favorite is also common in pink 'Rosea Plena' and white 'Alba Plena'. Both are early bloomers, softly scented, and fully double in form.

'Bunker Hill', 'Catharina Fontijn', and 'West Elkton' peonies

Avoid any heavy material that might compact the soil and smother the plant.

Then take a hiatus. Peonies thrive on benign neglect.

In spring, remove the mulch and, if your peonies may be exposed to strong winds or heavy spring rains, support the stems. Three-legged metal peony rings (like tomato cages, which will do the job) support stems and allow them to grow through the rings. Set the support early in season; if you wait too long, you risk breaking stems wrangling them into the rings.

Deadhead peony flowers as soon as they begin to fade, cutting to a strong leaf so that the stem does not protrude from the foliage. Cut the foliage to the ground in fall to avoid any overwintering disease. Don't cut back tree peonies.

Learn to Love Ant Antics

Ants love peonies. The flower buds have tiny (nearly invisible) nectaries, specialized tissues that secrete nectar at the edge of their bud scales, those delicate leafy structures that swath the buds. The

Photos, from left: Iuliia Azarova/Shutterstock; Christa Brand-Höllberg Gardens/GAP Photos

It wasn't just love *powering* us through the outage and the storm, it was preparation.

Times like this remind you how *your life*, and how you live, are worth overprotecting.

GARDENING

GROW TOGETHER

The American Peony Society (americanpeonysociety.org), founded in 1903, endeavors to promote, encourage, and foster the development and improvement of *Paeonia*. Its work involves new and unusual cultivars, award programs, an annual meeting, and providing a wealth of information.

The Canadian Peony Society (peony.ca) was founded in 1998. Today, the organization has more than 300 members, from Newfoundland to British Columbia, who conduct plant sales, plant shows, and garden tours.

Both organizations welcome newcomers from beyond their borders.

nectaries contain a sweet, nutritious blend of sugars, proteins, and amino acids that attracts ants to the buds. In exchange, supping ants provide protections: They attack bud-eating pests by biting or stinging them or spraying them with acid and tossing them off the plant. It's pure symbiosis: The ants protect their food supply and the peonies are safeguarded.

Never spray the ants with water or poison. Instead, perhaps, lean in and watch them: They are helping to bring the flowers into bloom.

Tree Peonies Are Solo Acts

Sometimes called the "king of flowers," tree peonies differ considerably from the more common herbaceous peonies. Hybrids of *P. suffruticosa*, tree peonies are deciduous shrubs with lovely branching foliage and exquisite ephemeral flowers. Slow to develop and hardy in Zones 4 to 8, tree peonies do not die down in the fall, and they thrive in partial shade. Native to the windy hills of western China, tree peonies are tough plants, despite the exquisite delicacy of their flowers, which range from singles to "thousand petal" flowers in luminous colors from deep wine to snow white. ∎

Cynthia Van Hazinga, a frequent contributor to *Old Farmer's Almanac* publications, gardens in New Hampshire.

'Going Bananas' peony

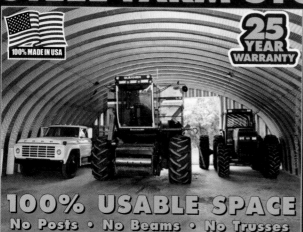

LET'S CHAT
About Chicken

We're scratching through history to learn the finger-lickin' reasons why we're chowing down on chicken.

BY SARAH PERREAULT

Chicken has been
on the menu
since ancient times,
but it has never
been as popular
as it is today.

(continued)

The ancestor of today's domestic chicken was *Gallus gallus,* a native of India and Southeast Asia. Commonly known as the red jungle fowl, it was raised mainly for cockfighting. So, who first decided that chicken would be good eatin'?

Ancient Romans dined on mashed chicken brains and stuffed their birds before roasting. In Maresha, an Israeli city dating from 400 B.C., archeologists have found thousands of chicken bones with visible knife marks. Roman naturalist Pliny the Elder recommended chicken soup as a cure for dysentery.

The first American cookbook to endorse the bird was the 48-page *American Cookery,* published by Amelia Simmons in 1796. It bears the first known recipe calling for chicken—a pie—along with Simmons's advice: "The yellow leg'd [are] the best and their taste the sweetest."

Chickens roaming in backyards were common by the 1800s. They were most prized for their eggs, but with enterprising farmers selling their broods during dormant laying months to supplement their income, hens occasionally became the main course of Sunday dinner.

The production of chickens solely for meat began with the development of broiler chickens. Cecile Steele of Delaware was the first person to raise broilers for profit—and she did it by accident. In 1923, she ordered 50 chicks for her farm. Mistakenly, she received 500. She sold more than 300 of these when they reached 2¼ pounds—and never looked back. By 1926, she was raising 10,000 broilers. Sussex County, Steele's home area, now produces more broilers than any other U.S. county.

Today, according to the National Chicken Council, about 90 pounds of chicken are consumed per person each year in the United States. It is the most commonly eaten meat in North America, and there is no shortage of ways to prepare it. Turn the page for some of our favorite chicken dishes.

(continued)

Sarah Perreault is the food editor of *The Old Farmer's Almanac.*

A COLONIST COOKS A HEN

The chicken pie recipe from *American Cookery;* we think you'll find ours tastier . . .

Pick and clean six chickens, (without scalding) take out their innards and wash the birds while whole, then joint the birds, salt and pepper the pieces and innards. Roll one inch thick crust and cover a deep dish, and double at the rim or edge of the dish, put thereto a layer of chickens and a layer of thin slices of butter, till the chickens and one and a half pounds butter are expended, which cover with a thick crust ; bake one and a half hours.

CHICKEN RECIPES
to Crow About

We love these dishes! Find more recipes
at Almanac.com/Chicken
and on pages 254–256.

CHICKEN POTPIE
p. 254

FRIED CHICKEN WITH CHEESE
p. 255

SLOW COOKER CHICKEN TACOS
p. 256

Photography:
BECKY LUIGART-STAYNER
Food Stylist:
KELLIE KELLY
Prop Stylist:
JAN GAUTRO

FIRST PRIZE: $250
**NO-CHURN SWEET POTATO
CASSEROLE ICE CREAM**
P. 257

SECOND PRIZE: $150
**SWEET POTATO LENTIL
COCONUT CURRY**
P. 258

2017
SWEET POTATO
RECIPE CONTEST
WINNERS

Many thanks to the hundreds of you who submitted recipes!

Enter this year's recipe contest. See page 267 for details.

THIRD PRIZE: $100
ROASTED GARLIC SWEET POTATO MAC-'N-CHEESE
P. 258

FORAGE
FOR FUN AND FEASTING

Edible adventures are at your feet.

BY MARTIE MAJOROS

Foraging—finding food in the wild—is a timeless tradition. Today, the foraging trend is gaining popularity as more people are seeking fresh, locally grown, "free" foods. With a little practice, knowledge, and a good identification guide, you can find ingredients for your next meal in nearby fields, woods, and—if you're lucky—even your own backyard. Dig in!

Look for **WATERCRESS** *(Nasturtium officinale)* near bodies of water. It can be found in every state and much of southern Canada. Although often considered a harbinger of spring, it can be picked year-round in some locations. Carefully cut the edible leaves at the surface of the water; be careful not to pull up the roots. Use in salads, soups, and sandwiches. *(continued)*

WATERCRESS
Nasturtium officinale

WINTER CRESS
Barbarea vulgaris

WINTER CRESS
(Barbarea vulgaris)
gets its botanical name
from St. Barbara,
whose feast day is
December 4. The leaves
can be harvested all
winter but are best in
February and March,
before they become
bitter. Look for it in
low, rich ground near
streams in ditches and
fields across most of
North America. Use
young leaves in salads
or as cooked greens.

Not to be confused with
the banana-like fruit
(*Musa* spp.), **PLANTAIN**
*(Plantago major; P.
lanceolata)* is valued for
the leaves that grow
from the base of the
plant and form 6- to
12-inch-wide rosettes.
Native Americans
believed that eating the
leaves could cure ulcers,

PLANTAIN
Plantago major

and they referred to it
as "white-man's foot"
because it grew near
colonists' settlements.
Early Americans made
a poultice of cooked
leaves to relieve the
itch of insect bites.
Today, plantain can be
found growing in rich
soil throughout North
America. Pick tender
young leaves in early
spring to use in salads.
As they mature, the
leaves become tough
and need to be cooked.

MORELS (*Morchella*
spp.), aka sponge
mushrooms, grow about
2 to 4 inches tall, with a
beige-brown hollow cap
that is ridged and pitted
and attached directly
to the stem. Search for
morels around dead
trees in forests, in
abandoned orchards,
and on burned-over
ground. They appear in
early spring long before
other mushrooms,
making them easy to
identify. Use the stems
and caps as you would
use any mushrooms.
   Although many
first-time foragers are
apprehensive about
gathering mushrooms,

ADVANCED HEARING AID TECHNOLOGY
Costs 90% Less

I am ecstatic! My hearing has improved so much I can not believe it!

Barbra B, January 2017

How can a Hearing Aid be every bit as good as one that sells for $4,000 or more, yet costs 90% less?

<u>The answer:</u>

Although tremendous strides have been made in Advanced Hearing Aid Technology, those cost reductions have not been passed on to you. Until now...

The **MDHearingAid** *AIR*® uses the same kind of Advanced Digital Hearing Aid Technology incorporated into hearing aids that cost thousands more at a small fraction of the price.

Over 75,000 satisfied *AIR* customers agree: High quality FDA registered hearing aids don't have to cost a fortune.

The fact is, you don't need to spend thousands for a medical-grade digital hearing aid. **MDHearingAid** *AIR*® gives you a sophisticated high-performance hearing aid that works right out of the box with no time-consuming "adjustment" appointments. You can contact a hearing specialist conveniently online or by phone—even after sale at no cost. No other company provides such extensive support.

Now that you know... why pay more?

BIG SOUND. TINY PRICE.

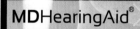
MDHearingAid®

TAKE ADVANTAGE OF OUR 45-DAY RISK-FREE TRIAL!

Hearing is believing and we invite you to try this nearly invisible hearing aid with no annoying whistling or background noise for yourself.
If you are not completely satisfied, simply return it within that time period for a *100% refund of your purchase price.*

For the Lowest Price Call
800-491-9204
GetMDHearingAid.com

Nearly Invisible

BATTERIES INCLUDED!
READY TO USE RIGHT OUT OF THE BOX!

Use Code **DD24**
and get **FREE** Batteries for 1 Year
Plus **FREE** Shipping

MORELS
Morchella spp.

or to prepare as cooked greens. Harvest the plant's long taproot and cook it as you would potatoes—boiled, roasted, or in soups and stews. If you feel adventurous, use the roots as coffee. With a moist cloth, clean off all dirt; slice and dry the roots in the sun or oven. When the slices are completely dry, spread them on a baking sheet and roast at 300°F until brown. When cool, grind them into a powder.

experienced foragers claim that edible mushrooms aren't any more difficult to identify than other wild plants. They recommend beginning with morels, as there are no poisonous varieties. Note that *Morchella* species are similar in appearance to the False Morel (*Gyromitra* spp.); the false specimen's caps are wrinkled, not pitted, and, when cut open, reveal chambers, not an all-hollow interior.

The blue flowers of **CHICORY** (*Cichorium intybus)* are a common sight along roadsides and in fields and vacant lots, yet it is the leaves and root that are eaten. Pick tender leaves in early spring for salads

CHICORY
Cichorium intybus

Native Americans called the **ELDERBERRY TREE** (*Sambucus nigra* ssp. *canadensis*) the "tree of music" because they made instruments from its hollow stems. The 8- to 10-foot-tall trees can be found throughout North America along streams or riverbeds, in shallow canyons, and in abandoned fields. In summer, the trees produce white blossoms that later become umbrels of tiny purple berries. Pick the flower clusters in midsummer for elder blow (or blau) pancakes or fritters (see recipe, page 256). Wait

ELDERBERRY TREE
Sambucus nigra ssp. *canadensis*

until mid- to late August to pick the berries for use in jams or pies. Pick only purple berries, as there is a poisonous variety with red berries. Avoid the leaves, stems, and roots, as they are poisonous.

For many foragers, **CATTAILS** *(Typha latifolia)* are the holy grail. The roots and young stalks are most commonly eaten, but even its pollen can be gathered and used in recipes for muffins (substitute for one-quarter of the flour) and pancakes (swap for up to half of the flour). In early summer, pick the new stalks by pulling back the green, fibrous outer layers to expose the white stalk. Harvest the stalk's tender 6- to 8-inch bottoms; its flavor is similar to that of cucumber or celery. Eat them raw, if desired, but be aware that doing so may cause a tingling sensation in the throat. To be safe, boil them for 10 to 20 minutes.

Gather pollen from the tip of the spike (male part) just above

IF YOU GO . . .
• Sign up for a local foraging tour.

• Identify plants with 100% certainty, cross-referencing at least two sources.

• Use the scientific name to identify plants. Common names can be misleading and vary from one region to another.

• Begin foraging in pesticide-free areas for common, easily identified plants such as dandelions.

• Harvest carefully. Leave some plants to guarantee a harvest next year.

• Consult with your state's cooperative extension service to confirm that none of the plants is on an endangered species list.

• Bring your kids. They will enjoy the adventure and learn new skills.

• Learn how to identify poison ivy. Your found food won't taste good if you're covered in an itchy rash!

• Dress properly: Steve Brill, who leads foraging tours throughout the New York City area and shared his expertise for this article, recommends comfortable, seasonal clothes and hiking shoes for rugged terrain or rubber boots for wet areas. Where ticks abound, wear light-color pants tucked into light-color socks. Bring a hat and gloves with fingertips cut off of your dominant hand's glove.

• Be sure to rinse all plants before using.

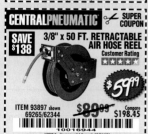

CATTAILS
Typha latifolia

are easy to spot: Cattail stalks are round, and each leaf is wrapped around the stem. The stalks of water iris are flat, and the leaves fan out from the stalk.

MILKWEED (*Asclepias syriaca*) is often recognized by the pods that form in late summer and then burst open in the fall to expose white, silky fibers. In the spring and summer, milkweed can be seen growing in clusters of erect stalks, about 2 to 5 feet tall. As the plant matures, it can be identified by its gray-green, oblong leaves. Pick young sprouts in the spring when they are about 6 inches tall

the brown, sausage-like section (female part). Hold each stalk over a cloth or pail and shake it. Just above the root, or rhizome, is the "heart" of the plant. Peel and cook these as you would prepare potatoes. Although cattail is similar in appearance to the toxic water iris, the differences

and resemble asparagus spears. The new leaves can be picked and eaten cooked, as you would with spinach. The unopened flower buds can be picked and cooked like broccoli. In late summer, pick the immature pods before the downy fibers form inside and prepare them as you would okra. All parts of the plant will taste somewhat bitter if not cooked properly, so when preparing sprouts, flower buds, or pods, boil for 1 minute, rinse, and repeat. Some foragers avoid picking milkweed shoots because they are similar in appearance to poisonous dogbane (*Apocynum* spp.). However, milkweed sprouts are slightly hairy; dogbane's are smooth. Do not eat raw milkweed as it contains resins that can cause severe stomach upset, as well as difficulty breathing, high temperatures, and muscle spasms. ∎

Turn to page 256 for forage recipes.

Martie Majoros forages for wild plants in her Burlington, Vermont, neighborhood.

MILKWEED
Asclepias syriaca

ONE OVER TWO, TWO OVER ONE

Secrets of stone walls laid bare

BY KEVIN GARDNER

In 1871, the only known census of stone walls in the U.S. Northeast took place, carried out by the newly created U.S. Department of Agriculture as part of a nationwide inventory of fencing. In the six New England states plus New York, the survey located more than 250,000 miles of stone wall, enough to circle Earth 10 times or even reach to the Moon.

The USDA's findings were impressive. They were also wildly off the mark—on the low side! The survey excluded thousands of other stone structures: foundations, causeways, ramps, bridges, dams, culverts, wells, and town pounds, all built the same way as the walls. The ubiquitous presence of such structures in almost every corner of the region has inspired the assertion that there is more dry-laid stone here than in all of the rest of

Photo: Sharon Cobo/Shutterstock

EVERY WALL
IS A DOOR.
–Ralph Waldo Emerson,
American poet (1803–82)

the world combined.

Although stone walls may have appeared as early as 1607 in the short-lived colony at Sagadahoc, Maine, and certainly did along the relatively tree-less coast of Rhode Island by the 1640s, they were not pioneers' first choice for fencing. Barriers of pulled stumps, split rails, and even brush—the vast detritus of clearing away the forest—served instead. At the same time, plowing and planting began to turn up huge quantities of glacially deposited stone. At first, farmers simply hauled the stone to the sides of their fields. As the early fences broke down and disappeared, they began to reorganize the growing rock mounds into taller, more carefully assembled structures.

Stone walls are far more durable than stumps and rails. They look better, too. Once under way, stone wall construction became a primary activity on the region's farms. Already well established in the decades leading up to the American Revolution, it accelerated after independence; the years between 1775 and 1825 witnessed a "frenzy of wall building." After 1810, when the appearance of the merino breed set off a profitable craze for sheep raising, hundreds of thousands more acres became enclosed in stone, especially in the region's still-developing northern states.

Stone wall building has one essential rule, which is to offset each row, layer, or *course* of stone over the joints (the cracks between stones) in the course below, so that individual stones are settled on more than one other. "One over two, two over one" is a common way of putting it, although in practice builders are just as likely to lay seven over three or two over nine. When properly constructed, stone walls become

THE YEARS BETWEEN 1775 AND 1825 WITNESSED A "FRENZY OF WALL BUILDING."

POST & BEAM

BARNS | GARAGES | PAVILIONS

gctimberframes.com
(860) 454-9103

Build Services &
Timber Frame Kits

GREAT COUNTRY
TIMBER FRAMES

IN STRUCTURAL TERMS THERE ARE REALLY ONLY TWO KINDS OF STONE WALLS: THE FREESTANDING AND THE RETAINER.

integrated but flexible units, able to adjust to settling and minor disturbances over time because each stone is held in place by several others rather than only one or two.

Still, the implication of "one over two"—that all stones are the same thickness—is a comical proposition in the Northeast, where tectonic collision, volcanic eruption, and implacable glaciation have left us with a mighty mess of stone of every conceivable shape, type, and size, much of it worn and rounded. New England wall builders responded to the dysfunctional diversity of their stone supply by building rougher and frequently thicker structures than wallers elsewhere. Wider walls with generous interior space offered room to store not just sheer volume, but also the peculiar stone shapes that make New

England wall building, in one commentator's words, "a real challenge."

The Northeast's random riot of stone types produces considerable variety in the way that walls can be made to look, but in structural terms there are really only two kinds: the freestanding and the retainer. Freestanding walls, which show faces on both sides, are generally built at least three-quarters as wide as they are tall. Retainers, which show a face on only one side and are built to hold back ("retain") a higher bank of earth on the other side, are built more thickly, often as wide as they are tall, or even wider, especially if they are foundations for buildings. The familiar single stack, or farmer's wall, just one stone thick, dispenses with formulas

Photo: Jay Boucher/Shutterstock

How To: Fix Crepe Skin

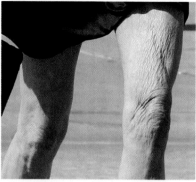

and faces altogether but still tends to run from wider to narrower as it rises, even though its individual stones are balanced, not clamped, in place.

The evolution of style in the Northeast's stone walls followed a path roughly similar to that of barns, houses, and land development. From the low rounded mounds of early settlement days, alongside log cabins, primitive lean-tos for animals, and stump-pocked clearings, stone walls developed and diversified. As the familiar landscape of large Colonial-era houses and barns amid a patchwork of open pastures, meadows, gardens, and woodlots emerged, stone walls took on a more sophisticated aspect, with tighter, more selective fitting, vertical faces, and formal ends and caps. Dimensions became purpose-built, from the 6- and 8-foot-wide containment walls stuffed with tons of garden-picked rubble to the formidable 4- and 5-foot-high single stacks to keep the sheep at home, to the blocky, bulky precision of foundations under barns and houses.

After 1840 or so, farming in the

TIPS OFF THE OL' BLOCK
Want to build a stone wall? Start here:

• Gather the largest supply of stone that you can. Variety in shape and size, with everything from "baseballs" to "bushel baskets," will give you the range of choices you need to match the requirements of the project as you go. It's much harder to build effectively from a supply that's too small.

• Learn to recognize useful shapes. Ideal building stones are often shaped like loaves of bread with flattened ends. Place them so that their long sides run back into the wall where they can be gripped by the structure's mass. Stones on the outside of a wall that are too shallow will squeeze out and fall away much sooner than longer ones.

• Work forward, not backward: Begin each placement at the wall, not the pile of stones. Look for holes, gaps, or platforms that will accept a particular shape, then search for something like it in your supply. If you begin by picking a stone and then starting a quest for its spot in the wall, you'll waste a lot of energy. If you know where every stone is going before you pick it up, your stamina will be much extended.

• Build on a section of some length rather than a single spot. An 8- or 10-foot stretch offers more possibilities for placement than one of a foot or two. If the wall is double-faced, build both sides and the middle all at once rather than by turns. This will help you to integrate its sections so that they support one another structurally.

• Pack as tightly as you can, even on the inside. Leaving too much space between stones allows them to move over time, accelerating the inevitable loosening (and eventual tumbling) that takes place in all walls.

PARK SEED

Superior Germination Guaranteed!

15%OFF

Your Next Order!

USE CODE: DELIGHTS
EXPIRES: 6/1/2018

parkseed.com   1.800.845.3369

1) 52782-PK-P1 Patio Choice Yellow Tomato 2) 51995-PK-P1 Zinnia Queen Red Lime 3) 52782-PK-P1 Tomato Midnight Snack 4) 52006-PK-P1 Penstemon Twizzle Purple 5) 52774-PK-P1 Pepper Sweetie Pie Bell Pepper 6) 51042-PK-P1 Cosmos Cupcakes Mix 7) 52747-PK-P1 Giant Garden Paste Tomato

THE LURE OF THE OLD NEW ENGLAND LANDSCAPE IS IRRESISTIBLE FOR MANY.

Northeast began to fall on hard times. Even before the Civil War, abandonment of upland homesteads had begun, and the postwar years saw alarming out-migration from many parts of the area. By the time barbed wire came along in the early 1870s, farmers had all but stopped building and maintaining their stone walls. But the craft was kept alive, often by recent immigrants familiar with stonework from their home countries and working for the railroads, on civic projects, or for the wealthy.

The residential building booms from the late 1970s on and off to the present have created a renaissance for wall building. At first almost entirely associated with landscaping, it blossomed into the restoration of older structures. Today, there are many more men and women—from professionals to inspired amateurs—engaged in traditional New England stonework than at any time in the past century. It seems unlikely that the craft will be forgotten anytime soon.

Although most contemporary wall building is decorative rather than rough-and-ready traditional work, the lure of the old New England landscape is irresistible for many. "Please don't make it look too nice!" they say. For them, a new wall isn't a good one unless it looks like an old one. ∎

Kevin Gardner is a writer, teacher, and tradesman living in Hopkinton, New Hampshire. He has been building traditional New England stone walls for more than 40 years. His latest book is *Stone Building: How to Make New England–Style Walls and Other Structures the Old Way* (The Countryman Press, 2017).

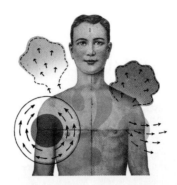

COMMON SCENTS

THROUGH THE AGES

Our fondness for fragrance is no accident.

By Ruth Graham
Illustrations by Tim Robinson

Americans spend $18 billion a year on deodorant and antiperspirants. That's $18 billion of proof that no one likes to smell bad. Read on to learn what history, science, and plain ol' common sense tell about our funky fragrance.

(continued)

THE SMALL STUFF

• We humans sweat all over our bodies, but most of our noticeable body odor comes from areas where we have a distinct variety of sweat glands called apocrine glands. Their excretions combine with the billions of bacteria that live on our bodies to create that unique aroma.

• "Deodorant" and "antiperspirant" are often used interchangeably, but they are slightly different products: Deodorant controls odor only, while antiperspirant is also meant to prevent sweat.

Early remedies for armpit odor included consuming chestnuts, celery, asparagus, and wine. But body odor hasn't always been something to be banished. One 4th-century mystic claimed to be able to diagnose a person's moral character through the smell of his body. More commonly, the smell of a person's sweat would have helped to identify him or her—even where he or she were from. A leather craftsman would smell like hides, for example, and a fisherman, like the ocean or the catch.

Some people found personal odors alluring. Napoleon so enjoyed Josephine's aroma that he told her, "Don't wash." In that era, even some members of royal families emitted odors that would stand out to modern noses, says Jonathan Reinarz, the author of *Past Scents,* a book about the history of smell. But "if even royalty stinks, it gives it a respectability," he says. In other words, if everyone smells, then nobody does.

In France, especially, strong perfume was often used by the aristocracy to cover B.O. But when bathing became customary and perfume more widespread, it was no longer chic to reek. In the Victorian era, people wore cotton or rubber

Horses sweat, men perspire, and ladies glow.

–Victorian etiquette guide

> **Common sense is like deodorant . . . the people who need it almost never use it.**
>
> *–Unknown*

pads in their armpits to protect their clothes from sweat.

The first deodorant, called Mum, was a cream that users rubbed into their armpits. It often left a greasy residue on clothes. (The product's name is not about "keeping mum"—being silent, say, about using it. The word was a nickname for the inventor's nurse.)

Mum was trademarked in 1888, and an antiperspirant called Everdry hit the market 15 years later. Advertisers told women that they would never catch a husband without applying the right odor-banishing products. But it took another few decades for deodorant-makers to try selling their wares to men because smelling "all natural" was considered manly.

Despite the proliferation of body odor blockers and inhibitors in the past century, modern science suggests that you might be better off—or at least no worse—without them. For example, one very small study in Belgium suggested that antiperspirants increased the levels of foul-smelling bacteria in the armpit. Then there is this other . . . er . . . evidence:

REUSE YOUR ROLL-ONS
Wash and refill empty roll-on deodorant bottles with bath oil, suntan lotion, water for moistening stamps and envelopes, or paint for kids.

VINEGAR

TO CLEAR THE AIR

● **Consume more citrus.**
The acids in fresh citrus fruit, particularly lemons, may help to flush out some of the toxins that can lead to stench.

● **Make your own deodorants.**
1. Combine equal parts apple cider vinegar and water in a spray bottle. Spritz odor-prone areas. The vinegar's smell dissipates within a few minutes, while its antibacterial power remains.

2. Mix ¼ cup baking soda with ¼ cup of cornstarch or arrowroot powder. If desired, add a few drops of essential oil (e.g., lavender and/or tea tree; both are antimicrobial). Shake to mix well. Pat on odor-prone areas with a damp washcloth or cotton ball.
  Variation: Add 3 to 5 tablespoons coconut oil and stir well to form a thick paste. Transfer to an empty, clean deodorant dispenser and use it as you would a commercial product.

Red meat can make you rank. Scientists in the Czech Republic put a group of men on a meat or vegetarian diet for 2 weeks. The next month, the same men swapped: Those who had previously eaten meat went vegetarian and vice versa. When women rated how the men smelled, the veggie diet was judged "more attractive, more pleasant, and less intense."

Some people's armpits don't smell at all. That's thanks to a rare genetic mutation. Even so, a recent study showed that the vast majority of women with the lucky mutation still use deodorant every day.

What Napoleon knew: Most people think of body odor as the opposite of alluring, which is why we put on perfume before dates and apply an extra layer of deodorant before a big meeting. But scientists are finding that body odor is not always a repellent. One study showed that men can smell when women are most fertile, for example. The men weren't sniffing for fertility, but they rated fertile women as smelling more "pleasant" and "desirable."

Ruth Graham is a freelance journalist who lives in New Hampshire.

Success is a great deodorant. It takes away all your past smells.
–*Elizabeth Taylor, American actress (1932–2011)*

THE FUTURE OF SMELLING NICE

What's next for one of the oldest smells in human history? Here are some possibilities.

- From "pee-ewe" to "love you." In preparation for "pheromone parties," guests sleep in the same T-shirt for 3 nights. They then bring it to the party in a bag. People sniff each other's bags, and if a scent appeals, they follow their nose.

A dating service called "Smell Dating, the first mail odor dating service," works similarly. The service sends subscribers a clean shirt to wear for 3 days and 3 nights. Then it mails swatches of the used garment to potential matches. If two users like each other's smell, the service connects them.

- How to tell if you smell? There's an app for that. A German company and a Vietnamese ad agency created a mobile phone cover that works as an "electronic nose." A user activates a special app and then waves his phone near his armpits. The app lets him know if he smells A-OK or if he needs to reapply ASAP.

- Slather on a super-smart deodorant. Dark, moist armpits make good homes for bacteria. But it was only recently that scientists figured out which bacteria cause that funky odor. The culprits include *Staphylococcus hominis,* which combines with sweat to produce one of the main components of B.O. This research means that someday your deodorant could target only certain bacteria, rather than killing off harmless or even beneficial strains, too. That's the sweet smell of success! –R. G. ■

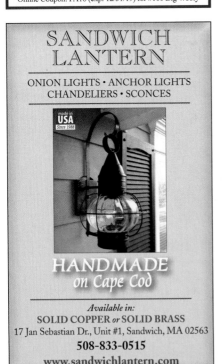

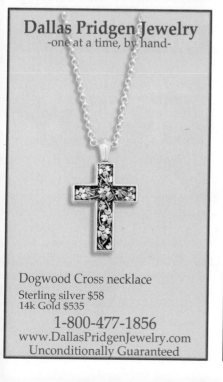

WINTER 2017-18

Cold, snowy

Mild, wet

Mild, dry

Mild, snowy

Cold, dry

Mild, snowy

Mild, snowy

Mild, snowy

Cold, wet

Cold, snowy

Mild, snowy

Mild, wet

Mild, wet

Cold, wet

Mild, wet

Cold, snowy

Cold, snowy

Cold, wet

Mild, wet

Cold, wet

Cold, wet

Mild, wet

These weather maps correspond to the winter (November through March) and summer (June through August) predictions in the General Weather Forecast (opposite). Forecast terms here represent deviations from the normals; learn more on page 217.

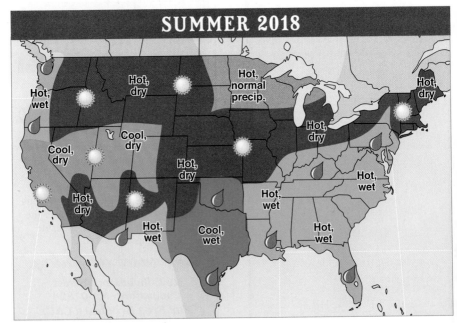

SUMMER 2018

Hot, wet

Hot, dry

Hot, normal precip.

Hot, dry

Cool, dry

Cool, dry

Hot, dry

Hot, dry

Hot, dry

Hot, wet

Hot, wet

Cool, wet

Hot, wet

Hot, wet

THE GENERAL WEATHER REPORT AND FORECAST

FOR REGIONAL FORECASTS, SEE PAGES 220-237.

What's shaping the weather? Solar Cycle 24, the smallest in more than 100 years, is well into its declining phase after reaching double peaks in late 2011 and early 2014. As solar activity continues to decline from these low peaks toward the minima in early 2019, we expect temperatures in much of the nation to be colder than last winter but still above normal. The winter of 2017–18 will feature above-normal snowfall in much of New England, from New Mexico eastward to the Tennessee Valley, in the central Plains and the Intermountain region, and in the California mountains, with below-normal snowfall in other areas.

With last winter's weak La Niña most likely to be replaced by a weak El Niño this winter, cold air masses will be able to slide into the Intermountain region but will have difficulty making any prolonged inroads into the northern Plains, Great Lakes, or northeastern states. Other important factors in the coming weather pattern include the Atlantic Multidecadal Oscillation in a continued warm phase, the North Atlantic Oscillation (NAO) in a neutral phase, and the Pacific Decadal Oscillation (PDO) in the early stages of its warm cycle. Oscillations are linked ocean–atmosphere patterns that influence the weather over periods of weeks to years.

WINTER temperatures will be much colder than last winter—but still above normal—from Maine southward to most of Florida and westward through the Great Lakes, Midwest, Heartland, and Northern Plains. Below-normal temperatures will be the rule from the Gulf States westward to California and from the Intermountain region westward to the Pacific Northwest. Precipitation will be above normal in much of the country, with above-normal snowfall in northern and central New England, from the Tennessee Valley westward to New Mexico, and in the central Great Lakes, the central Plains, and the Intermountain region.

SPRING will be warmer than normal in Florida, the Lower Lakes, the Intermountain region, the Pacific Northwest, and interior portions of the Pacific Southwest and near or cooler than normal elsewhere. Spring precipitation will be below normal from North Carolina southward to Florida and in the Lower Lakes, the Intermountain region, and the Pacific Coast states; it will be above normal in most other areas.

SUMMER temperatures will be below normal in much of California, the southern Intermountain region, and Texas–Oklahoma but above normal elsewhere. Rainfall will be above normal from the mid-Atlantic southward to Florida, in the Tennessee and Ohio Valleys and the Deep South, from Texas–Oklahoma westward into southeastern Arizona, and in the Pacific Northwest; it will be below normal elsewhere.

The best chances for a major **HURRICANE** strike are in late August and early September along the western and central Gulf regions, with a tropical storm threat in early to mid-September from Florida to North Carolina.

AUTUMN temperatures will be cooler than normal in much of the Northeast, from the High Plains westward to the Pacific, and in the Desert Southwest and warmer than normal in most other areas. Precipitation will be above normal in Florida, the Deep South, the Ohio Valley, and Texas; from Illinois westward to the Intermountain region; and in the central Pacific region. It will be near or below normal elsewhere.

TO LEARN HOW WE MAKE OUR WEATHER PREDICTIONS, TURN TO PAGE 217;
TO GET A SUMMARY OF THE RESULTS OF OUR FORECAST FOR LAST WINTER, TURN TO PAGE 218.

WEATHER

THE OLD
FARMER'S ALMANAC

Established in 1792 and published every year thereafter
ROBERT B. THOMAS, *founder* (1766–1846)

YANKEE PUBLISHING INC.

EDITORIAL AND PUBLISHING OFFICES
P.O. Box 520, 1121 Main Street, Dublin, NH 03444
Phone: 603-563-8111 • Fax: 603-563-8252

EDITOR *(13th since 1792):* Janice Stillman
ART DIRECTOR: Colleen Quinnell
MANAGING EDITOR: Jack Burnett
SENIOR EDITORS: Sarah Perreault, Heidi Stonehill
EDITORIAL ASSISTANTS: Tim Clark,
Mare-Anne Jarvela, Benjamin Kilbride
WEATHER GRAPHICS AND CONSULTATION:
AccuWeather, Inc.

V.P., NEW MEDIA AND PRODUCTION:
Paul Belliveau
PRODUCTION DIRECTORS:
Susan Gross, David Ziarnowski
SENIOR PRODUCTION ARTISTS:
Rachel Kipka, Jennifer Freeman, Janet Selle

WEB SITE: ALMANAC.COM
DIGITAL EDITOR: Catherine Boeckmann
DIGITAL ASSISTANT EDITOR: Christopher Burnett
NEW MEDIA DESIGNERS: Lou S. Eastman, Amy O'Brien
E-COMMERCE DIRECTOR: Alan Henning
PROGRAMMING: Peter Rukavina

CONTACT US
We welcome your questions and comments about articles in and topics for this Almanac. Mail all editorial correspondence to Editor, The Old Farmer's Almanac, P.O. Box 520, Dublin, NH 03444-0520; fax us at 603-563-8252; or contact us through Almanac.com/Feedback. *The Old Farmer's Almanac* can not accept responsibility for unsolicited manuscripts and will not acknowledge any hard-copy queries or manuscripts that do not include a stamped and addressed return envelope.

All printing inks used in this edition of *The Old Farmer's Almanac* are soy-based. This product is recyclable. Consult local recycling regulations for the right way to do it.

Thank you for buying this Almanac! We hope that you find it "useful, with a pleasant degree of humor." Thanks, too, to everyone who had a hand in it, including advertisers, distributors, printers, and sales and delivery people.

OUR CONTRIBUTORS

Bob Berman, our astronomy editor, is the director of Overlook Observatory in Woodstock and Storm King Observatory in Cornwall, both in New York. In 1976, he founded the Catskill Astronomical Society. Bob has led many aurora and eclipse expeditions, venturing as far as the Arctic and Antarctic.

Tim Clark, a retired high school English teacher from New Hampshire, wrote the Farmer's Calendar essays that appear in this edition. His recordings of them are available free at Almanac.com/Podcast. He has composed the weather doggerel on the Calendar Pages since 1980.

Bethany E. Cobb, our astronomer, earned a Ph.D. in astronomy at Yale University and is an Assistant Professor of Honors and Physics at George Washington University. She also conducts research on gamma-ray bursts and follows numerous astronomy pursuits, including teaching astronomy to adults at the Osher Lifelong Learning Institute at UC Berkeley. When she is not scanning the sky, she enjoys playing the violin, figure skating, and reading science fiction.

Celeste Longacre, our astrologer, often refers to astrology as "a study of timing, and timing is everything." A New Hampshire native, she has been a practicing astrologer for more than 25 years. Her book, *Celeste's Garden Delights* (2015), is available for sale on her Web site, www.celestelongacre.com.

Michael Steinberg, our meteorologist, has been forecasting weather for the Almanac since 1996. In addition to college degrees in atmospheric science and meteorology, he brings a lifetime of experience to the task: He began predicting weather when he attended the only high school in the world with weather Teletypes and radar.

ADVERTISEMENT

"My friends all hate their cell phones... I love mine!" Here's why.

Say good-bye to everything you hate about cell phones. Say hello to the Jitterbug Flip.

"Cell phones have gotten so small, I can barely dial mine." Not the Jitterbug® Flip. It features a large keypad for easier dialing. It even has a larger display and a powerful, hearing aid compatible speaker, so it's easy to see and conversations are clear.

"I'd like a cell phone to use in an emergency." Now you can turn your phone into a personal safety device with 5Star® Service. In any uncertain or unsafe situation, simply press the 5Star button to speak immediately with a highly-trained Urgent Response Agent who will confirm your location, evaluate your situation and get you the help you need, 24/7.

Monthly Plan	$14.99/mo¹	$19.99/mo¹
Monthly Minutes	200	600
Personal Operator Assistance	24/7	24/7
Long Distance Calls	No add'l charge	No add'l charge
Voice Dial	FREE	FREE
Nationwide Coverage	YES	YES
30-Day Return Policy²	YES	YES

More minute plans and Health & Safety Packages available. Ask your Jitterbug expert for details.

Enough talk. Isn't it time you found out more about the cell phone that's changing all the rules? Call now! Jitterbug product experts are standing by.

Order now and receive a **FREE Car Charger** for your Jitterbug Flip – a $25 value. Call now!

Available in Red (shown) and Graphite.

Call toll-free to get your
Jitterbug Flip Cell Phone
Please mention promotional code 106301.

1-877-566-2254
www.JitterbugDirect.com

47667

THE OLD

FARMER'S ALMANAC

Established in 1792 and published every year thereafter

ROBERT B. THOMAS, *founder* (1766–1846)

YANKEE PUBLISHING INC.
P.O. Box 520, 1121 Main Street, Dublin, NH 03444
Phone: 603-563-8111 • Fax: 603-563-8252

PUBLISHER *(23rd since 1792)*: Sherin Pierce
EDITOR IN CHIEF: Judson D. Hale Sr.

FOR DISPLAY ADVERTISING RATES
Go to Almanac.com/AdvertisingInfo or
Call 800-895-9265, ext. 109

Stephanie Bernbach-Crowe • 914-827-0015
Steve Hall • 800-736-1100, ext. 320
Susan Lyman • 646-221-4169

FOR CLASSIFIED ADVERTISING
Cindy Levine, RJ Media • 212-986-0016

AD PRODUCTION COORDINATOR:
Janet Selle • 800-895-9265, ext. 168

PUBLIC RELATIONS
Quinn/Brein • 206-842-8922
ginger@quinnbrein.com

CONSUMER MAIL ORDERS
Call 800-ALMANAC (800-256-2622)
or go to Almanac.com/Shop

CONSUMER MARKETING MANAGER:
Kate McPherson • 800-895-9265, ext. 188

RETAIL SALES
Stacey Korpi • 800-895-9265, ext. 160
Janice Edson, ext. 126

DISTRIBUTORS
NATIONAL: Curtis Circulation Company
New Milford, NJ
BOOKSTORE: Houghton Mifflin Harcourt
Boston, MA

Old Farmer's Almanac publications are available for sales promotions or premiums. Contact Beacon Promotions, info@beaconpromotions.com.

YANKEE PUBLISHING INCORPORATED

Jamie Trowbridge, *President;* Judson D. Hale Sr., *Senior Vice President;* Paul Belliveau, Jody Bugbee, Judson D. Hale Jr., Brook Holmberg, Sherin Pierce, *Vice Presidents.*

PRINTED IN U.S.A.

How To: Fix Your Fatigue and Get More Energy

According to patients at the Center for Restorative Medicine, a discovery has completely transformed their lives.

Founder and Director **Dr. Steven Gundry** is a world-renowned heart surgeon, a best-selling author, and the personal physician to many celebrities. But his breakthrough could be the most important accomplishment of his career.

"They're reporting natural, long-lasting energy without a 'crash' and they're feeling slim, fit and active," he revealed yesterday.

Dr. Gundry has unveiled a simple — yet highly effective — solution to issues that plague millions of Americans over 40: low energy, low metabolism and constant fatigue.

"When you're feeling low energy, that's your body screaming **HELP!**" Dr. Gundry's radical solution was inspired by a breakthrough with a "hopeless" patient who had been massively overweight, chronically fatigued and suffering from severely clogged arteries.

The secret to his breakthrough? **"There are key 'micronutrients' missing from your diet,"** Dr. Gundry said, "If you can replenish them in very high dosages, the results can be astonishing."

This unorthodox philosophy is what led Dr. Gundry to create an at-home method for fatigue — which has since become remarkably successful with his patients.

Dr. Gundry's team released a **comprehensive video presentation**, so that the public can be educated as to exactly how it works.

Watch the presentation here at **www.GetEnergy52.com**

Within just a few hours, this video had gotten thousands of hits, and is now considered to have gone viral. One viewer commented: "If this works, it's exactly what I've been praying for my whole life. I've never seen anything like this solution before…the truth about my diet was shocking and eye-opening."

It makes a lot of sense, and it sounds great in theory, but we'll have to wait and see what the results are. Knowing Dr. Gundry, however, there is a great deal of potential.

See his presentation here at **www.GetEnergy52.com**

There will be five eclipses in 2018, three of the Sun and two of the Moon. Solar eclipses are visible only in certain areas and require eye protection to be viewed safely. Lunar eclipses are technically visible from the entire night side of Earth, but during a penumbral eclipse, the dimming of the Moon's illumination is slight. See the **Astronomical Glossary, page 126,** for explanations of the different types of eclipses.

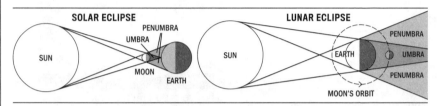

JANUARY 31: TOTAL ECLIPSE OF THE MOON. This eclipse is best viewed from central and western North America; in the east, the Moon will be setting soon after it enters the umbra. The Moon will enter the penumbra at 5:50 A.M. ET (2:50 A.M. PT) and the umbra at 6:48 A.M. ET (3:48 A.M. PT). The Moon will leave the umbra at 10:12 A.M. ET (7:12 A.M. PT) and the prenumbra at 11:10 A.M. ET (8:10 A.M. PT).

FEBRUARY 15: PARTIAL ECLIPSE OF THE SUN. This eclipse is not visible from North America but can be viewed from Antarctica, southern South America, and the Falkland Islands.

JULY 13: PARTIAL ECLIPSE OF THE SUN. This eclipse is not visible from North America but can be viewed from Antarctica, Tasmania, southern South Australia, and Stewart Island.

JULY 27: TOTAL ECLIPSE OF THE MOON. This eclipse is not visible from North America but can be viewed from Antarctica, Australia, Asia, Africa, Europe, and central and eastern South America.

AUGUST 11: PARTIAL ECLIPSE OF THE SUN. This eclipse is visible in North America only from very northeastern Canada but can also be seen from Greenland, Iceland, northernmost UK, most of Scandinavia and Russia, Kazakhstan, Kyrgyzstan, Mongolia, and China.

NEXT TOTAL ECLIPSES OF THE SUN. *July 2, 2019:* visible from South America and the South Pacific Ocean. *December 14, 2020:* visible from South America and Antarctica. The next total solar eclipse visible from North America will occur on April 8, 2024.

THE MOON'S PATH

The Moon's path across the sky changes with the seasons. Full Moons are very high in the sky (at midnight) between November and February and very low in the sky between May and July.

FULL-MOON DATES (ET)					
	2018	2019	2020	2021	2022
JAN.	1 & 31	21	10	28	17
FEB.	–	19	9	27	16
MAR.	1 & 31	20	9	28	18
APR.	29	19	7	26	16
MAY	29	18	7	26	16
JUNE	28	17	5	24	14
JULY	27	16	5	23	13
AUG.	26	15	3	22	11
SEPT.	24	14	2	20	10
OCT.	24	13	1 & 31	20	9
NOV.	23	12	30	19	8
DEC.	22	12	29	18	7

BRIGHT STARS

TRANSIT TIMES

This table shows the time (ET) and altitude of a star as it transits the meridian (i.e., reaches its highest elevation while passing over the horizon's south point) at Boston on the dates shown. The transit time on any other date differs from that of the nearest date listed by approximately 4 minutes per day. To find the time of a star's transit for your location, convert its time at Boston using Key Letter C (see Time Corrections, page 130).

STAR	CONSTELLATION	MAGNITUDE	JAN. 1	MAR. 1	MAY 1	JULY 1	SEPT. 1	NOV. 1	ALTITUDE (DEGREES)
			TIME OF TRANSIT (ET) BOLD = P.M. LIGHT = A.M.						
Altair	Aquila	0.8	**12:51**	8:59	5:59	1:59	**9:51**	**5:51**	56.3
Deneb	Cygnus	1.3	**1:41**	9:49	6:49	2:49	**10:41**	**6:42**	92.8
Fomalhaut	Psc. Aus.	1.2	**3:57**	**12:05**	9:05	5:05	1:02	**8:58**	17.8
Algol	Perseus	2.2	**8:07**	**4:15**	**1:15**	9:15	5:12	1:12	88.5
Aldebaran	Taurus	0.9	**9:34**	**5:42**	**2:43**	10:43	6:39	2:39	64.1
Rigel	Orion	0.1	**10:13**	**6:21**	**3:21**	11:21	7:17	3:18	39.4
Capella	Auriga	0.1	**10:15**	**6:23**	**3:24**	11:24	7:20	3:20	93.6
Bellatrix	Orion	1.6	**10:23**	**6:31**	**3:32**	11:32	7:28	3:28	54.0
Betelgeuse	Orion	var. 0.4	**10:53**	**7:01**	**4:02**	**12:02**	7:58	3:58	55.0
Sirius	Can. Maj.	−1.4	**11:43**	**7:51**	**4:51**	**12:51**	8:48	4:48	31.0
Procyon	Can. Min.	0.4	12:41	**8:45**	**5:45**	**1:46**	9:42	5:42	52.9
Pollux	Gemini	1.2	12:47	**8:51**	**5:52**	**1:52**	9:48	5:48	75.7
Regulus	Leo	1.4	3:10	**11:14**	**8:14**	**4:14**	**12:10**	8:11	59.7
Spica	Virgo	var. 1.0	6:26	2:34	**11:30**	**7:31**	**3:27**	11:27	36.6
Arcturus	Boötes	−0.1	7:16	3:24	12:25	**8:21**	**4:17**	**12:17**	66.9
Antares	Scorpius	var. 0.9	9:30	5:38	2:38	**10:34**	**6:31**	**2:31**	21.3
Vega	Lyra	0	11:37	7:45	4:45	12:45	**8:37**	**4:37**	86.4

RISE AND SET TIMES

To find the time of a star's rising at Boston on any date, subtract the interval shown at right from the star's transit time on that date; add the interval to find the star's setting time. To find the rising and setting times for your city, convert the Boston transit times above using the Key Letter shown at right before applying the interval (see Time Corrections, page 130). Deneb, Algol, Capella, and Vega are circumpolar stars—they never set but appear to circle the celestial north pole.

STAR	INTERVAL (H. M.)	RISING KEY	RISING DIR.*	SETTING KEY	SETTING DIR.*
Altair	6 36	B	EbN	E	WbN
Fomalhaut	3 59	E	SE	D	SW
Aldebaran	7 06	B	ENE	D	WNW
Rigel	5 33	D	EbS	B	WbS
Bellatrix	6 27	B	EbN	D	WbN
Betelgeuse	6 31	B	EbN	D	WbN
Sirius	5 00	D	ESE	B	WSW
Procyon	6 23	B	EbN	D	WbN
Pollux	8 01	A	NE	E	NW
Regulus	6 49	B	EbN	D	WbN
Spica	5 23	D	EbS	B	WbS
Arcturus	7 19	A	ENE	E	WNW
Antares	4 17	E	SEbE	A	SWbW

*b = "by"

Breakthrough technology converts phone calls to captions.

New amplified phone lets you hear AND see the conversation.

The Hamilton® CapTel® Captioned Telephone coverts phone conversations to easy-to-read captions for individuals with hearing loss.

A simple idea... made possible with sophisticated technology. If you have trouble understanding a call, captioned telephone can change your life. During a phone call the words spoken to you appear on the phone's screen – similar to closed captioning on TV. So when you make or receive a call, the words spoken to you are not only amplified by the phone, but scroll across the phone so you can listen while reading everything that's said to

hello grandma this is Kaitlynn how are you today? I wanted to say thank you for the birthday card

SEE what you've been missing!

you. Each call is routed through a call center, where computer technology – aided by a live representative – generates voice-to-text translations. The captioning is real-time, accurate and readable. Your conversation is private and the captioning service doesn't cost you a penny. Internet Protocol Captioned Telephone Service (IP CTS) is regulated and funded by the Federal Communications Commission (FCC) and is designed exclusively for individuals with hearing loss. To learn more, visit www.fcc.gov. The Hamilton CapTel phone requires telephone service and high-speed Internet access. WiFi Capable. Callers do not need special equipment or a captioned telephone in order to speak with you.

Finally... a phone you can use again. The Hamilton CapTel phone is also packed with features to help make phone calls easier. The keypad has large, easy to use buttons. You get adjustable volume amplification along with the ability to save captions for review later. It even has an answering machine that provides you with the captions of each message.

See for yourself with our exclusive home trial. Try a captioned telephone in your own home and if you are not completely amazed, simply return it within 60-days for a refund of the product purchase price. It even comes with a 5-year warranty.

Captioned Telephone
Call now for our special introductory price!

Call now Toll-Free
1-877-671-2905

Please mention promotion code 106302.

THE TWILIGHT ZONE/METEOR SHOWERS

Twilight is the time when the sky is partially illuminated preceding sunrise and again following sunset. The ranges of twilight are defined according to the Sun's position below the horizon. **Civil twilight** occurs when the Sun's center is between the horizon and 6 degrees below the horizon (visually, the horizon is clearly defined). **Nautical twilight** occurs when the center is between 6 and 12 degrees below the horizon (the horizon is distinct). **Astronomical twilight** occurs when the center is between 12 and 18 degrees below the horizon (sky illumination is imperceptible). When the center is at 18 degrees (**dawn** or **dark**) or below, there is no illumination.

LENGTH OF ASTRONOMICAL TWILIGHT (HOURS AND MINUTES)

LATITUDE	JAN. 1- APR. 10	APR. 11- MAY 2	MAY 3- MAY 14	MAY 15- MAY 25	MAY 26- JULY 22	JULY 23- AUG. 3	AUG. 4- AUG. 14	AUG. 15- SEPT. 5	SEPT. 6- DEC. 31
25°N to 30°N	1 20	1 23	1 26	1 29	1 32	1 29	1 26	1 23	1 20
31°N to 36°N	1 26	1 28	1 34	1 38	1 43	1 38	1 34	1 28	1 26
37°N to 42°N	1 33	1 39	1 47	1 52	1 59	1 52	1 47	1 39	1 33
43°N to 47°N	1 42	1 51	2 02	2 13	2 27	2 13	2 02	1 51	1 42
48°N to 49°N	1 50	2 04	2 22	2 42	–	2 42	2 22	2 04	1 50

TO DETERMINE THE LENGTH OF TWILIGHT: The length of twilight changes with latitude and the time of year. See the **Time Corrections, page 130,** to find the latitude of your city or the city nearest you. Use that figure in the chart above with the appropriate date to calculate the length of twilight in your area.

TO DETERMINE ARRIVAL OF DAWN OR DARK: Calculate the sunrise/sunset times for your locality using the instructions in **How to Use This Almanac, page 136.**

Subtract the length of twilight from the time of sunrise to determine when dawn breaks. Add the length of twilight to the time of sunset to determine when dark descends.

EXAMPLE:
BOSTON, MASS. (LATITUDE 42°22')

Sunrise, August 1	5:37 A.M. ET
Length of twilight	- 1 52
Dawn breaks	3:45 A.M.
Sunset, August 1	8:04 P.M. ET
Length of twilight	+1 52
Dark descends	9:56 P.M.

PRINCIPAL METEOR SHOWERS

SHOWER	BEST VIEWING	POINT OF ORIGIN	DATE OF MAXIMUM*	NO. PER HOUR**	ASSOCIATED COMET
Quadrantid	**Predawn**	**N**	**Jan. 4**	**25**	–
Lyrid	Predawn	S	Apr. 22	10	Thatcher
Eta Aquarid	Predawn	SE	May 4	10	Halley
Delta Aquarid	Predawn	S	July 30	10	–
Perseid	**Predawn**	**NE**	**Aug. 11-13**	**50**	**Swift-Tuttle**
Draconid	Late evening	NW	Oct. 9	6	Giacobini-Zinner
Orionid	Predawn	S	Oct. 21-22	15	Halley
Taurid	Late evening	S	Nov. 9	3	Encke
Leonid	Predawn	S	Nov. 17-18	10	Tempel-Tuttle
Andromedid	Late evening	S	Nov. 25-27	5	Biela
Geminid	**All night**	**NE**	**Dec. 13-14**	**75**	–
Ursid	Predawn	N	Dec. 22	5	Tuttle

*May vary by 1 or 2 days   **In a moonless, rural sky   **Bold** = most prominent

THE VISIBLE PLANETS

Listed here for Boston are viewing suggestions for and the rise and set times (ET) of Venus, Mars, Jupiter, and Saturn on specific days each month, as well as when it is best to view Mercury. Approximate rise and set times for other days can be found by interpolation. Use the Key Letters at the right of each listing to convert the times for other localities **(see pages 130 and 136)**.

FOR ALL PLANET RISE AND SET TIMES BY ZIP CODE, VISIT ALMANAC.COM/ASTRONOMY.

VENUS

This is a very good year for the cloud-covered planet. It starts 2018 invisibly, behind the Sun on January 9, but can be glimpsed low in the west in mid-February. It gets higher and brighter thereafter and will catch the world's attention as a brilliant evening star throughout the spring. It's highest in May, when it sets before 11:00 P.M.; then, still brightening, it gets lower through the summer. Its greatest brilliancy is in September, but by then it has sunk into the evening twilight. Venus vanishes in October, then rapidly returns as a morning star in mid-November, near Virgo's Spica, and is prominent at month's end. It reaches greatest brilliancy in December, while nicely high at dawn at a shadow-casting magnitude –4.9.

Jan. 1	rise	7:10	E	Apr. 1	set	**8:51**	D	July 1	set	**10:44**	E	Oct. 1	set	**7:04**	A
Jan. 11	rise	7:20	E	Apr. 11	set	**9:17**	E	July 11	set	**10:31**	D	Oct. 11	set	**6:21**	A
Jan. 21	set	**4:54**	B	Apr. 21	set	**9:42**	E	July 21	set	**10:14**	D	Oct. 21	rise	8:05	E
Feb. 1	set	**5:23**	B	May 1	set	**10:06**	E	Aug. 1	set	**9:53**	C	Nov. 1	rise	6:42	D
Feb. 11	set	**5:49**	B	May 11	set	**10:27**	E	Aug. 11	set	**9:32**	C	Nov. 11	rise	4:37	D
Feb. 21	set	**6:14**	C	May 21	set	**10:44**	E	Aug. 21	set	**9:09**	B	Nov. 21	rise	3:53	D
Mar. 1	set	**6:34**	C	June 1	set	**10:54**	E	Sept. 1	set	**8:41**	B	Dec. 1	rise	3:28	D
Mar. 11	set	**7:59**	C	June 11	set	**10:57**	E	Sept. 11	set	**8:13**	B	Dec. 11	rise	3:18	D
Mar. 21	set	**8:24**	D	June 21	set	**10:53**	E	Sept. 21	set	**7:42**	A	Dec. 21	rise	3:18	D
												Dec. 31	rise	3:25	D

MARS

This is Mars's most brilliant year since its historic 2003 close approach. It is visible every month. After starting in Libra as a medium-bright predawn "star," Mars rapidly brightens and reaches zero magnitude in April, after having a close conjunction with Saturn from April 1 to 3 in Sagittarius. The Red Planet attains a dazzling magnitude –2.8 on July 31, at its closest approach, when it outshines even Jupiter. It's then 24 arcseconds across—its widest appearance of the past 15 years—although it's quite low. Even at its highest nightly point in the south, it's lower than the winter solstice Sun. Mars fades thereafter, rapidly gains elevation in late autumn, and finishes the year in Pisces. It's then highest at nightfall, shining at a still respectable magnitude zero.

Jan. 1	rise	2:44	D	Apr. 1	rise	2:12	E	July 1	**rise**	**10:23**	E	Oct. 1	set	1:17	A
Jan. 11	rise	2:37	E	Apr. 11	rise	1:55	E	July 11	**rise**	**9:44**	E	Oct. 11	set	1:02	B
Jan. 21	rise	2:29	E	Apr. 21	rise	1:37	E	July 21	**rise**	**9:01**	E	Oct. 21	set	12:51	B
Feb. 1	rise	2:20	E	May 1	rise	1:16	E	Aug. 1	**rise**	**8:10**	E	Nov. 1	set	12:41	B
Feb. 11	rise	2:11	E	May 11	rise	12:54	E	Aug. 11	set	3:58	A	Nov. 11	**set**	**11:32**	B
Feb. 21	rise	2:02	E	May 21	rise	12:30	E	Aug. 21	set	3:12	A	Nov. 21	**set**	**11:26**	B
Mar. 1	rise	1:53	E	June 1	rise	12:02	E	Sept. 1	set	2:30	A	Dec. 1	**set**	**11:20**	C
Mar. 11	rise	1:41	E	June 11	**rise**	**11:30**	E	Sept. 11	set	2:00	A	Dec. 11	**set**	**11:15**	C
Mar. 21	rise	2:28	E	June 21	**rise**	**10:58**	E	Sept. 21	set	1:36	A	Dec. 21	**set**	**11:10**	C
												Dec. 31	**set**	**11:05**	C

BOLD = P.M. LIGHT = A.M.

JUPITER

The largest planet spends most of the year in Libra, starting out near Mars in the predawn sky; it hovers quite close to the Red Planet on January 6–7. Jupiter rises about 2 hours earlier each month and by mid-April can be seen in the east after 10:00 P.M. Jupiter reaches opposition on May 8–9, when it's out all night, shining at a brilliant magnitude –2.5, a bit below its normal maximum brightness. It remains well placed through the summer, gets low in the evening sky in autumn, and vanishes in early November. Jupiter reappears in December, low in the predawn sky. It sits next to Mercury on the winter solstice (December 21).

Jan. 1	rise	2:57	D	Apr. 1	rise	10:26	E	July 1	set	2:00	B	Oct. 1	set	8:18	B
Jan. 11	rise	2:26	D	Apr. 11	rise	9:42	E	July 11	set	1:20	B	Oct. 11	set	7:44	B
Jan. 21	rise	1:53	D	Apr. 21	rise	8:57	E	July 21	set	12:41	B	Oct. 21	set	7:11	B
Feb. 1	rise	1:17	D	May 1	rise	8:12	D	Aug. 1	set	11:55	B	Nov. 1	set	6:35	B
Feb. 11	rise	12:42	E	May 11	rise	7:26	D	Aug. 11	set	11:18	B	Nov. 11	set	5:03	A
Feb. 21	rise	12:06	E	May 21	set	4:51	B	Aug. 21	set	10:41	B	Nov. 21	set	4:31	A
Mar. 1	rise	11:32	E	June 1	set	4:04	B	Sept. 1	set	10:02	B	Dec. 1	rise	6:33	E
Mar. 11	rise	11:53	E	June 11	set	3:22	B	Sept. 11	set	9:27	B	Dec. 11	rise	6:04	E
Mar. 21	rise	11:12	E	June 21	set	2:41	B	Sept. 21	set	8:52	B	Dec. 21	rise	5:36	E
												Dec. 31	rise	5:07	E

SATURN

The most beautiful planet has its rings wide open this year, a treat through backyard telescopes. In Sagittarius, it starts appearing low in the predawn eastern sky in mid-January. It has a lovely close conjunction with orange Mars from April 1 to 3, but still doesn't rise until after 2:00 A.M. Saturn reaches opposition on June 27—the same night that it's strikingly close to the almost full Moon—and is out all night. The Ringed Planet remains well placed through the summer and early fall, gets low in November, and becomes hidden by solar glare soon thereafter.

Jan. 1	rise	6:32	E	Apr. 1	rise	2:09	E	July 1	set	5:06	A	Oct. 1	set	10:48	A
Jan. 11	rise	5:57	E	Apr. 11	rise	1:30	E	July 11	set	4:23	A	Oct. 11	set	10:11	A
Jan. 21	rise	5:23	E	Apr. 21	rise	12:51	E	July 21	set	3:41	A	Oct. 21	set	9:34	A
Feb. 1	rise	4:44	E	May 1	rise	12:11	E	Aug. 1	set	2:55	A	Nov. 1	set	8:55	A
Feb. 11	rise	4:09	E	May 11	rise	11:26	E	Aug. 11	set	2:13	A	Nov. 11	set	7:19	A
Feb. 21	rise	3:33	E	May 21	rise	10:45	E	Aug. 21	set	1:32	A	Nov. 21	set	6:44	A
Mar. 1	rise	3:04	E	June 1	rise	10:00	E	Sept. 1	set	12:48	A	Dec. 1	set	6:10	A
Mar. 11	rise	3:28	E	June 11	rise	9:18	E	Sept. 11	set	12:09	A	Dec. 11	set	5:35	A
Mar. 21	rise	2:50	E	June 21	rise	8:36	E	Sept. 21	set	11:26	A	Dec. 21	set	5:01	A
												Dec. 31	set	4:27	A

MERCURY

The innermost planet plays its usual hide-and-seek with the Sun. As an evening star shining in the western twilight, Mercury is not hard to find in March, particularly when it's close to Venus from the 5th to the 18th. Mercury has a lower, much less favorable evening star apparition during the first half of July, when it floats between Venus and the sunset point. The planet enjoys two good showings as a morning star: The first starts on August 24 and continues until September 8. The tiny orange planet returns to the predawn scene from December 5 to 21, when it hovers first above and then below bright Jupiter and is easy to spot.

DO NOT CONFUSE: *Mars with Saturn, April 1–3, in the predawn east: Mars is orange and brighter. • Jupiter with Mars, Jan. 6–7, in the predawn east: Jupiter is much brighter. • Jupiter with Mercury, Dec. 18–21, low in the predawn east: Jupiter is brighter.*

APHELION (APH.): The point in a planet's orbit that is farthest from the Sun.

APOGEE (APO.): The point in the Moon's orbit that is farthest from Earth.

CELESTIAL EQUATOR (EQ.): The imaginary circle around the celestial sphere that can be thought of as the plane of Earth's equator projected out onto the sphere.

CELESTIAL SPHERE: An imaginary sphere projected into space that represents the entire sky, with an observer on Earth at its center. All celestial bodies other than Earth are imagined as being on its inside surface.

CIRCUMPOLAR: Always visible above the horizon, such as a circumpolar star.

CONJUNCTION: The time at which two or more celestial bodies appear closest in the sky. **Inferior (Inf.):** Mercury or Venus is between the Sun and Earth. **Superior (Sup.):** The Sun is between a planet and Earth. Actual dates for conjunctions are given on the **Right-Hand Calendar Pages, 141–167;** the best times for viewing the closely aligned bodies are given in **Sky Watch** on the **Left-Hand Calendar Pages, 140–166.**

DECLINATION: The celestial latitude of an object in the sky, measured in degrees north or south of the celestial equator; comparable to latitude on Earth. This Almanac gives the Sun's declination at noon.

ECLIPSE, LUNAR: The full Moon enters the shadow of Earth, which cuts off all or part of the sunlight reflected off the Moon. **Total:** The Moon passes completely through the umbra (central dark part) of Earth's shadow. **Partial:** Only part of the Moon passes through the umbra. **Penumbral:** The Moon passes through only the penumbra (area of partial darkness surrounding the umbra). **See page 118** for more information about eclipses.

ECLIPSE, SOLAR: Earth enters the shadow of the new Moon, which cuts off all or part of the Sun's light. **Total:** Earth passes through the umbra (central dark part) of the Moon's shadow, resulting in totality for observers within a narrow band on Earth. **Annular:** The Moon appears silhouetted against the Sun, with a ring of sunlight showing around it. **Partial:** The Moon blocks only part of the Sun.

ECLIPTIC: The apparent annual path of the Sun around the celestial sphere. The plane of the ecliptic is tipped 23½° from the celestial equator.

ELONGATION: The difference in degrees between the celestial longitudes of a planet and the Sun. **Greatest Elongation (Gr. Elong.):** The greatest apparent distance of a planet from the Sun, as seen from Earth.

EPACT: A number from 1 to 30 that indicates the Moon's age on January 1 at Greenwich, England; used in determining the date of Easter.

EQUINOX: When the Sun crosses the celestial equator. This event occurs two times each year: **Vernal** is around March 20 and **Autumnal** is around September 22.

EVENING STAR: A planet that is above the western horizon at sunset and less than 180° east of the Sun in right ascension.

GOLDEN NUMBER: A number in the 19-year Metonic cycle of the Moon, used in determining the date of Easter. See **page 169** for this year's Golden Number.

MAGNITUDE: A measure of a celestial object's brightness. **Apparent magnitude** measures the brightness of an object as seen from Earth. Objects with an apparent magnitude of 6 or less are observable to the naked eye. The lower the magnitude, the greater the brightness; an object with a magnitude of –1, e.g., is

ASTRONOMICAL GLOSSARY

brighter than one with a magnitude of +1.

MIDNIGHT: Astronomically, the time when the Sun is opposite its highest point in the sky. Both 12 hours before and after noon (so, technically, both A.M. and P.M.), midnight in civil time is usually treated as the beginning of the day. It is displayed as 12:00 A.M. on 12-hour digital clocks. On a 24-hour cycle, 00:00, not 24:00, usually indicates midnight.

MOON ON EQUATOR: The Moon is on the celestial equator.

MOON RIDES HIGH/RUNS LOW: The Moon is highest above or farthest below the celestial equator.

MOONRISE/MOONSET: When the Moon rises above or sets below the horizon.

MOON'S PHASES: The changing appearance of the Moon, caused by the different angles at which it is illuminated by the Sun. **First Quarter:** Right half of the Moon is illuminated. **Full:** The Sun and the Moon are in opposition; the entire disk of the Moon is illuminated. **Last Quarter:** Left half of the Moon is illuminated. **New:** The Sun and the Moon are in conjunction; the Moon is darkened because it lines up between Earth and the Sun.

MOON'S PLACE, Astronomical: The position of the Moon within the constellations on the celestial sphere at midnight. **Astrological:** The position of the Moon within the tropical zodiac, whose twelve 30° segments (signs) along the ecliptic were named more than 2,000 years ago after constellations within each area. Because of precession and other factors, the zodiac signs no longer match actual constellation positions.

MORNING STAR: A planet that is above the eastern horizon at sunrise and less than 180° west of the Sun in right ascension.

NODE: Either of the two points where a celestial body's orbit intersects the ecliptic. **Ascending:** When the body is moving from south to north of the ecliptic. **Descending:** When the body is moving from north to south of the ecliptic.

OPPOSITION: The Moon or a planet appears on the opposite side of the sky from the Sun (elongation 180°).

PERIGEE (PERIG.): The point in the Moon's orbit that is closest to Earth.

PERIHELION (PERIH.): The point in a planet's orbit that is closest to the Sun.

PRECESSION: The slowly changing position of the stars and equinoxes in the sky caused by a slight wobble as Earth rotates around its axis.

RIGHT ASCENSION (R.A.): The celestial longitude of an object in the sky, measured eastward along the celestial equator in hours of time from the vernal equinox; comparable to longitude on Earth.

SOLSTICE, Summer: When the Sun reaches its greatest declination (23½°) north of the celestial equator, around June 21. **Winter:** When the Sun reaches its greatest declination (23½°) south of the celestial equator, around December 21.

STATIONARY (STAT.): The brief period of apparent halted movement of a planet against the background of the stars shortly before it appears to move backward/westward (retrograde motion) or forward/eastward (direct motion).

SUN FAST/SLOW: When a sundial is ahead of (fast) or behind (slow) clock time.

SUNRISE/SUNSET: The visible rising/setting of the upper edge of the Sun's disk across the unobstructed horizon of an observer whose eyes are 15 feet above ground level.

TWILIGHT: See **page 122**. ∎

PAIN & INFLAMMATION?

If you suffer from pain due to inflammation related ailments such as arthritis, tendonitis, sprains, stiffness or swelling, you should know that help is available. Many people are putting up with the pain because they are not aware of this new, innovative treatment for topical pain management.

73% of study participants found MagniLife® Pain & Inflammation Relief Gel's proprietary formula to be more effective than their current treatments (including prescription drugs) at reducing pain. Non-greasy formula is aspirin-free and menthol-free.

MagniLife® Pain & Inflammation Relief Gel is **sold at select Walgreens**. Order risk free for $14.99 ($5.95 S&H) for a 2 oz. tube. **Get a FREE tube** when you order two for $29.98 ($5.95 S&H). Send payment to: MagniLife IC-FA6, PO Box 6789, McKinney, TX 75071 or call **1-800-299-1875**. Satisfaction guaranteed. Order at **www.InflammationGel.com**

MUSCLE & JOINT PAIN?

Are you one of 16 million people suffering from deep muscle pain and tenderness, joint stiffness, difficulty sleeping, or the feeling of little or no energy? You should know relief is available.

MagniLife® Pain & Fatigue Relief combines 11 active ingredients to relieve deep muscle pain and soreness, arthritis pain, aching joints, and back and neck pain. *"These tablets have just been WONDERFUL. I'd recommend them to anyone and everyone!"* - Debra, WV. Tablets are safe to take with other medications. *"They also help me immensely with my sleep!"* - Cathy W.

MagniLife® Pain & Fatigue Relief is **sold at CVS/pharmacy and Rite Aid**. Order risk free for $19.99 ($5.95 S&H) for 125 tablets. Get a **FREE** bottle when you order two for $39.98 ($9.95 S&H). Send payment to: MagniLife F-FA6, PO Box 6789, McKinney, TX 75071 or call **1-800-299-1875**. Satisfaction guaranteed. Order now at **www.PainFatigue.com**

AGE SPOTS?

Are unsightly brown spots on your face and body making you uncomfortable? Liver spots, also known as age spots, affect the cosmetic surface of the skin and can add years to your appearance. Many people try to cover them with makeup, or bleach them with harsh chemicals because they are not aware of this new topical treatment that gently and effectively lightens the shade of the skin.

MagniLife® Age Spot Cream uses botanicals, such as licorice root extract to naturally fade age spots, freckles, and other age-associated discolorations, while protecting against harmful external factors. *"It is fading my liver spots. This product actually works!!!"* - Patricia C., NJ.

MagniLife® Age Spot Cream can be ordered risk free for $19.99 ($5.95 S&H) for a 2 oz jar. **Get a FREE jar** when you order two for $39.98 ($9.95 S&H). Send payment to: MagniLife AC-FA6, PO Box 6789, McKinney, TX 75071 or call **1-800-299-1875**. Satisfaction guaranteed. Order now at **www.AgeSpotSolution.com**

TIME CORRECTIONS

Astronomical data for Boston are given on pages **120, 124–125,** and **140–166.** Use the Key Letters shown on those pages with this table to find the number of minutes that you must add to or subtract from Boston time to get the approximate time for your locale. Time zone codes here represent standard time. Atlantic is –1, Eastern is 0, Central is 1, Mountain is 2, Pacific is 3, Alaska is 4, and Hawaii-Aleutian is 5. For more information on the use of Key Letters, see **How to Use This Almanac, page 136.**

GET EXACT TIMES EASILY: Download astronomical times calculated for your zip code and presented as Left-Hand Calendar Pages at **Almanac.com/Access.**

STATE	CITY	NORTH LATITUDE °	NORTH LATITUDE ′	WEST LONGITUDE °	WEST LONGITUDE ′	TIME ZONE CODE	KEY LETTERS (MINUTES) A	B	C	D	E
EAST AND MIDWEST											
CT	Hartford–New Britain	41	46	72	41	0	+8	+7	+6	+5	+4
DC	Washington	38	54	77	1	0	+35	+28	+23	+18	+13
DE	Wilmington	39	45	75	33	0	+26	+21	+18	+13	+10
IA	Des Moines	41	35	93	37	1	+32	+31	+30	+28	+27
IA	Dubuque	42	30	90	41	1	+17	+18	+18	+18	+18
IL	Chicago–Oak Park	41	52	87	38	1	+7	+6	+6	+5	+4
IL	Springfield	39	48	89	39	1	+22	+18	+14	+10	+6
IN	Fort Wayne	41	4	85	9	0	+60	+58	+56	+54	+52
IN	Indianapolis	39	46	86	10	0	+69	+64	+60	+56	+52
IN	Terre Haute	39	28	87	24	0	+74	+69	+65	+60	+56
KS	Oakley	39	8	100	51	1	+69	+63	+59	+53	+49
KS	Topeka	39	3	95	40	1	+49	+43	+38	+32	+28
KS	Wichita	37	42	97	20	1	+60	+51	+45	+37	+31
MA	Springfield–Holyoke	42	6	72	36	0	+6	+6	+6	+5	+5
MD	Baltimore	39	17	76	37	0	+32	+26	+22	+17	+13
MD	Hagerstown	39	39	77	43	0	+35	+30	+26	+22	+18
MD	Salisbury	38	22	75	36	0	+31	+23	+18	+11	+6
ME	Eastport	44	54	67	0	0	–26	–20	–16	–11	–8
ME	Portland	43	40	70	15	0	–8	–5	–3	–1	0
ME	Presque Isle	46	41	68	1	0	–29	–19	–12	–4	+2
MI	Cheboygan	45	39	84	29	0	+40	+47	+53	+59	+64
MI	Detroit–Dearborn	42	20	83	3	0	+47	+47	+47	+47	+47
MI	Ironwood	46	27	90	9	1	0	+9	+15	+23	+29
MI	Lansing	42	44	84	33	0	+52	+53	+53	+54	+54
MI	Traverse City	44	46	85	38	0	+49	+54	+57	+62	+65
MN	Bemidji	47	28	94	53	1	+14	+26	+34	+44	+52
MN	Minneapolis–St. Paul	44	59	93	16	1	+18	+24	+28	+33	+37
MO	Jefferson City	38	34	92	10	1	+36	+29	+24	+18	+13
MO	Kansas City	39	1	94	20	1	+44	+37	+33	+27	+23
MO	St. Louis	38	37	90	12	1	+28	+21	+16	+10	+5
MO	Springfield	37	13	93	18	1	+45	+36	+29	+20	+14
NE	North Platte	41	8	100	46	1	+62	+60	+58	+56	+54
NE	Omaha	41	16	95	56	1	+43	+40	+39	+37	+36
NH	Manchester–Concord	42	59	71	28	0	0	0	+1	+2	+3
NJ	Atlantic City	39	22	74	26	0	+23	+17	+13	+8	+4
NJ	Trenton	40	13	74	46	0	+21	+17	+14	+11	+8
NY	Buffalo	42	53	78	52	0	+29	+30	+30	+31	+32
NY	New York	40	45	74	0	0	+17	+14	+11	+9	+6
NY	Syracuse	43	3	76	9	0	+17	+19	+20	+21	+22

STATE	CITY	NORTH LATITUDE °	NORTH LATITUDE ′	WEST LONGITUDE °	WEST LONGITUDE ′	TIME ZONE CODE	A	B	C	D	E
ND	Bismarck	46	48	100	47	1	+41	+50	+58	+66	+73
ND	Fargo	46	53	96	47	1	+24	+34	+42	+50	+57
ND	Williston	48	9	103	37	1	+46	+59	+69	+80	+90
OH	Cleveland-Lakewood	41	30	81	42	0	+45	+43	+42	+40	+39
OH	Columbus	39	57	83	1	0	+55	+51	+47	+43	+40
OH	Toledo	41	39	83	33	0	+52	+50	+49	+48	+47
PA	Erie	42	7	80	5	0	+36	+36	+35	+35	+35
PA	Harrisburg	40	16	76	53	0	+30	+26	+23	+19	+16
PA	Philadelphia-Chester	39	57	75	9	0	+24	+19	+16	+12	+9
PA	Pittsburgh-McKeesport	40	26	80	0	0	+42	+38	+35	+32	+29
PA	Scranton-Wilkes-Barre	41	25	75	40	0	+21	+19	+18	+16	+15
RI	Providence	41	50	71	25	0	+3	+2	+1	0	0
SD	Aberdeen	45	28	98	29	1	+37	+44	+49	+54	+59
SD	Rapid City	44	5	103	14	2	+2	+5	+8	+11	+13
SD	Sioux Falls	43	33	96	44	1	+38	+40	+42	+44	+46
VT	Brattleboro	42	51	72	34	0	+4	+5	+5	+6	+7
VT	Burlington	44	29	73	13	0	0	+4	+8	+12	+15
WI	Eau Claire	44	49	91	30	1	+12	+17	+21	+25	+29
WI	Green Bay	44	31	88	0	1	0	+3	+7	+11	+14
WI	Milwaukee	43	2	87	54	1	+4	+6	+7	+8	+9

SOUTH

STATE	CITY	NORTH LATITUDE °	NORTH LATITUDE ′	WEST LONGITUDE °	WEST LONGITUDE ′	TIME ZONE CODE	A	B	C	D	E
AL	Birmingham	33	31	86	49	1	+30	+15	+3	−10	−20
AL	Decatur	34	36	86	59	1	+27	+14	+4	−7	−17
AL	Mobile	30	42	88	3	1	+42	+23	+8	−8	−22
AR	Fort Smith	35	23	94	25	1	+55	+43	+33	+22	+14
AR	Little Rock	34	45	92	17	1	+48	+35	+25	+13	+4
FL	Jacksonville	30	20	81	40	0	+77	+58	+43	+25	+11
FL	Miami	25	47	80	12	0	+88	+57	+37	+14	−3
FL	Orlando	28	32	81	22	0	+80	+59	+42	+22	+6
FL	Pensacola	30	25	87	13	1	+39	+20	+5	−12	−26
FL	St. Petersburg	27	46	82	39	0	+87	+65	+47	+26	+10
GA	Atlanta	33	45	84	24	0	+79	+65	+53	+40	+30
GA	Augusta	33	28	81	58	0	+70	+55	+44	+30	+19
GA	Savannah	32	5	81	6	0	+70	+54	+40	+25	+13
KY	Lexington-Frankfort	38	3	84	30	0	+67	+59	+53	+46	+41
KY	Louisville	38	15	85	46	0	+72	+64	+58	+52	+46
LA	Lake Charles	30	14	93	13	1	+64	+44	+29	+11	−2
LA	New Orleans	29	57	90	4	1	+52	+32	+16	−1	−15
LA	Shreveport	32	31	93	45	1	+60	+44	+31	+16	+4
MS	Biloxi	30	24	88	53	1	+46	+27	+11	−5	−19
MS	Jackson	32	18	90	11	1	+46	+30	+17	+1	−10
MS	Tupelo	34	16	88	34	1	+35	+21	+10	−2	−11
NC	Asheville	35	36	82	33	0	+67	+55	+46	+35	+27
NC	Charlotte	35	14	80	51	0	+61	+49	+39	+28	+19
NC	Raleigh	35	47	78	38	0	+51	+39	+30	+20	+12
NC	Wilmington	34	14	77	55	0	+52	+38	+27	+15	+5
OK	Oklahoma City	35	28	97	31	1	+67	+55	+46	+35	+26
OK	Tulsa	36	9	95	60	1	+59	+48	+40	+30	+22
SC	Charleston	32	47	79	56	0	+64	+48	+36	+21	+10
SC	Columbia	34	0	81	2	0	+65	+51	+40	+27	+17
SC	Spartanburg	34	56	81	57	0	+66	+53	+43	+32	+23
TN	Knoxville	35	58	83	55	0	+71	+60	+51	+41	+33
TN	Memphis	35	9	90	3	1	+38	+26	+16	+5	−3
TN	Nashville	36	10	86	47	1	+22	+11	+3	−6	−14
TX	Amarillo	35	12	101	50	1	+85	+73	+63	+52	+43
TX	Dallas-Fort Worth	32	47	96	48	1	+71	+55	+43	+28	+17

(continued)

TIME CORRECTIONS

STATE/PROVINCE	CITY	NORTH LATITUDE °	'	WEST LONGITUDE °	'	TIME ZONE CODE	A	B	C	D	E
TX	El Paso	31	45	106	29	2	+53	+35	+22	+6	−6
TX	Houston	29	45	95	22	1	+73	+53	+37	+19	+5
TX	McAllen	26	12	98	14	1	+93	+69	+49	+26	+9
TX	San Antonio	29	25	98	30	1	+87	+66	+50	+31	+16
VA	Charlottesville	38	2	78	30	0	+43	+35	+29	+22	+17
VA	Richmond	37	32	77	26	0	+41	+32	+25	+17	+11
VA	Roanoke	37	16	79	57	0	+51	+42	+35	+27	+21
VA	Winchester	39	11	78	10	0	+38	+33	+28	+23	+19
WV	Charleston	38	21	81	38	0	+55	+48	+42	+35	+30
WEST											
AK	Anchorage	61	10	149	59	4	−46	+27	+71	+122	+171
AK	Fairbanks	64	48	147	51	4	−127	+2	+61	+131	+205
AK	Juneau	58	18	134	25	4	−76	−23	+10	+49	+86
AZ	Phoenix	33	27	112	4	2	+71	+56	+44	+30	+20
AZ	Tucson	32	13	110	58	2	+70	+53	+40	+24	+12
CA	Bakersfield	35	23	119	1	3	+33	+21	+12	+1	−7
CA	Fresno	36	44	119	47	3	+32	+22	+15	+6	0
CA	Los Angeles-Pasadena-Santa Monica	34	3	118	14	3	+34	+20	+9	−3	−13
CA	Redding	40	35	122	24	3	+31	+27	+25	+22	+19
CA	San Francisco-Oakland-San Jose	37	47	122	25	3	+40	+31	+25	+18	+12
CO	Craig	40	31	107	33	2	+32	+28	+25	+22	+20
CO	Denver-Boulder	39	44	104	59	2	+24	+19	+15	+11	+7
CO	Grand Junction	39	4	108	33	2	+40	+34	+29	+24	+20
HI	Hilo	19	44	155	5	5	+94	+62	+37	+7	−15
HI	Honolulu	21	18	157	52	5	+102	+72	+48	+19	−1
ID	Boise	43	37	116	12	2	+55	+58	+60	+62	+64
ID	Pocatello	42	52	112	27	2	+43	+44	+45	+46	+46
MT	Billings	45	47	108	30	2	+16	+23	+29	+35	+40
MT	Great Falls	47	30	111	17	2	+20	+31	+39	+49	+58
NM	Albuquerque	35	5	106	39	2	+45	+32	+22	+11	+2
NM	Las Cruces	32	19	106	47	2	+53	+36	+23	+8	−3
NV	Carson City-Reno	39	10	119	46	3	+25	+19	+14	+9	+5
NV	Las Vegas	36	10	115	9	3	+16	+4	−3	−13	−20
OR	Pendleton	45	40	118	47	3	−1	+4	+10	+16	+21
OR	Portland	45	31	122	41	3	+14	+20	+25	+31	+36
OR	Salem	44	57	123	1	3	+17	+23	+27	+31	+35
UT	Moab	38	35	109	33	2	+46	+39	+33	+27	+22
UT	Salt Lake City	40	45	111	53	2	+48	+45	+43	+40	+38
WA	Seattle-Tacoma-Olympia	47	37	122	20	3	+3	+15	+24	+34	+42
WA	Spokane	47	40	117	24	3	−16	−4	+4	+14	+23
WY	Casper	42	51	106	19	2	+19	+19	+20	+21	+22
WY	Cheyenne	41	8	104	49	2	+19	+16	+14	+12	+11
WY	Sheridan	44	48	106	58	2	+14	+19	+23	+27	+31
CANADA											
AB	Calgary	51	5	114	5	2	+13	+35	+50	+68	+84
BC	Vancouver	49	13	123	6	3	0	+15	+26	+40	+52
MB	Winnipeg	49	53	97	10	1	+12	+30	+43	+58	+71
NB	Saint John	45	16	66	3	−1	+28	+34	+39	+44	+49
NS	Halifax	44	38	63	35	−1	+21	+26	+29	+33	+37
ON	Ottawa	45	25	75	43	0	+6	+13	+18	+23	+28
ON	Thunder Bay	48	27	89	12	0	+47	+61	+71	+83	+93
ON	Toronto	43	39	79	23	0	+28	+30	+32	+35	+37
QC	Montreal	45	28	73	39	0	−1	+4	+9	+15	+20
SK	Saskatoon	52	10	106	40	1	+37	+63	+80	+101	+119

Why Viagra Is Failing Men

Soaring demand expected for new scientific advance made just for older men. Works on both men's physical ability and their desire in bed.

New men's pill overwhelms your senses with sexual desire as well as firmer, long-lasting erections. There's never been anything like it before.

By Harlan S. Waxman
Health News Syndicate

New York – If you're like the rest of us guys over 50; you probably already know the truth… Prescription ED pills don't work! Simply getting an erection doesn't fix the problem" says Dr. Bassam Damaj, chief scientific officer at the world famous Innovus Pharma Laboratories.

As we get older, we need more help in bed. Not only does our desire fade; but erections can be soft or feeble, one of the main complaints with prescription pills. Besides, they're expensive… costing as much as $50.00 each

Plus, it does nothing to stimulate your brain to want sex. "I don't care what you take, if you aren't interested in sex, you can't get or keep an erection. It's physiologically impossible," said Dr. Damaj.

MADE JUST FOR MEN OVER 50

But now, for the first time ever, there's a pill made just for older men. It's called Vesele®. A new pill that helps you get an erection by stimulating your body and your brainwaves. So Vesele® can work even when nothing else worked before.

The new men's pill is not a drug. It's something completely different Because you don't need a prescription for Vesele®, sales are exploding. The maker just can't produce enough of it to keep up with demand. Even doctors are having a tough time getting their hands on it. So what's all the fuss about?

WORKS ON YOUR HEAD AND YOUR BODY

The new formula takes on erectile problems with a whole new twist. It doesn't just address the physical problems of getting older; it works on the mental part of sex too. Unlike the expensive prescriptions, the new pill stimulates your sexual brain chemistry as well. Actually helping you regain the passion and burning desire you had for your partner again.

THE BRAIN/ERECTION CONNECTION

Vesele takes off where Viagra® only begins. Thanks to a discovery made by 3 Nobel-Prize winning scientists; Vesele® has become the first ever patented supplement to harden you and your libido. So you regain your desire as well as the ability to act on it.

JAW-DROPPING CLINICAL PROOF

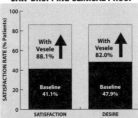

	Vesele	Baseline
Satisfaction	88.1%	41.4%
Frequency	79.5%	44.9%
Desire	82%	47.9%
Hardness	85.7%	36.2%
Duration	79.5%	35%
Ability to Satisfy	83.3%	44.1%

In a 16-week clinical study; scientists from the U.S.A. joined forces to prove Nitric Oxide's effects on the cardio vascular system. They showed that Nitric Oxide could not only increase your ability to get an erection, it would also work on your brainwaves to stimulate your desire for sex. The results were remarkable and published in the world's most respected medical journals.

THE SCIENCE OF SEX

The study asked men, 45 to 65 years old to take the main ingredient in Vesele® once a day. Then they were instructed not to change the way they eat or exercise but to take Vesele® twice a day. What happened next was remarkable. Virtually every man in the study who took Vesele® twice a day reported a huge difference in their desire for sex. They also experienced harder erections that lasted for almost 20 minutes. The placebo controlled group (who received sugar pills) mostly saw no difference.

The study results even showed an impressive increase in the energy, brain-power and memory of the participants.

"VESELE® PASSED THE TEST"

"As an expert in the development of sexual dysfunction, I've studied the effectiveness of Nitric Oxide on the body and the brain. I'm impressed by the way it increases cerebral and penile blood flow. The result is evident in the creation of Vesele®. It's sure-fire proof that the mind/body connection is unbeatable when achieving and maintaining an erection and the results are remarkable" said Dr. Damaj.

HOW TO GET VESELE®

In order to get the word out about Vesele®, Innovus Pharma is offering special introductory discounts to all who call. Discounts will automatically be applied to all callers, but don't wait. This offer may not last forever. **Call toll-free: 1-800-611-1445.**

2017

JANUARY

S	M	T	W	T	F	S
1	2	3	4	5	6	7
8	9	10	11	12	13	14
15	16	17	18	19	20	21
22	23	24	25	26	27	28
29	30	31				

FEBRUARY

S	M	T	W	T	F	S
			1	2	3	4
5	6	7	8	9	10	11
12	13	14	15	16	17	18
19	20	21	22	23	24	25
26	27	28				

MARCH

S	M	T	W	T	F	S
			1	2	3	4
5	6	7	8	9	10	11
12	13	14	15	16	17	18
19	20	21	22	23	24	25
26	27	28	29	30	31	

APRIL

S	M	T	W	T	F	S
						1
2	3	4	5	6	7	8
9	10	11	12	13	14	15
16	17	18	19	20	21	22
23	24	25	26	27	28	29
30						

MAY

S	M	T	W	T	F	S
	1	2	3	4	5	6
7	8	9	10	11	12	13
14	15	16	17	18	19	20
21	22	23	24	25	26	27
28	29	30	31			

JUNE

S	M	T	W	T	F	S
				1	2	3
4	5	6	7	8	9	10
11	12	13	14	15	16	17
18	19	20	21	22	23	24
25	26	27	28	29	30	

JULY

S	M	T	W	T	F	S
						1
2	3	4	5	6	7	8
9	10	11	12	13	14	15
16	17	18	19	20	21	22
23	24	25	26	27	28	29
30	31					

AUGUST

S	M	T	W	T	F	S
		1	2	3	4	5
6	7	8	9	10	11	12
13	14	15	16	17	18	19
20	21	22	23	24	25	26
27	28	29	30	31		

SEPTEMBER

S	M	T	W	T	F	S
					1	2
3	4	5	6	7	8	9
10	11	12	13	14	15	16
17	18	19	20	21	22	23
24	25	26	27	28	29	30

OCTOBER

S	M	T	W	T	F	S
1	2	3	4	5	6	7
8	9	10	11	12	13	14
15	16	17	18	19	20	21
22	23	24	25	26	27	28
29	30	31				

NOVEMBER

S	M	T	W	T	F	S
			1	2	3	4
5	6	7	8	9	10	11
12	13	14	15	16	17	18
19	20	21	22	23	24	25
26	27	28	29	30		

DECEMBER

S	M	T	W	T	F	S
					1	2
3	4	5	6	7	8	9
10	11	12	13	14	15	16
17	18	19	20	21	22	23
24	25	26	27	28	29	30
31						

2018

JANUARY

S	M	T	W	T	F	S
	1	2	3	4	5	6
7	8	9	10	11	12	13
14	15	16	17	18	19	20
21	22	23	24	25	26	27
28	29	30	31			

FEBRUARY

S	M	T	W	T	F	S
				1	2	3
4	5	6	7	8	9	10
11	12	13	14	15	16	17
18	19	20	21	22	23	24
25	26	27	28			

MARCH

S	M	T	W	T	F	S
				1	2	3
4	5	6	7	8	9	10
11	12	13	14	15	16	17
18	19	20	21	22	23	24
25	26	27	28	29	30	31

APRIL

S	M	T	W	T	F	S
1	2	3	4	5	6	7
8	9	10	11	12	13	14
15	16	17	18	19	20	21
22	23	24	25	26	27	28
29	30					

MAY

S	M	T	W	T	F	S
		1	2	3	4	5
6	7	8	9	10	11	12
13	14	15	16	17	18	19
20	21	22	23	24	25	26
27	28	29	30	31		

JUNE

S	M	T	W	T	F	S
					1	2
3	4	5	6	7	8	9
10	11	12	13	14	15	16
17	18	19	20	21	22	23
24	25	26	27	28	29	30

JULY

S	M	T	W	T	F	S
1	2	3	4	5	6	7
8	9	10	11	12	13	14
15	16	17	18	19	20	21
22	23	24	25	26	27	28
29	30	31				

AUGUST

S	M	T	W	T	F	S
			1	2	3	4
5	6	7	8	9	10	11
12	13	14	15	16	17	18
19	20	21	22	23	24	25
26	27	28	29	30	31	

SEPTEMBER

S	M	T	W	T	F	S
						1
2	3	4	5	6	7	8
9	10	11	12	13	14	15
16	17	18	19	20	21	22
23	24	25	26	27	28	29
30						

OCTOBER

S	M	T	W	T	F	S
	1	2	3	4	5	6
7	8	9	10	11	12	13
14	15	16	17	18	19	20
21	22	23	24	25	26	27
28	29	30	31			

NOVEMBER

S	M	T	W	T	F	S
				1	2	3
4	5	6	7	8	9	10
11	12	13	14	15	16	17
18	19	20	21	22	23	24
25	26	27	28	29	30	

DECEMBER

S	M	T	W	T	F	S
						1
2	3	4	5	6	7	8
9	10	11	12	13	14	15
16	17	18	19	20	21	22
23	24	25	26	27	28	29
30	31					

2019

JANUARY

S	M	T	W	T	F	S
		1	2	3	4	5
6	7	8	9	10	11	12
13	14	15	16	17	18	19
20	21	22	23	24	25	26
27	28	29	30	31		

FEBRUARY

S	M	T	W	T	F	S
					1	2
3	4	5	6	7	8	9
10	11	12	13	14	15	16
17	18	19	20	21	22	23
24	25	26	27	28		

MARCH

S	M	T	W	T	F	S
					1	2
3	4	5	6	7	8	9
10	11	12	13	14	15	16
17	18	19	20	21	22	23
24	25	26	27	28	29	30
31						

APRIL

S	M	T	W	T	F	S
	1	2	3	4	5	6
7	8	9	10	11	12	13
14	15	16	17	18	19	20
21	22	23	24	25	26	27
28	29	30				

MAY

S	M	T	W	T	F	S
			1	2	3	4
5	6	7	8	9	10	11
12	13	14	15	16	17	18
19	20	21	22	23	24	25
26	27	28	29	30	31	

JUNE

S	M	T	W	T	F	S
						1
2	3	4	5	6	7	8
9	10	11	12	13	14	15
16	17	18	19	20	21	22
23	24	25	26	27	28	29
30						

JULY

S	M	T	W	T	F	S
	1	2	3	4	5	6
7	8	9	10	11	12	13
14	15	16	17	18	19	20
21	22	23	24	25	26	27
28	29	30	31			

AUGUST

S	M	T	W	T	F	S
				1	2	3
4	5	6	7	8	9	10
11	12	13	14	15	16	17
18	19	20	21	22	23	24
25	26	27	28	29	30	31

SEPTEMBER

S	M	T	W	T	F	S
1	2	3	4	5	6	7
8	9	10	11	12	13	14
15	16	17	18	19	20	21
22	23	24	25	26	27	28
29	30					

OCTOBER

S	M	T	W	T	F	S
		1	2	3	4	5
6	7	8	9	10	11	12
13	14	15	16	17	18	19
20	21	22	23	24	25	26
27	28	29	30	31		

NOVEMBER

S	M	T	W	T	F	S
					1	2
3	4	5	6	7	8	9
10	11	12	13	14	15	16
17	18	19	20	21	22	23
24	25	26	27	28	29	30

DECEMBER

S	M	T	W	T	F	S
1	2	3	4	5	6	7
8	9	10	11	12	13	14
15	16	17	18	19	20	21
22	23	24	25	26	27	28
29	30	31				

A CALENDAR OF THE HEAVENS FOR 2018

–Beth Krommes

The Calendar Pages (140–167) are the heart of *The Old Farmer's Almanac*. They present sky sightings and astronomical data for the entire year and are what make this book a true almanac, a "calendar of the heavens." In essence, these pages are unchanged since 1792, when Robert B. Thomas published his first edition. The long columns of numbers and symbols reveal all of nature's precision, rhythm, and glory, providing an astronomical look at the year 2018.

HOW TO USE THE CALENDAR PAGES

The astronomical data on the **Calendar Pages (140–167)** are calculated for Boston (where Robert B. Thomas learned to calculate the data for his first Almanac). Guidance for calculating the times of these events for your locale appears on **pages 136–137**. Note that the results will be *approximate*. For the *exact* time of any astronomical event at your locale, go to **Almanac.com/ Astronomy** and enter your zip code. While you're there, print the month's "Sky Map," useful for viewing with "Sky Watch" in the Calendar Pages.

TO OUR READERS: In the interest of our tradition of useful simplicity and because much more localized astronomical information is now instantly available at **Almanac.com/Astronomy,** beginning with this year, our previous Western and Southern editions will be supplanted by this new, more robust National edition that is usable throughout the United States. If you previously used our Western or Southern edition, we hope that you enjoy the improvement. As we endeavor to ensure that this Almanac is "Old" but not old-fashioned, we embrace yet one more innovation for the 21st century.

SPECIAL NOTES: 1. All times are given in ET (Eastern Time), except where otherwise noted as AT (Atlantic Time, +1 hour), CT (Central Time, –1), MT (Mountain Time, –2), PT (Pacific Time, –3), AKT (Alaska Time, –4), or HAT (Hawaii-Aleutian Time, –5). Between 2:00 A.M., March 11, and 2:00 A.M., November 4, Daylight Saving Time is assumed in those locales where it is observed. **2.** For tide heights and times, please visit **Almanac.com/Tides.**

The Left-Hand Calendar Pages, 140 to 166

On these pages are the year's astronomical predictions for Boston. Learn how to calculate the times of these events for your locale here or go to **Almanac.com/Astronomy/Rise** and enter your zip code.

A SAMPLE MONTH

SKY WATCH: The paragraph at the top of each Left-Hand Calendar Page describes the best times to view conjunctions, meteor showers, planets, and more. (Also see **How to Use the Right-Hand Calendar Pages, p. 138.**)

			① RISES	① RISE KEY	② SETS	② SET KEY	③ LENGTH OF DAY	④ SUN FAST	SUN DECLINATION		⑤ RISES	⑤ RISE KEY	SETS	SET KEY	⑥ ASTRON. PLACE	⑦ AGE	⑧ ASTROL. PLACE
DAY OF YEAR	DAY OF MONTH	DAY OF WEEK	H. M.		H. M.		H. M.	M.	°	'	H. M.		H. M.				
60	1	Th.	6:20	D	5:34	C	11 14	4	7 s. 25		5:19	C	6:14	E	LEO	14	VIR
61	2	Fr.	6:18	D	5:35	C	11 17	4	7 s. 02		6:30	D	6:50	D	LEO	15	VIR
62	3	Sa.	6:16	D	5:37	C	11 21	4	6 s. 39		7:39	D	7:23	D	VIR	16	LIB
63	4	**G**	6:15	D	5:38	C	11 23	4	6 s. 16		8:45	E	7:54	C	VIR	17	LIB

1. To calculate the sunrise time in your locale: Choose a day. Note its Sun Rise Key Letter. Find your (nearest) city on **page 130**. Add or subtract the minutes that correspond to the Sun Rise Key Letter to/from the sunrise time for Boston.

EXAMPLE:

To calculate the sunrise time in Denver, Colorado, on day 1:

Sunrise, Boston, with Key Letter D (above)	6:20 A.M. ET
Value of Key Letter D for Denver (p. 132)	+ 11 minutes
Sunrise, Denver	6:31 A.M. MT

To calculate your sunset time, repeat, using Boston's sunset time and its Sun Set Key Letter value.

2. To calculate the length of day: Choose a day. Note the Sun Rise and Sun Set Key Letters. Find your (nearest) city on **page 130**. Add or subtract the minutes that correspond to the Sun Set Key Letter to/from Boston's length of day. *Reverse* the sign (e.g., minus to plus) of the Sun Rise Key Letter minutes. Add or subtract it to/from the first result.

EXAMPLE:

To calculate the length of day in Richmond, Virginia, on day 1:

Length of day, Boston (above)	11h.14m.
Sunset Key Letter C for Richmond (p. 132)	+ 25m.
	11h.39m.
Reverse sunrise Key Letter D for Richmond (p. 132, +17 to –17)	– 17m.
Length of day, Richmond	11h.22m.

3. Use Sun Fast to change sundial time to clock time. A sundial reads natural (Sun) time, which is neither Standard nor Daylight time.

–Beth Krommes

To calculate clock time on a sundial in Boston, subtract the minutes given in this column; add the minutes when preceded by an asterisk [*]. To convert the time to your (nearest) city, use Key Letter C on **page 130.**

EXAMPLE:

To change sundial to clock time in Boston or Salem, Oregon, on day 1:

Sundial reading (Boston or Salem)	12:00 noon
Subtract Sun Fast (p. 136)	− 4 minutes
Clock time, Boston	11:56 A.M. ET
Use Key Letter C for Salem (p. 132)	+ 27 minutes
Clock time, Salem	12:23 P.M. PT

4. This column gives the degrees and minutes of the Sun from the celestial equator at noon ET.

5. To calculate the moonrise time in your locale: Choose a day. Note the Moon Rise Key Letter. Find your (nearest) city on **page 130.** Add or subtract the minutes that correspond to the Moon Rise Key Letter to/from the moonrise time given for Boston. (A dash indicates that the moonrise occurs on/after midnight and is recorded on the next day.) Find the longitude of your (nearest) city on **page 130.** Add a correction in minutes for your city's longitude:

LONGITUDE OF CITY	CORRECTION MINUTES	LONGITUDE OF CITY	CORRECTION MINUTES
58°–76°	0	116°–127°	+4
77°–89°	+1	128°–141°	+5
90°–102°	+2	142°–155°	+6
103°–115°	+3		

Use the same procedure with Boston's moonset time and the Moon Set Key Letter value to calculate the time of moonset in your locale.

EXAMPLE:

To calculate the time of moonset in Lansing, Michigan, on day 1:

Moonset, Boston, with Key Letter E (p. 136)	6:14 A.M. ET
Value of Key Letter E for Lansing (p. 130)	+ 54 minutes
Correction for Lansing longitude, 84°33'	+ 1 minute
Moonset, Lansing	7:09 A.M. ET

6. This column gives the Moon's *astronomical* position among the constellations (not zodiac) at midnight.

Constellations have irregular borders; on successive nights, the midnight Moon may enter one, cross into another, and then move to a new area of the previous. It visits the 12 zodiacal constellations, as well as Auriga **(AUR),** a northern constellation between Perseus and Gemini; Cetus **(CET),** which lies south of the zodiac, just south of Pisces and Aries; Ophiuchus **(OPH),** primarily north of the zodiac but with a small corner between Scorpius and Sagittarius; Orion **(ORI),** whose northern limit first reaches the zodiac between Taurus and Gemini; and Sextans **(SEX),** which lies south of the zodiac except for a corner that just touches it near Leo.

7. This column gives the Moon's age: the number of days since the previous new Moon. (The average length of the lunar month is 29.53 days.)

8. This column gives the Moon's *astrological* position in the zodiac at noon. For more astrological data, see **pages 238–241.** *(continued)*

The Right-Hand Calendar Pages, 141 to 167

The Right-Hand Calendar Pages contain celestial events; religious observances; proverbs and poems; civil holidays; historical events; folklore; weather prediction rhymes; Farmer's Calendar essays; and more.

A SAMPLE MONTH

	1	**2** **3** **4** **5**	**6**	**7**	**8**	**9**
1	Fr.	ALL FOOLS' •	*If you want to make a fool of yourself, you'll find a lot of people ready to help you.*	*Flakes*	an inch long, who v
2	Sa.	Tap dancer Charles "Honi" Coles born, 1911		*alive!*	in fresh water, pro pond across the r
3	**B**	2nd ⅀. of Easter •	Writer F. Scott Fitzgerald married Zelda Sayre, 1920	*Spring's*	emerged a month (
4	M.	Annunciation^T • ♂♆☾ •	*Ben Hur* won 11 Academy Awards, 1960	*arrived!*	to spend the next 3
5	Tu.	☾ AT ☍ •	Blizzard left 27.2" snow, St. John's, Nfld., 1999	*Or is this*	on land before ret their wet world.
6	W.	☾ ON EQ. • ♂♀☾ •	Twin mongoose lemurs born, Busch Gardens, Tampa, Fla., 2012	*warmth*	You can't mis

1. The bold letter is the Dominical Letter (from A to G), a traditional ecclesiastical designation for Sunday determined by the date on which the year's first Sunday falls. For 2018, the Dominical Letter is **G.**

2. Civil holidays and astronomical events.

3. Religious feasts: A^T indicates a major feast that the church has this year temporarily transferred to a date other than its usual one.

4. Sundays and special holy days.

5. Symbols for notable celestial events. For example, ♂♆☾ on the 4th day of the month means that on that date a conjunction (♂) of Neptune (♆) and the Moon (☾) occurs: They are aligned along the same celestial longitude and appear to be closest together in the sky.

6. Proverbs, poems, and adages.

7. Noteworthy historical events, folklore, and legends.

8. Weather prediction rhyme.

9. Farmer's Calendar essay.

Celestial Symbols

☉ Sun	⊕ Earth	♅ Uranus	♂ Conjunction	☋ Descending node
○●☾ Moon	♂ Mars	♆ Neptune	(on the same	☌ Opposition
☿ Mercury	♃ Jupiter	♇ Pluto	celestial longitude)	(180 degrees
♀ Venus	♄ Saturn		☊ Ascending node	from Sun)

PREDICTING EARTHQUAKES

Note the dates in the Right-Hand Calendar Pages when the Moon rides high or runs low. The date of the high begins the most likely 5-day period of earthquakes in the Northern Hemisphere; the date of the low indicates a similar 5-day period in the Southern Hemisphere. Also noted are the 2 days each month when the Moon is on the celestial equator, indicating the most likely time for earthquakes in either hemisphere.

EARTH AT PERIHELION AND APHELION

Perihelion: January 3, 2018 (ET). Earth will be 91,402,062 miles from the Sun. **Aphelion:** July 6, 2018 (ET). Earth will be 94,507,885 miles from the Sun.

Why We Have Seasons

−Beth Krommes

The seasons occur because as Earth revolves around the Sun, its axis remains tilted at 23.5 degrees from the perpendicular. This tilt causes different latitudes on Earth to receive varying amounts of sunlight throughout the year.

In the Northern Hemisphere, the summer solstice marks the beginning of summer and occurs when the North Pole is tilted toward the Sun. The winter solstice marks the beginning of winter and occurs when the North Pole is tilted away from the Sun.

The equinoxes occur when the hemispheres equally face the Sun. At this time, the Sun rises due east and sets due west. The vernal equinox marks the beginning of spring; the autumnal equinox marks the beginning of autumn.

In the Southern Hemisphere, the seasons are the reverse of those in the Northern Hemisphere.

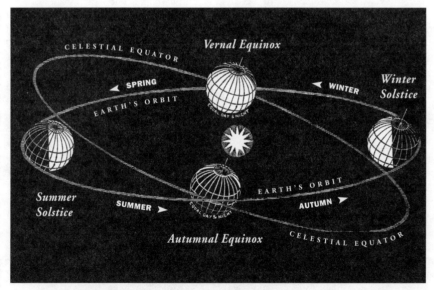

THE FIRST DAYS OF THE 2018 SEASONS

VERNAL (SPRING) EQUINOX: March 20, 12:15 P.M. ET	
SUMMER SOLSTICE: June 21, 6:07 A.M. ET	
AUTUMNAL (FALL) EQUINOX: Sept. 22, 9:54 P.M. ET	
WINTER SOLSTICE: Dec. 21, 5:23 P.M. ET	

NOVEMBER

SKY WATCH: No planet remains high or conspicuous this month. Saturn has become low in the southwest at nightfall. In the predawn east, Venus, now near blue Spica, is also getting very low. From the 12th to the 14th (especially on the 13th), the planet has an extremely close conjunction with Jupiter but will be only a few degrees above the horizon. On the 14th, the Moon forms a straight line with Mars and Spica, then hovers above Venus on the 16th and to the left of Venus on the 17th. On the 20th, the crescent Moon stands to the right of Saturn and above Mercury. The innermost planet, Mercury, is quite bright but just 8 degrees high at dusk.

○ **FULL MOON**	4th day 1:23 A.M.	● **NEW MOON**	18th day 6:42 A.M.
◑ **LAST QUARTER**	10th day 3:36 P.M.	◐ **FIRST QUARTER**	26th day 12:03 P.M.

After 2:00 A.M. on Nov. 4, EST is given. For CT, subtract 1 hour; MT, –2; PT, –3; AKT, –4; HAT, –5.

GET THESE PAGES WITH TIMES SET TO YOUR ZIP CODE AT ALMANAC.COM/ACCESS.

FOR LOCAL TIDE TIMES AND HEIGHTS, GO TO ALMANAC.COM/TIDES.

DAY OF YEAR	DAY OF MONTH	DAY OF WEEK	☼ RISES H. M.	RISE KEY	☼ SETS H. M.	SET KEY	LENGTH OF DAY H. M.	SUN FAST M.	SUN DECLINATION ° '	☾ RISES H. M.	RISE KEY	☾ SETS H. M.	SET KEY	☾ ASTRON. PLACE	☾ AGE	☾ ASTROL. PLACE
305	1	W.	7:18	D	**5:37**	B	10 19	32	14 s. 38	**4:36**	D	3:58	D	PSC	13	ARI
306	2	Th.	7:19	D	**5:36**	B	10 17	32	14 s. 57	**5:08**	C	5:07	D	CET	14	ARI
307	3	Fr.	7:20	D	**5:35**	B	10 15	32	15 s. 16	**5:43**	C	6:18	E	PSC	15	TAU
308	4	Sa.	7:22	D	**5:34**	B	10 12	32	15 s. 34	**6:22**	B	7:31	E	ARI	16	TAU
309	5	**A**	6:23	D	**4:32**	B	10 09	32	15 s. 52	**6:07**	B	7:44	E	TAU	17	GEM
310	6	M.	6:24	E	**4:31**	B	10 07	32	16 s. 10	**6:58**	B	8:56	E	TAU	18	GEM
311	7	Tu.	6:25	E	**4:30**	B	10 05	32	16 s. 28	**7:55**	B	10:03	E	TAU	19	CAN
312	8	W.	6:27	E	**4:29**	B	10 02	32	16 s. 45	**8:58**	B	11:03	E	GEM	20	CAN
313	9	Th.	6:28	E	**4:28**	B	10 00	32	17 s. 02	**10:04**	C	11:55	E	GEM	21	LEO
314	10	Fr.	6:29	E	**4:27**	B	9 58	32	17 s. 19	**11:11**	C	12:39	E	CAN	22	LEO
315	11	Sa.	6:30	E	**4:26**	B	9 56	32	17 s. 36	—	–	1:17	E	LEO	23	VIR
316	12	**A**	6:32	E	**4:25**	B	9 53	32	17 s. 52	12:18	C	**1:51**	D	LEO	24	VIR
317	13	M.	6:33	E	**4:24**	B	9 51	31	18 s. 08	1:23	D	**2:22**	D	LEO	25	VIR
318	14	Tu.	6:34	E	**4:23**	B	9 49	31	18 s. 23	2:26	D	**2:51**	C	VIR	26	LIB
319	15	W.	6:35	E	**4:22**	B	9 47	31	18 s. 38	3:28	D	**3:19**	C	VIR	27	LIB
320	16	Th.	6:36	E	**4:21**	B	9 45	31	18 s. 53	4:29	E	**3:49**	C	VIR	28	SCO
321	17	Fr.	6:38	E	**4:20**	B	9 42	31	19 s. 08	5:30	E	**4:20**	B	LIB	29	SCO
322	18	Sa.	6:39	E	**4:20**	B	9 41	31	19 s. 22	6:29	E	**4:53**	B	LIB	0	SCO
323	19	**A**	6:40	E	**4:19**	B	9 39	30	19 s. 36	7:26	E	**5:30**	B	SCO	1	SAG
324	20	M.	6:41	E	**4:18**	B	9 37	30	19 s. 50	8:21	E	**6:11**	B	OPH	2	SAG
325	21	Tu.	6:43	E	**4:17**	B	9 34	30	20 s. 03	9:13	E	**6:57**	B	SAG	3	CAP
326	22	W.	6:44	E	**4:17**	B	9 33	30	20 s. 16	10:01	E	**7:46**	B	SAG	4	CAP
327	23	Th.	6:45	E	**4:16**	B	9 31	29	20 s. 28	10:44	E	**8:39**	B	SAG	5	CAP
328	24	Fr.	6:46	E	**4:16**	B	9 30	29	20 s. 40	11:23	E	**9:36**	B	CAP	6	AQU
329	25	Sa.	6:47	E	**4:15**	A	9 28	29	20 s. 52	11:59	E	**10:34**	C	CAP	7	AQU
330	26	**A**	6:48	E	**4:14**	A	9 26	28	21 s. 03	12:32	E	**11:35**	C	AQU	8	PSC
331	27	M.	6:50	E	**4:14**	A	9 24	28	21 s. 14	1:03	D	—	–	AQU	9	PSC
332	28	Tu.	6:51	E	**4:14**	A	9 23	28	21 s. 25	1:33	D	12:38	D	AQU	10	ARI
333	29	W.	6:52	E	**4:13**	A	9 21	27	21 s. 35	2:04	C	1:44	D	CET	11	ARI
334	30	Th.	6:53	E	**4:13**	A	9 20	27	21 s. 44	2:37	C	2:52	E	PSC	12	ARI

To use this page, see p. 136; for Key Letters, see p. 130. LIGHT = A.M. BOLD = P.M. 2018

THE ELEVENTH MONTH • 2017 **NOVEMBER** NOVEMBER HATH 30 DAYS

The wind one morning sprang up from sleep,
Saying, "Now for a frolic! Now for a leap!"
–**William Howitt**

DAY OF MONTH	DAY OF WEEK	DATES, FEASTS, FACTS, & ASPECTS	
1	W.	All Saints' • ☾ ON EQ. • Sculptor Antonio Canova born, 1757	*Hocus-*
2	Th.	All Souls' • ☌♅☾ • *Ice in November Brings mud in December.*	*pocus,*
3	Fr.	Canada's first bank, Bank of Montreal, opened, Que., 1817	*drizzles*
4	Sa.	Sadie Hawkins Day • FULL BEAVER ○ • Future U.S. president Abraham Lincoln wed Mary Todd, 1842	*will*
5	**A**	**22nd S. af. P.** • **DAYLIGHT SAVING TIME ENDS, 2:00 A.M.** • ☾ AT PERIG.	*soak*
6	M.	First recorded sightings of supernova in Cassiopeia, 1572 • 87°F, Charleston, S.C., 2003	*us.*
7	Tu.	**ELECTION DAY** • ☾ RIDES HIGH • Chemist Marie Curie born, 1867	*Flaky*
8	W.	Black bears head to winter dens now.	*flurries*
9	Th.	First issue of *Rolling Stone* magazine, 1967	*and*
10	Fr.	☾ AT ☊ • SS *Edmund Fitzgerald*, with 29 aboard, sank during storm, Lake Superior, 1975	*cold*
11	Sa.	St. Martin of Tours • **VETERANS DAY** • Actress Demi Moore born, 1962	*that's*
12	**A**	**23rd S. af. P.** • Indian Summer	*biting—*
13	M.	☌♀♃ • Lobsters move to offshore waters.	*anyone*
14	Tu.	☾ ON EQ. • ☌♂☾ • First caboose-less Canadian Pacific train left Winnipeg, Man., for Thunder Bay, Ont., 1989	*had*
15	W.	*Nothing is a man's truly, but what he came by duly.*	*a*
16	Th.	☌♃☾ • Napoleon E. Guerin granted patent for cork life preserver, 1841	*Sun*
17	Fr.	St. Hugh of Lincoln • ☌♀☾ • Capt. Nathaniel B. Palmer sighted Antarctica, 1820	*sighting?*
18	Sa.	St. Hilda of Whitby • NEW ● • First commercial push-button telephone introduced, Pa., 1963	*Warm*
19	**A**	**24th S. af. P.** • Crab apples are ripe now.	*hiatus*
20	M.	☌☿☾ • ☌♄☾ • U.S. suffragette Harriot Stanton Blatch died, 1940	*lets*
21	Tu.	☾ RUNS LOW • ☾ AT APO. • Writer Voltaire born, 1694	*a*
22	W.	☌♇☾ • ♆ STAT. • Actress Lillian Russell debuted at Tony Pastor's Theatre, N.Y.C., 1880	*storm*
23	Th.	St. Clement • **THANKSGIVING DAY** • ☿ GR. ELONG. (22° EAST)	*deflate*
24	Fr.	239-lb. yellowfin tuna caught off Catalina Island, Calif., 1984	*us!*
25	Sa.	☾ AT ☋ • American College of Surgeons incorporated, 1912	*How*
26	**A**	**25th S. af. P.** • Movie *Casablanca* premiered, N.Y.C., 1942	*long*
27	M.	☌♆☾ • *Howdy Doody* host Buffalo Bob Smith born, 1917	*till*
28	Tu.	☌☿♄ • Drag racer Dale Armstrong died, 2014	*they*
29	W.	☾ ON EQ. • *If today will not, tomorrow may.*	*excavate*
30	Th.	St. Andrew • ☌♅☾ • Writer Jonathan Swift born, 1667	*us?*

Farmer's Calendar

Wild turkeys are such a familiar sight now that they are as likely to inspire annoyance as awe. When we see two hens bringing a couple dozen poults across a road—one hen on each side of the crossing, herding the little ones on—we may honk the horn to hurry them up.

Biologists call such a group a brood flock. A hen lays 10 to 12 eggs, and there's no evolutionary advantage in an unrelated hen looking after the young. They apparently find some efficiency, or increased safety, or sheer pleasure in combining forces with another mother. Maybe it's as simple as having one adult on each side of the roads that must be crossed.

In the brood flock that hangs out in our neighborhood, the poults are adult-size now. They likely hatched in June. The two other brood flocks farther up the road have smaller poults, probably mothered by hens that renested in late summer and brought off a second brood.

By winter, the young turkeys will have separated by age and sex into larger flocks, stalking through the snowy woods, leaving four-toed tracks like the dinosaurs that were their ancestors. Watching them now, it seems amazing it took so long to see the resemblance.

DECEMBER

SKY WATCH: A strange configuration rules the sky after Saturn and Mercury vanish on the 7th. Not a single naked-eye planet can be seen virtually all night, from nightfall until Mars and Jupiter finally rise before dawn. But 2017's best meteor shower, the Geminids, delivers a superb show on the 13th, starting at around 9:00 P.M. A thin crescent Moon will not interfere. Jupiter has a close meeting with the Moon on the 14th. The year's most distant Moon is the new Moon on the 18th. Winter arrives with the solstice on the 21st at 11:28 A.M. At month's end, Jupiter rises about 3 hours before the Sun. Looking ahead: Jupiter, now in Libra, approaches Mars and will very closely meet the Red Planet on January 6 and 7.

○ **FULL MOON** 3rd day 10:47 A.M. ● **NEW MOON** 18th day 1:30 A.M.
◐ **LAST QUARTER** 10th day 2:51 A.M. ◑ **FIRST QUARTER** 26th day 4:20 A.M.

All times are given in EST. For CT, subtract 1 hour; MT, –2; PT, –3; AKT, –4; HAT, –5.

GET THESE PAGES WITH TIMES SET TO YOUR ZIP CODE AT ALMANAC.COM/ACCESS.

FOR LOCAL TIDE TIMES AND HEIGHTS, GO TO ALMANAC.COM/TIDES.

DAY OF YEAR	DAY OF MONTH	DAY OF WEEK	☼ RISES H. M.	RISE KEY	☼ SETS H. M.	SET KEY	LENGTH OF DAY H. M.	SUN FAST M.	SUN DECLINATION ° '	☾ RISES H. M.	RISE KEY	☾ SETS H. M.	SET KEY	☾ ASTRON. PLACE	☾ AGE	☾ ASTROL. PLACE
335	1	Fr.	6:54	E	4:13	A	9 19	27	21 s. 54	3:13	C	4:03	E	CET	13	TAU
336	2	Sa.	6:55	E	4:12	A	9 17	26	22 s. 02	3:54	C	5:17	E	ARI	14	TAU
337	3	**A**	6:56	E	4:12	A	9 16	26	22 s. 11	4:43	B	6:31	E	TAU	15	GEM
338	4	M.	6:57	E	4:12	A	9 15	25	22 s. 19	5:38	B	7:43	E	TAU	16	GEM
339	5	Tu.	6:58	E	4:12	A	9 14	25	22 s. 26	6:41	B	8:49	E	GEM	17	CAN
340	6	W.	6:59	E	4:12	A	9 13	25	22 s. 33	7:49	B	9:47	E	GEM	18	CAN
341	7	Th.	7:00	E	4:12	A	9 12	24	22 s. 40	8:58	C	10:36	E	CAN	19	LEO
342	8	Fr.	7:01	E	4:11	A	9 10	24	22 s. 46	10:07	C	11:18	E	LEO	20	LEO
343	9	Sa.	7:02	E	4:12	A	9 10	23	22 s. 52	11:14	D	11:54	E	LEO	21	VIR
344	10	**A**	7:03	E	4:12	A	9 09	23	22 s. 57	—	–	12:26	D	LEO	22	VIR
345	11	M.	7:03	E	4:12	A	9 09	22	23 s. 02	12:19	D	12:56	D	VIR	23	LIB
346	12	Tu.	7:04	E	4:12	A	9 08	22	23 s. 07	1:22	D	1:24	C	VIR	24	LIB
347	13	W.	7:05	E	4:12	A	9 07	21	23 s. 11	2:23	E	1:53	C	VIR	25	SCO
348	14	Th.	7:06	E	4:12	A	9 06	21	23 s. 14	3:23	E	2:23	C	LIB	26	SCO
349	15	Fr.	7:06	E	4:12	A	9 06	20	23 s. 17	4:22	E	2:55	B	LIB	27	SCO
350	16	Sa.	7:07	E	4:13	A	9 06	20	23 s. 20	5:20	E	3:30	B	SCO	28	SAG
351	17	**A**	7:08	E	4:13	A	9 05	19	23 s. 22	6:16	E	4:09	B	OPH	29	SAG
352	18	M.	7:08	E	4:13	A	9 05	19	23 s. 23	7:09	E	4:53	B	SAG	0	CAP
353	19	Tu.	7:09	E	4:14	A	9 05	19	23 s. 25	7:58	E	5:41	B	SAG	1	CAP
354	20	W.	7:10	E	4:15	A	9 05	18	23 s. 25	8:43	E	6:33	B	SAG	2	CAP
355	21	Th.	7:10	E	4:15	A	9 05	18	23 s. 26	9:24	E	7:28	B	CAP	3	AQU
356	22	Fr.	7:11	E	4:16	A	9 05	17	23 s. 25	10:01	E	8:26	C	CAP	4	AQU
357	23	Sa.	7:11	E	4:16	A	9 05	17	23 s. 25	10:34	E	9:25	C	CAP	5	PSC
358	24	**A**	7:11	E	4:16	A	9 05	16	23 s. 23	11:05	D	10:26	D	AQU	6	PSC
359	25	M.	7:12	E	4:17	A	9 05	16	23 s. 22	11:35	D	11:29	D	AQU	7	PSC
360	26	Tu.	7:12	E	4:18	A	9 06	15	23 s. 20	12:04	D	—	–	PSC	8	ARI
361	27	W.	7:12	E	4:18	A	9 06	15	23 s. 17	12:34	C	12:33	D	CET	9	ARI
362	28	Th.	7:13	E	4:19	A	9 06	14	23 s. 14	1:07	C	1:40	E	PSC	10	TAU
363	29	Fr.	7:13	E	4:20	A	9 07	14	23 s. 10	1:44	C	2:50	E	ARI	11	TAU
364	30	Sa.	7:13	E	4:21	A	9 08	13	23 s. 06	2:27	B	4:02	E	TAU	12	GEM
365	31	**A**	7:13	E	4:22	A	9 09	13	23 s. 02	3:18	B	5:15	E	TAU	13	GEM

DECEMBER

DECEMBER HATH 31 DAYS

For a welcome guest is expected soon,
And he comes on the crest of the rising Moon.
–J. T. Burton Wollaston

DAY OF MONTH	DAY OF WEEK	DATES, FEASTS, FACTS, & ASPECTS	
1	Fr.	National gas rationing began in U.S., 1942	*So*
2	Sa.	St. Viviana • First televised human birth, Denver, Colo., 1952	*many*
3	**A**	**1st S. of Advent** • FULL COLD ○ • ☿ STAT. • Last run of *20th Century Limited* train, 1967	*feathers*
4	M.	☾ AT PERIG. • National Grange of the Order of Patrons of Husbandry founded, 1867	*in*
5	Tu.	☾ RIDES HIGH • *If wind rises at night, it will fall at daylight.*	*the*
6	W.	St. Nicholas • ☌☿♄ • Ship explosion devastated Halifax, N.S., 1917	*sky,*
7	Th.	St. Ambrose • **NAT'L PEARL HARBOR REMEMBRANCE DAY** • ☾ AT ☊	*there*
8	Fr.	Winterberry fruit especially showy now.	*must*
9	Sa.	Numismatic Society of Montreal formed, 1862	*be a*
10	**A**	**2nd S. of Advent** • Mississippi admitted to Union as 20th state, 1817	*pillow*
11	M.	☾ ON EQ. • British king Edward VIII abdicated throne to marry Wallis Simpson, 1936	*fight*
12	Tu.	**Our Lady of Guadalupe** • Chanukah begins at sundown • ☿ IN INF. ☌	*going*
13	W.	St. Lucia • ☌♂☾ • *What has been, may be.*	*on high!*
14	Th.	Halcyon Days begin. • ☌♃☾ • First recorded meteorite in New World fell, Weston, Conn., 1807	*Not*
15	Fr.	☌☿♀ • First rendezvous of two manned spacecraft, *Gemini 6* and *Gemini 7*, 1965	*much*
16	Sa.	Ice jam closed Ohio R. from Warsaw, Ky., to Rising Sun, Ind., 1917	*of*
17	**A**	**3rd S. of Advent** • ☌☿☾ • ☌♀☾	*a*
18	M.	NEW ● • ☾ AT APO. • ☌♄☾ • Film director Steven Spielberg born, 1946	*crowd*
19	Tu.	☾ RUNS LOW • ☌♇☾ • Beware the Pogonip.	*out—*
20	W.	Ember Day • Drop from 40° to 0°F froze chickens in their tracks, central Ill., 1836	*nobody's*
21	Th.	St. Thomas • **WINTER SOLSTICE** • ☌♄☉	*plowed*
22	Fr.	Ember Day • ☾ IN ☋ • ☿ STAT.	*out!*
23	Sa.	Ember Day • Saturn moon Rhea discovered, 1672 • Transistor first demonstrated, 1947	*We're*
24	**A**	**4th S. of Advent** • ☌♆☾ • Actor Jack Klugman died, 2012	*asking*
25	M.	**Christmas** • ☌♀♄ • *A gift with a kind countenance is a double present.*	*Santa*
26	Tu.	St. Stephen • **BOXING DAY (CANADA)** • **FIRST DAY OF KWANZAA** • ☾ ON EQ.	*for*
27	W.	St. John • ☌♅☾ • Radio City Music Hall opened, N.Y.C., 1932	*a*
28	Th.	Holy Innocents • U.S. vice president John C. Calhoun resigned, 1832	*great*
29	Fr.	William Lyon Mackenzie King became prime minister of Canada, 1921	*scene*
30	Sa.	Figure skater David Pelletier wed skating partner Jamie Salé, 2005	*in*
31	**A**	**1st S. af. Ch.** • Explorer Jacques Cartier born, 1491	*2018!*

Farmer's Calendar

Temperatures falling, skies threatening, the dogs and I started our afternoon walk a little before 3:00, heading uphill. The plan was to follow the road to the top.

It climbs sharply at the end, and the prospect is magnificent there. In addition to a broad view of the Wapack Range and a few buildings in Peterborough, there was light glinting off the waters of Thorndike Pond and steam rising from the match factory in Jaffrey.

By 4:00, we were in a field just beyond the last two houses on the road—summer places, to judge from the absence of cars and the window shades pulled down. Not surprising; the winter heating bills must be as spectacular as the views. In general here, the houses with the best views are unoccupied in December.

When we started home, we flushed a massive buck that bounded farther up the wooded hill, headed north. The dogs didn't see him, but they got wildly excited when they caught his scent at the point where he began his flight and started to tug frantically on their leashes. The dogs wanted to follow him into the forest.

So did I, but it was getting dark. There will be other opportunities to track deer when the light comes back.

JANUARY

SKY WATCH: The year begins auspiciously with a full Moon on the 1st that is also the closest Moon of 2018—a "Supermoon." On the 3rd, Earth arrives at its annual point nearest to the Sun, perihelion. Venus is invisible at superior conjunction on the 9th, but Jupiter, in Libra, is brilliant and up in the east at dawn. It hovers wonderfully close to medium-bright Mars from the 5th to the 8th; they are closest together on the 6th and 7th and visible after 4:00 A.M. The crescent Moon joins them on the 11th. The year's only eclipse for North America is a lunar totality just before dawn on the 31st. Its total phase can be seen west of the Mississippi and from western Canada.

○ **FULL MOON** 1st day 9:24 P.M.   ◐ **FIRST QUARTER** 24th day 5:20 P.M.
◑ **LAST QUARTER** 8th day 5:25 P.M.   ○ **FULL MOON** 31st day 8:27 A.M.
● **NEW MOON** 16th day 9:17 P.M.

All times are given in EST. For CT, subtract 1 hour; MT, –2; PT, –3; AKT, –4; HAT, –5.
GET THESE PAGES WITH TIMES SET TO YOUR ZIP CODE AT ALMANAC.COM/ACCESS.

FOR LOCAL TIDE TIMES AND HEIGHTS, GO TO ALMANAC.COM/TIDES.

DAY OF YEAR	DAY OF MONTH	DAY OF WEEK	☼ RISES H.M.	RISE KEY	☼ SETS H.M.	SET KEY	LENGTH OF DAY H.M.	SUN FAST M.	SUN DECLINATION ° '	☾ RISES H.M.	RISE KEY	☾ SETS H.M.	SET KEY	☾ ASTRON. PLACE	☾ AGE	☾ ASTROL. PLACE
1	1	M.	7:13	E	4:22	A	9 09	12	22 s. 57	4:17	B	6:25	E	ORI	14	CAN
2	2	Tu.	7:13	E	4:23	A	9 10	12	22 s. 52	5:24	B	7:29	E	GEM	15	CAN
3	3	W.	7:13	E	4:24	A	9 11	11	22 s. 46	6:35	C	8:24	E	CAN	16	LEO
4	4	Th.	7:13	E	4:25	A	9 12	11	22 s. 40	7:47	C	9:12	E	CAN	17	LEO
5	5	Fr.	7:13	E	4:26	A	9 13	10	22 s. 33	8:58	C	9:52	E	LEO	18	VIR
6	6	Sa.	7:13	E	4:27	A	9 14	10	22 s. 26	10:06	D	10:27	D	LEO	19	VIR
7	7	**G**	7:13	E	4:28	A	9 15	10	22 s. 18	11:12	D	10:58	D	VIR	20	LIB
8	8	M.	7:13	E	4:29	A	9 16	9	22 s. 10	—	–	11:28	C	VIR	21	LIB
9	9	Tu.	7:13	E	4:30	A	9 17	9	22 s. 02	12:15	D	11:57	C	VIR	22	LIB
10	10	W.	7:13	E	4:31	A	9 18	8	21 s. 53	1:16	E	12:26	C	VIR	23	SCO
11	11	Th.	7:12	E	4:32	A	9 20	8	21 s. 43	2:15	E	12:57	B	LIB	24	SCO
12	12	Fr.	7:12	E	4:33	A	9 21	7	21 s. 34	3:13	E	1:31	B	LIB	25	SAG
13	13	Sa.	7:12	E	4:35	A	9 23	7	21 s. 23	4:10	E	2:09	B	OPH	26	SAG
14	14	**G**	7:11	E	4:36	A	9 25	7	21 s. 13	5:04	E	2:51	B	OPH	27	SAG
15	15	M.	7:11	E	4:37	A	9 26	6	21 s. 02	5:55	E	3:37	B	SAG	28	CAP
16	16	Tu.	7:10	E	4:38	A	9 28	6	20 s. 50	6:42	E	4:28	B	SAG	0	CAP
17	17	W.	7:10	E	4:39	A	9 29	6	20 s. 39	7:24	E	5:23	B	SAG	1	AQU
18	18	Th.	7:09	E	4:41	A	9 32	5	20 s. 26	8:02	E	6:20	C	CAP	2	AQU
19	19	Fr.	7:09	E	4:42	A	9 33	5	20 s. 14	8:37	E	7:19	C	CAP	3	AQU
20	20	Sa.	7:08	E	4:43	B	9 35	5	20 s. 01	9:09	D	8:19	C	AQU	4	PSC
21	21	**G**	7:07	E	4:44	B	9 37	5	19 s. 47	9:38	D	9:21	D	AQU	5	PSC
22	22	M.	7:07	E	4:45	B	9 38	4	19 s. 34	10:07	D	10:23	D	PSC	6	ARI
23	23	Tu.	7:06	E	4:47	B	9 41	4	19 s. 20	10:36	C	11:28	E	CET	7	ARI
24	24	W.	7:05	E	4:48	B	9 43	4	19 s. 05	11:07	C	—	–	PSC	8	TAU
25	25	Th.	7:04	E	4:49	B	9 45	4	18 s. 50	11:41	C	12:34	E	CET	9	TAU
26	26	Fr.	7:03	E	4:51	B	9 48	3	18 s. 35	12:19	B	1:42	E	TAU	10	TAU
27	27	Sa.	7:03	E	4:52	B	9 49	3	18 s. 20	1:04	B	2:52	E	TAU	11	GEM
28	28	**G**	7:02	E	4:53	B	9 51	3	18 s. 04	1:57	B	4:01	E	TAU	12	GEM
29	29	M.	7:01	E	4:54	B	9 53	3	17 s. 48	2:58	B	5:07	E	GEM	13	CAN
30	30	Tu.	7:00	E	4:56	B	9 56	3	17 s. 32	4:07	B	6:06	E	GEM	14	CAN
31	31	W.	6:59	E	4:57	B	9 58	2	17 s. 15	5:19	C	6:58	E	CAN	15	LEO

RUSH!
Priority Order!

BUSINESS REPLY MAIL
FIRST-CLASS MAIL   PERMIT NO 500   MT MORRIS IL

POSTAGE WILL BE PAID BY ADDRESSEE

The Old Farmer's Almanac
Subscriptions
PO BOX 450
MT MORRIS IL 61054-9902

RUSH!
Priority Order!

NO POSTAGE
NECESSARY
IF MAILED
IN THE
UNITED STATES

BUSINESS REPLY MAIL
FIRST-CLASS MAIL   PERMIT NO 500   MT MORRIS IL

POSTAGE WILL BE PAID BY ADDRESSEE

The Old Farmer's Almanac
Subscriptions
PO BOX 450
MT MORRIS IL 61054-9902

JANUARY

JANUARY HATH 31 DAYS

Another year is opening, and another year is gone,
We have passed the darkness of the night, we are in the early morn.
–Unknown

DAY OF MONTH	DAY OF WEEK	DATES, FEASTS, FACTS, & ASPECTS	
1	M.	Holy Name • NEW YEAR'S DAY • FULL WOLF ○ • ☾ RIDES HIGH • ☾ AT PERIG. • ☿ GR. ELONG. (23° WEST)	
2	Tu.	♅ STAT. • *Jack Frost in Janiveer / Nips the nose of the nascent year.*	*We'll*
3	W.	⊕ AT PERIHELION • First free kindergarten opened, Florence, Mass., 1876	*be*
4	Th.	St. Elizabeth Ann Seton • ☾ AT ☊	*singing*
5	Fr.	Twelfth Night • Athlete Myrtle Alice Cook McGowan born, 1902	*"Cold*
6	Sa.	**Epiphany** • ☌♂♃ • 14.9" snow, Chicago, Ill., 1918	*Lang*
7	**G**	**1st S. af. Ep.** • Distaff Day • Am. Rev. War general Israel Putnam born, 1718	*Shine."*
8	M.	Plough Monday • ☾ ON EQ. • Operation Recuperation began after ice storm, N.B., Ont., Que., 1998	*Flurries*
9	Tu.	☌♀♇ • ☌♇☉ • ♀ IN SUP. ☌ • First successful U.S. balloon flight, Pa., 1793	*stinging,*
10	W.	*A goose quill is more dangerous than a lion's claw.*	*then*
11	Th.	☌♂☾ • ☌♃☾ • Composer Francis Scott Key died, 1843	*mildness*
12	Fr.	Schoolchildren's Blizzard killed 235 people, Great Plains, 1888	*divine.*
13	Sa.	St. Hilary • ☌☿♄ • Existence of monkey clone Tetra announced, 2000	*Raindrops*
14	**G**	**2nd S. af. Ep.** • ☌♄☾ • ☾ AT APO. • Actor Conrad Bain died, 2013	*flake*
15	M.	**MARTIN LUTHER KING JR.'S BIRTHDAY** • ☾ RUNS LOW • ☌☿☾ • Pentagon built, Va., 1943	*out;*
16	Tu.	NEW ● • ☌♇☾ • Roman Senate granted Gaius Octavius title of Augustus, 27 B.C.	*powers*
17	W.	☌♀☾ • U.S. statesman Benjamin Franklin born, 1706	*of showers!*
18	Th.	☾ AT ☋ • 4-lb. 8-oz. Heller's barracuda caught, Molokai, Hawaii, 2005	*Sunbeams*
19	Fr.	*Keep a thing 7 years, and you will find a use for it.*	*break*
20	Sa.	☌♆☾ • Actress Audrey Hepburn died, 1993	*out;*
21	**G**	**3rd S. af. Ep.** • Inventor John Fitch born, 1743	*snowing*
22	M.	St. Vincent • ☾ ON EQ. • Roberta Bondar became first Canadian woman in space, 1992	*for*
23	Tu.	☌♅☾ • Int'l Polar Bear Conservation Centre opened, Winnipeg, Man., 2012	*hours!*
24	W.	☌☿♇ • Percy Spencer granted patent for microwave oven, 1950	*Solar,*
25	Th.	Conversion of Paul • January thaw traditionally begins about now.	*polar,*
26	Fr.	Sts. Timothy & Titus • Ohio R. 28' above flood stage, Cincinnati, Ohio, 1937	*then*
27	Sa.	Thomas Edison granted patent for incandescent electric lamp, 1880	*rainy,*
28	**G**	**Septuagesima** • Explorer Henry Morton Stanley born, 1841	*stormish;*
29	M.	☾ RIDES HIGH • Fields full of snow rollers, Weld County, Colo., 2001	*sunny*
30	Tu.	☾ AT PERIG. • Raccoons mate now.	*and*
31	W.	FULL OLD ○ • ECLIPSE ☾ • ☾ AT ☊	*warmish.*

Farmer's Calendar

My plow guy lives up the street. Over a cup of coffee in his kitchen, he talked about his work. It's tough on family life. "The hardest are the 24-hour storms, when you're up all night, and then your kid wants to play as soon as you get home."

On the other hand, he says, nature's beauty is on show. "I see the glowing green eyes of enormous owls. The first time I saw a bobcat was when I was plowing snow."

My plow guy describes his clients as "the good, the bad, and the ugly." The good (95 percent) pay on time and park their cars out of his way on snowy nights. One brings him hot coffee and muffins on the job.

The bad are slow to pay and quick to complain: "Why do you always come at 2:00 in the morning? Do you have to use those blinking lights?"

The ugly have steep, twisty driveways, "and once you start sliding backward, you're stuck—any plow guy who says he never gets stuck is a liar."

Plow guys help each other out whenever possible—it's the Code of the Plow—but there are limits. After pulling Plow Guy out a few times, one of his competitors handed him a set of chains and said, "Good luck."

This, too, is the Code of the Plow.

FEBRUARY

SKY WATCH: Mars brightens to magnitude 1 as it floats to the upper left of Antares in Scorpius, low in the east at dawn. The Moon passes to the left of Mars on the 9th. Jupiter now rises by 2:00 A.M. and is the brightest "star" in the east. Saturn, its gorgeous rings wide open, begins to be seen easily this month, 15 degrees high just before dawn. The crescent Moon floats above Saturn on the 15th. In the evening sky, by midmonth, Venus starts to emerge low in western twilight. A thin, waxing crescent Moon floats above it on the 16th. Every planet is brightening and getting higher.

<table>
<tr><td>◐ LAST QUARTER</td><td>7th day 10:54 A.M.</td><td>◑ FIRST QUARTER</td><td>23rd day 3:09 A.M.</td></tr>
<tr><td>● NEW MOON</td><td>15th day 4:05 P.M.</td><td></td><td></td></tr>
</table>

All times are given in EST. For CT, subtract 1 hour; MT, –2; PT, –3; AKT, –4; HAT, –5.
GET THESE PAGES WITH TIMES SET TO YOUR ZIP CODE AT ALMANAC.COM/ACCESS.

FOR LOCAL TIDE TIMES AND HEIGHTS, GO TO ALMANAC.COM/TIDES.

DAY OF YEAR	DAY OF MONTH	DAY OF WEEK	☼ RISES H. M.	RISE KEY	☼ SETS H. M.	SET KEY	LENGTH OF DAY H. M.	SUN FAST M.	SUN DECLINATION ° '	☾ RISES H. M.	RISE KEY	☾ SETS H. M.	SET KEY	☾ ASTRON. PLACE	☾ AGE	☾ ASTROL. PLACE
32	1	Th.	6:58	E	4:58	B	10 00	2	16 s. 58	6:32	C	7:43	E	LEO	16	LEO
33	2	Fr.	6:57	E	5:00	B	10 03	2	16 s. 40	7:44	D	8:22	E	LEO	17	VIR
34	3	Sa.	6:56	D	5:01	B	10 05	2	16 s. 23	8:53	D	8:56	D	LEO	18	VIR
35	4	G	6:54	D	5:02	B	10 08	2	16 s. 05	10:00	D	9:27	D	VIR	19	LIB
36	5	M.	6:53	D	5:04	B	10 11	2	15 s. 47	11:03	E	9:57	C	VIR	20	LIB
37	6	Tu.	6:52	D	5:05	B	10 13	2	15 s. 28	—	–	10:27	C	VIR	21	SCO
38	7	W.	6:51	D	5:06	B	10 15	2	15 s. 09	12:05	E	10:58	C	LIB	22	SCO
39	8	Th.	6:50	D	5:07	B	10 17	2	14 s. 51	1:05	E	11:31	B	LIB	23	SAG
40	9	Fr.	6:48	D	5:09	B	10 21	2	14 s. 31	2:03	E	12:08	B	OPH	24	SAG
41	10	Sa.	6:47	D	5:10	B	10 23	2	14 s. 12	2:58	E	12:48	B	OPH	25	SAG
42	11	G	6:46	D	5:11	B	10 25	2	13 s. 52	3:50	E	1:33	B	SAG	26	CAP
43	12	M.	6:45	D	5:13	B	10 28	2	13 s. 32	4:38	E	2:22	B	SAG	27	CAP
44	13	Tu.	6:43	D	5:14	B	10 31	2	13 s. 12	5:22	E	3:16	B	SAG	28	AQU
45	14	W.	6:42	D	5:15	B	10 33	2	12 s. 52	6:02	E	4:12	C	CAP	29	AQU
46	15	Th.	6:41	D	5:17	B	10 36	2	12 s. 31	6:38	E	5:11	C	CAP	0	AQU
47	16	Fr.	6:39	D	5:18	B	10 39	2	12 s. 10	7:11	E	6:12	C	AQU	1	PSC
48	17	Sa.	6:38	D	5:19	B	10 41	2	11 s. 49	7:42	D	7:14	D	AQU	2	PSC
49	18	G	6:36	D	5:20	B	10 44	2	11 s. 28	8:11	D	8:17	D	AQU	3	ARI
50	19	M.	6:35	D	5:22	B	10 47	2	11 s. 07	8:40	C	9:21	D	CET	4	ARI
51	20	Tu.	6:33	D	5:23	B	10 50	2	10 s. 45	9:10	C	10:26	E	PSC	5	ARI
52	21	W.	6:32	D	5:24	B	10 52	2	10 s. 23	9:42	C	11:33	E	CET	6	TAU
53	22	Th.	6:30	D	5:25	B	10 55	2	10 s. 02	10:18	B	—	–	ARI	7	TAU
54	23	Fr.	6:29	D	5:27	B	10 58	3	9 s. 40	10:59	B	12:40	E	TAU	8	GEM
55	24	Sa.	6:27	D	5:28	B	11 01	3	9 s. 17	11:47	B	1:47	E	TAU	9	GEM
56	25	G	6:26	D	5:29	B	11 03	3	8 s. 55	12:43	B	2:52	E	ORI	10	CAN
57	26	M.	6:24	D	5:30	C	11 06	3	8 s. 33	1:46	B	3:52	E	GEM	11	CAN
58	27	Tu.	6:23	D	5:32	C	11 09	3	8 s. 10	2:54	C	4:46	E	CAN	12	LEO
59	28	W.	6:21	D	5:33	C	11 12	3	7 s. 47	4:06	C	5:33	E	CAN	13	LEO

To use this page, see p. 136; for Key Letters, see p. 130. LIGHT = A.M. BOLD = P.M.   2018

THE SECOND MONTH • 2018 **FEBRUARY** FEBRUARY HATH 28 DAYS

Behold within the north a crimson light
That reaches to the heavens' farthest height.
–**Clinton Scollard,** of the aurora borealis

DAY OF MONTH	DAY OF WEEK	DATES, FEASTS, FACTS, & ASPECTS	
1	Th.	St. Brigid • *As long as the sunbeam comes in on Bridget's feast day, the snow comes before May Day.*	*Sunshine's*
2	Fr.	Candlemas • Groundhog Day • Cardiff Giant hoax revealed, 1870	*scary:*
3	Sa.	The "Four Chaplains" gave their life jackets to others, drowned when SS *Dorchester* sank, WWII, 1943	*Groundhogs*
4	**G**	**Sexagesima** • ☾ ON EQ. • Canadian senator Cairine Reay Wilson born, 1885	*get*
5	M.	St. Agatha • Dozens of twisters reported in Ala., Ark., Ky., Miss., and Tenn., 2008	*buried.*
6	Tu.	Mass. joined Union, becoming 6th state, 1788	*Call in*
7	W.	☌♃☾ • Writer Laura Ingalls Wilder born, 1867	*the*
8	Th.	College of William & Mary chartered, 1693	*plowers,*
9	Fr.	☌♂☾ • *He who speaks without care, shall remember with sorrow.*	*shovel*
10	Sa.	Comedian Jimmy Durante born, 1893	*the*
11	**G**	**Quinquagesima** • ☾ RUNS LOW • ☾ AT APO. • ☌♄☾	*walks;*
12	M.	☌♇☾ • U.S. president Abraham Lincoln born, 1809	*shrug*
13	Tu.	Shrove Tuesday • Calgary, Alta., Winter Olympics began, 1988	*off*
14	W.	**Ash Wednesday** • **VALENTINE'S DAY** • ☾ AT ☋	*showers,*
15	Th.	**NATIONAL FLAG OF CANADA DAY** • NEW ● • ECLIPSE ☉ • ☌☿☾ • S. B. Anthony born, 1820	
16	Fr.	**CHINESE NEW YEAR (DOG)** • ☌♀☾ • ☌♆☾ • Winter's back breaks.	*put on*
17	Sa.	☿ IN SUP. ☌ • Baron Karl von Drais de Sauerbrun patented draisine (bicycle precursor), 1818	*thermal*
18	**G**	**1st S. in Lent** • First coiled postage stamps issued, 1908	*socks!*
19	M.	Clean Monday • **PRESIDENTS' DAY** • ☾ ON EQ.	*The*
20	Tu.	☌♅☾ • V-2 rocket launched fruit flies to 68-mile altitude, 1947	*mercury's*
21	W.	Ember Day • ☌♀♆ • –33° to 50°F, Granville, N.Dak., 1918	*mercurial:*
22	Th.	U.S. president George Washington born, 1732 • 11" snow, Blue Lick, Mo., 2013	*A*
23	Fr.	Ember Day • Chloe Hegland kept soccer ball aloft with 163 touches in 30 seconds, 2008	*flurry'll*
24	Sa.	St. Matthias • Ember Day • Skunks mate now.	*come*
25	**G**	**2nd S. in Lent** • ☾ RIDES HIGH • ☌☿♆	*pelting,*
26	M.	Michael Jackson's *Thriller* album hit number 1 on *Billboard 200* chart and remained there for 37 weeks, 1983	*then*
27	Tu.	☾ AT PERIG. • Actress Lillian Gish died, 1993	*everything's*
28	W.	St. Romanus • ☾ AT ☊ • *Speech is the picture of the mind.*	*melting.*

How does a pig write home? With a pig pen.

Farmer's Calendar

The dogs and I walked south today in bright sun, with the mercury rising to 35°F. But the spectacle of two pileated woodpeckers whirling around a grove of beeches turned our winter ramble into a Mardi Gras parade.

Bigger than other woodpeckers, these exotic creatures boast brilliant plumage of black and white as formal as tuxedos, with a blood-red crest on their heads. Unlike the machine-gun rattles of downy and hairy woodpeckers or the syncopated beat of yellow-bellied sapsuckers, the sound that the pileated species makes while excavating large holes in trees is a slow, percussive "Thock! Thock! Thock!"

This krewe of two chased each other around the pearl-gray trunks, occasionally hovering in midair, beak to beak, wings flashing and heads bobbing. Were they fighting or flirting? Males and females are about the same size, with equally vivid colors, so it was hard to tell.

Their battle—or dance—took my breath away. The dogs stood perfectly still and watched the birds with close attention, rare for them.

Then, suddenly, as if they'd noticed us staring, the birds disappeared into the darker hemlocks that lay just beyond the beeches. The parade was over.

MARCH

SKY WATCH: Mercury has its best evening star showing of the year. To the right of brilliant returning Venus, it begins low in evening twilight but gets higher and brighter and looks best from the 5th to the 18th, still to the right of Venus. It's strikingly joined by the thin crescent Moon on the 18th. Jupiter rises at around midnight, with the Moon nearby on the night of the 6th–7th. In the predawn, the Moon hovers between Mars and Saturn on the 10th. These two planets meet on the last two mornings of the month. Spring begins with the equinox on the 20th, at 12:15 P.M. ET.

○ **FULL MOON**	1st day 7:51 P.M.	◐ **FIRST QUARTER**	24th day 11:35 A.M.
◑ **LAST QUARTER**	9th day 6:20 A.M.	○ **FULL MOON**	31st day 8:37 A.M.
● **NEW MOON**	17th day 9:12 A.M.		

After 2:00 A.M. on Mar. 11, EDT is given. For CT, subtract 1 hour; MT, −2; PT, −3; AKT, −4; HAT, −5 (−6 in Hawaii).

GET THESE PAGES WITH TIMES SET TO YOUR ZIP CODE AT ALMANAC.COM/ACCESS.

FOR LOCAL TIDE TIMES AND HEIGHTS, GO TO ALMANAC.COM/TIDES.

DAY OF YEAR	DAY OF MONTH	DAY OF WEEK	☼ RISES H.M.	RISE KEY	☼ SETS H.M.	SET KEY	LENGTH OF DAY H.M.	SUN FAST M.	SUN DECLINATION ° '	☾ RISES H.M.	RISE KEY	☾ SETS H.M.	SET KEY	☾ ASTRON. PLACE	☾ AGE	☾ ASTROL. PLACE
60	1	Th.	6:20	D	5:34	C	11 14	4	7 s. 25	5:19	C	6:14	E	LEO	14	VIR
61	2	Fr.	6:18	D	5:35	C	11 17	4	7 s. 02	6:30	D	6:50	D	LEO	15	VIR
62	3	Sa.	6:16	D	5:37	C	11 21	4	6 s. 39	7:39	D	7:23	D	VIR	16	LIB
63	4	**G**	6:15	D	5:38	C	11 23	4	6 s. 16	8:45	E	7:54	C	VIR	17	LIB
64	5	M.	6:13	D	5:39	C	11 26	4	5 s. 53	9:50	E	8:25	C	VIR	18	SCO
65	6	Tu.	6:11	D	5:40	C	11 29	5	5 s. 29	10:52	E	8:56	C	LIB	19	SCO
66	7	W.	6:10	C	5:41	C	11 31	5	5 s. 06	11:52	E	9:29	B	LIB	20	SCO
67	8	Th.	6:08	C	5:42	C	11 34	5	4 s. 43	—	–	10:05	B	SCO	21	SAG
68	9	Fr.	6:06	C	5:44	C	11 38	5	4 s. 19	12:49	E	10:44	B	OPH	22	SAG
69	10	Sa.	6:05	C	5:45	C	11 40	6	3 s. 56	1:43	E	11:27	B	SAG	23	CAP
70	11	**G**	7:03	C	6:46	C	11 43	6	3 s. 32	3:32	E	1:15	B	SAG	24	CAP
71	12	M.	7:01	C	6:47	C	11 46	6	3 s. 08	4:18	E	2:06	B	SAG	25	CAP
72	13	Tu.	7:00	C	6:48	C	11 48	6	2 s. 45	4:59	E	3:02	B	CAP	26	AQU
73	14	W.	6:58	C	6:50	C	11 52	7	2 s. 21	5:37	E	4:00	C	CAP	27	AQU
74	15	Th.	6:56	C	6:51	C	11 55	7	1 s. 57	6:11	E	5:01	C	AQU	28	PSC
75	16	Fr.	6:54	C	6:52	C	11 58	7	1 s. 34	6:42	D	6:03	C	AQU	29	PSC
76	17	Sa.	6:53	C	6:53	C	12 00	8	1 s. 10	7:13	D	7:07	D	AQU	0	PSC
77	18	**G**	6:51	C	6:54	C	12 03	8	0 s. 46	7:42	D	8:11	D	CET	1	ARI
78	19	M.	6:49	C	6:55	C	12 06	8	0 s. 22	8:12	C	9:18	E	PSC	2	ARI
79	20	Tu.	6:47	C	6:56	C	12 09	8	0 N. 00	8:44	C	10:25	E	CET	3	TAU
80	21	W.	6:46	C	6:58	C	12 12	9	0 N. 24	9:19	B	11:33	E	ARI	4	TAU
81	22	Th.	6:44	C	6:59	C	12 15	9	0 N. 48	9:58	B	—	–	TAU	5	GEM
82	23	Fr.	6:42	C	7:00	C	12 18	9	1 N. 11	10:43	B	12:40	E	TAU	6	GEM
83	24	Sa.	6:41	C	7:01	C	12 20	10	1 N. 35	11:36	B	1:45	E	ORI	7	CAN
84	25	**G**	6:39	C	7:02	C	12 23	10	1 N. 58	12:35	B	2:46	E	GEM	8	CAN
85	26	M.	6:37	C	7:03	C	12 26	10	2 N. 22	1:40	B	3:40	E	GEM	9	LEO
86	27	Tu.	6:35	C	7:04	C	12 29	11	2 N. 46	2:49	B	4:28	E	CAN	10	LEO
87	28	W.	6:34	C	7:06	C	12 32	11	3 N. 09	3:59	C	5:10	E	LEO	11	VIR
88	29	Th.	6:32	C	7:07	C	12 35	11	3 N. 32	5:09	D	5:46	E	LEO	12	VIR
89	30	Fr.	6:30	C	7:08	D	12 38	11	3 N. 56	6:18	D	6:20	D	VIR	13	VIR
90	31	Sa.	6:28	C	7:09	D	12 41	12	4 N. 19	7:26	D	6:51	D	VIR	14	LIB

To use this page, see p. 136; for Key Letters, see p. 130. LIGHT = A.M. **BOLD = P.M.** 2018

THE THIRD MONTH • 2018 **MARCH** MARCH HATH 31 DAYS

What is the roar of a lion,
If it ends in the bleat of a lamb, March?
–**Marc Cook**

DAY OF MONTH	DAY OF WEEK	DATES, FEASTS, FACTS, & ASPECTS	
1	Th.	St. David • FULL WORM ○ • Johnny Cash wed June Carter, 1968	*Less*
2	Fr.	St. Chad • *No weather is ill / If the wind be still.*	*harsh*
3	Sa.	☾ ON EQ. • F5 "Candlestick Park" tornado struck Jackson, Miss., 1966	*than*
4	**G**	3rd S. in Lent • ☌♆☉ • FDR: ". . . the only thing we have to fear is fear itself," 1933	*marsh;*
5	M.	St. Piran • ☌☿♀ • Inventor Emmett J. Culligan born, 1893	*it's*
6	Tu.	U.S. First Lady Nancy Reagan died, 2016	*dreary*
7	W.	St. Perpetua • ☌♃☾ • Toronto Stock Exchange incorporated, 1878	*and*
8	Th.	3,902-lb. meteorite fell, Jilin Province, China, 1976	*drippery.*
9	Fr.	☌♂☾ • ♃ STAT. • Champion chess player Bobby Fischer born, 1943	*Temperatures*
10	Sa.	☌♄☾ • Hummingbirds migrate north now.	*drop,*
11	**G**	**4th S. in Lent** • DAYLIGHT SAVING TIME BEGINS, 2:00 A.M. • ☾ AT APO. • ☾ RUNS LOW	
12	M.	☌♇☾ • *A quiet conscience sleeps in thunder.*	*and roads*
13	Tu.	☾ AT ☋ • Joseph Priestley, chemist and oxygen discoverer, born, 1733	*get*
14	W.	Red snow fell in parts of Italy and present-day Slovenia, 1813	*slippery!*
15	Th.	Beware the ides of March. • ☿ GR. ELONG. (18° EAST)	*You'll*
16	Fr.	☌♆☾ • Storm brought 80-mph wind gust, Centerville, Utah, 1988	*need*
17	Sa.	ST. PATRICK'S DAY • NEW ● • ☌☿♀	*rubbers*
18	**G**	**5th S. in Lent** • ☾ ON EQ. • ☌☿☾ • ☌♀☾	*for*
19	M.	St. Joseph • ☌⛢☾ • Daylight Saving Time first enacted in U.S., 1918	*St. Pat's*
20	Tu.	VERNAL EQUINOX • First Farm Bureau in U.S. formed, Binghamton, N.Y., 1911	*suppers.*
21	W.	Order of Canada, to honor outstanding contributions to society and country, instituted, 1967	*Sunny*
22	Th.	☿ STAT. • Chipmunks emerge from hibernation now.	*out,*
23	Fr.	Oil refinery explosion, Texas City, Tex., 2005	*and*
24	Sa.	☾ RIDES HIGH • Beaver became a symbol of Canadian sovereignty, 1975	*warmer*
25	**G**	**Palm Sunday** • D.C.'s *Daily News* first U.S. newspaper with perfumed ad, 1937	*than*
26	M.	☾ AT PERIG. • Dr. Jonas Salk announced development of polio vaccine, 1953	*you'd*
27	Tu.	☾ AT ☊ • Pope Gregory XI died, 1378	*guess:*
28	W.	☌♀⛢ • *Judge not of a ship as she lieth on the stocks.*	*a*
29	Th.	Maundy Thursday • Catherine Callbeck first woman elected provincial premier (P.E.I.), 1993	*slushy,*
30	Fr.	**Good Friday** • Passover begins at sundown	*sloppy*
31	Sa.	FULL SAP ○ • ☾ ON EQ. • Illustrator Bob Clarke died, 2013	*mess!*

Farmer's Calendar

8:00 A.M.: Town Meeting won't start for an hour, but my wife May has to open the elementary school (she's the principal). As Town Moderator, I need to ensure that the wooden ballot boxes have been brought down from the town hall, which is too small for this meeting. The sky is blue and the sun is bright. I leave my topcoat at home.

1:00 P.M.: Meeting's over. Some folks got agitated about a $350,000 bond issue for the new fire truck, and a long-winded presentation on traffic calming didn't improve anyone's mood. Nor did going outside, where it's snowing hard. I miss my topcoat.

2:00 P.M.: Lunch and a springlike shift in the weather cheers us up. We take the dogs for a walk, wearing light jackets and dark glasses (us, not the dogs).

4:00 P.M.: Time to set up the St. Patrick's Day supper at church. As we put up the folding tables and chairs, the south wind backs into the northwest and the temperature drops abruptly. People arrive in the steaming vestry wearing epaulets of snow.

8:00 P.M.: Stuffed with corned beef, onions, cabbage, carrots, potatoes, and bread pudding, we shuffle out of church. In a clear sky, the Full Worm Moon hangs benevolently, unperturbed by all of these vernal reversals.

CALENDAR

APRIL

SKY WATCH: Mars and Saturn continue their conjunction in predawn Sagittarius from the 1st to the 3rd, as the Red Planet reaches magnitude zero. Its brightening is now accelerating rapidly. The Moon joins them on the 7th, with those planets now rising just after 2:00 A.M. and up at dawn. On the 2nd and 3rd, the Moon is near brilliant Jupiter, which rises just after 10:00 P.M. Venus is 15 degrees high as evening twilight deepens; it is brilliant but far from the maximum dazzle that it will attain at summer's end. The crescent Moon passes to Venus's right on the 17th. Venus glides just to the left of the Pleiades star cluster from the 24th to the 27th—a fine sight in binoculars.

◑ **LAST QUARTER** 8th day 3:18 A.M.	◐ **FIRST QUARTER** 22nd day 5:46 P.M.
● **NEW MOON** 15th day 9:57 P.M.	○ **FULL MOON** 29th day 8:58 P.M.

All times are given in EDT. For CT, subtract 1 hour; MT, -2; PT, -3; AKT, -4; HAT, -5 (-6 in Hawaii).

GET THESE PAGES WITH TIMES SET TO YOUR ZIP CODE AT ALMANAC.COM/ACCESS.

FOR LOCAL TIDE TIMES AND HEIGHTS, GO TO ALMANAC.COM/TIDES.

DAY OF YEAR	DAY OF MONTH	DAY OF WEEK	☼ RISES H. M.	RISE KEY	☼ SETS H. M.	SET KEY	LENGTH OF DAY H. M.	SUN FAST M.	SUN DECLINATION ° ′	☾ RISES H. M.	RISE KEY	☾ SETS H. M.	SET KEY	☾ ASTRON. PLACE	☾ AGE	☾ ASTROL. PLACE
91	1	**G**	6:27	C	**7:10**	D	12 43	12	4 N. 42	**8:32**	E	7:22	C	VIR	15	LIB
92	2	M.	6:25	C	**7:11**	D	12 46	12	5 N. 05	**9:36**	E	7:52	C	VIR	16	SCO
93	3	Tu.	6:23	C	**7:12**	D	12 49	13	5 N. 28	**10:38**	E	8:25	B	LIB	17	SCO
94	4	W.	6:22	C	**7:13**	D	12 51	13	5 N. 51	**11:37**	E	9:00	B	LIB	18	SAG
95	5	Th.	6:20	C	**7:15**	D	12 55	13	6 N. 14	—	–	9:38	B	OPH	19	SAG
96	6	Fr.	6:18	C	**7:16**	D	12 58	13	6 N. 36	12:34	E	10:20	B	OPH	20	SAG
97	7	Sa.	6:16	C	**7:17**	D	13 01	14	6 N. 59	1:26	E	11:06	B	SAG	21	CAP
98	8	**G**	6:15	B	**7:18**	D	13 03	14	7 N. 21	2:13	E	11:56	B	SAG	22	CAP
99	9	M.	6:13	B	**7:19**	D	13 06	14	7 N. 44	2:56	E	**12:50**	B	SAG	23	AQU
100	10	Tu.	6:11	B	**7:20**	D	13 09	15	8 N. 06	3:35	E	**1:47**	C	CAP	24	AQU
101	11	W.	6:10	B	**7:21**	D	13 11	15	8 N. 28	4:10	E	**2:47**	C	CAP	25	AQU
102	12	Th.	6:08	B	**7:22**	D	13 14	15	8 N. 50	4:42	E	**3:48**	C	AQU	26	PSC
103	13	Fr.	6:06	B	**7:24**	D	13 18	15	9 N. 12	5:12	D	**4:51**	D	AQU	27	PSC
104	14	Sa.	6:05	B	**7:25**	D	13 20	16	9 N. 33	5:42	D	**5:56**	D	PSC	28	ARI
105	15	**G**	6:03	B	**7:26**	D	13 23	16	9 N. 55	6:12	C	**7:03**	E	CET	0	ARI
106	16	M.	6:02	B	**7:27**	D	13 25	16	10 N. 16	6:43	C	**8:12**	E	PSC	1	TAU
107	17	Tu.	6:00	B	**7:28**	D	13 28	16	10 N. 37	7:17	C	**9:21**	E	ARI	2	TAU
108	18	W.	5:58	B	**7:29**	D	13 31	16	10 N. 58	7:56	B	**10:31**	E	TAU	3	GEM
109	19	Th.	5:57	B	**7:30**	D	13 33	17	11 N. 19	8:40	B	**11:39**	E	TAU	4	GEM
110	20	Fr.	5:55	B	**7:32**	D	13 37	17	11 N. 40	9:31	B	—	–	TAU	5	CAN
111	21	Sa.	5:54	B	**7:33**	D	13 39	17	12 N. 00	10:28	B	**12:42**	E	GEM	6	CAN
112	22	**G**	5:52	B	**7:34**	D	13 42	17	12 N. 20	11:32	B	**1:39**	E	GEM	7	CAN
113	23	M.	5:51	B	**7:35**	D	13 44	17	12 N. 40	**12:39**	C	**2:28**	E	CAN	8	LEO
114	24	Tu.	5:49	B	**7:36**	D	13 47	18	13 N. 00	**1:48**	C	**3:11**	E	LEO	9	LEO
115	25	W.	5:48	B	**7:37**	D	13 49	18	13 N. 19	**2:57**	C	**3:48**	E	LEO	10	VIR
116	26	Th.	5:46	B	**7:38**	D	13 52	18	13 N. 39	**4:05**	D	**4:21**	D	LEO	11	VIR
117	27	Fr.	5:45	B	**7:39**	E	13 54	18	13 N. 58	**5:11**	D	**4:52**	D	VIR	12	LIB
118	28	Sa.	5:44	B	**7:41**	E	13 57	18	14 N. 17	**6:17**	C	**5:22**	C	VIR	13	LIB
119	29	**G**	5:42	B	**7:42**	E	14 00	18	14 N. 35	**7:21**	E	**5:51**	C	VIR	14	SCO
120	30	M.	5:41	B	**7:43**	E	14 02	19	14 N. 54	**8:24**	E	6:23	C	LIB	15	SCO

CALENDAR

Heavy with ruddy buds, the trees
Shake off the light flakes, while below
Rejoicing, the beholder sees
The young grass peeping through the snow.
–**Elizabeth Anne Chase Akers Allen**

DAY OF MONTH	DAY OF WEEK	DATES, FEASTS, FACTS, & ASPECTS	
1	G	**Easter** • ALL FOOLS' • ☿ IN INF. ☌	*Fools*
2	M.	Easter Monday • ☌♂♄ • 7.9 earthquake triggered tsunami, Hawaii, 1868	*cool,*
3	Tu.	St. Richard of Chichester • ☌♃☾ • Actor Leslie Howard born, 1893	*rainy*
4	W.	Civil rights leader Martin Luther King Jr. assassinated, Memphis, Tenn., 1968	*as a rule.*
5	Th.	N.Y. Chamber of Commerce formed, 1768	*Hosannas!*
6	Fr.	*Plant your 'taters when you will, They won't come up before April.*	*Springlike;*
7	Sa.	☾ RUNS LOW • ☌♂☾ • ☌♄☾ • Jack Nicklaus won Masters Golf Tournament, 1963	*robins*
8	G	**2nd S. of Easter** • Orthodox Easter • ☾ AT APO. • ☌♇☾	*sing*
9	M.	Annunciation[T] • F5 tornado hit Glazier and Higgins, Tex., and Woodward, Okla., 1947	*like*
10	Tu.	☾ AT ☋ • 253-mph wind gust, Barrow Island, Australia, 1996	*prima*
11	W.	U.S. Navy bought its first commissioned submarine, USS *Holland,* 1900	*donnas!*
12	Th.	☌♆☾ • *Penny and penny laid up will be many.*	*Daffodils*
13	Fr.	☿ STAT. • U.S. president Thomas Jefferson born, 1743 • Thomas Jefferson Memorial dedicated, D.C., 1943	
14	Sa.	☾ ON EQ. • ☌☿☾ • Don Calhoun won $1 million by making 79-foot shot in basketball contest, 1993	*arrive*
15	G	**3rd S. of Easter** • NEW ● • ☌♅☾	*with*
16	M.	Annie Oakley hit 100 clay targets in a row, setting women's record, 1922	*chills*
17	Tu.	☌♀☾ • ♄ STAT. • Song "Hail! Hail! The Gang's All Here" copyrighted, 1908	*and*
18	W.	☌♅☉ • Astronomer Édouard Albert Roche died, 1883	*romping*
19	Th.	Colonial minutemen and British exchanged fire on Lexington Green, Mass., 1775	*rills.*
20	Fr.	☾ AT PERIG. • Sculptor Daniel Chester French born, 1850	*Just*
21	Sa.	☾ RIDES HIGH • Aviator Manfred von Richthofen (the "Red Baron") died, 1918	*our luck,*
22	G	**4th S. of Easter** • ♇ STAT. • U.S. Proclamation of Neutrality issued, 1793	*it's*
23	M.	St. George • ☾ AT ☊ • First postage stamps issued in Canada, 1851	*raining*
24	Tu.	*Old Farmer's Almanac* founder Robert B. Thomas born, 1766	*buckets!*
25	W.	St. Mark • ☌♂♇ • Singer Ella Fitzgerald born, 1918	*Diminishing,*
26	Th.	*East or west, / Home is best.*	*dark is;*
27	Fr.	☾ ON EQ. • 102°F, Los Angeles, Calif., 2004	*we*
28	Sa.	At age 98, Walter Sitch of Halifax, N.S., became a great-great-great-grandfather, 1968	*don't*
29	G	**5th S. of Easter** • FULL PINK ○ • ☿ GR. ELONG. (27° WEST)	*need*
30	M.	☌♃☾ • Poplars leaf out about now.	*parkas!*

CALENDAR

Farmer's Calendar

A harbinger of spring around here is a wildflower called red trillium *(Trillium erectum).* Ages ago, people called it wake-robin, because it appears just as the first robins arrive in spring.

It's an elegant plant, whose single flower has three maroon-red petals that droop toward the ground, making it hard to spot from above. It grows in most of the eastern states and provinces, some of which have given it protected status, so check before you attempt to transplant it.

The color mimics the appearance of rotting meat, as does its gamy scent. Called "stinking Benjamin," the plant attracts carrion flies, insects that normally lay their eggs in rotting meat, which pollinate the flowers. Once again, fair is foul and foul is fair.

But why "Benjamin"? It turns out to be a corruption of the word "benzoin," or "benjoin," a substance found in Southeast Asia and used in the manufacture of perfumes. Another evocative name for the plant is "wet dog trillium." It's not a strong odor; rather a faint whiff of *eau de dump.* The trick is to keep your nose at a safe distance. That way, stinking Benjamin can be one of the fairest flowers of the spring.

MAY

SKY WATCH: Brilliant Jupiter now rises before 9:00 P.M. and is visible the rest of the night. The Moon passes to the left of the Giant Planet on the 1st; Jupiter comes to opposition on May 8–9 and shines at its brightest of the year. It is easily recognized as the most dazzling "star" in the midnight sky. Venus attains its highest 2018 position in the west after nightfall and sets before 11:00 P.M. all month. (This is, however, far below the elevation that it reaches in other years.) The Moon passes between Mars and Saturn on the 5th, hovers to the left of Venus on the 17th, and is to the left of Jupiter on the 27th.

◐ LAST QUARTER	7th day 10:09 P.M.	◑ FIRST QUARTER	21st day 11:49 P.M.
● NEW MOON	15th day 7:48 A.M.	○ FULL MOON	29th day 10:20 A.M.

All times are given in EDT. For CT, subtract 1 hour; MT, -2; PT, -3; AKT, -4; HAT, -5 (-6 in Hawaii).

GET THESE PAGES WITH TIMES SET TO YOUR ZIP CODE AT ALMANAC.COM/ACCESS.

FOR LOCAL TIDE TIMES AND HEIGHTS, GO TO ALMANAC.COM/TIDES.

DAY OF YEAR	DAY OF MONTH	DAY OF WEEK	☀ RISES H. M.	RISE KEY	☀ SETS H. M.	SET KEY	LENGTH OF DAY H. M.	SUN FAST M.	SUN DECLINATION ° '	☾ RISES H. M.	RISE KEY	☾ SETS H. M.	SET KEY	☾ ASTRON. PLACE	☾ AGE	☾ ASTROL. PLACE
121	1	Tu.	5:39	B	7:44	E	14 05	19	15 N. 12	9:25	E	6:56	B	LIB	16	SAG
122	2	W.	5:38	B	7:45	E	14 07	19	15 N. 30	10:24	E	7:33	B	OPH	17	SAG
123	3	Th.	5:37	B	7:46	E	14 09	19	15 N. 48	11:18	E	8:13	B	OPH	18	SAG
124	4	Fr.	5:35	B	7:47	E	14 12	19	16 N. 05	—	–	8:58	B	SAG	19	CAP
125	5	Sa.	5:34	B	7:48	E	14 14	19	16 N. 22	12:08	E	9:47	B	SAG	20	CAP
126	6	**G**	5:33	B	7:49	E	14 16	19	16 N. 39	12:53	E	10:39	B	SAG	21	AQU
127	7	M.	5:32	B	7:50	E	14 18	19	16 N. 55	1:33	E	11:35	B	CAP	22	AQU
128	8	Tu.	5:30	B	7:52	E	14 22	19	17 N. 12	2:09	E	12:33	C	CAP	23	AQU
129	9	W.	5:29	B	7:53	E	14 24	19	17 N. 28	2:42	E	1:33	C	AQU	24	PSC
130	10	Th.	5:28	B	7:54	E	14 26	19	17 N. 43	3:12	D	2:34	D	AQU	25	PSC
131	11	Fr.	5:27	B	7:55	E	14 28	19	17 N. 59	3:41	D	3:38	D	AQU	26	ARI
132	12	Sa.	5:26	B	7:56	E	14 30	19	18 N. 14	4:10	D	4:43	D	CET	27	ARI
133	13	**G**	5:25	B	7:57	E	14 32	19	18 N. 29	4:40	C	5:51	E	PSC	28	ARI
134	14	M.	5:24	B	7:58	E	14 34	19	18 N. 43	5:13	C	7:02	E	CET	29	TAU
135	15	Tu.	5:23	A	7:59	E	14 36	19	18 N. 58	5:50	B	8:13	E	ARI	0	TAU
136	16	W.	5:22	A	8:00	E	14 38	19	19 N. 11	6:32	B	9:25	E	TAU	1	GEM
137	17	Th.	5:21	A	8:01	E	14 40	19	19 N. 25	7:21	B	10:32	E	TAU	2	GEM
138	18	Fr.	5:20	A	8:02	E	14 42	19	19 N. 38	8:18	B	11:34	E	GEM	3	CAN
139	19	Sa.	5:19	A	8:03	E	14 44	19	19 N. 51	9:22	B	—	–	GEM	4	CAN
140	20	**G**	5:18	A	8:04	E	14 46	19	20 N. 04	10:30	B	12:27	E	CAN	5	LEO
141	21	M.	5:17	A	8:05	E	14 48	19	20 N. 16	11:39	C	1:12	E	LEO	6	LEO
142	22	Tu.	5:16	A	8:06	E	14 50	19	20 N. 28	12:48	C	1:51	E	LEO	7	VIR
143	23	W.	5:16	A	8:07	E	14 51	19	20 N. 39	1:56	D	2:25	D	LEO	8	VIR
144	24	Th.	5:15	A	8:08	E	14 53	19	20 N. 50	3:02	D	2:56	D	VIR	9	LIB
145	25	Fr.	5:14	A	8:09	E	14 55	19	21 N. 01	4:07	E	3:25	D	VIR	10	LIB
146	26	Sa.	5:13	A	8:10	E	14 57	19	21 N. 11	5:11	E	3:54	C	VIR	11	SCO
147	27	**G**	5:13	A	8:10	E	14 57	18	21 N. 21	6:14	E	4:24	C	LIB	12	SCO
148	28	M.	5:12	A	8:11	E	14 59	18	21 N. 31	7:15	E	4:56	B	LIB	13	SCO
149	29	Tu.	5:11	A	8:12	E	15 01	18	21 N. 40	8:14	E	5:31	B	SCO	14	SAG
150	30	W.	5:11	A	8:13	E	15 02	18	21 N. 49	9:11	E	6:09	B	OPH	15	SAG
151	31	Th.	5:10	A	8:14	E	15 04	18	21 N. 58	10:03	E	6:52	B	SAG	16	CAP

To use this page, see p. 136; for Key Letters, see p. 130. LIGHT = A.M. **BOLD = P.M.**

The apple trees with bloom are all aglow:
Soft drifts of perfumed light.
–**Horatio Nelson Powers**

DAY OF MONTH	DAY OF WEEK	DATES, FEASTS, FACTS, & ASPECTS	
1	Tu.	Sts. Philip & James • **MAY DAY** • Entertainer Jack Paar born, 1918	*Sopping,*
2	W.	St. Athanasius • Hudson's Bay Co. chartered, 1670	*with*
3	Th.	First U.S. telecast of a book review, 1938	*no*
4	F.	☾ RUNS LOW • ☌♄☾ • *A dry May is followed by a wet June.*	*signs*
5	Sa.	☾ AT APO. • ☌♇☾ • Actor Michael Palin born, 1943	*of stopping.*
6	**G**	**Rogation Sunday** • ☌♂☾ • London and Gore Railroad Co. incorporated, 1834	
7	M.	☾ AT ☋ • Composer Johannes Brahms born, 1833	*Fine*
8	Tu.	St. Julian of Norwich • ♃ AT ☍ • Grapefruit-size hail, Dallas and Fort Worth, Tex., 1981	*days*
9	W.	St. Gregory of Nazianzus • First American political cartoon, 1754	*for*
10	Th.	**Ascension** • ☌♆☾ • U.S. patriot Paul Revere died, 1818	*fish;*
11	Fr.	*Fish are not to be caught with a bird call.* • Three	*every*
12	Sa.	☾ ON EQ. • ☌☿♅ • U.S. Commerce Dept.: Hurricanes will also be named after men, 1978 • Chilly	*step*
13	**G**	**1st S. af. Asc.** • **MOTHER'S DAY** • ☌☿☾ • ☌♅☾ • Saints	*you*
14	M.	Louis XIV became king of France at age 4, 1643 • Horse Winning Brew ran 43.97 mph, 2008	*take goes*
15	Tu.	Ramadan begins at sundown • NEW ● • J. Kepler verified 3rd Law of Planetary Motion, 1618	squish.
16	W.	Canadian Victoria Cross unveiled, 2008 • Cranberries in bud now.	*Is*
17	Th.	Orthodox Ascension • ☾ AT PERIG. • ☌♀☾	*that*
18	Fr.	☾ RIDES HIGH • Aviator Jackie Cochran first woman to exceed Mach 1, 1953	*the*
19	Sa.	St. Dunstan • Shavuot begins at sundown	*Sun,*
20	**G**	**Whit S.** • **Pentecost** • ☾ AT ☊ • U.S. First Lady Dolley Madison born, 1768	*or*
21	M.	**VICTORIA DAY (CANADA)** • Windsor Agricultural Fair (North America's oldest) founded, N.S., 1765	*am I*
22	Tu.	Train of 100+ wagons left Independence, Mo., for Oreg., 1843	*crazy?*
23	W.	Ember Day • Explorer William Clark: "Water freeses on the oars" in what is now Mont., 1805	*Thunder*
24	Th.	☾ ON EQ. • Astronomer Nicolaus Copernicus died, 1543	*rolls:*
25	Fr.	St. Bede • Ember Day • Father Stephen Badin first Catholic priest ordained in U.S., 1793	*it's*
26	Sa.	Ember Day • *Drive not away what never came near you.*	*hot*
27	**G**	**Trinity** • Orthodox Pentecost • ☌♃☾ • Reformer Amelia Bloomer born, 1818	*and*
28	M.	**MEMORIAL DAY, OBSERVED** • Hubble Space Telescope photographed unknown object TMR-1C, 1998	*hazy.*
29	Tu.	Vesak • **FULL FLOWER** ○ • Ramona Trinidad Iglesias-Jordan died at 114 years 272 days, 2004	*Fresh*
30	W.	First U.S. national celebration of Memorial (Decoration) Day, Arlington National Cemetery, Va., 1868	*as a*
31	Th.	Visit of Mary • ☌♄☾ • Governor-general of Canada Sir Victor Cavendish born, 1868	*daisy.*

Farmer's Calendar

While walking the dogs on the road yesterday, I spotted something unusual in the leaves and garbage unveiled by the melting snow: the clean, dry, elegantly curved skull of a small deer.

It was a hard winter for deer. The snow came early and piled deep. No thaw in January, February, March; even April was grim and gray. The smaller critters were safe and warm under the snow, but it was near impossible for deer to move. It made them easy prey for coyotes and for dogs whose owners allow them to run loose in the winter.

Wildlife experts know that such a winter kills more deer. It's natural. It's expected. It goes into the state's calculation of how many deer should be harvested this fall to best maintain the health of the herd. Authorities estimate that there will be about 15 percent fewer deer, so they will plan the hunting season accordingly.

I put the skull in a plastic bag and set it aside to give to my grandson, Sam, who is curious about nature and not squeamish about bones. To him, it will be a mystery to investigate and perhaps a step down the long path that leads to becoming a scientist. To me, it is a *memento mori,* a Latin phrase that means "remember you must die."

JUNE

SKY WATCH: Jupiter spends the first week close to Libra's brightest star, Zubeneschamali. Mars rises at midnight at a blazing magnitude –1.7. The only naked-eye asteroid, Vesta, attains a rare brilliancy. At magnitude 5.3, it is faint but easily seen (away from city lights) to the upper right of Saturn during the moonless period from the 5th to the 15th. The Moon stands above Venus on the 15th and to the left of Venus on the 16th. The Moon then passes close to Saturn on the 27th—the very night the Ringed Planet comes to opposition, its nearest and brightest position of the year. The solstice brings summer on the 21st at 6:07 A.M. ET.

◐ LAST QUARTER	6th day	2:32 P.M.
● NEW MOON	13th day	3:43 P.M.
◑ FIRST QUARTER	20th day	6:51 A.M.
○ FULL MOON	28th day	12:53 A.M.

All times are given in EDT. For CT, subtract 1 hour; MT, –2; PT, –3; AKT, –4; HAT, –5 (–6 in Hawaii).

GET THESE PAGES WITH TIMES SET TO YOUR ZIP CODE AT ALMANAC.COM/ACCESS.

FOR LOCAL TIDE TIMES AND HEIGHTS, GO TO ALMANAC.COM/TIDES.

DAY OF YEAR	DAY OF MONTH	DAY OF WEEK	☼ RISES H. M.	RISE KEY	☼ SETS H. M.	SET KEY	LENGTH OF DAY H. M.	SUN FAST M.	SUN DECLINATION ° ′	☽ RISES H. M.	RISE KEY	☽ SETS H. M.	SET KEY	☽ ASTRON. PLACE	☽ AGE	☽ ASTROL. PLACE
152	1	Fr.	5:10	A	**8:15**	E	15 05	18	22 N. 06	**10:50**	E	7:39	B	SAG	17	CAP
153	2	Sa.	5:09	A	**8:15**	E	15 06	18	22 N. 14	**11:32**	E	8:30	B	SAG	18	CAP
154	3	**G**	5:09	A	**8:16**	E	15 07	17	22 N. 21	—	–	9:25	B	CAP	19	AQU
155	4	M.	5:09	A	**8:17**	E	15 08	17	22 N. 28	12:09	E	10:22	B	CAP	20	AQU
156	5	Tu.	5:08	A	**8:17**	E	15 09	17	22 N. 35	12:43	E	11:20	C	AQU	21	PSC
157	6	W.	5:08	A	**8:18**	E	15 10	17	22 N. 41	1:13	E	**12:20**	C	AQU	22	PSC
158	7	Th.	5:08	A	**8:19**	E	15 11	17	22 N. 47	1:42	D	**1:21**	D	AQU	23	PSC
159	8	Fr.	5:07	A	**8:19**	E	15 12	17	22 N. 52	2:10	D	**2:25**	D	PSC	24	ARI
160	9	Sa.	5:07	A	**8:20**	E	15 13	16	22 N. 57	2:39	C	**3:30**	E	CET	25	ARI
161	10	**G**	5:07	A	**8:21**	E	15 14	16	23 N. 02	3:09	C	**4:38**	E	PSC	26	TAU
162	11	M.	5:07	A	**8:21**	E	15 14	16	23 N. 06	3:43	C	**5:49**	E	ARI	27	TAU
163	12	Tu.	5:07	A	**8:22**	E	15 15	16	23 N. 10	4:22	B	**7:02**	E	TAU	28	GEM
164	13	W.	5:07	A	**8:22**	E	15 15	16	23 N. 13	5:08	B	**8:13**	E	TAU	0	GEM
165	14	Th.	5:07	A	**8:22**	E	15 15	15	23 N. 16	6:02	B	**9:19**	E	ORI	1	CAN
166	15	Fr.	5:07	A	**8:23**	E	15 16	15	23 N. 19	7:05	B	**10:18**	E	GEM	2	CAN
167	16	Sa.	5:07	A	**8:23**	E	15 16	15	23 N. 21	8:13	B	**11:09**	E	CAN	3	LEO
168	17	**G**	5:07	A	**8:24**	E	15 17	15	23 N. 23	9:25	C	**11:51**	E	CAN	4	LEO
169	18	M.	5:07	A	**8:24**	E	15 17	14	23 N. 24	10:37	C	—	–	LEO	5	VIR
170	19	Tu.	5:07	A	**8:24**	E	15 17	14	23 N. 25	11:47	D	12:28	D	LEO	6	VIR
171	20	W.	5:07	A	**8:24**	E	15 17	14	23 N. 26	**12:55**	D	1:00	D	VIR	7	LIB
172	21	Th.	5:07	A	**8:25**	E	15 18	14	23 N. 26	**2:00**	D	1:30	D	VIR	8	LIB
173	22	Fr.	5:08	A	**8:25**	E	15 17	14	23 N. 25	**3:04**	E	1:59	C	VIR	9	LIB
174	23	Sa.	5:08	A	**8:25**	E	15 17	13	23 N. 25	**4:07**	E	2:28	C	VIR	10	SCO
175	24	**G**	5:08	A	**8:25**	E	15 17	13	23 N. 23	**5:08**	E	2:59	B	LIB	11	SCO
176	25	M.	5:09	A	**8:25**	E	15 16	13	23 N. 22	**6:07**	E	3:32	B	LIB	12	SAG
177	26	Tu.	5:09	A	**8:25**	E	15 16	13	23 N. 20	**7:05**	E	4:08	B	OPH	13	SAG
178	27	W.	5:09	A	**8:25**	E	15 16	13	23 N. 17	**7:58**	E	4:49	B	OPH	14	CAP
179	28	Th.	5:10	A	**8:25**	E	15 15	12	23 N. 15	**8:47**	E	5:35	B	SAG	15	CAP
180	29	Fr.	5:10	A	**8:25**	E	15 15	12	23 N. 11	**9:31**	E	6:24	B	SAG	16	CAP
181	30	Sa.	5:11	A	**8:25**	E	15 14	12	23 N. 08	**10:10**	E	7:18	B	CAP	17	AQU

CALENDAR

THE SIXTH MONTH • 2018 **JUNE** JUNE HATH 30 DAYS

When on smooth petals he would slip
Or over tangled stamens trip,
And headlong in the pollen rolled,
Crawl out quite dusted o'er with gold.
–**Henry Augustin Beers,** of the bumblebee

DAY OF MONTH	DAY OF WEEK	DATES, FEASTS, FACTS, & ASPECTS	
1	Fr.	☾ RUNS LOW • ☌♇☾ • U.S. president James Buchanan died, 1868	*Each night's*
2	Sa.	☾ AT APO. • Kraft's Velveeta invented, 1928	*a*
3	**G**	Corpus Christi • Orthodox All Saints' • ☾ AT ☋ • ☌♂☾	*thrill—*
4	M.	Ernest Poole first to win Pulitzer Prize for novel, 1918	*are we*
5	Tu.	St. Boniface • ☿ IN SUP. ☌ • Sen. Robert F. Kennedy shot, 1968	*listening*
6	W.	D-Day, 1944 • ☌♆☾ • First U.S. drive-in movie theater opened, Camden, N.J., 1933	*to*
7	Th.	*You can not hide an eel in a sack.*	*summer's*
8	Fr.	☾ ON EQ. • Jennifer Reinke spelled "chihuahua" to win Scripps bee, 1967	*artillery?*
9	Sa.	☌♅☾ • Deadly tornado struck Worcester County, Mass., 1953	*Sunny*
10	**G**	**3rd S. af. P.** • Canadian prime minister Sir Robert Borden died, 1937	*and*
11	M.	St. Barnabas • U.S. patriot Joseph Warren born, 1741	*cool;*
12	Tu.	*A misty morning may be a clear day.*	*farewell*
13	W.	NEW ● • Cedar River crested at 31.12', Cedar Rapids, Iowa, 2008	*to*
14	Th.	St. Basil • FLAG DAY • ☾ RIDES HIGH • ☾ AT PERIG. • ☌☿☾	*school!*
15	Fr.	Composer Edvard Grieg born, 1843	*Mortarboards*
16	Sa.	☾ AT ☊ • ☌♀☾ • Football player Brian Piccolo died, 1970	*fly*
17	**G**	**4th S. af. P.** • FATHER'S DAY • Astronomer James Ludlow Elliot born, 1943	*in*
18	M.	Sally K. Ride first U.S. woman in space, 1983	*a*
19	Tu.	♆ STAT. • Mathematician Blaise Pascal born, 1623	*threatening*
20	W.	Fred H. Howard rec'd patent for hybrid tea rose with "clear rose red color which does not fade or turn blue," 1950	*sky,*
21	Th.	SUMMER SOLSTICE • ☾ ON EQ. • First bachelor of medicine degree in U.S. issued, 1768	*and*
22	Fr.	St. Alban • Pluto's moon Charon discovered, 1978 • U.S. First Lady Pat Nixon died, 1993	*many*
23	Sa.	☌♃☾ • William Penn signed treaty of friendship with the Lenni Lenape, 1683	*a*
24	**G**	**5th S. af. P.** • MIDSUMMER DAY • 9 UFOs reported, Mt. Rainier, Wash., 1947	*bride*
25	M.	Nativ. John the Baptist[T] • 121°F, Willow Beach, Ariz., 1981	*has*
26	Tu.	*Love rules his kingdom without a sword.*	*a*
27	W.	♄ AT ☍ • ☌♄☾ • Joseph Walker flew X-15 at Mach 5.92 (4,104 mph), 1962	*tear*
28	Th.	St. Irenaeus • FULL STRAWBERRY ○ • ☾ RUNS LOW • ♂ STAT.	*in*
29	Fr.	Sts. Peter & Paul • ☾ AT APO. • ☌♇☾	*her*
30	Sa.	☾ AT ☋ • ☌♂☾ • Tunguska fireball in sky, Russia, 1908	*eye!*

Farmer's Calendar

A rainy spring speaks with many voices. Dripping gutters plink like banjos. Sleet makes a ticking sound on the windows. A hard rain, the kind folks call a "gullywasher" or a "frog-strangler," is so loud that you might have to shout to be heard over it, even without thunder. But a soft rain, the kind that's slow and steady and good for the garden, murmurs like a lullaby.

On average, an inch of rain that falls evenly on 1 acre drops about 113 tons of water—more than 27,000 gallons. Add it all up, and that's enough, in an average year, to cover the 48 contiguous states with 30 inches of water, if it stood still.

But it doesn't. In North America, 70 percent of this water goes back into the atmosphere through evaporation and transpiration. The remainder seeps underground or runs downhill into waterways, creating an average stream flow of 1,200 billion gallons per day.

Those are the other voices, from the whisper of a tiny rivulet that you have to bend over to hear to the whitewater roar of a river bursting over its banks. Where we live, on the eastern flank of a mountain, the streams are the first thing we hear when we wake up after a rainy night—not a single melody, but an oratorio.

CALENDAR

JULY

SKY WATCH: Venus grows brighter but sinks lower in the west. Mercury is low at twilight during the first half of the month, between Venus and the sunset point. Earth reaches its annual far point from the Sun, aphelion, on the 6th. The Moon performs wonderfully close conjunctions this month, passing very near Mercury on the 14th, close to Venus on the 15th, above Jupiter on the 20th, close above Saturn on the 24th, and above Mars on the 27th. Mars is the headliner; on the 27th, it reaches its closest opposition since 2003. It is nearest on the 31st, at a stunning magnitude –2.8, which is brighter than Jupiter. But its low location, even at midnight, may make its fine 24-arcsecond disk smudgy through telescopes.

◗ LAST QUARTER	6th day	3:51 A.M.	◐ FIRST QUARTER	19th day	3:52 P.M.
● NEW MOON	12th day	10:48 P.M.	○ FULL MOON	27th day	4:20 P.M.

All times are given in EDT. For CT, subtract 1 hour; MT, –2; PT, –3; AKT, –4; HAT, –5 (–6 in Hawaii).

GET THESE PAGES WITH TIMES SET TO YOUR ZIP CODE AT ALMANAC.COM/ACCESS.

CALENDAR

FOR LOCAL TIDE TIMES AND HEIGHTS, GO TO ALMANAC.COM/TIDES.

DAY OF YEAR	DAY OF MONTH	DAY OF WEEK	☼ RISES H. M.	RISE KEY	☼ SETS H. M.	SET KEY	LENGTH OF DAY H. M.	SUN FAST M.	SUN DECLINATION ° ′	☾ RISES H. M.	RISE KEY	☾ SETS H. M.	SET KEY	☾ ASTRON. PLACE	☾ AGE	☾ ASTROL. PLACE
182	1	**G**	5:11	A	8:25	E	15 14	12	23 N. 04	**10:45**	E	8:14	B	CAP	18	AQU
183	2	M.	5:12	A	8:25	E	15 13	12	22 N. 59	**11:16**	E	9:12	C	CAP	19	PSC
184	3	Tu.	5:12	A	8:24	E	15 12	11	22 N. 55	**11:45**	D	10:11	C	AQU	20	PSC
185	4	W.	5:13	A	8:24	E	15 11	11	22 N. 49	—	–	11:10	D	AQU	21	PSC
186	5	Th.	5:13	A	8:24	E	15 11	11	22 N. 44	12:13	D	**12:12**	D	PSC	22	ARI
187	6	Fr.	5:14	A	8:24	E	15 10	11	22 N. 38	12:40	D	**1:14**	D	CET	23	ARI
188	7	Sa.	5:15	A	8:23	E	15 08	11	22 N. 31	1:09	C	**2:19**	E	PSC	24	TAU
189	8	**G**	5:15	A	8:23	E	15 08	11	22 N. 25	1:40	C	**3:27**	E	CET	25	TAU
190	9	M.	5:16	A	8:22	E	15 06	10	22 N. 17	2:15	B	**4:37**	E	TAU	26	GEM
191	10	Tu.	5:17	A	8:22	E	15 05	10	22 N. 10	2:56	B	**5:48**	E	TAU	27	GEM
192	11	W.	5:18	A	8:22	E	15 04	10	22 N. 02	3:45	B	**6:57**	E	TAU	28	GEM
193	12	Th.	5:18	A	8:21	E	15 03	10	21 N. 54	4:43	B	**8:01**	E	GEM	0	CAN
194	13	Fr.	5:19	A	8:20	E	15 01	10	21 N. 45	5:50	B	**8:57**	E	GEM	1	CAN
195	14	Sa.	5:20	A	8:20	E	15 00	10	21 N. 36	7:02	C	**9:45**	E	CAN	2	LEO
196	15	**G**	5:21	A	8:19	E	14 58	10	21 N. 26	8:17	C	**10:25**	E	LEO	3	LEO
197	16	M.	5:22	A	8:19	E	14 57	10	21 N. 17	9:30	C	**11:00**	D	LEO	4	VIR
198	17	Tu.	5:22	A	8:18	E	14 56	10	21 N. 06	10:41	D	**11:32**	D	LEO	5	VIR
199	18	W.	5:23	A	8:17	E	14 54	9	20 N. 56	11:50	D	—	–	VIR	6	LIB
200	19	Th.	5:24	A	8:16	E	14 52	9	20 N. 45	**12:55**	E	12:02	C	VIR	7	LIB
201	20	Fr.	5:25	A	8:16	E	14 51	9	20 N. 34	**1:59**	E	12:32	C	VIR	8	SCO
202	21	Sa.	5:26	A	8:15	E	14 49	9	20 N. 22	**3:01**	E	1:02	C	LIB	9	SCO
203	22	**G**	5:27	A	8:14	E	14 47	9	20 N. 10	**4:01**	E	1:34	B	LIB	10	SAG
204	23	M.	5:28	A	8:13	E	14 45	9	19 N. 58	**4:59**	E	2:09	B	OPH	11	SAG
205	24	Tu.	5:29	A	8:12	E	14 43	9	19 N. 46	**5:54**	E	2:48	B	OPH	12	SAG
206	25	W.	5:30	A	8:11	E	14 41	9	19 N. 33	**6:44**	E	3:32	B	SAG	13	CAP
207	26	Th.	5:31	A	8:10	E	14 39	9	19 N. 19	**7:29**	E	4:20	B	SAG	14	CAP
208	27	Fr.	5:32	A	8:09	E	14 37	9	19 N. 06	**8:10**	E	5:13	B	SAG	15	AQU
209	28	Sa.	5:33	A	8:08	E	14 35	9	18 N. 52	**8:46**	E	6:08	B	CAP	16	AQU
210	29	**G**	5:34	B	8:07	E	14 33	9	18 N. 38	**9:19**	E	7:05	C	CAP	17	AQU
211	30	M.	5:35	B	8:06	E	14 31	9	18 N. 23	**9:48**	D	8:04	C	AQU	18	PSC
212	31	Tu.	5:36	B	8:05	E	14 29	9	18 N. 09	**10:16**	D	9:04	C	AQU	19	PSC

The Sun, midway upon his tireless march,
Eyes languidly the green earth's sleepy face.
–James Benjamin Kenyon

DAY OF MONTH	DAY OF WEEK	DATES, FEASTS, FACTS, & ASPECTS	
1	**G**	**6th S. af. P.** • CANADA DAY • Intelligence and Security Branch of U.S. Army established, 1962	*Hot*
2	M.	Alligator fell from sky during storm, Charleston, S.C., 1843	*and*
3	Tu.	Dog Days begin. • ☌♆☾ • *Hear twice before you speak once.*	*breathless*
4	W.	INDEPENDENCE DAY • Advice columnists "Ann Landers" and "Abigail Van Buren" born, 1918	*for*
5	Th.	☾ ON EQ. • Governor John Winthrop recorded "sudden gust" in N.E. Mass., 1643	*heroes*
6	Fr.	⊕ AT APHELION • Armadillos mate now.	*deathless.*
7	Sa.	☌♅☾ • First 6 women sworn in to regular U.S. Navy, 1948 • Actress Veronica Lake died, 1973	*Heat*
8	**G**	**7th S. af. P.** • Josh became first dromedary to summit Mt. Washington, N.H., 2009	*eases*
9	M.	14th Amendment to U.S. Constitution ratified, 1868	*with*
10	Tu.	♃ STAT. • 134°F, Greenland Ranch, Death Valley, Calif., 1913	*mountain*
11	W.	Cornscateous air is everywhere.	*breezes.*
12	Th.	NEW ● • ECLIPSE ☉ • ☾ RIDES HIGH • ♇ AT ☍ • ☿ GR. ELONG. (26° EAST)	
13	Fr.	☾ AT ☊ • ☾ AT PERIG. • Poet John Clare born, 1793	*Peachy!*
14	Sa.	Bastille Day • ☌☿☾ • First world's fair in U.S. opened, N.Y., 1853	*Spend*
15	**G**	**8th S. af. P.** • St. Swithin • ☌♀☾	*a week*
16	M.	*July, God send thee calm and fayre, That happy harvest we may see.*	*at the*
17	Tu.	First photo taken of star other than Sun (Vega), Harvard College Observatory, 1850	*beach—whee!*
18	W.	☾ ON EQ. • Marie and Pierre Curie discovered polonium, named after Poland, 1898	*Thunderstorms*
19	Th.	Canada/U.S. agreed to transfer certain prisoners who wish to finish sentence in own country, 1978	*fire*
20	Fr.	☌♃☾ • First International Special Olympics held, Chicago, Ill., 1968	*salutes*
21	Sa.	Black-eyed Susans in bloom now.	*while*
22	**G**	**9th S. af P.** • Prince George Alexander Louis of Cambridge born, England, 2013	*we*
23	M.	St. Mary Magdalene[T] • *Hearts may agree though heads differ.*	*bask*
24	Tu.	9-yr.-old Emma Houlston became youngest person to pilot plane across Canada (Victoria, B.C., to St. John's, N.L.), 1988	*in*
25	W.	St. James • ☾ RUNS LOW • ☌♄☾ • ☿ STAT.	*bathing*
26	Th.	St. Anne • ☌♇☾ • Singer Sir Michael Philip "Mick" Jagger born, 1943	*suits.*
27	Fr.	FULL BUCK ○ • ECLIPSE ☾ • ☾ AT ☋ • ☾ AT APO. • ☌♂☾ • ♂ AT ☍	
28	Sa.	Adult gypsy moths emerge.	*Thirsty gardens*
29	**G**	**10th S. af. P.** • National Aeronautics and Space Administration (NASA) created, 1958	*get*
30	M.	Writer Emily Brontë born, 1818	*brief*
31	Tu.	St. Ignatius of Loyola • ☌♆☾ • ♂ AT CLOSEST APPROACH	*relief.*

Farmer's Calendar

We've been visiting this shoreline for more than 40 summers, and now, for the first time, there are egrets around the offshore rocks.

Those rocks were once the exclusive province of double-crested cormorants. You can still see a few cormorants there, spreading their wings to dry, but nowhere near as many as in the past.

This little piece of waterfront also used to be the haunt of long-established families who came back every summer to relax and play with their cousins in the other houses. There were softball games and Sunday evening hymn sings.

That's changing, too. As children and grandchildren multiply, it's harder to share the old houses and pay the steep property taxes. So old families cash in and sell the Victorian-era "cottages" to high-tech millionaires, some of whom immediately tear them down and build new palaces on the beach. It's a succession as natural as that of the birds.

But something is lost. There are fewer softball games, and when it's time to haul the big swimming raft in or out of the bay, there are fewer strong young bodies to do the hard work. And the Sunday evening hymn sings are disappearing, like the cormorants.

CALENDAR

AUGUST

SKY WATCH: Mars remains spectacular and is brighter than Jupiter all month. Its only negative is a southerly declination of –25 degrees, which places it lower in the sky than even the winter solstice Sun. Meanwhile, Venus brightens but continues to sink lower, thanks to the increasingly horizontal slant of the post-sunset zodiac. The Perseid meteor shower should be ideal on the 11th and 12th, as the Moon is completely absent. The Moon stands above Venus on the 14th, near Jupiter on the 16th and 17th, to the right of Saturn on the 20th, and above Mars on the 22nd and 23rd. Mercury begins a good morning star apparition on the 24th. Far to the left of Sirius, it stands 10 degrees high as morning twilight brightens.

◐ LAST QUARTER 4th day 2:18 P.M.   ◑ FIRST QUARTER 18th day 3:49 A.M.
● NEW MOON 11th day 5:58 A.M.   ○ FULL MOON 26th day 7:56 A.M.

All times are given in EDT. For CT, subtract 1 hour; MT, –2; PT, –3; AKT, –4; HAT, –5 (–6 in Hawaii).

GET THESE PAGES WITH TIMES SET TO YOUR ZIP CODE AT ALMANAC.COM/ACCESS.

FOR LOCAL TIDE TIMES AND HEIGHTS, GO TO ALMANAC.COM/TIDES.

DAY OF YEAR	DAY OF MONTH	DAY OF WEEK	☀ RISES H. M.	RISE KEY	☀ SETS H. M.	SET KEY	LENGTH OF DAY H. M.	SUN FAST M.	SUN DECLINATION ° '	☽ RISES H. M.	RISE KEY	☽ SETS H. M.	SET KEY	☽ ASTRON. PLACE	☽ AGE	☽ ASTROL. PLACE
213	1	W.	5:37	B	8:04	E	14 27	9	17 N. 53	10:43	D	10:04	D	PSC	20	ARI
214	2	Th.	5:38	B	8:03	E	14 25	10	17 N. 38	11:11	C	11:05	D	CET	21	ARI
215	3	Fr.	5:39	B	8:01	E	14 22	10	17 N. 22	11:40	C	12:08	E	PSC	22	ARI
216	4	Sa.	5:40	B	8:00	E	14 20	10	17 N. 07	—	–	1:13	E	CET	23	TAU
217	5	**G**	5:41	B	7:59	E	14 18	10	16 N. 50	12:12	C	2:20	E	ARI	24	TAU
218	6	M.	5:42	B	7:58	E	14 16	10	16 N. 34	12:49	B	3:28	E	TAU	25	GEM
219	7	Tu.	5:43	B	7:56	E	14 13	10	16 N. 17	1:33	B	4:36	E	TAU	26	GEM
220	8	W.	5:44	B	7:55	E	14 11	10	16 N. 00	2:25	B	5:41	E	ORI	27	CAN
221	9	Th.	5:45	B	7:54	E	14 09	10	15 N. 43	3:26	C	6:41	E	GEM	28	CAN
222	10	Fr.	5:46	B	7:52	E	14 06	10	15 N. 25	4:35	C	7:32	E	CAN	29	LEO
223	11	Sa.	5:47	B	7:51	D	14 04	11	15 N. 07	5:49	C	8:17	E	CAN	0	LEO
224	12	**G**	5:48	B	7:50	D	14 02	11	14 N. 49	7:05	C	8:56	E	LEO	1	VIR
225	13	M.	5:49	B	7:48	D	13 59	11	14 N. 31	8:19	D	9:30	D	LEO	2	VIR
226	14	Tu.	5:50	B	7:47	D	13 57	11	14 N. 13	9:31	D	10:01	D	VIR	3	LIB
227	15	W.	5:51	B	7:45	D	13 54	11	13 N. 54	10:41	D	10:32	C	VIR	4	LIB
228	16	Th.	5:52	B	7:44	D	13 52	12	13 N. 35	11:47	E	11:02	C	VIR	5	SCO
229	17	Fr.	5:53	B	7:42	D	13 49	12	13 N. 16	12:51	E	11:35	B	LIB	6	SCO
230	18	Sa.	5:54	B	7:41	D	13 47	12	12 N. 57	1:53	E	—	–	LIB	7	SAG
231	19	**G**	5:56	B	7:39	D	13 43	12	12 N. 37	2:53	E	12:09	B	OPH	8	SAG
232	20	M.	5:57	B	7:38	D	13 41	12	12 N. 17	3:49	E	12:47	B	OPH	9	SAG
233	21	Tu.	5:58	B	7:36	D	13 38	12	11 N. 57	4:40	E	1:30	B	SAG	10	CAP
234	22	W.	5:59	B	7:35	D	13 36	13	11 N. 37	5:27	E	2:16	B	SAG	11	CAP
235	23	Th.	6:00	B	7:33	D	13 33	13	11 N. 17	6:10	E	3:07	B	SAG	12	AQU
236	24	Fr.	6:01	B	7:31	D	13 30	14	10 N. 56	6:47	E	4:02	B	CAP	13	AQU
237	25	Sa.	6:02	B	7:30	D	13 28	14	10 N. 36	7:21	E	4:59	B	CAP	14	AQU
238	26	**G**	6:03	B	7:28	D	13 25	14	10 N. 15	7:52	D	5:57	C	AQU	15	PSC
239	27	M.	6:04	B	7:27	D	13 23	14	9 N. 54	8:20	D	6:57	C	AQU	16	PSC
240	28	Tu.	6:05	B	7:25	D	13 20	15	9 N. 33	8:47	D	7:58	D	AQU	17	ARI
241	29	W.	6:06	B	7:23	D	13 17	15	9 N. 11	9:15	C	8:59	D	CET	18	ARI
242	30	Th.	6:07	B	7:22	D	13 15	15	8 N. 50	9:43	C	10:01	E	PSC	19	ARI
243	31	Fr.	6:08	B	7:20	D	13 12	16	8 N. 28	10:14	C	11:05	E	CET	20	TAU

To use this page, see p. 136; for Key Letters, see p. 130. LIGHT = A.M. BOLD = P.M.   2018

AUGUST

AUGUST HATH 31 DAYS

What is hotter than that voice of thine!
Like a sunbeam stinging sharp and fine.
–**William Wetmore Story,** of the locust

DAY OF MONTH	DAY OF WEEK	DATES, FEASTS, FACTS, & ASPECTS	
1	W.	Lammas Day • Astronomer Maria Mitchell born, 1818 • Missouri River crested at 49.47', St. Louis, Mo., 1993	
2	Th.	☾ ON EQ. • Official signing of enlarged copy of U.S. Declaration of Independence, 1776	*Scorchin'!*
3	F.	☌♅☾ • Hail injured locked-out workers after lightning triggered fire alarm, Fort Collins, Colo., 1988	*Find a*
4	Sa.	*August rain gives honey, wine, and saffron.*	*porch in*
5	**G.**	**11th S. af. P.** • Gray squirrels have second litters now.	*the*
6	M.	Transfiguration • **Civic Holiday (Canada)** • Shakespeare's Anne Hathaway died, 1623	*shade,*
7	Tu.	♅ STAT. • 108°F, Claysville, Pa., 1918	*and you'll*
8	W.	St. Dominic • ☾ RIDES HIGH • ☿ IN INF. ☌	*have*
9	Th.	Writer Izaak Walton born, 1593 • Actress Gillian Anderson born, 1968	*it*
10	Fr.	St. Lawrence • ☾ AT PERIG. • ☾ AT ☊ • ☌☿☾	*made.*
11	Sa.	St. Clare • Dog Days end. • **NEW** ● • **ECLIPSE** ☉	*Enjoy*
12	**G.**	**12th S. af. P.** • *Though the fox runs, the chicken hath wings.*	*the*
13	M.	Swimmer Michael Phelps won his 10th and 11th Olympic gold medals, 2008	*evening*
14	Tu.	☾ ON EQ. • ☌♀☾ • Oliver Shallenberger rec'd patent for electric meter, 1888	*fusillade.*
15	W.	Assumption • Penguin Nils Olav knighted, Edinburgh Zoo, Scotland, 2008	*Cooler,*
16	Th.	Ragweed in bloom. • Baseball player Babe Ruth died, 1948	*drier:*
17	Fr.	Cat Nights commence. • ☌♃☾ • ♀ GR. ELONG. (46° EAST)	*Take*
18	Sa.	☿ STAT. • Sir H. C. K. Petty-Fitzmaurice, Lord Lansdowne, named governor-general of Canada, 1883	*a*
19	**G**	**13th S. af. P.** • Engineer James Geddes died, 1838	*fishin'*
20	M.	Millions of *Velella* hydrozoans (jellyfish relations) washed up on Pacific shores during summer, 2014	*expedition,*
21	Tu.	☾ RUNS LOW • ☌♄☾ • American Bar Association founded, 1878	*while*
22	W.	☌♇☾ • Okanagan Mountain Park wildfire strengthened, Kelowna, B.C., 2003	*Thor*
23	Th.	☾ AT APO. • ☌♂☾ • Poet Edgar Lee Masters born, 1868	*reloads*
24	Fr.	St. Bartholomew • ☾ AT ☋ • *The more noble, the more humble.*	*his*
25	Sa.	New Orleans, La., founded, 1718 • Composer Leonard Bernstein born, 1918	*ammunition.*
26	**G**	**14th S. af. P.** • **FULL STURGEON** ○ • ☿ GR. ELONG. (18° WEST)	*Still*
27	M.	☌♆☾ • York (later renamed Toronto), Upper Canada, founded, 1793	*more*
28	Tu.	St. Augustine of Hippo • ♂ STAT. • Hummingbirds migrate south.	*booming,*
29	W.	St. John the Baptist • ☾ ON EQ. • Chemist Christian Friedrich Schönbein died, 1868	*but*
30	Th.	☌♅☾ • Astronaut Guion Bluford became first African-American in space, 1983	*autumn's*
31	Fr.	Hurricane Emily crossed Outer Banks, N.C., 1993	*looming.*

Farmer's Calendar

Our town has only 1,500 full-time residents, but it boasts five churches, in part because we used to have a considerable number of "summer people." Most come for the quiet, the mountain, and the historic Lake Club.

It's hard to say how many summer people there are now. You can keep a rough tally by counting the number of tanned, fit ladies in tennis dresses in the General Store.

Two of our five churches are relics of the summer people. Now a private home, the former Our Lady of the Snows was built for the mostly Irish, mostly Catholic servants who cooked and cleaned for the summer people.

There's also Emmanuel Church, open only in the summer. A friend who belonged to a subcategory called "winter summer people"—those who eventually settled here year-round—used to call it "the Lake Club at prayer."

Winter summer people often come to the community church on Main Street. The other two churches serve a more conservative population outside the village limits.

Why so many houses of worship? Perhaps it's because, with the center of town nearly 1,500 feet above sea level, we're the highest village in New England. Some of us like to think that this means we're closer to heaven.

SEPTEMBER

SKY WATCH: The planets are still all highly visible but will soon decline. Venus reaches greatest brilliancy at magnitude –4.8 in the latter half of this month, but it has gotten much lower. Mercury is bright at magnitude –1 in the predawn east from the 1st to the 6th, when it meets Leo's blue star, Regulus. Jupiter stands above Venus; their separation narrows each evening. The Moon passes to the right of Jupiter on the 13th, to the left of still-optimal Saturn on the 17th, and above Mars on the 19th. Mars fades to magnitude –1.6 at midmonth, matching Sirius, the night's brightest true star. Autumn arrives with the equinox on the 22nd at 9:54 P.M. ET.

☽ **LAST QUARTER**	2nd day	10:37 P.M.
● **NEW MOON**	9th day	2:01 P.M.
☽ **FIRST QUARTER**	16th day	7:15 P.M.
○ **FULL MOON**	24th day	10:52 P.M.

All times are given in EDT. For CT, subtract 1 hour; MT, –2; PT, –3; AKT, –4; HAT, –5 (–6 in Hawaii).
GET THESE PAGES WITH TIMES SET TO YOUR ZIP CODE AT ALMANAC.COM/ACCESS.

FOR LOCAL TIDE TIMES AND HEIGHTS, GO TO ALMANAC.COM/TIDES.

DAY OF YEAR	DAY OF MONTH	DAY OF WEEK	☀ RISES H. M.	RISE KEY	☀ SETS H. M.	SET KEY	LENGTH OF DAY H. M.	SUN FAST M.	SUN DECLINATION ° ′	☾ RISES H. M.	RISE KEY	☾ SETS H. M.	SET KEY	☾ ASTRON. PLACE	☾ AGE	☾ ASTROL. PLACE
244	1	Sa.	6:09	B	7:18	D	13 09	16	8 N.07	10:48	B	12:10	E	ARI	21	TAU
245	2	G	6:10	C	7:17	D	13 07	16	7 N.45	11:28	B	1:16	E	TAU	22	GEM
246	3	M.	6:11	C	7:15	D	13 04	17	7 N.23	—	–	2:23	E	TAU	23	GEM
247	4	Tu.	6:12	C	7:13	D	13 01	17	7 N.01	12:15	B	3:27	E	TAU	24	CAN
248	5	W.	6:14	C	7:11	D	12 57	17	6 N.38	1:10	B	4:27	E	GEM	25	CAN
249	6	Th.	6:15	C	7:10	D	12 55	18	6 N.16	2:14	B	5:21	E	GEM	26	LEO
250	7	Fr.	6:16	C	7:08	D	12 52	18	5 N.54	3:24	C	6:07	E	CAN	27	LEO
251	8	Sa.	6:17	C	7:06	D	12 49	18	5 N.31	4:38	C	6:48	E	LEO	28	VIR
252	9	G	6:18	C	7:04	D	12 46	19	5 N.08	5:53	C	7:24	D	LEO	0	VIR
253	10	M.	6:19	C	7:03	D	12 44	19	4 N.46	7:07	D	7:57	D	VIR	1	LIB
254	11	Tu.	6:20	C	7:01	D	12 41	19	4 N.23	8:19	D	8:29	C	VIR	2	LIB
255	12	W.	6:21	C	6:59	D	12 38	20	4 N.00	9:28	E	9:00	C	VIR	3	LIB
256	13	Th.	6:22	C	6:57	D	12 35	20	3 N.37	10:36	E	9:32	C	LIB	4	SCO
257	14	Fr.	6:23	C	6:56	C	12 33	20	3 N.14	11:41	E	10:06	B	LIB	5	SCO
258	15	Sa.	6:24	C	6:54	C	12 30	21	2 N.51	12:42	E	10:44	B	SCO	6	SAG
259	16	G	6:25	C	6:52	C	12 27	21	2 N.28	1:41	E	11:25	B	OPH	7	SAG
260	17	M.	6:26	C	6:50	C	12 24	21	2 N.05	2:35	E	—	–	SAG	8	CAP
261	18	Tu.	6:27	C	6:49	C	12 22	22	1 N.41	3:24	E	12:10	B	SAG	9	CAP
262	19	W.	6:28	C	6:47	C	12 19	22	1 N.18	4:08	E	1:00	B	SAG	10	CAP
263	20	Th.	6:29	C	6:45	C	12 16	22	0 N.55	4:47	E	1:54	B	CAP	11	AQU
264	21	Fr.	6:30	C	6:43	C	12 13	23	0 N.31	5:22	E	2:50	B	CAP	12	AQU
265	22	Sa.	6:31	C	6:41	C	12 10	23	0 N.08	5:53	E	3:48	C	AQU	13	PSC
266	23	G	6:33	C	6:40	C	12 07	24	0 S.14	6:23	D	4:48	C	AQU	14	PSC
267	24	M.	6:34	C	6:38	C	12 04	24	0 S.38	6:50	D	5:49	D	AQU	15	PSC
268	25	Tu.	6:35	C	6:36	C	12 01	24	1 S.01	7:18	C	6:51	D	PSC	16	ARI
269	26	W.	6:36	C	6:34	C	11 58	25	1 S.24	7:46	C	7:53	E	CET	17	ARI
270	27	Th.	6:37	C	6:33	C	11 56	25	1 S.48	8:16	C	8:58	E	PSC	18	TAU
271	28	Fr.	6:38	C	6:31	C	11 53	25	2 S.11	8:49	B	10:03	E	ARI	19	TAU
272	29	Sa.	6:39	C	6:29	C	11 50	26	2 S.34	9:27	B	11:10	E	TAU	20	GEM
273	30	G	6:40	C	6:27	C	11 47	26	2 S.58	10:11	B	12:16	E	TAU	21	GEM

CALENDAR

THE NINTH MONTH • 2018 **SEPTEMBER** SEPTEMBER HATH 30 DAYS

Farmers mighty combines ride
Soybeans, wheat, and corn to thresh
Harvesting in silhouette
Framed in sunset's closing tide.
–Edith D. Plettner

DAY OF MONTH	DAY OF WEEK	DATES, FEASTS, FACTS, & ASPECTS	
1	Sa.	*Fair on September first, / Fair for the month.*	*Shivering*
2	**G**	15th S. af. P. • Diana Nyad first to swim from Cuba to Fla. w/o shark cage, 2013	*scholars*
3	M.	LABOR DAY • 89°F, Stampede Pass, Wash., 1988	*turn up*
4	Tu.	Radio personality Paul Harvey born, 1918	*their*
5	W.	☾ RIDES HIGH • Russia's Peter the Great levied tax on beards, 1698	*collars.*
6	Th.	☾ AT ☊ • ♄ STAT. • Librarian Charles Ammi Cutter died, 1903	*Damper:*
7	F.	☾ AT PERIG. • ♆ AT ☍ • Cranberry bog harvest begins, Cape Cod, Mass.	*Put*
8	Sa.	☌☿☾ • Black rhino born, Pittsburgh Zoo, Pa., 2012	*away*
9	**G**	16th S. af. P. • Rosh Hashanah begins at sundown • NEW ●	*that*
10	M.	First of Muharram begins at sundown • Elias Howe patented his lockstitch sewing machine, 1846	*picnic*
11	Tu.	PATRIOT DAY • ☾ ON EQ. • Hawaii's first theater opened, 1847	*hamper.*
12	W.	☌♀☾ • Actor Raymond Burr died, 1993	*Golden*
13	Th.	☌♃☾ • Chocolate co. founder Milton Hershey born, 1857	*shafts*
14	Fr.	Holy Cross • *Zond 5* launched; 4 days later became first spacecraft to circle Moon and return, 1968	*illuminate*
15	Sa.	First U.S. milch goat show began, Rochester, N.Y., 1913 • 22 lb. 7-oz. summer flounder caught, Montauk, N.Y., 1975	*apple*
16	**G**	17th S. af. P. • *Zeal without knowledge is frenzy.*	*boughs*
17	M.	☌♄☾ • 23.6" snow, Lander, Wyo., 1965	*that sag*
18	Tu.	Yom Kippur begins at sundown • ☾ RUNS LOW • ☌♇☾	*with*
19	W.	Ember Day • ☾ AT APO. • Baseball player Joe Morgan born, 1943	*freight.*
20	Th.	☾ AT ☋ • ☌♂☾ • ☿ IN SUP. ☌	*Harvest*
21	Fr.	St. Matthew • Ember Day • ♀ AT GR. ILLUM. EXT.	*song:*
22	Sa.	Ember Day • Harvest Home • AUTUMNAL EQUINOX	*mild*
23	**G**	18th S. af. P. • Sukkoth begins at sundown • ☌♆☾	*and*
24	M.	FULL HARVEST ○ • First TV newsmagazine, *60 Minutes,* debuted, 1968	*moist*
25	Tu.	☾ ON EQ. • TAT-1 first transatlantic telephone cable to link North America and U.K., 1956	*as*
26	W.	Woodchucks hibernate now. • 42.1" cucumber set world record, 2011	*pickers*
27	Th.	St. Vincent de Paul • ☌♅☾ • Singer Shaun Cassidy born, 1958	*hoist*
28	Fr.	Explorer Juan Rodriguez Cabrillo reached what is now San Diego Bay, 1542	*their*
29	Sa.	St. Michael • 31 ears of corn husked by 4 people in 1 min., Markham, Ont., 2012	*ladders*
30	**G**	19th S. af. P. • ♇ STAT. • *Care and diligence bring luck.*	*long.*

Farmer's Calendar

Looks like it's going to be a big acorn season: The clatter sometimes sounds like a hailstorm. Walking under an oak tree is like walking on marbles; you risk a sprained ankle every time. If only we could eat acorns!

We can. There are two main ways to turn acorns into meal for cooking. One involves shelling and boiling them and discarding the dark brown, tannin-bearing water until it runs clear.

This is a pain in the neck. You must keep two pots boiling at once so that you can dump the hot acorns straight into fresh boiling water. If put into cold water, the bitter-tasting tannins will bind with the meat. It takes several hours, and that's the quick way.

The slow way requires soaking the shelled acorns in cold water until the water turns dark, tossing it out and adding fresh water, and repeating until the water stays clear. Depending on the kind of acorns, this can take anywhere from several days to more than a week. Then you have to dry the acorn meal. Grind it into a fine powder and refrigerate or freeze it.

If you're determined to live like our ancestors, that's okay. But I'll bet that our ancestors did it only because they couldn't go down to the store and buy flour.

OCTOBER

SKY WATCH: The summer spectacle is ending, with all planets now losing their luster simultaneously. Venus starts very low and then vanishes into the solar glare. Jupiter is up only 10 degrees as twilight ends. Mars, highest soon after nightfall, is rapidly fading, and Saturn is visible only in the first part of the night. The solitary bright star far to Mars's lower left is Fomalhaut. The Moon stands below Jupiter on the 11th, to the right of Saturn on the 14th, to the right of Mars on the 17th, and to the left of Mars on the 18th. Uranus reaches opposition on the 23rd–24th in Aries, at a dimly visible magnitude +5.7. Venus meets the Sun in inferior conjunction on the 26th.

◑ **LAST QUARTER** 2nd day 5:45 A.M.	○ **FULL MOON** 24th day 12:45 P.M.	
● **NEW MOON** 8th day 11:47 P.M.	◐ **LAST QUARTER** 31st day 12:40 P.M.	
◗ **FIRST QUARTER** 16th day 2:02 P.M.		

All times are given in EDT. For CT, subtract 1 hour; MT, –2; PT, –3; AKT, –4; HAT, –5 (–6 in Hawaii).

GET THESE PAGES WITH TIMES SET TO YOUR ZIP CODE AT ALMANAC.COM/ACCESS.

FOR LOCAL TIDE TIMES AND HEIGHTS, GO TO ALMANAC.COM/TIDES.

DAY OF YEAR	DAY OF MONTH	DAY OF WEEK	☼ RISES H.M.	RISE KEY	☼ SETS H.M.	SET KEY	LENGTH OF DAY H. M.	SUN FAST M.	SUN DECLINATION ° '	☾ RISES H.M.	RISE KEY	☾ SETS H.M.	SET KEY	☾ ASTRON. PLACE	☾ AGE	☾ ASTROL. PLACE
274	1	M.	6:41	C	6:26	C	11 45	26	3 s. 21	11:03	B	1:20	E	TAU	22	GEM
275	2	Tu.	6:42	C	6:24	C	11 42	27	3 s. 44	—	–	2:20	E	GEM	23	CAN
276	3	W.	6:43	C	6:22	C	11 39	27	4 s. 07	12:02	B	3:15	E	GEM	24	CAN
277	4	Th.	6:44	C	6:21	C	11 37	27	4 s. 30	1:08	B	4:02	E	CAN	25	LEO
278	5	Fr.	6:46	C	6:19	C	11 33	27	4 s. 53	2:19	C	4:44	E	LEO	26	LEO
279	6	Sa.	6:47	D	6:17	C	11 27	28	5 s. 16	3:31	C	5:20	D	LEO	27	VIR
280	7	**G**	6:48	D	6:15	C	11 27	28	5 s. 39	4:44	D	5:53	D	LEO	28	VIR
281	8	M.	6:49	D	6:14	C	11 25	28	6 s. 02	5:56	D	6:25	C	VIR	0	LIB
282	9	Tu.	6:50	D	6:12	C	11 22	29	6 s. 25	7:07	D	6:56	C	VIR	1	LIB
283	10	W.	6:51	D	6:10	C	11 19	29	6 s. 48	8:16	E	7:28	C	VIR	2	SCO
284	11	Th.	6:52	D	6:09	C	11 17	29	7 s. 11	9:23	E	8:01	B	LIB	3	SCO
285	12	Fr.	6:54	C	6:07	C	11 13	29	7 s. 33	10:28	E	8:38	B	LIB	4	SAG
286	13	Sa.	6:55	C	6:05	C	11 10	30	7 s. 55	11:29	E	9:18	B	OPH	5	SAG
287	14	**G**	6:56	D	6:04	B	11 08	30	8 s. 18	12:26	E	10:02	B	OPH	6	SAG
288	15	M.	6:57	D	6:02	B	11 05	30	8 s. 40	1:18	E	10:51	B	SAG	7	CAP
289	16	Tu.	6:58	D	6:01	B	11 03	30	9 s. 02	2:04	E	11:43	B	SAG	8	CAP
290	17	W.	6:59	D	5:59	B	11 00	30	9 s. 24	2:45	E	—	–	SAG	9	AQU
291	18	Th.	7:00	D	5:58	B	10 58	31	9 s. 46	3:22	E	12:39	B	CAP	10	AQU
292	19	Fr.	7:02	D	5:56	B	10 54	31	10 s. 08	3:54	E	1:36	C	CAP	11	AQU
293	20	Sa.	7:03	D	5:54	B	10 51	31	10 s. 29	4:24	D	2:36	C	AQU	12	PSC
294	21	**G**	7:04	D	5:53	B	10 49	31	10 s. 50	4:52	D	3:36	C	AQU	13	PSC
295	22	M.	7:05	D	5:51	B	10 46	31	11 s. 12	5:19	D	4:38	D	PSC	14	ARI
296	23	Tu.	7:06	D	5:50	B	10 44	32	11 s. 33	5:47	C	5:41	D	CET	15	ARI
297	24	W.	7:08	D	5:48	B	10 40	32	11 s. 53	6:16	C	6:45	E	PSC	16	TAU
298	25	Th.	7:09	D	5:47	B	10 38	32	12 s. 14	6:49	B	7:52	E	CET	17	TAU
299	26	Fr.	7:10	D	5:46	B	10 36	32	12 s. 35	7:25	B	9:00	E	TAU	18	TAU
300	27	Sa.	7:11	D	5:44	B	10 33	32	12 s. 55	8:08	B	10:08	E	TAU	19	GEM
301	28	**G**	7:13	D	5:43	B	10 30	32	13 s. 15	8:58	B	11:15	E	TAU	20	GEM
302	29	M.	7:14	D	5:41	B	10 27	32	13 s. 35	9:55	B	12:17	E	ORI	21	CAN
303	30	Tu.	7:15	D	5:40	B	10 25	32	13 s. 55	10:59	B	1:13	E	GEM	22	CAN
304	31	W.	7:16	D	5:39	B	10 23	32	14 s. 14	—	–	2:02	E	CAN	23	LEO

THE TENTH MONTH • 2018 OCTOBER OCTOBER HATH 31 DAYS

These moments are the richest gifts of time;
When day is fading, and the pale stars climb.
–**Charles Lotin Hildreth**

DAY OF MONTH	DAY OF WEEK	DATES, FEASTS, FACTS, & ASPECTS	
1	M.	Watch for banded woolly bear caterpillars now.	*Foliage*
2	Tu.	☾ RIDES HIGH • U.S. president Johnson signed bill establishing Redwood National Park in Calif., 1968	*freaks*
3	W.	☾ AT ☊ • Cherokee Nation chief John Ross born, 1790	*and*
4	Th.	St. Francis of Assisi • Pigeon Cher Ami's message saved 194 U.S. soldiers, WWI, 1918	*flocks*
5	Fr.	☾ AT PERIG. • ♀ STAT. • Tom Green's jet car reached 413.199 mph, 1964	*of*
6	Sa.	American Chess Association founded, 1857	*geese*
7	**G**	**20th S. af. P.** • Hurricane Daisy moved to Canadian waters near N.L., 1962	*encounter*
8	M.	**COLUMBUS DAY, OBSERVED** • **THANKSGIVING DAY (CANADA)** • NEW ● • ☾ ON EQ.	*rain*
9	Tu.	☌☿☾ • "Cape Kennedy" restored to original name of "Cape Canaveral," Fla., 1973	*and*
10	W.	☌♀☾ • Little brown bats hibernate now.	*chills;*
11	Th.	☌♃☾ • *A slip of the foot may be soon recovered, but that of the tongue, perhaps never.*	*undeterred,*
12	Fr.	Canadian prime minister Lester Pearson won Nobel Peace Prize, 1957	*both*
13	Sa.	B'nai B'rith founded, 1843 • Copyright for "Happy Birthday to You" tune registered, 1893	*bus*
14	**G**	**21st S. af. P.** • ☌☿♀ • ☌♄☾ • Astronomer Sir Edward Sabine born, 1788	*and*
15	M.	☾ RUNS LOW • First U.S. Agriculture Bureau scientific publication issued, 1862	*bird*
16	Tu.	☌♇☾ • Former French queen Marie Antoinette executed, 1793	*press on*
17	W.	St. Ignatius of Antioch • ☾ AT ☋ • ☾ AT APO.	*to*
18	Th.	St. Luke • ☌♂☾ • St. Luke's little summer.	*yonder*
19	Fr.	Streptomycin, first antibiotic remedy for tuberculosis, first isolated, Rutgers University, N.J., 1943	*hills,*
20	Sa.	☌♆☾ • *What is not wisdom is danger.*	*where*
21	**G**	**22nd S. af. P.** • Baseball player Edward Charles "Whitey" Ford born, 1928	*maples*
22	M.	☾ ON EQ. • Astronaut Donald H. Peterson born, 1933	*pose*
23	Tu.	St. James of Jerusalem • ♅ AT ☍ • Flood "swept all the fences off," Newbury, Vt., 1785	*for*
24	W.	FULL HUNTER'S ○ • ☌♅☾ • Last *Concorde* flight landed, London, 2003	*selfies*
25	Th.	Actor Vincent Price died, 1993	*splendid,*
26	Fr.	♀ IN INF. ☌ • 1,496-lb. tuna caught near Auld's Cove, N.S., 1979	*till*
27	Sa.	Timber rattlesnakes move to winter dens.	*snows*
28	**G**	**23rd S. af. P.** • U.S. First Lady Abigail Adams died, 1818	*proclaim*
29	M.	Sts. Simon & Jude[T] • ☾ RIDES HIGH • ☌☿♃	*the*
30	Tu.	☾ AT ☊ • *If owls hoot at night, expect fair weather.*	*game*
31	W.	All Hallows' Eve • Reformation Day • ☾ AT PERIG.	*is ended.*

Farmer's Calendar

Colored leaves and acorns are not the only objects that fall in autumn. Five of the 12 principal meteor showers occur in October and November. Nobody knows why.

These showers—the Draconids, the Orionids, the Taurids, the Leonids, and the Andromedids—are not the most spectacular meteor showers. Only one, the Orionids, usually offers 15 meteors per hour.

So when I saw a shooting star in the predawn darkness on October 24, I didn't make much of it. But 5 minutes later, when another flashed across the sky, I realized that this was the Orionids.

I've stayed up late to see the Perseids, the most prolific meteor shower of all. They frightened my 9-year-old granddaughter so much that I had to take her inside. Perhaps it had occurred to her, as it has to me, that although we look up to see them, it makes just as much sense to say that we are looking down at them, clinging desperately to the grass in the backyard lest we, too, fall into a dark and infinite well, from which even Lassie can not save us.

This chance encounter with the Orionids was better. There was no plan, no lawn chair or blankets to spread out in the backyard, no tedium, no terror.

It was a surprise, an unexpected gift.

NOVEMBER

SKY WATCH: Mars, having resumed its normal eastward motion against the stars, speeds from Capricornus into Aquarius, gaining elevation to stand about a third of the way up the southern sky at nightfall. Just 12 arcseconds wide and at magnitude zero, it's lost half its width and is now too small to show useful detail in telescopes. On the 1st, Jupiter meets Mercury low in the west; both soon vanish. The Moon floats left of ever-lower Saturn on the 11th, close below Mars on the 15th, and to the left of Taurus's main star, Aldebaran, on the 23rd. The action switches to the predawn sky, where the Moon meets returning Venus on the 6th. Venus hovers near Virgo's Spica from the 6th to the 12th and stands 25 degrees high by month's end.

● **NEW MOON** 7th day 11:02 A.M.	○ **FULL MOON** 23rd day 12:39 A.M.
☽ **FIRST QUARTER** 15th day 9:54 A.M.	☽ **LAST QUARTER** 29th day 7:19 P.M.

After 2:00 A.M. on Nov. 4, EST is given. For CT, subtract 1 hour; MT, –2; PT, –3; AKT, –4; HAT, –5.

GET THESE PAGES WITH TIMES SET TO YOUR ZIP CODE AT ALMANAC.COM/ACCESS.

FOR LOCAL TIDE TIMES AND HEIGHTS, GO TO ALMANAC.COM/TIDES.

DAY OF YEAR	DAY OF MONTH	DAY OF WEEK	☼ RISES H. M.	RISE KEY	☼ SETS H. M.	SET KEY	LENGTH OF DAY H. M.	SUN FAST M.	SUN DECLINATION ° ′	☾ RISES H. M.	RISE KEY	☾ SETS H. M.	SET KEY	☾ ASTRON. PLACE	☾ AGE	☾ ASTROL. PLACE
305	1	Th.	7:17	D	5:38	B	10 21	32	14 s. 33	12:07	B	2:44	E	CAN	24	LEO
306	2	Fr.	7:19	D	5:36	B	10 17	32	14 s. 52	1:18	C	3:21	E	LEO	25	VIR
307	3	Sa.	7:20	D	5:35	B	10 15	32	15 s. 11	2:29	C	3:54	D	LEO	26	VIR
308	4	**G**	6:21	D	4:34	B	10 13	32	15 s. 30	2:39	D	3:25	D	VIR	27	LIB
309	5	M.	6:22	D	4:33	B	10 11	32	15 s. 48	3:49	D	3:55	C	VIR	28	LIB
310	6	Tu.	6:24	D	4:31	B	10 07	32	16 s. 06	4:57	E	4:25	C	VIR	29	SCO
311	7	W.	6:25	E	4:30	B	10 05	32	16 s. 24	6:05	E	4:57	C	LIB	0	SCO
312	8	Th.	6:26	E	4:29	B	10 03	32	16 s. 41	7:11	E	5:32	B	LIB	1	SCO
313	9	Fr.	6:27	E	4:28	B	10 01	32	16 s. 58	8:15	E	6:11	B	SCO	2	SAG
314	10	Sa.	6:29	E	4:27	B	9 58	32	17 s. 15	9:15	E	6:53	B	OPH	3	SAG
315	11	**G**	6:30	E	4:26	B	9 56	32	17 s. 32	10:10	E	7:41	B	SAG	4	CAP
316	12	M.	6:31	E	4:25	B	9 54	32	17 s. 48	10:59	E	8:32	B	SAG	5	CAP
317	13	Tu.	6:32	E	4:24	B	9 52	31	18 s. 04	11:43	E	9:27	B	SAG	6	AQU
318	14	W.	6:34	E	4:23	B	9 49	31	18 s. 20	12:21	E	10:24	B	CAP	7	AQU
319	15	Th.	6:35	E	4:22	B	9 47	31	18 s. 35	12:55	E	11:22	C	CAP	8	AQU
320	16	Fr.	6:36	E	4:21	B	9 45	31	18 s. 50	1:25	E	—	–	AQU	9	PSC
321	17	Sa.	6:37	E	4:21	B	9 44	31	19 s. 05	1:53	D	12:21	C	AQU	10	PSC
322	18	**G**	6:39	E	4:20	B	9 41	31	19 s. 19	2:20	D	1:22	D	AQU	11	ARI
323	19	M.	6:40	E	4:19	B	9 39	30	19 s. 33	2:47	C	2:24	D	CET	12	ARI
324	20	Tu.	6:41	E	4:18	B	9 37	30	19 s. 46	3:15	C	3:27	E	PSC	13	ARI
325	21	W.	6:42	E	4:18	B	9 36	30	20 s. 00	3:46	C	4:33	E	CET	14	TAU
326	22	Th.	6:43	E	4:17	A	9 34	30	20 s. 13	4:21	B	5:42	E	ARI	15	TAU
327	23	Fr.	6:45	E	4:16	A	9 31	29	20 s. 25	5:02	B	6:52	E	TAU	16	GEM
328	24	Sa.	6:46	E	4:16	A	9 30	29	20 s. 37	5:50	B	8:02	E	TAU	17	GEM
329	25	**G**	6:47	E	4:15	A	9 28	29	20 s. 49	6:46	B	9:08	E	ORI	18	CAN
330	26	M.	6:48	E	4:15	A	9 27	28	21 s. 00	7:49	B	10:09	E	GEM	19	CAN
331	27	Tu.	6:49	E	4:14	A	9 25	28	21 s. 11	8:58	B	11:01	E	CAN	20	LEO
332	28	W.	6:50	E	4:14	A	9 24	28	21 s. 22	10:09	C	11:46	E	CAN	21	LEO
333	29	Th.	6:51	E	4:13	A	9 22	27	21 s. 32	11:20	C	12:24	E	LEO	22	VIR
334	30	Fr.	6:53	E	4:13	A	9 20	27	21 s. 42	—	–	12:58	D	LEO	23	VIR

To use this page, see p. 136; for Key Letters, see p. 130. LIGHT = A.M. **BOLD = P.M.** **2018**

CALENDAR

NOVEMBER

NOVEMBER HATH 30 DAYS

Shorter and shorter now the twilight clips
The days, as through the sunset gate they crowd . . .
–Alice Cary

DAY OF MONTH	DAY OF WEEK	DATES, FEASTS, FACTS, & ASPECTS	
1	Th.	All Saints' • Architect James Renwick Jr. born, 1818 • First direct flight from Canada to USSR, 1966	*Dank*
2	Fr.	All Souls' • Storm blocked Ben Franklin's view of lunar eclipse, Philadelphia, 1743	*and*
3	Sa.	Sadie Hawkins Day • *Mariner 10* spacecraft launched, Cape Canaveral, Fla., 1973	*dismal,*
4	**G**	**24th S. af. P.** • **Daylight Saving Time ends, 2:00 A.M.** • ☾ ON EQ.	*dearie.*
5	M.	☌♀☾ • *In the evening, one may praise the day.*	*Just*
6	Tu.	**Election Day** • ☿ GR. ELONG. (23° EAST) • Composer Pyotr Ilyich Tchaikovsky died, 1893	*short*
7	W.	**NEW** ● • Evangelist Billy Graham born, 1918	*of*
8	Th.	☌♃☾ • Black bears head to winter dens now.	*abysmal;*
9	Fr.	☌☿☾ • Worst day of storm that caused 12 major shipwrecks on Great Lakes, U.S. and Canada, 1913	
10	Sa.	Statue of Our Lady of Prompt Succor first in U.S. to be canonically crowned, New Orleans, La., 1895	*hardly what*
11	**G**	**25th S. af. P.** • **Veterans Day** • ☾ RUNS LOW • ☌♄☾	*we'd*
12	M.	Indian Summer • ☌♇☾ • 208-mile-long, 60-mile-wide iceberg discovered, 1956	*call*
13	Tu.	☾ AT ☋ • ♀ STAT. • Lobsters move to offshore waters.	*cheery.*
14	W.	☾ AT APO. • Yale U. announced will admit women following fall, 1968	*Rain*
15	Th.	☌♂☾ • First gas-turbine electric locomotive in U.S. track-tested, Erie, Pa., 1948	*comes*
16	Fr.	Louis Riel, Métis leader and founder of Man., died, 1885	*and*
17	Sa.	St. Hugh of Lincoln • ☌♆☾ • ☿ STAT.	*goes:*
18	**G**	**26th S. af. P.** • Crab apples are ripe now.	*dreary!*
19	M.	☾ ON EQ. • Columbus first saw what is now Puerto Rico, 1493	*At*
20	Tu.	☌⛢☾ • *One sesame seed won't make oil.*	*least*
21	W.	Actress Marlo Thomas born, 1937 • Actor Bill Bixby died, 1993	*our*
22	Th.	**Thanksgiving Day** • Explorer La Salle born, 1643 • Pirate Blackbeard died, 1718	*turkey*
23	Fr.	St. Clement • **FULL BEAVER** ○ • Lake Merced water level dropped 30', Calif., 1852	*isn't*
24	Sa.	Artist Henri de Toulouse-Lautrec born, 1864 • Pianist Scott Joplin born, 1868	*jerky.*
25	**G**	**27th S. af. P.** • ☾ RIDES HIGH • ♆ STAT.	*Quirky:*
26	M.	☾ AT PERIG. • ☌♃☉ • First major football game played indoors, Chicago Coliseum, Ill., 1896	*mild,*
27	Tu.	☾ AT ☊ • ☌☿♃ • ☿ IN INF. ☌ • Blizzard with lightning struck parts of S.Dak., 1983	*wild,*
28	W.	North Pacific Canning Co. formed, B.C., 1888	*wet,*
29	Th.	Maj. Henry Hitchcock, Sherman's March, Ga., 1864: "Weather so warm that I could not wear any cape after 10 A.M."	*and*
30	Fr.	St. Andrew • *A heavy November snow will last until April.*	*murky.*

Farmer's Calendar

In late autumn, after most of the leaves have fallen, the forest suddenly becomes transparent. The contours of the land leap out in 3-D, exposing all kinds of subtleties. Many of them are small, bashful, the kind of sights that require us to look down instead of up.

For example, just before Thanksgiving, I noticed for the first time some spectacular maple leaves in colors—rose, bright yellow, hunter's orange—that had long since left the canopy above me. They were big leaves, 6 inches or more across, but they were growing on stems less than 18 inches tall.

Why do these tiny trees put forth such disproportionately large and brilliant leaves? Perhaps it's because now the sunlight streams down to the forest floor unhindered, where these previously shaded maples can suck up energy with their outsized solar collectors.

Once I noticed the first, the second, the third, I saw them everywhere. They fluttered, but there was no breeze. They looked like cops doing that palm-down hand-waggle that means, "You're not going fast enough for me to stop you, but you're going too fast."

The semaphore of the leaves has a similar message: "Slow down. You're going too fast to see me."

DECEMBER

SKY WATCH: Venus excels as a morning star, now at greatest brilliancy at a gorgeous, shadow-casting magnitude –4.9. High at predawn twilight, it's below the Moon on the 3rd. Mercury also begins a good morning apparition, below the Moon on the 5th. On the 6th, Jupiter takes its turn dangling below the crescent Moon. The Geminid meteors should be excellent on the 13th, after the Moon sets at around 10:00 P.M. Zero-magnitude Mars stands above the Moon on the 14th, with both about halfway up the southern sky at nightfall. Jupiter and Mercury hang out together most of the month and are quite close on the 21st, some 10 degrees high, 40 minutes before sunrise. Winter begins with the solstice, on the 21st at 5:23 P.M. ET.

● NEW MOON	7th day 2:20 A.M.	○ FULL MOON	22nd day 12:49 P.M.
◐ FIRST QUARTER	15th day 6:49 A.M.	◑ LAST QUARTER	29th day 4:34 A.M.

All times are given in EST. For CT, subtract 1 hour; MT, –2; PT, –3; AKT, –4; HAT, –5.

GET THESE PAGES WITH TIMES SET TO YOUR ZIP CODE AT ALMANAC.COM/ACCESS.

FOR LOCAL TIDE TIMES AND HEIGHTS, GO TO ALMANAC.COM/TIDES.

DAY OF YEAR	DAY OF MONTH	DAY OF WEEK	☼ RISES H. M.	RISE KEY	☼ SETS H. M.	SET KEY	LENGTH OF DAY H. M.	SUN FAST M.	SUN DECLINATION ° '	☾ RISES H. M.	RISE KEY	☾ SETS H. M.	SET KEY	☾ ASTRON. PLACE	☾ AGE	☾ ASTROL. PLACE
335	1	Sa.	6:54	E	4:13	A	9 19	27	21 s. 51	12:30	D	1:29	D	VIR	24	LIB
336	2	G	6:55	E	4:12	A	9 17	26	22 s. 00	1:38	D	1:58	C	VIR	25	LIB
337	3	M.	6:56	E	4:12	A	9 16	26	22 s. 09	2:46	E	2:27	C	VIR	26	LIB
338	4	Tu.	6:57	E	4:12	A	9 15	25	22 s. 17	3:52	E	2:57	C	VIR	27	SCO
339	5	W.	6:58	E	4:12	A	9 14	25	22 s. 24	4:58	E	3:30	B	LIB	28	SCO
340	6	Th.	6:59	E	4:12	A	9 13	25	22 s. 32	6:02	E	4:06	B	SCO	29	SAG
341	7	Fr.	7:00	E	4:12	A	9 12	24	22 s. 38	7:03	E	4:47	B	OPH	0	SAG
342	8	Sa.	7:01	E	4:12	A	9 11	24	22 s. 45	8:00	E	5:32	B	SAG	1	CAP
343	9	G	7:01	E	4:12	A	9 11	23	22 s. 51	8:53	E	6:22	B	SAG	2	CAP
344	10	M.	7:02	E	4:12	A	9 10	23	22 s. 56	9:39	E	7:16	B	SAG	3	CAP
345	11	Tu.	7:03	E	4:12	A	9 09	22	23 s. 01	10:19	E	8:12	B	CAP	4	AQU
346	12	W.	7:04	E	4:12	A	9 08	22	23 s. 06	10:55	E	9:10	C	CAP	5	AQU
347	13	Th.	7:05	E	4:12	A	9 07	22	23 s. 10	11:26	E	10:09	C	AQU	6	PSC
348	14	Fr.	7:06	E	4:12	A	9 06	21	23 s. 13	11:55	D	11:08	C	AQU	7	PSC
349	15	Sa.	7:06	E	4:12	A	9 06	21	23 s. 17	12:21	D	—	-	AQU	8	PSC
350	16	G	7:07	E	4:13	A	9 06	20	23 s. 19	12:47	D	12:08	D	PSC	9	ARI
351	17	M.	7:08	E	4:13	A	9 05	20	23 s. 21	1:14	C	1:09	D	CET	10	ARI
352	18	Tu.	7:08	E	4:13	A	9 05	19	23 s. 23	1:43	C	2:13	E	PSC	11	TAU
353	19	W.	7:09	E	4:14	A	9 05	19	23 s. 24	2:15	B	3:19	E	CET	12	TAU
354	20	Th.	7:09	E	4:14	A	9 05	18	23 s. 25	2:52	B	4:28	E	TAU	13	GEM
355	21	Fr.	7:10	E	4:15	A	9 05	18	23 s. 26	3:36	B	5:38	E	TAU	14	GEM
356	22	Sa.	7:10	E	4:15	A	9 05	17	23 s. 25	4:30	B	6:48	E	TAU	15	CAN
357	23	G	7:11	E	4:16	A	9 05	17	23 s. 25	5:32	B	7:54	E	GEM	16	CAN
358	24	M.	7:11	E	4:16	A	9 05	16	23 s. 24	6:41	B	8:52	E	GEM	17	CAN
359	25	Tu.	7:12	E	4:17	A	9 05	16	23 s. 22	7:54	C	9:42	E	CAN	18	LEO
360	26	W.	7:12	E	4:18	A	9 06	15	23 s. 20	9:08	C	10:25	E	LEO	19	LEO
361	27	Th.	7:12	E	4:18	A	9 06	15	23 s. 18	10:20	D	11:01	D	LEO	20	VIR
362	28	Fr.	7:13	E	4:19	A	9 06	14	23 s. 15	11:30	D	11:33	D	LEO	21	VIR
363	29	Sa.	7:13	E	4:20	A	9 07	14	23 s. 11	—	-	12:03	C	VIR	22	LIB
364	30	G	7:13	E	4:21	A	9 08	13	23 s. 08	12:38	D	12:32	C	VIR	23	LIB
365	31	M.	7:13	E	4:21	A	9 08	13	23 s. 03	1:44	E	1:01	C	VIR	24	SCO

THE TWELFTH MONTH · 2018 **DECEMBER** DECEMBER HATH 31 DAYS

Come give the holly a song;
For it helps to drive stern winter away.
–**Eliza Cook**

DAY OF MONTH	DAY OF WEEK	DATES, FEASTS, FACTS, & ASPECTS	
1	Sa.	♀ AT GR. ILLUM. EXTENT • –25.6°F, Fort Saskatchewan, Alta., 1990	*Shopping*
2	G	**1st S. of Advent** • Chanukah begins at sundown • ☾ ON EQ.	*rush*
3	M.	☌♀☾ • Ill. admitted to Union as 21st state, 1818	*slowed*
4	Tu.	Cardinal de Richelieu died, 1642	*by*
5	W.	☌☿☾ • Canada's first electric car debuted, Toronto, Ont., 1893	*slush;*
6	Th.	St. Nicholas • ☌♃☾ • ☿ STAT. • 5" snow, Savannah, Ga., 1740	*We'll*
7	Fr.	St. Ambrose • **NAT'L PEARL HARBOR REMEMBRANCE DAY** • **NEW** ● • ☌♂♆	*have*
8	Sa.	Winterberry fruits especially showy now.	*to mush!*
9	G	**2nd S. of Advent** • ☾ RUNS LOW • ☌♄☾ • ☌♇☾	*A*
10	M.	St. Eulalia • ☾ AT ☋ • *One ounce of discretion is worth a pound of wit.*	*snow*
11	Tu.	Astronomer Annie Jump Cannon born, 1863 • *Dec. 11–12:* Ice storm hit Northeast, 2008	*event*
12	W.	**Our Lady of Guadalupe** • ☾ AT APO. • U.S. diplomat Joel Roberts Poinsett died, 1851	*may*
13	Th.	St. Lucia • Wilson first U.S. president to visit Europe while in office, 1918	*leave*
14	Fr.	Halcyon Days begin. • ☌♂☾ • ☌♆☾ • "Diplogen" suggested for isotope name, 1933	*us*
15	Sa.	☿ GR. ELONG. (21° WEST) • Architect Alexandre Gustave Eiffel born, 1832	*wan,*
16	G	**3rd S. of Advent** • ☾ ON EQ. • Boston Tea Party occurred, 1773	*spent.*
17	M.	☌⛢☾ • *When the snow falls dry, it means to lie; But flakes light and soft bring rain oft.*	*Arctic*
18	Tu.	Beware the Pogonip. • Actress Zsa Zsa Gabor died, 2016	*blast*
19	W.	Ember Day • *Intelsat III F-2* communications satellite launched, 1968	*is*
20	Th.	Industrialist Harvey S. Firestone born, 1868	*quickly*
21	Fr.	St. Thomas • Ember Day • **WINTER SOLSTICE** • ☌☿♃	*past,*
22	Sa.	Ember Day • **FULL COLD** ○ • Writer Beatrix Potter died, 1943	*so*
23	G	**4th S. of Advent** • ☾ RIDES HIGH • Van Gogh cut off most of left ear, 1888	*Santa's*
24	M.	☾ AT ☊ • ☾ AT PERIG. • Pepper, a Bolivian gray titi monkey, born at Philadelphia Zoo, Pa., 2012	*not*
25	Tu.	**Christmas** • G. Washington's troops crossed Delaware R., Am. Revolution, 1776	*despondent.*
26	W.	St. Stephen • **BOXING DAY (CANADA)** • **FIRST DAY OF KWANZAA**	*Snowy*
27	Th.	St. John • Ill diarist, N.Y., 1864: *I don't see no need of being sick now that school is out. Darn it!*	*and shivery*
28	Fr.	Holy Innocents • First sudden-death overtime game in NFL, Baltimore Colts vs. N.Y. Giants, 1958	*for*
29	Sa.	☾ ON EQ. • Lake Washington Floating Bridge construction began, Seattle, Wash., 1938	*infant*
30	G	**1st S. af. Ch.** • *Good to begin well, better to end well.*	*'19's*
31	M.	St. Sylvester • Helium-filled sun shade patented, 1991	*delivery!*

Farmer's Calendar

Those of us who lived through the Great New England Ice Storm of December 11–12, 2008, still have posttraumatic stress disorder. The storm lasted 2 days, but the power was out for more than a week at our house. Now, when ice is predicted, we check our water supplies, our batteries, our candles. We sleep with a flashlight; we unplug the computers. We lie awake listening for the chatter of sleet on the windows or, God forbid, the rifle shots of branches breaking or the chandelier-fall crash of a treetop.

But in many ways this was the most joyous holiday season ever. People checked on their neighbors. The General Store contributed 200 turkey dinners to a supper at the elementary school so that people could enjoy a hot meal and some company. One couple went ahead with a church wedding, lit by candles. Bundled up like fur trappers, they left little puffs of fog when they said their vows.

We're just not quite ready to go through it all again. The worst part was going a week without a shower. Come to think of it: No, it was hauling water up from the creek in buckets. Actually: No, it was using up half a winter's firewood in a fortnight!

This ice storm followed the last big one by 12 years. We're about due for another.

HOLIDAYS AND OBSERVANCES

2018 HOLIDAYS
FEDERAL HOLIDAYS ARE LISTED IN BOLD.

JAN. 1: New Year's Day

JAN. 15: Martin Luther King Jr.'s Birthday

JAN. 19: Robert E. Lee Day *(Fla., Ky.)*

FEB. 2: Groundhog Day

FEB. 12: Abraham Lincoln's Birthday

FEB. 13: Mardi Gras *(Baldwin & Mobile counties, Ala.; La.)*

FEB. 14: Valentine's Day

FEB. 15: Susan B. Anthony's Birthday *(Fla.)*

FEB. 19: Presidents' Day

FEB. 22: George Washington's Birthday

MAR. 2: Texas Independence Day

MAR. 6: Town Meeting Day *(Vt.)*

MAR. 8: International Women's Day

MAR. 17: St. Patrick's Day
Evacuation Day *(Suffolk Co., Mass.)*

MAR. 26: Seward's Day *(Alaska)*

MAR. 31: César Chávez Day

APR. 2: Pascua Florida Day

APR. 16: Patriots Day *(Maine, Mass.)*

APR. 21: San Jacinto Day *(Tex.)*

APR. 22: Earth Day

APR. 27: National Arbor Day

MAY 5: Cinco de Mayo

MAY 8: Truman Day *(Mo.)*

MAY 13: Mother's Day

MAY 19: Armed Forces Day

MAY 21: Victoria Day *(Canada)*

MAY 22: National Maritime Day

MAY 28: Memorial Day, observed

JUNE 5: World Environment Day

JUNE 11: King Kamehameha I Day *(Hawaii)*

JUNE 14: Flag Day

JUNE 17: Father's Day
Bunker Hill Day *(Suffolk Co., Mass.)*

JUNE 19: Emancipation Day *(Tex.)*

JUNE 20: West Virginia Day

JULY 1: Canada Day

JULY 4: Independence Day

JULY 24: Pioneer Day *(Utah)*

AUG. 1: Colorado Day

AUG. 6: Civic Holiday *(parts of Canada)*

AUG. 16: Bennington Battle Day *(Vt.)*

AUG. 19: National Aviation Day

AUG. 26: Women's Equality Day

SEPT. 3: Labor Day

SEPT. 9: Grandparents Day
Admission Day *(Calif.)*

SEPT. 11: Patriot Day

SEPT. 17: Constitution Day

SEPT. 21: International Day of Peace

OCT. 1: Child Health Day

OCT. 8: Columbus Day, observed
Native Americans' Day *(S.Dak.)*
Thanksgiving Day *(Canada)*

OCT. 9: Leif Eriksson Day

OCT. 18: Alaska Day

OCT. 24: United Nations Day

OCT. 26: Nevada Day

OCT. 31: Halloween

NOV. 4: Will Rogers Day *(Okla.)*

NOV. 6: Election Day

NOV. 11: Veterans Day
Remembrance Day *(Canada)*

NOV. 19: Discovery of Puerto Rico Day	**DEC. 15:** Bill of Rights Day
NOV. 22: Thanksgiving Day	**DEC. 17:** Wright Brothers Day
NOV. 23: Acadian Day *(La.)*	**DEC. 25: Christmas Day**
DEC. 7: National Pearl Harbor Remembrance Day	**DEC. 26:** Boxing Day *(Canada)* First day of Kwanzaa

Movable Religious Observances

JAN. 28: Septuagesima Sunday	**MAY 15:** Ramadan begins at sundown
FEB. 13: Shrove Tuesday	**MAY 20:** Whitsunday–Pentecost
FEB. 14: Ash Wednesday	**MAY 27:** Trinity Sunday
MAR. 25: Palm Sunday	**JUNE 3:** Corpus Christi
MAR. 30: Good Friday Passover begins at sundown	**SEPT. 9:** Rosh Hashanah begins at sundown
APR. 1: Easter	**SEPT. 18:** Yom Kippur begins at sundown
APR. 8: Orthodox Easter	
MAY 6: Rogation Sunday	**DEC. 2:** First Sunday of Advent Chanukah begins at sundown
MAY 10: Ascension Day	

—Beth Krommes

CHRONOLOGICAL CYCLES

Dominical Letter **G**

Epact **13**

Golden Number (Lunar Cycle) **5**

Roman Indiction **11**

Solar Cycle **11**

Year of Julian Period **6731**

ERAS

ERA	YEAR	BEGINS
Byzantine	7527	September 14
Jewish (A.M.)*	5779	September 9
Chinese (Lunar) [Year of the Dog]	4716	February 16
Roman (A.U.C.)	2771	January 14
Nabonassar	2767	April 19
Japanese	2678	January 1
Grecian (Seleucidae)	2330	September 14 (or October 14)
Indian (Saka)	1940	March 22
Diocletian	1735	September 11
Islamic (Hegira)*	1440	September 10

*Year begins at sundown.

GLOSSARY OF ALMANAC ODDITIES

Many readers have expressed puzzlement over the rather obscure entries that appear on our **Right-Hand Calendar Pages, 141–167.** These "oddities" have long been fixtures in the Almanac, and we are pleased to provide some definitions. Once explained, they may not seem so odd after all!

−Beth Krommes

EMBER DAYS: These are the Wednesdays, Fridays, and Saturdays that occur in succession following (1) the First Sunday in Lent; (2) Whitsunday–Pentecost; (3) the Feast of the Holy Cross, September 14; and (4) the Feast of St. Lucia, December 13. The word *ember* is perhaps a corruption of the Latin *quatuor tempora,* "four times." The four periods are observed by some Christian denominations for prayer, fasting, and the ordination of clergy.

Folklore has it that the weather on each of the 3 days foretells the weather for the next 3 months; that is, in September, the first Ember Day, Wednesday, forecasts the weather for October; Friday predicts November; and Saturday foretells December.

DISTAFF DAY (JANUARY 7): This was the day after Epiphany, when women were expected to return to their spinning following the Christmas holiday. A distaff is the staff that women used for holding the flax or wool in spinning. (Hence the term "distaff" refers to women's work or the maternal side of the family.)

PLOUGH MONDAY (JANUARY): Traditionally, the first Monday after Epiphany was called Plough Monday because it was the day when men returned to their plough, or daily work, following the Christmas holiday. (Every few years, Plough Monday and Distaff Day fall on the same day.) It was customary at this time for farm laborers to draw a plough through the village, soliciting money for a "plough light,"

which was kept burning in the parish church all year. This traditional verse captures the spirit of it:

Yule is come and Yule is gone,
and we have feasted well;
so Jack must to his flail again
and Jenny to her wheel.

THREE CHILLY SAINTS (MAY): Mamertus, Pancras, and Gervais were three early Christian saints whose feast days, on May 11, 12, and 13, respectively, are traditionally cold; thus they have come to be known as the Three Chilly Saints. An old French saying translates to "St. Mamertus, St. Pancras, and St. Gervais do not pass without a frost."

MIDSUMMER DAY (JUNE 24): To the farmer, this day is the midpoint of the growing season, halfway between planting and harvest. The Anglican church considered it a "Quarter Day," one of the four major divisions of the liturgical year. It also marks the feast day of St. John the Baptist. (Midsummer Eve is an occasion for festivity and celebrates fertility.)

CORNSCATEOUS AIR (JULY): First used by early almanac makers, this term signifies warm, damp air. Although it signals ideal climatic conditions for growing corn, warm, damp air poses

One Simple Trick to Reversing Memory Loss

World's Leading Brain Expert and Winner of the Prestigious Kennedy Award, Unveils Exciting News For the Scattered, Unfocused and Forgetful

BY STEVEN WUZUBIA
HEALTH CORRESPONDENT;

Dr. Meir Shinitzky, Ph.D. a former visiting professor at Duke University and a recipient of the prestigious J.F. Kennedy Prize

Clearwater, Florida: Dr. Meir Shinitzky, Ph.D., is a former visiting professor at Duke University, recipient of the prestigious J.F. Kennedy Prize and author of more than 200 international scientific papers on human body cells. But now he's come up with what the medical world considers his greatest accomplishment — A vital compound. so powerful, it's reported to repair… even regrow damaged brain cells. In layman's terms — Bring back your memory power. And leave you feeling more focused and clear-headed than you have in years!

In his last speaking engagment, Dr. Shinitsky explains this phenomenon in simple terms; "Science has shown when your brain nutrient levels drop, you can start to experience memory problems and overall mental fatigue. Your ability to concentrate and stay focused becomes compromised. And gradually, a "mental fog" sets in. It can damage every aspect of your life". Not only do brain cells die but they become dysfunctional as if they begin to fade away as we age. This affects our ability to have mental clarity and focus and impacts our ability to remember things that were easy for us to do in our 20's and 30's.

Scientists think the biggest cause of brain deterioration in older people is the decreased functioning of membranes and molecules that surround the brain cells. These really are the transmitters that connect the tissues or the brain cells to one another that help us with our sharp memory, clear thinking and mental focus, even our powers to reason well. "When we are in our 20's" according to Dr. Shinitzky "our body produces key substances like phosphatidylserine and phosphatidic acid"…unfortunately they are believed to be critical essential nutrients that just fade away with age, much like our memories often do leading to further mental deterioration.

As we get older it becomes more frustrating as there is little comfort when you forget names… misplace your keys…or just feel "a little confused". And even though your foggy memory gets laughed off as just another "senior moment," it's not very funny when it keeps happening to you.

The Missing Link is Found and Tested

It's hard to pronounce that's for sure, but it certainly appears from the astounding clinical research that this one vital nutrient phosphatidylserine (PS) can really make a huge difference in our mental wellness. 17 different double blind studies with placebo controlled groups have been involved in the clinical research of PS with patients between the ages of 55-80 years of age. Periodically the researchers gave these patients memory and cognitive tests and the results were simply amazing:

1) PS patients outperformed placebo patients in All 5 Tests - 100% Success Rate

2) After only 45 days there was a measurable improvement in mental function

3) After 90 days, there was an impressive and amazing improvement in mental function

The group taking phosphatidylserine, not only enjoyed sharper memory, but listen to this… they were also more upbeat and remarkably more happy. By contrast, the moods of the individuals who took the placebo (starch pill), remained unaffected….no mental or mood improvement at all.

Vital Nutrient Reverses "Scatter Brain"

This incredible PS nutrient feeds your brain the vital nutrient it needs to stay healthy... PS now has the attention of some of the world's most prominent brain experts. It has been written up and published in leading science and medical journals and its findings have electrified the International scientific community.

Earth-Shaking Science

Published, clinical reports show replenishing your body's natural supply of Phosphatidylserine, not only helps sharpen your memory and concentration — but also helps "perk you up" and put you in a better mood. PS as it turns out also helps to reduce everyday stress and elevate your mood by lowering your body's production of the hormone cortisol. When cortisol levels are too high for too long you experience fatigue, bad moods and weakness. This drug-free brain-boosting formula enters your bloodstream fast (in as little as thirty minutes).

Officially Reviewed by the U.S. Food and Drug Administration: PS is the ONLY Health Supplement that has a "Qualified Health Claim" for both Cognitive Dysfunction and Dementia".

Special Opportunity For Our Readers

We've made arrangements with the distributor of this proprietary blend of PS, which combines with several other proven special brain boosting natural ingredients to give you the mental clarity and memory gain that you need, to give you a Risk-Free trial supply. This is a special "Readers Only Discount". This trial is 100% risk-free.

It's a terrific deal. If Lipogen PS Plus doesn't help you think better, remember more... and improve your mind, clarity and mood — you won't pay a penny! (Except S&H).

So don't wait. Now you can join the thousands of people who think better, remember more — and enjoy clear, "fog-free" memory. Think of it as making a "wake-up call" to your brain. **CALL NOW TOLL FREE 1-800-609-3558.**

a danger to those affected by asthma and other respiratory problems.

DOG DAYS (JULY 3-AUGUST 11): These 40 days are traditionally the year's hottest and unhealthiest. They once coincided with the year's heliacal (at sunrise) rising of the Dog Star, Sirius. Ancient folks thought that the "combined heat" of Sirius and the Sun caused summer's swelter.

LAMMAS DAY (AUGUST 1): Derived from the Old English *hlaf maesse,* meaning "loaf mass," Lammas Day marked the beginning of the harvest. Traditionally, loaves of bread were baked from the first-ripened grain and brought to the churches to be consecrated. Eventually, "loaf mass" became "Lammas." In Scotland, Lammastide fairs became famous as the time when trial marriages could be made. These marriages could end after a year with no strings attached.

CAT NIGHTS COMMENCE (AUGUST 17): This term harks back to the days when people believed in witches. An Irish legend says that a witch could turn into a cat and regain herself eight times, but on the ninth time (August 17), she couldn't change back and thus began her final life permanently as a cat. Hence the saying: "A cat has nine lives."

HARVEST HOME (SEPTEMBER): In Europe and Britain, this marked the conclusion of the harvest and a period of festivals for feasting and thanksgiving. It was also a time to hold elections, pay workers, and collect rents. These festivals usually took place around the autumnal equinox. Certain groups in the United States, e.g., the Pennsylvania Dutch, have kept the tradition alive.

ST. LUKE'S LITTLE SUMMER (OCTOBER): This is a period of warm weather that occurs on or near St. Luke's feast day (October 18) and is sometimes called Indian summer.

INDIAN SUMMER (NOVEMBER): A period of warm weather following a cold spell or a hard frost, Indian summer can occur between St. Martin's Day (November 11) and November 20. Although there are differing dates for its occurrence, for more than 225 years the Almanac has adhered to the saying "If All Saints' (November 1) brings out winter, St. Martin's brings out Indian summer." The term may have come from early Native Americans, some of whom believed that the condition was caused by a warm wind sent from the court of their southwestern god, Cautantowwit.

HALCYON DAYS (DECEMBER): This is a period of about 2 weeks of calm weather that often follows the blustery winds at autumn's end. Ancient Greeks and Romans experienced this weather around the time of the winter solstice, when the halcyon, or kingfisher, was thought to brood in a nest floating on the sea. The bird was said to have charmed the wind and waves so that the waters were especially calm at this time.

BEWARE THE POGONIP (DECEMBER): The word *pogonip* refers to frozen fog and was coined by Native Americans to describe the frozen fogs of fine ice needles that occur in the mountain valleys of the western United States and Canada. According to tradition, breathing the fog is injurious to the lungs. ∎

33 STELLAR
Moments in Time

BY BOB BERMAN

20 PHENOMENAL FIRSTS

1800: William Herschel discovers "invisible light" and calls it "calorific rays." Later, it's renamed "infrared" and found to be the Sun's biggest energy emission.

1801: Italian astronomer Giuseppe Piazzi finds a tiny "new planet" between Mars and Jupiter and names it Ceres. More are soon seen; Herschel suggests these be called "asteroids."

1838: Friedrich Bessel notices that Earth's orbit around the Sun causes stars to change position slightly. Using this "parallax" method, he finds the first true distance to a star.

1840: John Draper, professor of chemistry at N.Y.U., takes the first photograph of a full Moon.

1845: Irish astronomer William Parsons builds the world's largest telescope (its mirror is 72 inches in diameter). With it, he finds that some nebulae have a spiral structure. He has discovered galaxies.

1845: French physicists Léon Foucault and Louis Fizeau take the first photograph of the Sun.

1846: On September 23, the planet Neptune is discovered, in Aquarius—almost exactly where it had been predicted to be by French mathematician Urbain Le Verrier and, before him, hypothesized to be by English astronomer John Couch Adams.

1872: American astronomer Henry Draper takes the first photograph of a star (Vega) showing its spectrum, which reveals a star's hydrogen composition.

1916: German physicist Karl Schwarzschild uses Albert Einstein's general relativity theory from 1 year earlier to predict the possibility of black holes.

1920: Arthur Eddington explains that the Sun and stars shine because of nuclear fusion, in which elements release huge amounts of energy while transmuting into other elements. Until now, the Sun's continual 400 trillion trillion–watt brilliance had been a total mystery.

1929: Using the new, largest-ever telescope, with its 100-inch mirror, at Mount Wilson (Calif.), Edwin Hubble discovers that the universe is expanding and that galaxies farther away rush outward at faster speeds.

1930: Clyde Tombaugh announces discovery of the planet Pluto on March 13. In 2006, Pluto is reclassified as a "dwarf" planet, due to its tiny size and the presence of other similar-size bodies.

1930–32: Theorists calculate that very old stars can collapse to be as small as Earth (now called white dwarfs) or as little as 12 miles in diameter (now called neutron stars).

1933: Fritz Zwicky finds that all galaxies move strangely, revealing a strong, unseen gravity source. This mystery material is soon called "dark matter."

1948: The Palomar Mountain (Calif.) telescope is completed. Its 200-inch mirror reveals the Andromeda galaxy to be over 2 million light-years away.

1963: Mysterious radio sources found in 1960 are called "quasars" and identified as explosive galaxy cores, the most distant objects in the cosmos.

1965: Scientists Arno Penzias and Robert Wilson recognize that a weak radio signal coming from all parts of the sky must be remnant energy of the Big Bang from 13.8 billion years ago. This is the first evidence of the birth of the observable universe.

1967: British researcher Jocelyn Bell finds the first pulsar—a tiny neutron star, spinning hundreds of times per second, that is a remnant of a supernova explosion.

1995: The first extrasolar planet (one that orbits a star other than the Sun) is discovered: 51 Pegasi is 50 light-years away in Pegasus.

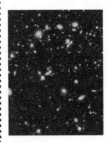

1998: Two independent teams find that the universe's expansion sped up about 5 billion years ago due to an enigmatic antigravity force, soon named "dark energy," that fills all of empty space.

10
SPECTACULAR SIGHTS

1833: Fifty meteors per second dazzle U.S. observers on November 13. Alas, this "meteor storm"—a rare flare-up of the annual Leonid meteor shower—is not repeated for more than a century.

1878: On July 29, millions in the U.S. view a total solar eclipse, during which Thomas Edison tries to measure the temperature of the Sun's corona—and fails.

1882: The Great Comet, perhaps the millennium's brightest at an estimated magnitude −15 to −20, can be seen in the blue sky of daytime.

1910: The Great January Comet appears and, being about five times brighter than Venus, is mistakenly thought by many to be Halley's Comet.

1925: On January 24, a solar eclipse over N.Y.C. is total north of 96th Street. A reporter coins the term "diamond ring" for its beautiful appearance just before totality.

1966: For over 2 hours, the Leonid meteor shower produces 60 "shooting stars" per second over the U.S. West.

1997: In March, Comet Hale-Bopp, the longest-lasting, at 18 months, and brightest comet, at magnitude −1, in at least 87 years, is easily seen over U.S. and Canadian locales.

2001: In the predawn hours of November 18, observers in the eastern half of the U.S. and Canada see five brilliant green meteors with glowing trains every minute, for hours. Such an extraordinary enhancement of the Leonid meteor shower is the finest display of our lifetimes and is not expected to repeat until 2099.

2004: Earth's nearest neighbor, Venus, partially covers the Sun in its first transit in 121 years.

2017: August 21 brings the first U.S. coast-to-coast solar eclipse totality since 1918.

3 WEIRD WONDERS

1965: On March 18, Russian cosmonaut Alexei Leonov becomes the first person to walk in space. When the vacuum expands his newly designed spacesuit far more than expected, Leonov can not fit through his spacecraft's hatch; he's trapped outside.

His spacewalk's scheduled length doubles before he finally manages

to release much of the suit's air, remain conscious, and squeeze through the opening. The onboard computer soon fails, and his craft lands 240 miles off course in a mountainous wilderness. It takes rescuers 2 days to find him.

1969: On July 20, astronaut Neil Armstrong

lands so gently on the Moon that the spacecraft's legs, designed to crush slightly, remain intact. As a result, he and Edwin "Buzz" Aldrin (whose mother's maiden name was Moon) must jump to the lunar surface from a much higher

distance than planned—a move that ruptures the urine bag in Aldrin's boot.

1992: On October 9, a brilliant meteor seen along the U.S. East Coast smashes through the trunk of a 1980 Chevy Malibu parked in Peekskill, N.Y. The 18-year-old owner, Michelle Knapp, is miserable, until a collector offers her $69,000 for the meteorite—and the car. ∎

Bob Berman, the *Old Farmer's Almanac* astronomy editor, is the director of Overlook Observatory in Woodstock and Storm King Observatory in Cornwall, both in New York.

The Shadowy Story of
Groundhogs

and the answer to "How much wood . . . ?"

BY KAREN L. KIRSCH

Groundhogs are North America's most widespread marmot.

What do groundhogs, wood-chucks, whistlepigs, grass-rats, landbeavers, rock-chucks and earthpigs have in common? They are all the same animal—members of the Sciuridae family of large ground squirrels. Their scientific name is *Marmota monax,* but we call them ground-hogs and they are North America's most widespread marmot. Groundhogs seem to be here, there, and everywhere.

It's believed that their populations are greater today than when the first Europeans arrived in North America. Forests cleared for farming created an ideal habitat for groundhogs, and they rapidly reproduced. Farmers soon be-gan a hunting tradition that continues today. Whatever you call them, they are here to stay—and this is not neces-sarily a bad thing, for they play some surprisingly beneficial roles.

Sources of their curious names are mostly regional, but some have indig-enous roots. "Woodchuck" is believed to be a distortion of *wuchak,* a Native American name for the animal, anoth-er of which is *monax,* meaning "the dig-ger." Dictionaries define "groundhog" as being the same as a "woodchuck." Presumably, "groundhog" refers to its voracious appetite and the fact that it spends time in the ground, but this may also have a culinary reference as its meat was sometimes a pork substitute.

(continued)

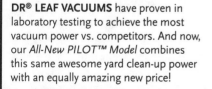

ANSWER: NONE

Contrary to the implication of the tongue twister "How much wood could a woodchuck chuck if a woodchuck could chuck wood?," the answer is none. "Woodchucks" neither chuck nor eat wood (except for a little bark) as beavers do, which leaves the origin of "landbeaver" a mystery. "Whistlepig" is a popular Appalachian moniker stemming from the animal's high-pitched sound of alarm or call to beckon its young.

The sturdy rodents weigh from 5 to 15 pounds, depending on the time of year. Being true hibernators, groundhogs are thin upon emerging from the den in early spring but quickly pile on the pounds to fatten up for the next winter's nap. Adult males are about 20 inches long, not including a bushy 4- to 7-inch tail. Females are slightly smaller. The pelt may vary from brownish gray to shades of cinnamon to blend into the landscape, but albinos and even some totally black groundhogs have been found.

Young pups are especially vulnerable to snakes, but around the end of August, they'll be independent.

generally solitary. Territories, however, may overlap. Communication is by visual acknowledgment, sound, scent marking, and a naso-oral "kiss."

Their burrows, usually located in open country and woodland edges, are masterful excavations with two to five entries and large underground chambers connected by tunnels that can be 5 feet deep and more than 40 feet long. Each chamber has a purpose: bedroom, nursery, "bathroom." A separately excavated hibernaculum (hibernation hole) is used each consecutive year.

CHUCKLING TIME

Males emerge from hibernation weeks before the females. They are thin, hungry, and eager to feast on spring vegetation and to mate. Once the females wake up, an enthusiastic courtship ensues. With his mission accomplished, each polygamous male moves on to visit other girls in the area. He may later return to check on his harems but spends most of the time eating and growing fat.

Meanwhile, the pregnant females take it easy to conserve energy during the monthlong gestation period, after which a litter of two to six pups, or chucklings, will demand attention. Young pups are especially vulnerable to snakes, but around the end of August, they'll be independent. Despite having a host of predators, man being the most prevalent, these enduring mammals can live 6 to 9 years in the wild, although 2 to 3 years is more likely.

Groundhogs have long been the subjects of songs, folklore, poetry, and

DIG THIS

The roly-poly omnivores are cute, but their form follows function: They are built for digging, with powerful front legs and long curved claws that act as little shovels. Their white incisors grow continuously. Ears and eyes near the top of the head allow them to remain inconspicuous in the burrow while scanning the landscape for food or predators. They can also climb trees and are excellent swimmers.

Some believe that groundhogs live in colonies like prairie dogs, but they are cookbooks. There's even a rock band called The Groundhogs, so why do so many regard them as pests? It's their diet and that darned digging.

The diurnal foragers feast for a couple of hours twice daily, with 20 percent of this time spent sitting up on back haunches checking for predators. Issuing a sharp whistle warns of danger. Their favorite foods include alfalfa, clover, dandelions, and many garden goodies, but they also snack on bark, leaves, bugs, and bird eggs. When not eating, they lounge in the sun or climb a tree and nap.

THE HOLE STORY

Farmers and equestrians loathe them because their holes pose a threat to live-stock. Gardeners resent sharing their produce with the freeloaders, and bird lovers go ballistic when eggs are on the menu. Once groundhogs discover an all-you-can-eat buffet, they are reluctant to leave; hence they become targets, especially for hunters—except in Wisconsin, where they've been protected from "sport hunting" since the mid–20th century. Kill for fun there, and get a fine.

Groundhogs do have some friends. Ecologists know that their excavations not only aerate the soil but also serve as dens for other wildlife. Because foxes and skunks eat mice and destructive field insects, by providing homes for these predators, groundhogs indirectly help the farmers who hate them. Groundhogs are also preyed upon

THE SHADOW KNOWS . . . OR DOES IT?

Each year on February 2, Pennsylvania's Punxsutawney Phil and Canada's Wiarton Willie (and a host of other groundhogs) predict spring's arrival. According to lore, if a groundhog sees his shadow when yanked from hibernation, 6 more weeks of winter will follow. Festivities here stem from Old World celebrations, which involved a hedgehog (or badger or bear or wolf, among other critters) in Europe but evolved to be a Pennsylvania groundhog in 1887. Such claims are without scientific basis, so don't put all your faith in the mammals.

Astronomically, the date marks the midpoint between the winter solstice and the spring equinox. In England, this was called Candlemas Day. Lighted candles honored the purification of the Virgin Mary, but traditional verse focused on the weather:

If Candlemas be fair and bright,
Come, winter, have another flight;
If Candlemas brings clouds and rain,
Go winter and come not again.

In Ireland and Scotland, February 2 was called Imbolc (im-MOLK, for lambs' milk), noting the start of lambing season; in Ireland, it was also Brigantia, named for the Celtic female deity of light and signaling longer days.

Groundhogs feast for a couple of hours twice daily.

by more tolerated creatures such as hawks and owls, but perhaps no one appreciates them more than the medical community.

In biomedical research, groundhogs are particularly beneficial in liver disease studies. Being susceptible to a virus similar to human hepatitis B, groundhogs have been valuable for research that has led to treatment discoveries for the human affliction. The groundhog virus is not transmittable to humans, and the Centers for Disease Control and Prevention also notes that it is extremely rare for groundhogs to carry rabies.

MOVING ACCOUNTS

Those unwilling to peacefully coexist with groundhogs might consider some nonlethal efforts to encourage their relocation. One possibility is baiting a live trap with their favorite foods and then taking the intruder on a road trip to a more remote location (check local laws first). But never do this while chuck-

lings are dependent upon the mom.

Fences are only marginally useful in discouraging groundhogs. Used cat litter spread around the burrows (never near plants intended for human consumption) is an effective deterrent, but little will keep a mother from her young. Epsom salts sprinkled on plants will also deter the snackers. So will ammonia-soaked rags in the garden, but both methods require post-rain refreshing. Motion-activated sprinklers, tin pie plates hanging on strings, pinwheels, and wind chimes will frighten groundhogs and condition them to avoid an area. Never use poisons. Groundhogs are shy, preferring to avoid humans, so perhaps the best deterrent is just going outside and doing something! ∎

Karen L. Kirsch lives in Louisville, Ohio, with three dogs, four cats, two donkeys, a flock of geriatric free-range chickens, and the occasional opossum. She writes about animal and environmental issues for numerous publications and in her blog, mysmallcountrylife.com.

THE
SECRETS
OF
SNAKE OIL

IT'S TIME TO SLITHER UP TO THE FACTS.

BY LISA HIX

THESE DAYS, "snake oil" is synonymous with quackery, the phoniest of phony medicines. A "snake oil salesman" promises you the world, takes your money, and is long gone by the time you realize that the product in your hands is completely worthless. But get this: At one time, snake oil was an effective and sought-after remedy.

In the 1860s, Chinese laborers immigrated to the United States to work on the Transcontinental Railroad. At night, they would rub their sore, tired muscles with ointment made from the Chinese water snake *(Enhydris chinensis).* They shared this ancient Chinese remedy with their grateful American coworkers.

Today, thanks in large part to California neurophysiology researcher Richard Kunin, we know that the "secret ingredient" in the oil was omega-3 acids. Kunin made the connection between Chinese water snake oil and omega-3 fatty acids in the 1980s. Knowing that cold-blooded animals produce more omega-3 fatty acids, that fatty acids are frequently found in fish, and that Chinese water snakes feed on fish, Kunin theorized that water snakes, being cold-blooded, might produce abundant omega-3 fatty acids.

To test his hunch,

Kunin purchased snake oil in San Francisco's Chinatown and had it analyzed, along with the subcutaneous fat of both a rattlesnake *(Crotalus viridis)* from southern California and a rattlesnake *(C. tigris)* from Arizona.

According to his report published in the *Western Journal of Medicine* in 1989, Chinese water

SNAKING AROUND

Snakes have been in medicine practically forever. The physician god of the ancient Sumerians had the body of a snake and the head of a man. The ancient Greeks' god of healing, Asklepios, was often depicted holding a staff with a snake coiled around it. Snakes were believed to be able to cure by touch. They were believed to represent the circle of life because they can shed their skin. The symbol in modern medicine of a snake wrapped around a staff descends from these traditions.

snake oil contains almost 20 percent eicosapentaenoic acid (EPA), one of several omega-3 fatty acids—triple the concentration found in the rattlesnakes. As a concentrated source of EPA, snake oil was deemed by Kunin to be a "credible anti-inflammatory agent . . . [and] since essential fatty acids are known to absorb transdermally, it is not far-fetched to think that inflamed skin and joints could benefit by the actual anti-inflammatory action of locally applied oil."

It wasn't until several years after Kunin's research that American scientists discovered that omega-3s are vital for human metabolism.

WHY THE BAD RAP?

So, why does snake oil have such a bad connotation?

Well, as the railroad advanced, hucksters who sold patent (or proprietary) medicine caught wind of the miraculous, muscle-soothing powers of snake oil. Naturally, they decided to sell their own versions—but Chinese

water snakes were hard to come by in the dry and dusty 19th-century Wild West. Undeterred, the charlatans quickly discovered that no one could tell the difference if they made products having no actual Chinese water snake connection whatsoever.

Already, to give their remedies credibility, these companies—in particular, the Kickapoo Indian Medicine

Company—had been claiming that their recipes came from Native American healers.

As it turns out, the Choctaws and other tribes did use rattlesnake grease to alleviate pain from rheumatoid arthritis. So, the hucksters claimed to be making their cure-all out of the most fearsome snake that most Americans ever encountered: the rattlesnake. What's more, the rattlesnake could be used to heighten the danger and excitement during their pitches.

STEP RIGHT UP!

To sell people on their products, these companies toured the West with elaborate, carnival-like "medicine shows," often featuring live music, puppetry, acrobatics, blackface performers, and sideshow acts. The medicine show always culminated with a dramatic demonstration of the remedy "healing" audience members, who usually were "shills" placed in the crowd by the company.

Rattlesnake wranglers became hugely popular gimmicks, as they would appear to slaughter a hisser in front of a crowd and then pretend to extract the oil from its body to make a liniment that could cure everything from measles to typhoid fever.

The most famous of these was a cowboy named Clark Stanley, also known as The Rattlesnake King, who said that he had gotten his Snake Oil Liniment formula from a Moki Pueblo

Snake oil is wonderful stuff!

tribesman. Wearing colorful western garb, he'd captivate crowds, such as one at the 1893 World's Columbian Exposition in Chicago, as he battled rattlers before their eyes.

Stanley's Snake Oil Liniment had many imitators, including Miller's Antiseptic Oil and Lincoln Oil. Eventually, people

became wary of these "snake oil salesmen," so the hustlers started putting their names and pictures on their bottle labels as a guarantee of their products.

THE END OF THE SHOW

Still, the tide was turning against patent medicine at the turn of the 20th century, as more and more American doctors began to subscribe to the Germ Theory of Disease posed by Robert Koch and Louis Pasteur. Then, in 1905, *Collier's* magazine published a scathing article indicting patent medicine pushers as fraudsters who often sold poisonous products. Public outrage led to

GENUINE SNAKE OIL

THANKS TO THE PEDDLERS

While we at this Almanac can not vouch for the efficacy of snake oil in any form or at any time in history, it and natural remedies have had a long association with this publication. John Pierce, former Almanac group publisher, once explained it this way: "In the early 19th century, before formal distribution channels came into being, copies of the Almanac were sold by itinerant peddlers, those salesmen with everything in their wagons that a farmer or pioneer might need—anything from pots and pans to potions and elixirs. Ever since then, the Almanac has been associated with snake oils, potions, and the like. They have come to be something that our readers expect to see in every issue."

the Pure Food and Drug Act of 1907.

In 1917, a shipment of Clark Stanley's Snake Oil Liniment was seized by the U.S. government and studied by scientists. Their research revealed that it contained mineral oil, red pepper (which warms the skin), traces of turpentine or camphor (for a medicinal smell), and just 1 percent of fatty oil, likely from cattle. But it contained not one ounce of snake oil—rattlesnake, water snake, or any other type.

It wasn't long before other "snake oils" started putting their true ingredients on the label. One of these was Old-Fashioned Snake Oil, produced by C. F. Sams of Durham, North Carolina. This contained mustard oil, pine oil, petroleum oil, paprika, camphor gum, and oil of wintergreen. Others, like Miller's, labeled their bottles with phrases like "known as snake oil" or "for years called snake oil but does not contain snake oil."

This period marked the beginning of the end for medicine-show hucksters. But was it the end for snake oil? Not entirely. True Chinese water snake oil has always been available in most urban Chinatowns. As the Chinese proverb goes, *All that is constant is change.* ■

–adapted, with permission, from Collectors Weekly, www.collectorsweekly.com

Lisa Hix, associate editor at collectorsweekly.com, explores how history informs who we are today. She has been widely published.

BORDER LINE

9 UNPARALLELED FACTS ABOUT THE **49TH**

The 49th parallel is a famous line separating much of Canada and the United States. As a border demarcation established in 1818, it designates who owns what territory—nationally speaking—from

BEHAVIOR

BY
SANDY NEWTON

ILLUSTRATIONS
BY TIM ROBINSON

PARALLEL AND THE CANADA–U.S. BORDER

Lake of the Woods in Ontario and Manitoba west to the Pacific. As the border along this parallel celebrates its 200th birthday, we offer some surprising facts about our distinctive dividing line.

THE "49TH PARALLEL" IS NOT EXACTLY AT 49° N LATITUDE . . .

1 A border on a line of latitude looks good on a map, gently following the curve of Earth. But when that imaginary line was transferred to the ground—in stages, by different teams of surveyors using imperfect 19th-century surveying equipment—it became crooked. In fact, the "line" of the 49th parallel zigzags from monument to monument (912 in all), now a bit to the north, now a bit to the south of 49° N, and sometimes missing the mark by as much as a few hundred feet.

(continued)

. . . BUT YOU CAN SEE IT FROM SPACE!

2 Examine a satellite image of North America: Zoom in on the 49th parallel, and *voilà*, you can actually see it! Or at least you can see a strip of seemingly barren ground where the border lies on land. Canada and the United States (through the International Boundary Commission, or IBC) work together to keep a 20-foot-wide "vista" cleared. The strip not only makes the border visible, but also makes it simpler to patrol and easier for authorities to spot anyone trying to cross illegally. And, yes, they are watching.

EX-TRA FACT
In border-speak, a bit of territory that is not attached by land to its own country is called an "exclave."

IT HAS A POWERFUL PRESENCE . . .

3 Our border could keep some people out even before the vista began to be maintained in 1908, when the IBC was formed, in part, to maintain it. A famous example of this occurred during the 1870s. Following years of strife capped by the Battle of the Little Bighorn, Chief Sitting Bull fled northward with many Sioux people, seeking safety or a place beyond which American soldiers refused to go. They found it in a 100-mile arid stretch of land between Montana and Saskatchewan. The place was at the 49th parallel, and it was the soldiers' recognition of international law that held them back from pursuing. Among the Sioux, this stretch of border was known as "the medicine line."

... PLUS A FEW ZIGS AND ZAGS ...

4 A string of treaties signed over several decades created the entire Canada–U.S. border that we know today. But applying words to land masses can be tricky, especially when a treaty specifies that "lines"—not terrestrial phenomena such as rivers or mountain ranges—will determine a border. Lines imagined in a faraway place can (and do) separate chunks of territory from the motherland when they are laid on the ground.

Take Point Roberts, Washington, and Minnesota's "The Angle," for example. Because the Convention of 1818 attached the border to the 49th parallel, both shoreline communities were cut off from the rest of the United States. Residents of these two American communities can reach the rest of their states directly by crossing a stretch of water, but the only way to get there overland is through Canada—and this requires a border crossing. Somewhat similarly, in the Bay of Fundy, Canadian Campobello Island has a single bridge to shore that delivers travelers to Lubec, Maine.

... AND HOUSES DIVIDED.

5 Words in treaties have also caused the border to run through towns and even right through buildings. One of the most celebrated examples of this is the Haskell Free Library and Opera House in both Derby Line, Vermont, and Stanstead, Quebec. Inside, the American library displays no books (they're on the Canadian side) and audiences sit in America to watch theater productions onstage in Canada. Border control has tightened in the 21st century and, lest anyone get any sneaky ideas, comings and goings are monitored—and some doors are now sealed to prevent untoward international travel.

Residences that straddle the border are known as "line houses." In northern New England, particularly, some line houses became locally (in)famous during the Prohibition years, when bootleggers and/or Americans longing for a drink could go in through the stateside door and then purchase liquor that had come in through the Canadian entrance. It wasn't long before this enterprising phenomenon spawned a law forbidding the construction of any more such border buildings. *(continued)*

THEN THERE'S THE GOLF SHOT THAT TAKES AN HOUR TO LAND . . .

6 A more sporting border situation exists in the twin towns of North Portal and Portal (Saskatchewan and North Dakota, respectively). There, the Gateway Cities Golf Course crosses the line, literally. The first eight holes of this semiprivate club are in Canada, but the final green and clubhouse are in the States. It's only a par 34, but the ninth hole makes it the only cross-border course in the country.

Curiously, when you play the last hole, your tee shot will seemingly fly for an hour. North Portal is not on Daylight Saving Time, so a ball driven at 4:00 P.M. lands shortly after 5:00 in the States.

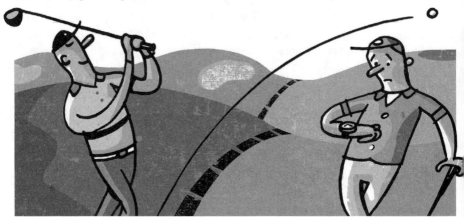

. . . AND THE ACCIDENTAL REFUGEES . . .

7 The Port Huron Float Down may take the cake for border line oddities. Staged off and on since the 1970s, this "group float" sees participants shove off from Lighthouse Beach in Port Huron, Michigan, on whatever inflatable device will take the weight of the crew on the third Sunday in August. Folks then drift 8 miles downstream on the St. Clair River to Chrysler Beach in Marysville, Michigan. That would be the same St. Clair River that forms the international border and contains the Great Lakes Waterway shipping lanes.

In 2016, about 2,500 people took part. Stormy weather blew about 1,500 floaters onto Canadian shores at Sarnia, causing some border consternation. Despite cries of alarm from some quarters, most participants seemed unruffled.

... AND THE INTERNATIONAL BRIDGE THAT ISN'T.

8 Despite what some Thousand Islands (NY/ON) tourism promoters will say, the 32-foot bridge between Zavikon and Little Zavikon islands is not the "world's shortest international bridge." The two islands are privately owned: one hosts a cottage in Canada; the other, its separate and reputedly American "backyard." And while there is a reference monument on Little Zavikon (to help pinpoint the border's location), the actual line is in the St. Lawrence River south of both islands.

MONUMENTAL OUTLIERS

Three border monuments near the Abbotsford, British Columbia, airport are the farthest north of 49° N (lying at 49°00'08.8"). The southernmost monument (#347) is located east of Coutts, Alberta, at 48°59'48" N.

FINALLY, SOME STRAIGHT TALK: IT'S LONG AND NOT WINDING.

9 Our total border length is not the longest on the planet; China's and Russia's are longer. And when it comes to "undefended," you'll find that "nonmilitarized" is the preferred term these days. Our border is the longest shared by just two countries. And the part aligned with the 49th parallel is the longest straight stretch of international border ... but by now you know that the record proclaimers define "straight" a little loosely. ■

Sandy Newton, a regular contributor to the Almanac, writes from the island of Newfoundland, which shares no border with the United States.

(continued from page 16)

Jamie Cruz
SPRINGDELL FARM
LITTLETON, MASSACHUSETTS

1. I always assumed that the farm would be here. But I saw myself doing something else. When I witnessed a potential threat to the farm's future, I decided that I should tend to it.

2. Juggling the retail, wholesale, and CSA worlds during the height of the season.

3. Picking kale!

4. "Staked and tied by the 4th of July."

5. Be optimistic! You can put your whole heart and soul into something—and in the blink of an eye, Mother Nature can knock it down.

6. Consumers need to remember that a human worked to produce their food.

Amanda Freund
FREUND'S FARM
EAST CANAAN, CONNECTICUT

1. My very persistent father frequently asked, "When are you coming back to take on this farm?" I guess you could say that persistence outweighs resistance!

2. Hearing misinformation spread about how food is produced.

3. Engaging with followers on social media, speaking at conferences, and hosting visitors.

4. Scouting our 200 acres of cornfields for cutworms and other pests in June, walking each field.

5. Build your network: Get to know other farmers, ag service providers, extension agents, government officials, and ag lenders.

6. Farming needs to adopt new technologies.

Aaron Golladay
STOKROSE FARMS
WARDEN, WASHINGTON

1. Love of the outdoors, T-shirts, and blue jeans.

2. Dealing with people.

3. Dealing with animals.

4. In the Midwest, the saying is "knee high by the 4th of July." Here we have a standard of "head high by the 4th of July."

5. Lose money the first year you farm. The lessons you learn make you successful for the rest of your career!

6. Farmers have to be optimists! No one else would work this hard for this many hours for a hope.

Linda Grinthal
SUNSET VISTA FARM
ANDOVER TOWNSHIP, NEW JERSEY

1. We wanted to raise children in the country. We saved enough money to buy 20 acres.

2. Dealing with weather and pests!

3. Conversations among family, friends, and volunteers in the fields.

4. Planting peas on St. Patrick's Day.

5. Plant lots of perennials! These crops come back, year after year.

6. More small local farms.

Giulia Iannitelli Grotenhuis
THE FARM IN HARMONY
HARMONY TOWNSHIP, NEW JERSEY

1. As first-generation Italian immigrants, my parents had a garden that was the envy of their neighbors and friends. Growing up, I did not know a time when food came from a restaurant, cans, or a box.

2. The unpredictability of it all.

3. We celebrate the rain and the growth spurt of our crop that follows (but so do the weeds!).

4. Fly-by-the-seat-of-the-pants gardening.

5. Be able to adapt and enjoy the ride.

6. Vertical farming.

Leslie Hamilton
TRIPLE H FARMS
GENESEO, NEW YORK

1. Growing up, I worked summers on the farm that my father and uncle run today.

2. Full-time dedication. We have a few head of beef cattle, and they always get out or need something during the most inopportune times.

3. Getting to work outdoors, alongside your family and animals, all while being your own boss.

4. Getting meals for each other during harvesttime.

5. Most farms need part-time or seasonal help.

6. Harnessing people's interest in where their food comes from.

Joël Hatch-Jensen
HATCH LIVESTOCK LLC
HUNTINGTON, UTAH

1. By marrying into the lifestyle.

2. The animals! I don't understand why they can't go through the open gate right in front of them, why the ewe doesn't like its babies, or why a calf is sick.

3. Seeing that the calves that were born are now ready to be shipped or that the alfalfa you planted and watered is now in a bale of hay in the stackyard.

4. Easter weekend means marking calves on the desert, the 4th of July means moving cows, and the "Fall Behind" time change means we are gathering cows off the mountain.

5. Be prepared to work harder than you have ever worked in your life— but also be prepared to receive great rewards. *(continued)*

6. Do more with less and for less—but do it, and keep doing it!

Mary Hull
HULL FOREST PRODUCTS INC.
POMFRET CENTER, CONNECTICUT

1. I was born into a family of tree farmers. My family still owns working forests that our ancestors were harvesting trees from in the 1700s.

2. Public scorn for timber harvesting; it can be disheartening.

3. Getting testimonials from our wide plank wood flooring.

4. I always plant corn when the oak leaves are as big as a squirrel's ear.

5. Study marketing and economics in addition to agriculture.

6. Helping farm and forestland owners to pass on their land, intact, to the next generation.

Dean Hutto
HUTTO BROTHERS PARTNERSHIP
HOLLY HILL, SOUTH CAROLINA

1. I came back to carry on the tradition after graduating from college.

2. Planning based on the weather. It always seems that when we start hoping for rain, it doesn't come, and vice versa.

3. Watching what you plant grow until harvest.

4. An old proverb is "Thunder in February means frost in April." If we get thunderstorms in February, we delay planting a few days.

5. Surround yourself with lots of people who know about as many different topics as possible!

6. The people who love this occupation need to stick together.

Julie Keene
FLINCHBAUGH'S ORCHARD & FARM MARKET
HELLAM, PENNSYLVANIA

1. It comes with ups and downs but always ends with fullness when you see your crop come to fruition. That crop might be peaches, soybeans, hogs—or a new generation of educated students after a farm tour.

2. Managing time.

3. Eating our harvest!

4. Nothing in particular.

5. Be open-minded to all avenues of agriculture.

6. Exciting!

Frank Kurylo
KIMBERTON CSA
PHOENIXVILLE, PENNSYLVANIA

1. After realizing that I could benefit the Earth better as a farmer than as a lawyer, I made farming my life. I wake up every morning with a giant smile.

2. Farming in a changing climate.

3. Knowing you're providing quality produce to many different families all living just as complex a life as you.

4. At the beginning of each growing season, we write on a sheet of paper what we wish to achieve. We ask the universe for these things, then burn the papers in a large bonfire, sending our words to the sky.

5. Work a farm first. Learn from others' mistakes.

6. Row cover for season extension and pest management.

Pam Lewison
ROBEL FARMS
MOSES LAKE, WASHINGTON

1. I was born into one of the original farm families to settle into the Columbia Basin of Washington State. I've pursued a life in agriculture because I love everything about it.

2. Establishing a connection with consumers who have lost touch with where their food truly comes from.

3. Seeing hard work come to fruition. You plant a seed in bare soil, water it, hope for warmth and sunshine, and, in a few short months, you've grown something edible.

4. We wait for water to start filling the East Low Canal alongside our farm. Watching that water start to roll by in spring is like hearing the starting gun at a track meet. It's a signal that it's time to start the sprint to harvest!

5. Be a positive voice for your profession.

6. Embrace technology, consumers, and any opportunity to be more efficiently productive.

Sarrah Lyons
MILL HILL FARMS
WILLIAMSBURG, PENNSYLVANIA

1. I was born into it, as part of the ninth generation to live and work on our dairy farm.

2. Things we can't control—like the weather!

3. Working with family and animals.

4. Taking a yearly family photo in front of the corn on July 4.

5. Be open to learning and change. Practices always evolve for the better!

6. We will need to rely on technology and ingenuity in order to feed the growing population of this world.

Kole Nielsen
K&R FARMS
WEST WEBER, UTAH

1. My grandfather was a dairy farmer. I developed a love for farming that I didn't know I had until he sold the cows while I was in high school. I have since started farming his land again so that I can raise my family around this wonderful lifestyle.

2. Having a full-time job on top of the farm!　　*(continued)*

3. Corn that is ready to harvest.

4. (No answer.)

5. Use the resources available—programs to help beginning farmers and agencies that can steer you in the right direction.

6. All farmers need to help fight for each other.

Kies Orr
FORT HILL FARMS
THOMPSON, CONNECTICUT

1. As a child, I loved being included in the day-to-day activities, such as milking and moving cows, feeding calves, and washing water tubs. My love for it grew only stronger.

2. Trying to keep all the cows calm and cool, and drinking plenty of water on 90-degree days.

3. Feeding calves. They melt my heart.

4. Plant any perennial ornamentals and trees and shrubs in April and May while there is "natural irrigation." Then do not water them so that their roots will "look" for water. Your plants will have deep roots, and you won't even have to water in a drought.

5. Don't let small problems waylay you!

6. Future generations need to start learning more about farming.

Rose Robson
ROBSON'S FARM
WRIGHTSTOWN, NEW JERSEY

1. I am an only child, and when my father passed away, something clicked.

I quit my corporate job and reopened the farm. I didn't want something so special to end with me.

2. No vacations.

3. I'm not sure there is just one. There are many joyful parts!

4. Planting pumpkins while everyone else is kicking off the start of summer. It speaks to the forward thinking of farming.

5. Work on an organic farm, a conventional farm, and a livestock farm. Understand and support your fellow farmers, no matter what!

6. Year-round production in areas where it has never been.

Tenisio Seanima
NATURE'S CANDY FARMS
ATLANTA, GEORGIA

1. Our property had not been farmed in several decades, but the older generation put the charge on the younger one to pick that back up. I always knew it was something that I would do.

2. Getting others to understand the true value of food and convincing people to pay the value it's worth.

3. Knowing that whatever happens, I can feed my family.

4. When you walk through a forest, you don't see any bare soil. I mulch the beds to mimic the forest floor.

5. Grow wherever you are. There's always a way.

6. People reaching out to neighbors and others in the community to increase their yield.

Raj Sinha
LIBERTY FARM
SANDYSTON, NEW JERSEY

1. I became a farmer for the challenge. I bought a historic circa 1790 farm desperately in need of restoration.

2. Government regulations, wildlife damage, and lack of time.

3. Watching families meet their local farmer, see how food grows, and learn about the value of good land stewardship.

4. We plant our garlic in early fall, just after the fall equinox, and harvest right after the summer solstice.

5. Do it! There is no greater reward than working your own land, being in charge of your destiny, and being rewarded with a bountiful harvest.

6. Agritourism.

Ken Suzuki
SUZUKI FARM
DELMAR, DELAWARE

1. When we moved here, we could not find the vegetables that we ate in

Japan. I started to grow them.

2. Farming is hard, hard work.

3. Bringing a healthy and bright life to our customers.

4. We do not use machinery. We do everything—seeding, planting, and harvesting—by hand.

5. Grow near your customers and sell straight to people.

6. Selling directly to customers.

Kevin Wilson
WILSON FARMS
SPRUCE PINE, NORTH CAROLINA

1. The "farming bug" bit me early in life. I have followed my dream of owning and operating my own farm.

2. Balancing professional life with farm life. There are many days at the office when I sit and daydream about being out on the farm.

3. Working on the farm! Knowing that I have been entrusted with a piece of God's creation makes me humble and appreciative.

4. We set tobacco on the new of the Moon. The plants live better and grow more aggressively.

5. Experiment. You may stumble upon the future of farming!

6. Efficiency. We must all learn how to produce more while using fewer resources and less labor. ■

LET'S HEAR

CHIF

FROM
RAGS

TO
REFINEMENT

TO
REFRESHMENT

by Martie Majoros

Who would guess that the word "chiffon" comes from the French *chiffe*, meaning "rag"? For some, "chiffon" conjures up images of diaphanous flowing fabric. Others may be reminded of a delicious light dessert. In either case, "chiffon" implies luxury. A derivative even conferred elegance on the lowliest ragpicker, aka a *chiffonnière*.

Once made only from the finest silk, chiffon became a status symbol, worn by society's wealthiest. Today, chiffon is made from silk, cotton, nylon, polyester, or rayon. The fabric's characteristic lightness is due to the way in which its threads are twisted: in two directions, to the right (S twist) or to the left (Z twist). The twists create a fine mesh, giving the fabric a sheer, slightly stretchy quality.

Chiffon is still associated with elegance and is often reserved for use in formal wear. Michelle Obama chose this luxurious fabric for her first inaugural gown. In 1909, Helen Taft also chose white silk chiffon for her inaugural gown.

IT FOR THE
FONS

Chiffon in Bloom

Among flowers, hibiscus is considered something of a show-off, flaunting colorful 4- to 5-inch petals. The cultivar Lavender Chiffon *(Hibiscus syriacus)* does not disappoint. In late summer, the deciduous shrub produces lavender blossoms on 8- to 9-foot branches. Hardy to Zone 5, it's a showy landscape plant, perfect for a border or privacy hedge.

The Blue Chiffon rose of Sharon *(Hibiscus syriacus)* is also a fast-growing deciduous shrub. It tops out at 8 to 10 feet tall and blooms from late spring through early fall, producing blue flowers with a burgundy center and blue inner petals, giving the 4- to 5-inch blooms a lacy appearance.

Lemon Chiffon water lily *(Nymphaea),* with its glossy green leaves and double lemon-yellow flowers, will add a touch of class to any pond or water garden.   *(continued)*

A Chorus of Chiffons

The Chiffons were one of the first all-girl singing groups that became popular in the 1960s. By '63, they had two hit songs, "One Fine Day" and "He's So Fine."

Chiffon Brownie is a pseudonym of Japanese rock/pop musician Shunsaku Okuda.

THE CHIFFOROBE

In the days before built-in closets, women stored scraps of fabric and needlework in a chest of drawers called a chiffonier. They used free-standing cupboards, or wardrobes, to hold clothes. In 1908, the Sears, Roebuck & Company catalog advertised a piece of furniture called a chifforobe, a single piece of furniture that was a combination of a chiffonier and a wardrobe: It contained a section to hang clothes and drawers to store smaller items.

CHIFFON FOOLERY

When whipped margarine was introduced in the 1950s and '60s, marketers at Anderson, Clayton, and Company (ACCO) emphasized its fluffiness by calling it "Chiffon." Although made with hydrogenated cottonseed oil, Chiffon was said to taste so much like butter that it would fool even Mother Nature. The slogan "It's not nice to fool Mother Nature" boosted sales and became part of American pop culture.

Pet Shiffons

Shiffon (pronounced shi-FON, like the fabric) dogs are a cross between the shih tzu and the Brussels griffon. They average about 16 pounds and 11 inches tall, making them a favorite for anyone living in an apartment or small house. Their smooth, silky coat may be black, tan, cream, or white. Shiffons have round faces, dark eyes, and a black snout. Their affectionate nature makes them an ideal family pet.

SENSATIONAL CHIFFON

Thank an insurance salesman and part-time caterer in Hollywood for creating the chiffon cake. In 1927, Harry Baker, in his quest for a light yet luscious cake, created a recipe that used oil instead of butter or margarine. He kept his recipe a secret until he sold it to General Mills in 1947. It was announced as the first new cake in 100 years and the "baking sensation of the century!" In the ensuing decade, hostesses who wanted to impress their dinner guests often served chiffon cake or pie for dessert. *(For recipes, see page 252.)*

Horrified Chiffon

In the 1986 film *Little Shop of Horrors,* Chiffon (right) is one of three female characters (Crystal and Ronette are the others) featured throughout the movie in nearly every song. Like a Greek chorus, they are aware of what is going on in the movie from beginning to end.

Chiffonade

Chiffonade refers to a method of chopping herbs such as basil into long, thin strips to use as garnish or in salads. To make a chiffonade, stack the leaves into a small pile, roll them tightly and then cut across the roll.

THE CHIFFON DIFFERENCE

Angel food, chiffon, and sponge cakes: What's the difference?

Angel food cake has no shortening, baking powder, or egg yolks and contains a high proportion of egg whites to flour. The whipped whites lend fluffiness, and the absence of egg yolks results in the cake's white appearance.

Sponge cake contains no leavening agent. It contains whole eggs; the yolks and whites are beaten separately for maximum lightness. Unlike angel food cake, sponge cake may contain a small amount of butter.

Chiffon cake contains vegetable oil; whole eggs, separated; and usually baking powder, unless the recipe also contains an acid, such as buttermilk. The whites are beaten to soft peaks before being folded into the batter. Chiffon cakes are moister than sponge or angel food cakes. ∎

AMUSEMENT

In Praise of Timeless Wisdom

Life holds more meaning when the past ties in to the present. When this happens, one gains assurance that the present will also tie in to the future.

–Robb Sagendorph (1900–70), 11th editor, *The Old Farmer's Almanac*

BY JACK SAVAGE

"Adjust your accounts; see that your expenditures do not exceed your incomes." Good advice, especially in our modern era of the seductive credit card offer. Yet such was the wisdom imparted in 1792 by founder Robert Bailey Thomas in his first edition of *The* [Old] *Farmer's Almanac.*

That Thomas saw the need for this advice tells us something else about his readers and others who were busy plowing up an arduous—and ideally virtuous—living in 18th-century New England: Failure to adjust one's accounts was not so uncommon.

Have we changed much in the intervening period? A random perusal of the past 225 Almanacs provides insights.

SEE ABOUT THE BEDBUGS

"Ladies, for mercy's sake, see about the bedbugs," Thomas implores in his "Farmer's Calendar" essay for July 1809. Centuries later, we may not find it appropriate to relegate this chore only to the ladies, but for mercy's sake, the bedbugs still need to be seen about.

"How is the barn and the woodhouse, and the door-yard, Mr. Snug?," asks the Almanac in 1812. "And the woodhouse filled with broken ploughs, dislocated wheelbarrows, hog's nests, and skunk skins? And your barn cramm'd with old barrels, sleighs, wheels, useless rakes, forks, gate posts, guide boards, and broken grindstones?"

Those of us with barns—or basements or attics—such as these more than two centuries later still need the Almanac's gentle prodding for a cleanup. (Note to self, courtesy of the 1946 edition: "What about those bookshelves? Don't tinker with the clocks.")

In service of its fundamental purpose, the Almanac marks the Sun's daily passage ("Hark to the music of the merry haymakers at the break of day!"), the Moon's phase, and the seasons' transition, and it augurs the weather accordingly.

208

Debate the accuracy of the forecasts as you please, but, as advised in 1840, "be prepared for all weathers." Be ready be it fair or foul, certainly, but be especially wary of the stroke that fells the oak, cautions the 1943 Almanac: "The nearest tall tree is not where you should go during a thunderstorm. It's better to get a little wet than end up a burned cookie."

Some might suggest that our 21st-century existence is more expansive and informed than that of an old-time rural New Englander. Could the 18th-century farmers who reached for the Almanac to guide planting by the phases of the Moon have imagined a man walking on it? Could 19th-century readers conceive of genetically modified seeds? Did early 20th-century patrons dream of weather satellites taking photos of hurricanes?

Likely not.

However, our predecessors would have known with precision every stone in the field that threatened the plough and every noxious weed that threatened the livestock. They understood intuitively where the streams flowed, where the hardwoods grew, and where the medicinal

"WHAT PLEASURE EXCEEDS THAT OF A FARMER?"

herbs might be found. They knew how to live in their time, something for which many of us today would be woefully unprepared. Well they knew, even before it appeared in a 1914 essay, that "there's a universe in a single ten-acre lot."

Surely, the passing of two-and-one-quarter centuries would have changed the Almanac's readers? After all, a New England farmer of the 1790s lived with remarkable uncertainty. There were no guarantees of a bountiful harvest or that the livestock would mature. Indeed, every day's survival demanded full attention; in 1808, "a little farm [would] furnish business enough for a considerable family."

But Almanac readers, changed? Likely not.

WHEN IT RAINS POTTAGE . . .

For all of our technological advances, accomplishments, and possessions, we are no more enlightened than our predecessors. We hold dear to the values inherent in what we think of as a simpler time. Today, as surely as in 1914: "The hours are now precious; [we must] husband them well." If you agree, pledge from now forward, at the most demanding times, to "keep your feet warm, your back straight, and your head cool"—an antidote for distress in 1800.

Be thankful, then, for the success

that you may attain and be aware that "the man who always keeps 2 weeks behind his work never makes a success in any business."

Know that good fortune has many forms: "Take an occasional ride with your family, thus making you all happier as well as healthier," "beware of too many pets," and, for heaven's sake, "when it rains pottage, hold out your dish."

AVOID VEXATION

Finally, consider Thomas's words in 1812: "Your corn may grow, your cattle may fatten, and your gardens be crowded with the exhuberance [sic] of the fields, but still you will be continually in a state of vexation unless you are out of debt."

Were Robert B. Thomas alive today, he would remind us to avoid vexation by turning off our modern gadgets for a moment, making sure that our expenditures do not exceed our incomes, and contemplating his words of 1809: "What pleasure exceeds that of the farmer? He picks his apples; he gathers his corn; he digs his potatoes, and dances around the cider mill with a delight that kings and emperors can not enjoy with all their pompous parade and tinsel splendor." ∎

Jack Savage lives on uneven floors in an old farmhouse in Middleton, New Hampshire, where he serves as town moderator.

How to Help Your Child Blossom

By Celeste Longacre

Focus
their energy.

ARIES

MARCH 21-APRIL 20
Aries children are inquisitive and energetic and love to start things. They will often bounce from one thing to the next as something new catches their eyes. Liking to be active, they sometimes have a problem sitting still. It's best for these children to have something to do before they head off to school. Walking a dog, playing with siblings, or shooting hoops outside could help to burn off some of their excessive energy. Sugary cereals and treats should be avoided.

Introduce
new ideas.

TAURUS

APRIL 21-MAY 20
Taurus children like things to stay the same, and they prefer to be comfortable. Watch them build a nest for themselves before they start their homework. Introduce new ideas slowly, one at a time. Visit an art museum this weekend and a science museum next. These children are not averse to doing new things but will appreciate your guidance. Make sure that they are not hungry or cold; they would not want to repeat activities associated with these conditions.

Reward
completed tasks.

GEMINI

MAY 21-JUNE 20
Gemini children like to laugh and roam; they bore easily. They notice every little thing and can easily become distracted when too much stimulus is available. Quiet, simple surroundings can help them to focus on the task at hand. Offering rewards such as a trip to the zoo or the movies for finishing projects can aid them in their studies. They love to socialize, but their social media time should be limited so that they will dedicate the proper time to their schoolwork.

Ever wonder why your child (grandchild, young neighbor, student, or other little one) behaves a certain way? Why he or she has a certain personality? Take a clue from the zodiac.

Involve
in family activities.

CANCER

JUNE 21-JULY 22

Cancer children love to be home with their families. They see Mom and Dad as true heroes and will want to be just like them. Setting a good example is important here. Showing children how to be involved in family routines and chores will help them to feel noticed and appreciated. Sensitive in the extreme, these young people respond much better to praise and encouragement than to criticism and correction. Expressing your love is especially valuable here.

Notice their
accomplishments.

LEO

JULY 23-AUGUST 22

Leo children love to be the center of attention, and their larger-than-life personalities fit the bill perfectly. They need pats on the back the way the rest of us need air to breathe, so it's wise to keep noticing their accomplishments. Praise given in bits and pieces on a daily basis will ensure that they keep trying to please you. These children tend to dream big, so make sure that you encourage them to reach for the stars.

Explore
the outdoors.

VIRGO

AUGUST 23- SEPTEMBER 22

Virgo children are detail-oriented and able to instantly spot the flaws. They abhor chaos and will want everything to stay in its place. Encouragement is very important here, as well as a soft, peaceful, individual resting place. Their scientific minds are restless for data, so bringing them out into nature—hiking, camping, swimming, or just walking around barefoot—can help to relax them. Discourage any judgment of others as it reflects their too high expectations of themselves.

Their creativity
needs an outlet.

LIBRA

SEPTEMBER 23-OCTOBER 22

Libra children need interaction with others and a truly clean habitat. Relationship is so important to them that—when alone—they relate to their surroundings. Regular play dates and an extensive array of friends keep these children happy. They also often have a strong sense of art and design, so be sure that their creativity has an outlet. Crayons, pipe cleaners, colored pencils, building blocks, or clay should be provided regularly.

Involve them
in outdoor activities.

SCORPIO

OCTOBER 23-NOVEMBER 22

Scorpio children are passionate and intense. They like to look deeply into things and can ferret out secrets better than most. These children are worldly and will want to succeed in life. Involving them in outdoor activities like hiking or biking or enrolling them in organized sports helps them to calm down and sleep at night. Bringing them to museums or the theater confirms their aspirations. Deep feelers, they forget nothing, so tread lightly here.

Be honest
with these little ones.

SAGITTARIUS

NOVEMBER 23-DECEMBER 21

Sagittarius children are restless and eager to move around. They love adventure and will pursue freedom with a passion. Encouraging them to be a bit more gentle with the truth (which they love) can help them to hang on to their friends. Getting them outside for a walk or run in the morning will benefit their study time. Be honest with these little ones; they can tell the difference.

Encourage
a sense of humor.

CAPRICORN

**DECEMBER 22-
JANUARY 19**

Capricorn children
know that society
has levels, and they
are determined not
to be stuck at the
bottom. Studious and
hardworking, they
pursue their futures
with patience and a
plan. Encouraging a
sense of humor will
help them to lighten
up and enjoy at least
a part of every day.
Gifts intended to
impart knowledge are
greatly appreciated
here. Teaching them
to play difficult
games like chess
complements their
intelligence.

Listen
to their reasoning.

AQUARIUS

**JANUARY 20-
FEBRUARY 19**

Aquarius children
are friendly and
future-oriented. They
often dance to the
beat of a different
drummer, so giving
them the freedom
to be themselves is
truly appreciated
here. Humanitarian
in the extreme, these
individuals take up
causes, so don't be
surprised. Listen
to their reasoning,
and you might learn
something. Be open
to new possibilities,
and you'll find some
unique answers here.

Give them
true alone time.

PISCES

**FEBRUARY 20-
MARCH 20**

Pisces children are
understanding and
compassionate. They
have the ability to
identify with anyone
and will do so time
after time. Making
sure that they get
some true alone time
will help them to
understand who they
are. Because they
are often musical or
artistic, encouraging
them to play an
instrument or tinker
with paints can be quite
successful. Taking
them out to lunch or a
play, one-on-one, helps
them to maintain their
uniqueness. ∎

Celeste Longacre is the author of *Visitor's Guide to Planet Earth: An Astrological Primer*
(Flaming Arrow, 1984) and *Celeste's Garden Delights* (Longacre, 2015).
She has been the Almanac's astrologer for 21 years.

BURPEE.

Since 1876

We are fiercely proud to offer the highest quality seeds, plants and supplies in the industry. We value quality above all else, and strive to bring breakthrough varieties to market year after year.

And yet, at the end of the day and at the heart of our success, is you, the Burpee gardener. For that, I'd like to say "Thank You."

Here's to another great season!

George

George Ball, CEO

HOW WE PREDICT THE WEATHER

We derive our weather forecasts from a secret formula that was devised by the founder of this Almanac, Robert B. Thomas, in 1792. Thomas believed that weather on Earth was influenced by sunspots, which are magnetic storms on the surface of the Sun.

Over the years, we have refined and enhanced this formula with state-of-the-art technology and modern scientific calculations. We employ three scientific disciplines to make our long-range predictions: solar science, the study of sunspots and other solar activity; climatology, the study of prevailing weather patterns; and meteorology, the study of the atmosphere. We predict weather trends and events by comparing solar patterns and historical weather conditions with current solar activity.

Our forecasts emphasize temperature and precipitation deviations from averages, or normals. These are based on 30-year statistical averages prepared by government meteorological agencies and updated every 10 years. The most-recent tabulations span the period 1981 through 2010.

The borders of the 16 weather regions of the contiguous states (page 219) are based primarily on climatology and the movement of weather systems. For example, while the average weather in Richmond, Virginia, and Boston, Massachusetts, is very different (although both are in Region 2), both areas tend to be affected by the same storms and high-pressure centers and have weather deviations from normal that are similar.

We believe that nothing in the universe happens haphazardly, that there is a cause-and-effect pattern to all phenomena. However, although neither we nor any other forecasters have as yet gained sufficient insight into the mysteries of the universe to predict the weather with total accuracy, our results are almost always very close to our traditional claim of 80%.

WEATHER

HOW ACCURATE WAS OUR FORECAST LAST WINTER?

Our overall accuracy rates in forecasting the direction of change from normal in the 2016–17 winter was 77.8% in temperature and 83.3% in precipitation. This 80.6% overall accuracy rate was slightly above our historical average rate of 80%.

After the historically warm 2015–16 winter, we gave ourselves an extra challenge, forecasting not only that "we expect temperatures in much of the nation to be . . . above normal," but also that temperatures would be "much colder than last winter." This forecast turned out to be correct in 72.2% of the regions, as most of the areas with exceptional warmth in 2015–16 cooled off some this past winter but did still remain above normal.

Our forecast for greater-than-normal snowfall in most of the Northeast and northern Atlantic Corridor was correct, while we were incorrect in forecasting above-normal snowfall in the Ohio Valley and northern Deep South. Our forecast for greater-than-normal snowfall was also correct in eastern and northern portions of the Upper Midwest but wrong in the southwest portion. While we were correct to forecast that some parts of the High Plains and Heartland would have above-normal snowfall and other portions would have below-normal snowfall, we were wrong in the precise locations of these departures. And while we were correct that most of the Pacific Northwest would have above-normal snowfall, the northern Intermountain region and the California mountains were snowier than forecast. Elsewhere across the nation, we were correct in our forecast for below-normal snowfall in those areas that normally receive snow.

The table below shows how the actual average temperature differed from our forecast for November through March for one city in each region. On average, the actual winter temperatures differed from our forecasts by 1.75 degrees.

REGION/ CITY	Nov.-Mar. Temp Variations From Normal (degrees) PREDICTED	ACTUAL	REGION/ CITY	Nov.-Mar. Temp Variations From Normal (degrees) PREDICTED	ACTUAL
1. Augusta, ME	–1.4	1.2	10. Kansas City, MO	1.3	4.7
2. Boston, MA	0.8	1.7	11. Oklahoma City, OK	2.8	3.8
3. Elmira, NY	0.2	3.6	12. Rapid City, SD	0.1	0.3
4. Raleigh, VA	1.6	3.3	13. Reno, NV	1.7	1.5
5. Miami, FL	2.4	2.8	14. Phoenix, AZ	0.9	2.4
6. Syracuse, NY	0.5	2.0	15. Eugene, OR	–0.2	–0.1
7. Charleston, WV	0.8	3.8	16. San Francisco, CA	–0.8	–1.3
8. Little Rock, AR	2.8	3.9	17. Juneau, AK	1.0	–1.0
9. Marquette, MI	–1.4	4.1	18. Honolulu, HI	–0.6	0.5

WEATHER REGIONS

Local 7-day weather forecasts for postal codes in the United States and Canada, as well as long-range weather predictions and weather history, are available at Almanac.com/Weather.

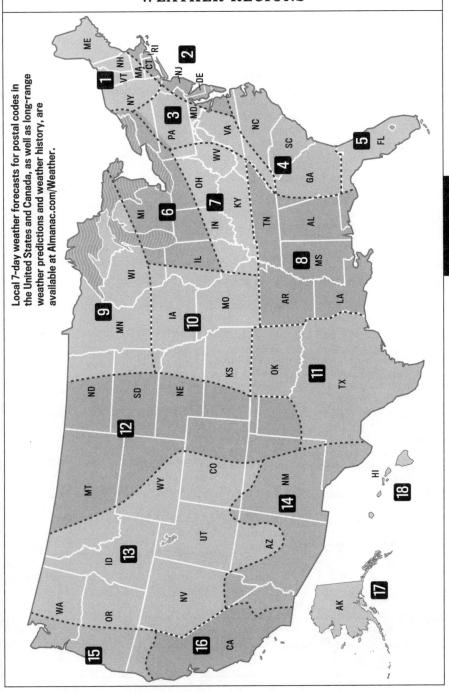

WEATHER

Illustrations of U.S. map and regional maps 1–16: Rob Schuster

NORTHEAST

SUMMARY: Winter will be milder than normal, on average, with above-normal precipitation and snowfall. The coldest periods will be in late December and early February. The snowiest periods will be in late November, early to mid-December, mid- to late January, and early to mid-February. **April** and **May** will be rainier than normal, with near-normal temperatures. **Summer** will be hotter and slightly drier than normal, with the hottest periods in early June, early and mid-July, and early August. **September** and **October** will be slightly cooler and drier than normal.

NOV. 2017: Temp. 35° (4° below avg.); precip. 5" (1.5" above avg.). 1–6 Rain, then flurries north, showers south. 7–11 Snow, then sunny, cold. 12–17 Rain and snow, then flurries, cold. 18–21 Rainy, mild. 22–26 Snowstorm, then flurries, cold. 27–30 Showers, mild.

DEC. 2017: Temp. 28° (avg.); precip. 4" (1" above avg.). 1–7 Snowy periods, cold. 8–11 Snowstorm, then sunny, cold. 12–15 Rain and snow showers. 16–18 Sunny, mild. 19–23 Snow showers, cold. 24–26 Showers, mild. 27–31 Snow, then sunny, frigid.

JAN. 2018: Temp. 27° (4° above avg.); precip. 3" (avg.). 1–6 Sunny, cold. 7–11 Flurries, then sunny, mild. 12–14 Rain to snow. 15–20 Showers, then sunny, mild. 21–25 Snowstorm, then sunny, cold. 26–31 Showers, then sunny, mild.

FEB. 2018: Temp. 22° (1° below avg.); precip. 2" (0.5" below avg.). 1–4 Snow, then sunny, cold. 5–12 Snowstorm, then sunny, cold. 13–17 Rain and snow showers, mild. 18–21 Sunny, cold. 22–28 Snow showers, then sunny, mild.

MAR. 2018: Temp. 39° (5° above avg.); precip. 4" (1" above avg.). 1–10 Rainy periods, mild. 11–17 Rain and snow, then sunny, cool. 18–24 Showers, then sunny, warm. 25–28 Rainy, mild. 29–31 Rain and wet snow, chilly.

APR. 2018: Temp. 47° (1° above avg.); precip. 3" (1" above avg. north, 1" below south). 1–2 Sunny, cool. 3–7 Rain and snow, then sunny, cool. 8–13 Sunny, warm. 14–19 Showers, cooler. 20–23 Rainy periods. 24–30 Showers, seasonable.

MAY 2018: Temp. 54° (1° below avg.); precip. 5.5" (2" above avg.). 1–5 Rainy periods. 6–10 Showers, cool. 11–15 Rainy, cool. 16–20 Sunny, nice. 21–31 T-storms, then sunny, warm.

JUNE 2018: Temp. 69° (4° above avg.); precip. 4.5" (1" above avg.). 1–5 Scattered t-storms, hot. 6–11 Sunny, cool. 12–20 Scattered t-storms, warm. 21–30 A few t-storms, warm.

JULY 2018: Temp. 71° (1° above avg.); precip. 3" (1" below avg.). 1–2 Sunny, hot. 3–10 Scattered t-storms, cool. 11–18 Sunny, warm. 19–27 A few t-storms, hot. 28–31 Showers.

AUG. 2018: Temp. 71° (5° above avg.); precip. 3" (1" below avg.). 1–2 Sunny, hot. 3–8 T-storms, then sunny, cool. 9–14 Scattered t-storms, warm. 15–19 Sunny, cool. 20–29 Isolated t-storms, hot. 30–31 Sunny, cool.

SEPT. 2018: Temp. 57° (2° below avg.); precip. 3.5" (0.5" below avg.). 1–6 Sunny, cool. 7–15 Showers, cool. 16–22 Sunny, turning warm. 23–28 A few showers, mild. 29–30 Sunny, cool.

OCT. 2018: Temp. 49° (1° above avg.); precip. 2.5" (1" below avg.). 1–6 Sunny, mild. 7–13 A few showers, cool. 14–20 Sunny, mild. 21–27 Showers, mild. 28–31 Flurries, cold.

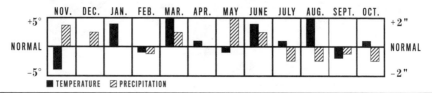

ATLANTIC CORRIDOR

SUMMARY: Winter temperatures will be above normal, on average, with the coldest periods in early to mid-December, late December, early January, and early February. Precipitation will be above normal, with below-normal snowfall. The snowiest periods will occur in late December and mid- to late January. **April** and **May** will be slightly rainier than normal, with near-normal temperatures. **Summer** will be hotter than normal, with the hottest periods in early June, early July, and early and mid- to late August. Rainfall will be below normal in the north and above in the south. **September** and **October** will be warmer and drier than normal.

WEATHER

NOV. 2017: Temp. 45° (2° below avg.); precip. 8.5" (5" above avg.). 1–3 Rainy, mild. 4–6 Sunny, cool. 7–11 Heavy rain, then sunny, cool. 12–18 Rain, then sunny, chilly. 19–24 Rainy periods, cool. 25–30 Rain and wet snow north; sunny, mild south.

DEC. 2017: Temp. 42° (1° above avg. north, 5° above south); precip. 4" (1" above avg.). 1–4 Rainy, mild. 5–11 Rain, then sunny, cold. 12–20 Rainy periods, mild. 21–23 Sunny, cold. 24–27 Rainy, mild. 28–31 Snow, then sunny, cold.

JAN. 2018: Temp. 38° (3° above avg.); precip. 4.5" (1" above avg.). 1–7 Sunny, cold. 8–21 Occasional rain, mild. 22–25 Rain to snow, then sunny, cold. 26–29 Heavy rain, then sunny, mild. 30–31 Rain and snow showers.

FEB. 2018: Temp. 33° (1° below avg.); precip. 1.5" (1.5" below avg.). 1–5 Sunny, cold. 6–9 Periods of rain and snow north, rain south. 10–13 Sunny; cold, then mild. 14–21 Rain and snow showers, turning cold. 22–28 Sunny, then rainy periods, mild.

MAR. 2018: Temp. 48° (4° above avg.); precip. 4.5" (0.5" above avg.). 1–10 A few showers, warm. 11–15 Rain and snow showers, cold. 16–18 Sunny, mild. 19–23 Showers, then sunny, cool. 24–31 Rainy periods, turning cool.

APR. 2018: Temp. 53° (1° above avg.); precip. 4" (0.5" above avg.). 1–7 Showers, then sunny, cool. 8–17 Scattered showers, turn-

ing warm. 18–20 Rainy, cool. 21–25 Showers, turning warm. 26–30 T-storms, then sunny, cool.

MAY 2018: Temp. 61° (1° below avg.); precip. 3" (avg.). 1–6 T-storms, then sunny, cool. 7–15 Rainy periods, cool. 16–21 Sunny north, rainy periods south; cool. 22–31 Scattered t-storms, warm.

JUNE 2018: Temp. 73° (2° above avg.); precip. 2.5" (1" below avg.). 1–5 Sunny, hot. 6–9 T-storms, then sunny, cool. 10–18 Scattered showers, cool. 19–28 A few t-storms, warm. 29–30 Sunny, hot.

JULY 2018: Temp. 76° (avg.); precip. 6" (1" above avg. north, 3" above south). 1–3 Sunny, hot. 4–7 T-storms, then sunny, cool. 8–12 T-storms, then sunny. 13–18 T-storms, then sunny, cool. 19–24 T-storms, then sunny, cool. 25–31 T-storms, then sunny, hot.

AUG. 2018: Temp. 77° (3° above avg.); precip. 3" (1" below avg.). 1–4 Sunny, hot. 5–15 A few t-storms, cool. 16–23 Sunny, turning hot. 24–31 Scattered t-storms, hot.

SEPT. 2018: Temp. 67.5° (0.5° above avg.); precip. 2.5" (1" below avg.). 1–5 T-storms, then sunny, cool. 6–15 Scattered t-storms, cool. 16–21 Sunny, warm. 22–30 Scattered t-storms, warm.

OCT. 2018: Temp. 57° (1° above avg.); precip. 3" (0.5" below avg.). 1–7 Sunny, warm. 8–15 Showers, then sunny, cool. 16–21 Sunny, warm. 22–26 Rainy, mild. 27–31 Sunny, chilly.

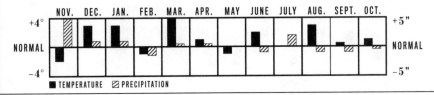

APPALACHIANS

Elmira
Scranton •
Harrisburg •
Frederick •
Roanoke •
Asheville

SUMMARY: Winter will be warmer than normal, with above-normal precipitation and below-normal snowfall. The coldest periods will be in late December, early and mid-January, and early and mid-February. The snowiest periods will be in mid- to late November, early and mid- to late January, and mid-March. **April** and **May** will be rainier and cooler than normal. **Summer** will be hotter and slightly rainier than normal, with the hottest periods in early June, early July, and late August. **September** and **October** will be warmer and slightly drier than normal.

NOV. 2017: Temp. 42.5° (4° below avg. north, 1° above south); precip. 6" (4" above avg. north, 1" above south). 1–7 Rain, some heavy. 8–11 Sunny, cold. 12–17 Rain, then flurries, cold. 18–22 Rain, then flurries. 23–26 Snow, then sunny, mild. 27–30 Rainy, mild.

DEC. 2017: Temp. 39° (3° above avg.); precip. 3" (avg.). 1–6 Rainy periods, mild. 7–11 Snow, then sunny, cold. 12–18 Rainy periods, mild. 19–22 Snow showers, cold. 23–25 Rainy, mild. 26–31 Snow, then sunny, cold.

JAN. 2018: Temp. 33° (3° above avg.); precip. 3" (avg.). 1–6 Snow, then sunny, cold. 7–11 Sunny, mild. 12–14 Rain, then sunny, cold. 15–21 Rainy periods, mild. 22–26 Snow, then sunny, cold. 27–31 Showers, mild.

FEB. 2018: Temp. 28° (2° below avg.); precip. 1.5" (1" below avg.). 1–6 Snow, then sunny, cold. 7–12 Snow, then sunny, cold. 13–20 Snow showers, cold. 21–28 Sunny, then rainy periods, mild.

MAR. 2018: Temp. 43° (3° above avg.); precip. 4" (1" above avg.). 1–9 Rainy periods, mild. 10–13 Rain to snow, then sunny, cold. 14–17 Rain to snow, then sunny, cold. 18–22 Rain, then sunny, cool. 23–31 Rainy periods, mild.

APR. 2018: Temp. 48° (2° below avg.); precip. 2.5" (avg.). 1–8 Rain, then sunny, cool. 9–17 Showers, warm. 18–21 Rainy, cool. 22–25 Sunny, turning warm. 26–30 Showers, then sunny, cool.

MAY 2018: Temp. 58° (2° below avg.); precip. 6" (2" above avg.). 1–7 Rain, then sunny, cool. 8–15 A few showers, cool. 16–21 Rainy periods, cool. 22–31 Scattered t-storms, turning warm.

JUNE 2018: Temp. 68° (1° above avg.); precip. 5" (1" above avg.). 1–4 Sunny, hot. 5–12 T-storms, then showers, cool. 13–19 Scattered t-storms, warm. 20–25 T-storms, then sunny, cool. 26–30 T-storms, warm.

JULY 2018: Temp. 72° (1° below avg.); precip. 4.5" (1" above avg.). 1–3 Sunny, hot. 4–6 T-storms, then sunny, cool. 7–12 T-storms, cool. 13–18 Sunny, cool. 19–27 Scattered t-storms, warm. 28–31 Sunny, warm.

AUG. 2018: Temp. 74° (3° above avg.); precip. 2" (1.5" below avg.). 1–9 Scattered t-storms, warm. 10–18 Sunny, cool. 19–31 Isolated t-storms, hot.

SEPT. 2018: Temp. 65° (1° above avg.); precip. 4" (0.5" above avg.). 1–6 Sunny north, t-storms south; cool. 7–10 T-storms, then sunny, cool. 11–22 A couple t-storms, turning warm. 23–25 Showers, cool. 26–30 T-storms, warm.

OCT. 2018: Temp. 54° (1° above avg.); precip. 1.5" (1.5" below avg.). 1–8 Sunny, warm. 9–16 Showers, then sunny, cool. 17–21 Sunny, warm. 22–25 Showers, cool. 26–28 Sunny, warm. 29–31 Rain to snow.

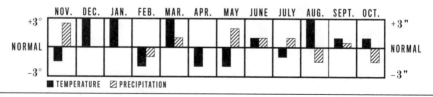

+3° .... +3"

NORMAL .... NORMAL

-3° .... -3"

NOV. DEC. JAN. FEB. MAR. APR. MAY JUNE JULY AUG. SEPT. OCT.

■ TEMPERATURE ▨ PRECIPITATION

WEATHER

SOUTHEAST

SUMMARY: Winter will be warmer and rainier than normal, with below-normal snowfall. The coldest periods will be in early January and early February. The best chances for snow will be in early January and early February. **April** and **May** will be drier than normal. Temperatures will be near normal in the south and below in the north. **Summer** will be slightly hotter than normal, on average, with above-normal rainfall. The hottest periods will be in early to mid-June, early August, and mid- to late August. Overall, **September** and **October** will be warmer and drier than normal. Watch for a tropical storm threat in early to mid-September.

NOV. 2017: Temp. 53° (2° below avg.); precip. 6" (3" above avg.). 1–5 Rain, then sunny, turning warm. 6–11 T-storms, then sunny, cold. 12–17 Showers, then sunny, cold. 18–24 Scattered showers, cool. 25–30 T-storms, turning warm.

DEC. 2017: Temp. 51° (4° above avg.); precip. 6.5" (3" above avg.). 1–3 Sunny, warm. 4–8 T-storms, mild. 9–12 Sunny, cold. 13–18 Rainy periods, mild. 19–22 Sunny, cool. 23–31 Rainy periods, mild.

JAN. 2018: Temp. 44° (1° above avg.); precip. 5.5" (1" above avg.). 1–7 Rain to snow, then sunny, cold. 8–11 Sunny, mild. 12–21 A few showers, mild. 22–24 Sunny, cold. 25–31 Heavy rain, then sunny, mild.

FEB. 2018: Temp. 44° (2° below avg.); precip. 4" (avg.). 1–6 Rain to snow, then sunny, very cold. 7–11 Rain, then sunny, very cold. 12–18 Sunny, cool. 19–22 Rain, then sunny, cool. 23–28 Rainy periods, mild.

MAR. 2018: Temp. 57° (2° above avg.); precip. 6.5" (2" above avg.). 1–4 Showers, mild. 5–8 Sunny, warm. 9–22 Showers, cool. 23–26 Rainy periods, mild. 27–31 Rainy, cool.

APR. 2018: Temp. 62° (1° below avg.); precip. 2" (1" below avg.). 1–9 Showers, then sunny, cool. 10–17 Scattered showers, warm. 18–23 T-storms, then sunny, cool. 24–30 A few showers, cool.

MAY 2018: Temp. 71° (1° below avg. north, 1° above south); precip. 2.5" (1" below avg.). 1–5 Scattered t-storms, warm. 6–9 Sunny, cool. 10–20 A few t-storms; cool north, turning warm south. 21–27 T-storms, then sunny, warm. 28–31 T-storms, warm.

JUNE 2018: Temp. 78.5° (0.5° above avg.); precip. 8.5" (4" above avg.). 1–5 Sunny, warm north; heavy t-storms south. 6–14 A few t-storms, hot. 15–21 T-storms, then sunny, cool. 22–30 A few t-storms, warm.

JULY 2018: Temp. 81.5° (0.5° below avg.); precip. 5.5" (1" above avg.). 1–11 A few t-storms; cool north, hot south. 12–14 Sunny, warm. 15–21 Scattered t-storms, warm. 22–31 A few t-storms; cool north, hot south.

AUG. 2018: Temp. 80.5° (0.5° above avg.); precip. 3" (2" below avg.). 1–3 Sunny, warm. 4–14 Scattered t-storms; hot, then cool. 15–23 Sunny inland, t-storms coast; turning hot. 24–31 Sunny inland, scattered t-storms coast; hot.

SEPT. 2018: Temp. 77° (3° above avg.); precip. 3.5" (1" below avg.). 1–6 Sunny, cool north; t-storms south. 7–9 Tropical storm threat. 10–16 T-storms, then sunny, warm. 17–21 Sunny north, t-storm south; hot. 22–30 T-storms, then sunny, warm.

OCT. 2018: Temp. 65° (1° above avg.); precip. 2" (2" below avg.). 1–9 T-storms, then sunny, warm. 10–15 Scattered t-storms, cool. 16–21 Sunny, warm. 22–24 Showers, cool. 25–28 Sunny, warm. 29–31 Rain, then cool.

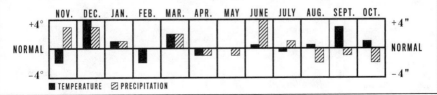

FLORIDA

SUMMARY: Winter will be milder than normal, with the coldest temperatures in early January, mid- to late January, and early February. Rainfall will be much above normal in the north and slightly above in the south. **April** and **May** will be a bit hotter and drier than normal. **Summer** will be slightly hotter than normal, with the hottest periods in early June, early July, and early to mid-August. Rainfall will be above normal, especially in the south. Overall, **September** and **October** will be warmer and rainier than normal. Watch for a tropical storm threat in mid-September.

NOV. 2017: Temp. 68° (1° below avg.); precip. 3.5" (1" above avg.). 1–5 Sunny, warm. 6–11 T-storms, then sunny, cool. 12–25 Scattered t-storms, cool. 26–30 Scattered t-storms, turning warm.

DEC. 2017: Temp. 67° (4° above avg.); precip. 1.5" (1" below avg.). 1–6 Sunny, warm. 7–11 T-storms, then sunny, cool. 12–16 Scattered t-storms, warm. 17–22 Sunny, cool. 23–31 Sunny, warm.

JAN. 2018: Temp. 60° (avg.); precip. 4.5" (2" above avg.). 1–5 T-storms, cool. 6–14 Sunny, turning warm. 15–21 Scattered showers, mild. 22–24 Sunny, chilly. 25–31 T-storms, then sunny, warm.

FEB. 2018: Temp. 60° (1° below avg.); precip. 2.5" (avg.). 1–6 T-storms, then sunny, cold. 7–8 Rainy, warm. 9–17 Sunny, chilly. 18–28 Showers, then sunny, warm.

MAR. 2018: Temp. 70° (3° above avg.); precip. 5" (5" above avg. north, 1" below south). 1–8 T-storms, then sunny, warm. 9–18 Scattered t-storms, cool. 19–31 Scattered t-storms north, sunny south; warm.

APR. 2018: Temp. 70° (1° below avg.); precip. 1" (1.5" below avg.). 1–6 Sunny, turning cool. 7–11 A few showers. 12–17 Sunny, warm. 18–30 T-storms, then sunny, cool.

MAY 2018: Temp. 79° (2° above avg.); precip. 5" (1" above avg.). 1–5 T-storms, then sunny, warm. 6–13 Showers, then sunny, cool. 14–25 A few t-storms, warm. 26–31 Sunny north, t-storms south; cool.

JUNE 2018: Temp. 83° (1° above avg.); precip. 7" (0.5" above avg.). 1–11 Several t-storms, hot. 12–19 A few t-storms, cool. 20–27 Sunny north, a few t-storms south; warm. 28–30 T-storms, warm.

JULY 2018: Temp. 83° (avg.); precip. 7.5" (1" above avg.). 1–13 Scattered t-storms; warm north and south, hot central. 14–19 Sunny north, a few t-storms central and south; warm. 20–31 Daily t-storms, seasonable.

AUG. 2018: Temp. 81.5° (0.5° below avg.); precip. 10" (1" below avg. north, 6" above south). 1–2 Sunny, cool north; heavy rain south. 3–9 A few t-storms, humid. 10–13 Sunny, hot north; t-storms, cool south. 14–16 T-storms, cool. 17–26 Daily t-storms, humid. 27–31 Sunny north, t-storms south; humid.

SEPT. 2018: Temp. 81° (1° above avg.); precip. 7.5" (2" above avg.). 1–9 Daily t-storms, humid. 10–14 Sunny, warm. 15–17 T-storms, warm. 18–20 Tropical storm threat. 21–24 Sunny, warm. 25–30 Scattered t-storms, warm.

OCT. 2018: Temp. 75° (avg.); precip. 3" (1" below avg.). 1–7 Scattered t-storms, warm. 8–13 Sunny, cool. 14–20 T-storms, then sunny, cool. 21–31 T-storms, then sunny, cool.

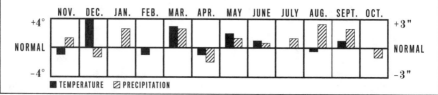

LOWER LAKES

SUMMARY: Winter will be warmer than normal, with slightly above-normal precipitation. The coldest periods will be in early to mid-December, early January, and mid-February. Snowfall will be above normal in Ohio and below normal elsewhere, with the snowiest periods in early to mid-December, late December, early January, and early February. **April** and **May** will be warmer and slightly drier than normal. **Summer** will be hotter and drier than normal. The hottest periods will be in early to mid- and late July and mid-August. **September** and **October** will be warmer than normal. Rainfall will be above normal in the west and below normal elsewhere.

WEATHER

NOV. 2017: Temp. 38° (3° below avg.); precip. 3.5" (1" above avg.). 1–6 Rainy periods, cool. 7–17 Rain to snow, then snow showers, cold. 18–24 Periods of rain and snow, chilly. 25–30 Lake snows, cold.

DEC. 2017: Temp. 33.5° (4° below avg. east, 1° below west); precip. 3" (avg.). 1–6 Rain and snow showers, mild east; snowy, cold west. 7–10 Lake snows, cold. 11–18 Rainy periods, mild. 19–22 Rain and snow showers. 23–25 Rainy, quite mild. 26–31 Rain to snow, then snow showers, cold.

JAN. 2018: Temp. 33° (6° above avg.); precip. 2" (0.5" below avg.). 1–5 Lake snows, cold. 6–11 Sunny, turning warm. 12–21 Rainy periods, mild. 22–24 Rain to snow. 25–31 Rainy periods, mild.

FEB. 2018: Temp. 27.5° (1° below avg. east, 2° above west); precip. 1.5" (0.5" below avg.). 1–6 Lake snows, cold. 7–11 Snow, then flurries, cold. 12–19 Rain and snow, then lake snows, cold. 20–23 Sunny, mild. 24–28 Showers, warm.

MAR. 2018: Temp. 44° (6° above avg.); precip. 4" (1" above avg.). 1–9 Rainy periods, warm. 10–15 Rain to snow, then flurries, cold. 16–22 Showers, mild. 23–27 Rainy periods, cooler. 28–31 Rain and snow showers, cool.

APR. 2018: Temp. 50° (2° above avg.); precip. 2.5" (1" below avg.). 1–7 Snow showers, then sunny, cool. 8–15 Rainy periods, warm. 16–19 Sunny, cool. 20–25 Rainy periods, turning warm. 26–30 Showers, cool.

MAY 2018: Temp. 57° (1° below avg.); precip. 4" (0.5" above avg.). 1–4 Showers, warm. 5–14 Rainy periods, cool. 15–23 Showers; warm east, cool west. 24–31 A few showers, turning warm.

JUNE 2018: Temp. 69° (3° above avg.); precip. 2.5" (1" below avg.). 1–4 Sunny, hot. 5–13 A few t-storms, warm. 14–21 Scattered t-storms; warm east, cool west. 22–25 Sunny, hot. 26–30 Scattered t-storms, warm.

JULY 2018: Temp. 71.5° (1° above avg.); precip. 4" (0.5" above avg.). 1–4 Sunny, cool. 5–7 T-storms, hot. 8–12 Sunny, warm. 13–25 A few t-storms, warm. 26–31 Sunny, turning hot.

AUG. 2018: Temp. 72° (3° above avg.); precip. 3" (1" below avg.). 1–4 T-storms, hot. 5–13 Scattered t-storms, warm. 14–17 Sunny east, showers west; cool. 18–27 Isolated t-storms, hot and humid. 28–31 T-storms, then sunny, cool.

SEPT. 2018: Temp. 63° (1° above avg.); precip. 4.5" (1" below avg. east, 1" above west). 1–6 Sunny, cool. 7–14 Scattered t-storms, cool. 15–22 Sunny east, showers west; warm. 23–30 Scattered t-storms, warm.

OCT. 2018: Temp. 54.5° (2.5° above avg.); precip. 2" (0.5" below avg.). 1–4 Sunny, warm. 5–10 T-storms, then sunny, cool. 11–19 Rain, then sunny, warm. 20–26 Rainy periods, mild. 27–31 Rain and snow showers, cold.

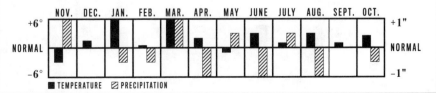

OHIO VALLEY

SUMMARY: Winter will be warmer than normal, with slightly above-normal precipitation and below-normal snowfall. The coldest periods will be in early to mid-December, late December, early January, and early and mid-February. The snowiest periods will be in mid-December, early February, and mid-March. **April** and **May** will be cooler and rainier than normal. **Summer** will be hotter and slightly rainier than normal, with the hottest periods in early July, early August, and mid- to late August. **September** and **October** will be rainier and warmer than normal.

NOV. 2017: Temp. 43° (3° below avg.); precip. 4" (0.5" above avg.). 1–7 Rainy periods, cool. 8–11 Flurries, cold. 12–17 Rain, then snow showers, cold. 18–24 Snowy periods, cold. 25–30 Rainy periods, mild.

DEC. 2017: Temp. 39.5° (4° above avg. east, 1° above west); precip. 4" (1" above avg.). 1–3 Rainy, mild. 4–7 Showers and flurries. 8–11 Snow showers, cold. 12–18 Rainy periods, mild. 19–22 Snow, then sunny, mild. 23–31 Showers, then flurries, cold.

JAN. 2018: Temp. 38° (5° above avg.); precip. 2" (1" below avg.). 1–6 Snow showers, very cold. 7–16 Showers, quite mild. 17–20 Snow showers, then rainy periods, mild. 21–24 Snow showers, cold. 25–31 Rainy periods, mild.

FEB. 2018: Temp. 34° (avg.); precip. 2" (1" below avg.). 1–6 Snow, then flurries, cold. 7–11 Rain to snow, then flurries, very cold. 12–18 Snow showers, cold. 19–23 Sunny, mild. 24–28 Rainy periods, quite mild.

MAR. 2018: Temp. 49° (4° above avg.); precip. 5" (1" above avg.). 1–4 Sunny, warm. 5–9 Rainy periods, warm. 10–16 Rain to snow, then flurries, cold. 17–25 A few showers, turning warm. 26–31 Rainy periods, cool.

APR. 2018: Temp. 54° (1° below avg.); precip. 4.5" (1" above avg.). 1–7 Rain and snow, then sunny, cool. 8–15 Rain, then sunny, warm. 16–22 Showers, turning cool. 23–25 Sunny, warm. 26–30 T-storms, then sunny, cool.

MAY 2018: Temp. 61° (2° below avg.); precip. 4" (0.5" above avg.). 1–4 Rainy periods, mild. 5–11 Showers, cool. 12–18 Rainy periods, cool. 19–22 Showers, warm. 23–31 Scattered t-storms; cool, then warm.

JUNE 2018: Temp. 75° (3° above avg.); precip. 4.5" (0.5" above avg.). 1–4 Sunny, hot. 5–8 T-storms, then sunny. 9–15 A few t-storms, warm. 16–23 Showers, then sunny, cool. 24–30 Scattered t-storms, warm.

JULY 2018: Temp. 75° (1° above avg. east, 1° below west); precip. 4.5" (0.5" above avg.). 1–2 Sunny, hot. 3–6 T-storms, then sunny, cool. 7–12 T-storms, then sunny, warm. 13–24 Scattered t-storms, warm. 25–31 Sunny, cool.

AUG. 2018: Temp. 76° (3° above avg.); precip. 3.5" (0.5" below avg.). 1–7 Scattered t-storms, hot. 8–14 A couple t-storms, cool. 15–27 Sunny, turning hot. 28–31 T-storms, then sunny, cool.

SEPT. 2018: Temp. 69° (2° above avg.); precip. 5" (2" above avg.). 1–13 A few showers, cool. 14–20 T-storms, then sunny, very warm. 21–30 Scattered t-storms, warm.

OCT. 2018: Temp. 58° (1° above avg.); precip. 3.5" (1" above avg.). 1–5 Sunny, warm. 6–12 Showers, then sunny, cool. 13–19 Sunny, warm. 20–26 Rainy periods, cool. 27–31 Showers and flurries, cold.

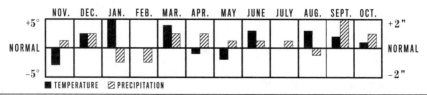

DEEP SOUTH

SUMMARY: Winter will be rainier and slightly cooler than normal, with near- or above-normal snowfall. The coldest periods will be in early to mid-December, early and mid-January, and early February, with snowfall most likely across the north in early to mid- and late December, early January, and early February. **April** and **May** will be cooler and rainier than normal. **Summer** will be hotter and rainier than normal, with the hottest periods in early and mid-July and mid-August. Watch for a tropical storm threat in late August. **September** and **October** will be warmer and rainier than normal. Expect a tropical storm threat in early September.

NOV. 2017: Temp. 52° (3° below avg.); precip. 4" (1" below avg.). 1–2 Sunny, cool. 3–6 Rainy, turning warm. 7–10 Sunny, cold. 11–23 Rainy periods, cool. 24–27 Sunny, mild. 28–30 Rainy, turning cold.

DEC. 2017: Temp. 49° (1° above avg.); precip. 8" (3" above avg.). 1–2 Rainy, mild. 3–8 Rain and snow, cool north; rainy, warm south. 9–11 Sunny, cold. 12–14 Rainy, mild. 15–21 Sunny, cool. 22–28 Rainy, mild. 29–31 Snow north, rain south.

JAN. 2018: Temp. 46° (1° above avg.); precip. 5" (1" above avg. north, 1" below south). 1–9 Rain and snow showers, then sunny, cold. 10–14 Rainy periods, warm. 15–18 Sunny, mild. 19–23 T-storms, then sunny, cold. 24–31 Rainy periods, mild.

FEB. 2018: Temp. 46° (1° below avg.); precip. 5" (avg.). 1–5 Rain to snow, then sunny, cold. 6–15 Rain, then sunny, cool. 16–21 Sunny, seasonable. 22–28 Rainy periods, mild.

MAR. 2018: Temp. 57° (1° above avg.); precip. 8" (2" above avg.). 1–9 Scattered t-storms, warm. 10–12 Sunny, cool. 13–16 T-storms, then sunny, cool. 17–31 Scattered t-storms; warm, then cool.

APR. 2018: Temp. 62° (1° below avg.); precip. 7.5" (3" above avg.). 1–7 Rain, then sunny, cool. 8–18 Rainy periods, warm. 19–23 Sunny, cool. 24–28 T-storms, then sunny, cool. 29–30 T-storms.

MAY 2018: Temp. 70° (1° below avg.); precip. 5" (avg.). 1–8 T-storms, then sunny, cool. 9–12 Scattered t-storms, cool. 13–20 Scattered t-storms, cool. 21–24 Sunny, cool. 25–31 A few t-storms, warm.

JUNE 2018: Temp. 79° (1° above avg.); precip. 6" (1" above avg.). 1–3 Sunny, warm. 4–12 A few t-storms, warm. 13–17 Sunny, cool. 18–30 Scattered t-storms, warm.

JULY 2018: Temp. 81° (1° below avg. north, 1° above south); precip. 5.5" (1" above avg.). 1–3 T-storms, hot. 4–6 Sunny, cool. 7–17 Scattered t-storms, turning hot. 18–22 T-storms, then sunny, cool. 23–31 T-storms, then sunny, cool.

AUG. 2018: Temp. 81° (2° above avg. north, avg. south); precip. 5.5" (1" above avg.). 1–9 Scattered t-storms, warm. 10–18 Sunny, warm. 19–28 Scattered t-storms, hot. 29–31 Tropical storm threat.

SEPT. 2018: Temp. 80° (4° above avg.); precip. 3.5" (1" below avg.). 1–4 T-storms, hot. 5–7 Tropical storm threat. 8–14 Sunny, cool. 15–30 Isolated t-storms, warm.

OCT. 2018: Temp. 68° (3° above avg.); precip. 6" (3" above avg.). 1–5 Sunny north, t-storms south; warm. 6–10 T-storms, then sunny, cool. 11–19 Sunny, warm. 20–24 Rainy, cool. 25–27 Sunny, warm. 28–31 T-storms, then sunny, cool.

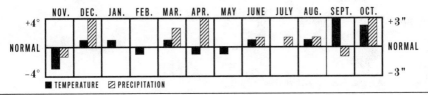

UPPER MIDWEST

SUMMARY: Winter will be warmer than normal, with the coldest periods in late November, early and late December, early January, and early February. Precipitation and snowfall will be below normal, with the snowiest periods in mid- to late December and early to mid-February. **April** and **May** will be cooler than normal, with near-normal precipitation. **Summer** will be hotter than normal, with near-normal precipitation. The hottest periods will be in late June, late July, and early to mid-August. **September** and **October** will be warmer and slightly drier than normal.

NOV. 2017: Temp. 25° (4° below avg.); precip. 1" (1" below avg.). 1–4 Sprinkles, mild. 5–10 Snow showers, cold. 11–20 Snow showers, cold east; showers, mild west. 21–30 Snow showers, very cold.

DEC. 2017: Temp. 13° (3° below avg.); precip. 1.5" (0.5" above avg.). 1–10 Snow showers, very cold. 11–21 Flurries, mild. 22–31 Snowstorm, then flurries, very cold.

JAN. 2018: Temp. 21° (8° above avg.); precip. 0.5" (0.5" below avg.). 1–4 Sunny, cold. 5–11 Sunny, quite mild. 12–18 Snow showers, mild. 19–26 Snow showers; cold, then mild. 27–31 Sunny, mild.

FEB. 2018: Temp. 16° (4° above avg.); precip. 1" (avg.). 1–5 Sunny; cold, then mild. 6–10 Snow, then flurries, cold. 11–17 Flurries; cold east, mild west. 18–25 Flurries, mild. 26–28 Showers, mild.

MAR. 2018: Temp. 35° (7° above avg.); precip. 2" (0.5" above avg.). 1–8 Rainy periods, mild. 9–14 Sunny; cool, then mild. 15–24 Showers, then sunny, mild. 25–31 Rain and snow, then showers, cool.

APR. 2018: Temp. 41° (1° below avg.); precip. 3" (1" above avg.). 1–8 Snow showers, cold. 9–14 Rainy periods, warm. 15–21 Sunny, cool. 22–26 Rain and snow showers, cool. 27–30 Showers, cool.

MAY 2018: Temp. 54° (1° below avg.); precip. 2" (1" below avg.). 1–10 Rain, then sunny, cool. 11–19 Showers, mild. 20–23 Sunny, cool. 24–31 A few t-storms, warm.

JUNE 2018: Temp. 64° (1° above avg.); precip. 3" (1" below avg.). 1–8 Scattered t-storms, warm. 9–18 A few t-storms, cool. 19–23 T-storms, then sunny, cool. 24–30 T-storms, then sunny, hot.

JULY 2018: Temp. 67° (1° below avg.); precip. 3.5" (avg.). 1–8 Isolated t-storms, cool. 9–17 A few t-storms; warm, then cool. 18–22 Showers, warm. 23–26 Rainy periods, cool. 27–31 Sunny, turning hot.

AUG. 2018: Temp. 70° (4° above avg.); precip. 4.5" (1" above avg.). 1–3 Showers, cool. 4–13 Isolated t-storms, turning hot. 14–18 A few t-storms, cool. 19–22 Sunny, hot. 23–31 T-storms, then sunny, cool.

SEPT. 2018: Temp. 57° (1° below avg.); precip. 3" (avg.). 1–5 Sunny, cool. 6–13 A few showers, chilly. 14–20 Rainy, mild. 21–26 Sunny, warm. 27–30 Showers, cool.

OCT. 2018: Temp. 50° (3° above avg.); precip. 2" (0.5" below avg.). 1–4 Rainy, warm. 5–11 Showers, then sunny, cool. 12–18 Sunny, warm. 19–25 Showers, turning cool. 26–31 Snow showers, cold.

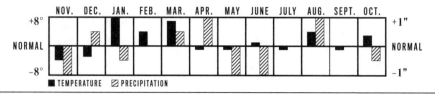

SUMMARY: Winter will be milder than normal, with above-normal precipitation and snowfall. The coldest periods will be from late November into early December, from late December into early January, and in early February. The snowiest periods will be in mid-November, early to mid- and late December, and early February. **April** and **May** will be cooler and rainier than normal. **Summer** will be hotter than normal, with slightly below normal rainfall. The hottest periods will be in early and late June, early and late July, and mid-August. **September** and **October** will be warmer and rainier than normal.

NOV. 2017: Temp. 38° (5° below avg.); precip. 2" (0.5" below avg.). 1–5 Rainy periods, cool. 6–8 Snowstorm north, showers south. 9–15 Sunny, cold north; snowstorm, then flurries south. 16–25 Rain and snow showers, then sunny, turning mild. 26–30 Snow showers, frigid.

DEC. 2017: Temp. 29° (3° below avg.); precip. 2" (0.5" above avg.). 1–3 Snow showers, frigid. 4–10 Heavy snow, then flurries, bitter cold. 11–19 Flurries north, a couple showers south; mild. 20–23 Rainy, mild. 24–26 Sunny. 27–31 Rain to snow, then sunny, cold.

JAN. 2018: Temp. 34° (5° above avg.); precip. 2" (1" above avg.). 1–5 Flurries, frigid. 6–12 Sunny, mild. 13–19 Rain, then sunny, mild. 20–22 Snow showers, cold. 23–31 Rain, then sunny, mild.

FEB. 2018: Temp. 32° (1° above avg.); precip. 1.5" (avg.). 1–4 Snow, then sunny, cold. 5–11 Rain and snow, then flurries, cold. 12–20 Sunny, turning mild. 21–28 Rainy periods, mild.

MAR. 2018: Temp. 47° (3° above avg.); precip. 3.5" (1" above avg.). 1–7 Rainy periods, warm. 8–11 Sunny, cool. 12–24 Rainy periods, turning warm. 25–31 Showers, cool.

APR. 2018: Temp. 53° (1° below avg.); precip. 5.5" (2" above avg.). 1–6 Rain to snow, then sunny, cool. 7–15 Rainy, turning mild. 16–21 Sunny north, rainy periods south;

turning cool. 22–27 Rain, then sunny, cool. 28–30 Rainy.

MAY 2018: Temp. 63° (1° below avg.); precip. 4.5" (avg.). 1–13 Rain, then sunny, cool. 14–19 Showers, cool. 20–24 T-storms, then sunny, warm. 25–31 T-storms, then sunny, warm.

JUNE 2018: Temp. 73° (1° above avg.); precip. 5.5" (1" above avg.). 1–4 Sunny, hot. 5–10 Scattered t-storms, warm. 11–21 A couple t-storms, cool. 22–30 T-storms, then sunny, hot.

JULY 2018: Temp. 76° (1° below avg.); precip. 3.5" (0.5" below avg.). 1–6 T-storms, then sunny, hot. 7–10 T-storms, then sunny, cool. 11–22 A few t-storms, cool. 23–27 Sunny, cool. 28–31 T-storms, hot.

AUG. 2018: Temp. 77.5° (4° above avg. north, 1° above south); precip. 2.5" (1" below avg.). 1–9 Showers; warm, then cool. 10–13 Sunny, hot. 14–17 T-storms. 18–23 Sunny, hot. 24–31 Scattered t-storms, turning cool.

SEPT. 2018: Temp. 68° (1° above avg.); precip. 4.5" (1" above avg.). 1–7 T-storms, then sunny, cool. 8–13 T-storms, then sunny, cool. 14–26 Scattered t-storms, warm. 27–30 Sunny, warm.

OCT. 2018: Temp. 58° (2° above avg.); precip. 3" (avg.). 1–2 Sunny, warm. 3–13 Rain, then sunny, mild. 14–18 Sunny, warm. 19–27 Rainy periods, cool. 28–31 Sunny, cold.

WEATHER

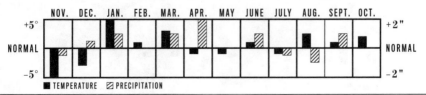

TEXAS–OKLAHOMA

Oklahoma City
Dallas
San Antonio
Houston

SUMMARY: Winter will be colder than normal, with above-normal precipitation. The coldest periods will be from late November into early December, from late December into early January, and in early February. Snowfall will be near to above normal, with the snowiest periods in late December and early to mid-February. **April** and **May** will be cooler and rainier than normal. **Summer** will be cooler and rainier than normal, with the hottest periods in mid-July and mid-August. Expect a hurricane threat in late August. **September** and **October** will be warmer and rainier than normal. Watch for a tropical storm threat in early September.

WEATHER

NOV. 2017: Temp. 53° (4° below avg.); precip. 3" (avg.). 1–2 Sunny, warm. 3–18 Rainy periods, cool. 19–26 Sunny; cool, then warm. 27–30 Rain, then misty, cold.

DEC. 2017: Temp. 51° (2° below avg.); precip. 3" (0.5" above avg.). 1–9 Flurries north, showers south; cold. 10–18 Rain, then sunny, mild. 19–24 Showers, mild. 25–27 Rainy, cool. 28–31 Snow north, rain south; cold.

JAN. 2018: Temp. 49° (1° below avg.); precip. 3" (1" above avg.). 1–4 Snow showers north, rain south; cold. 5–10 Sunny, turning warm. 11–16 Rainy, mild. 17–24 Showers, cool. 25–29 Sunny, mild. 30–31 Rainy.

FEB. 2018: Temp. 48° (2° below avg.); precip. 2" (1" below avg. north, 1" above south). 1–8 Sunny, cold. 9–15 Periods of rain and snow north, rain south; cool. 16–21 Sunny, cool. 22–28 Rainy periods, turning warm.

MAR. 2018: Temp. 60° (1° above avg.); precip. 3.5" (2" above avg. north, avg. south). 1–8 Showers, warm. 9–14 Sunny, cool. 15–18 Heavy rain north, sunny south; cool. 19–26 Showers, warm. 27–31 Sunny, cool.

APR. 2018: Temp. 65° (1° below avg.); precip. 5" (2" above avg.). 1–5 Rain, then sunny, cool. 6–12 Rainy, mild. 13–17 T-storms north, sunny south; warm. 18–22 Sunny, cool. 23–30 Scattered t-storms; warm, then cool.

MAY 2018: Temp. 73° (avg.); precip. 6" (1" above avg.). 1–3 Sunny, warm. 4–10 T-storms, then sunny, cool. 11–14 Sunny, warm. 15–20 A few t-storms, cool north; sunny, warm south. 21–24 Sunny. 25–31 T-storms, then sunny, cool.

JUNE 2018: Temp. 78° (1° below avg.); precip. 6" (avg. north, 4" above south). 1–3 Sunny, warm. 4–11 Scattered t-storms, warm. 12–20 Sunny north, t-storms south; cool. 21–30 Scattered t-storms, warm.

JULY 2018: Temp. 80° (1° below avg.); precip. 4" (1" above avg.). 1–8 Scattered t-storms north, sunny south; warm. 9–12 Sunny, warm. 13–16 T-storms north, sunny south; warm. 17–26 Scattered t-storms, warm. 27–31 Sunny, cool.

AUG. 2018: Temp. 80° (1° below avg.); precip. 3.5" (1" above avg.). 1–11 Scattered t-storms, warm. 12–18 Sunny; hot north, warm south. 19–27 Isolated t-storms, warm. 28–31 Hurricane threat.

SEPT. 2018: Temp. 76.5° (1° below avg. north, 2° above south); precip. 4.5" (1" above avg.). 1–3 Sunny, warm. 4–6 Tropical storm threat. 7–15 Sunny; cool, then warm. 16–20 T-storms, warm. 21–25 Sunny, warm. 26–30 Showers, warm.

OCT. 2018: Temp. 68.5° (1.5° above avg.); precip. 5" (1" above avg.). 1–3 Sunny, warm. 4–8 Heavy rain. 9–18 Sunny; warm. 19–25 Scattered t-storms, mild. 26–31 Sunny, cold north; t-storms, warm south.

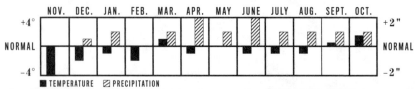

NOV. DEC. JAN. FEB. MAR. APR. MAY JUNE JULY AUG. SEPT. OCT.

+4° / NORMAL / −4°

+2" / NORMAL / −2"

■ TEMPERATURE ▨ PRECIPITATION

HIGH PLAINS

SUMMARY: Winter will be warmer than normal, with slightly above-normal precipitation. The coldest periods will be from late November into early December and from late December into early January. Snowfall will be below normal in the north and above in the south, with the snowiest periods in mid- and late November, mid- to late December, and early to mid-March. **April** and **May** will be cooler than normal, with precipitation a bit above normal. **Summer** will be a bit hotter than normal, with slightly below normal rainfall. The hottest periods will be in early and mid- to late July and mid-August. **September** and **October** will be cooler than normal, with slightly above normal rainfall.

Bismarck
Billings
Rapid City
Cheyenne
Denver
Amarillo

WEATHER

NOV. 2017: Temp. 31° (5° below avg.); precip. 1.5" (0.5" above avg.). 1–3 Showers, mild. 4–11 Snow showers, cold. 12–19 Sunny, mild north; snow showers, cold south. 20–23 Snow, then sunny, turning mild. 24–30 Snowy periods, turning bitterly cold.

DEC. 2017: Temp. 28° (3° below avg.); precip. 0.5" (avg.). 1–9 Snow showers, frigid. 10–15 Sunny, mild. 16–21 Snow showers, mild. 22–26 Snowy periods, mild. 27–31 Snow showers, frigid.

JAN. 2018: Temp. 36° (8° above avg.); precip. 0.5" (avg.). 1–3 Snow showers, frigid. 4–11 Sunny, turning warm. 12–18 Snow showers, then sunny, mild. 19–21 Snowy, cold. 22–28 Sunny, mild. 29–31 Snow showers, cold.

FEB. 2018: Temp. 32° (4° above avg.); precip. 0.3" (0.2" below avg.). 1–4 Sunny, turning mild. 5–9 Snow showers, cold. 10–15 Flurries, mild. 16–22 Sunny, mild. 23–28 Snow showers, mild.

MAR. 2018: Temp. 41° (2° above avg.); precip. 1.5" (0.5" above avg.). 1–5 Showers, mild. 6–10 Rain to snow, then sunny, mild. 11–19 Rain and snow showers, mild. 20–28 Sunny north, periods of rain and snow south; cool. 29–31 Snow showers, cold.

APR. 2018: Temp. 46° (2° above avg.); precip. 3" (1" above avg.). 1–5 Snow, then sunny, turning mild. 6–11 Showers, cool. 12–14 Snow north, showers south. 15–22 Rainy periods,

cool. 23–30 Snow, then showers, cool.

MAY 2018: Temp. 57° (1° below avg.); precip. 2" (0.5" below avg.). 1–5 Sunny, cool. 6–13 Showers, then sunny, warm. 14–27 A few showers, cool. 28–31 Sunny, warm.

JUNE 2018: Temp. 68° (1° above avg.); precip. 1.5" (1" below avg.). 1–4 Sunny, warm. 5–13 Scattered showers, cool. 14–22 Sunny, warm. 23–30 Showers, then sunny, warm.

JULY 2018: Temp. 70° (2° below avg.); precip. 1.5" (0.5" below avg.) 1–3 Sunny, hot. 4–11 Scattered showers, cool. 12–18 A couple t-storms, cool. 19–27 Sunny, turning hot. 28–31 T-storms, cool.

AUG. 2018: Temp. 73° (2° above avg.); precip. 2.5" (0.5" above avg.). 1–5 Scattered t-storms, warm. 6–11 Sunny, hot. 12–19 Scattered t-storms, warm north; sunny, hot south. 20–21 Sunny, hot. 22–29 T-storms, then sunny, cool. 30–31 T-storms, warm.

SEPT. 2018: Temp. 59° (2° below avg.); precip. 1" (0.5" below avg.). 1–5 Showers, then sunny, warm. 6–10 Rainy, cool. 11–15 Sunny; cool north, warm south. 16–24 Rain, then sunny, mild. 25–30 Showers, then sunny, warm.

OCT. 2018: Temp. 48° (1° below avg.); precip. 2" (1" above avg.). 1–5 Snow north, rain south, then sunny, cool. 6–17 Sunny, mild. 18–23 Scattered showers, cooler. 24–31 Snowy periods, some heavy, cold north; sunny, mild south.

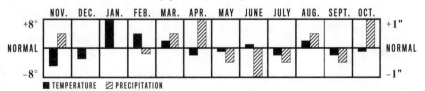

	NOV.	DEC.	JAN.	FEB.	MAR.	APR.	MAY	JUNE	JULY	AUG.	SEPT.	OCT.

+8° / +1"
NORMAL
−8° / −1"

■ TEMPERATURE ⬚ PRECIPITATION

SUMMARY: Winter will be colder than normal, especially in the south, with the coldest periods from late November into early December and in late December, mid-January, and early February. Precipitation will be slightly below normal in the north and above in the south, with above-normal snowfall in both. The snowiest periods will be in early and mid- to late December, mid-January, early and mid-February, and early March. **April** and **May** will be warmer and slightly drier than normal. **Summer** will be drier than normal, with temperatures warmer than normal in the north and cooler in the south. The hottest periods will be in late June, early and late July, and early and late August. **September** and **October** will be cooler than normal, with above-normal precipitation.

NOV. 2017: Temp. 39° (1° below avg.); precip. 1.5" (avg.). 1–11 Showers, mild north; periods of rain and snow south. 12–17 Sunny, cool. 18–23 Rain and snow showers, then sunny, mild. 24–30 Showers, then snowy periods, very cold.

DEC. 2017: Temp. 28° (5° below avg.); precip. 2.5" (avg. north, 2" above south). 1–4 Flurries north, snowstorm south; frigid. 5–8 Snow showers, frigid. 9–20 Rainy, mild north; flurries, cold south. 21–26 Flurries, mild north; heavy snow, then flurries, cold south. 27–31 Snow, then flurries, very cold.

JAN. 2018: Temp. 31° (2° above avg. north, 4° below south); precip. 1.5" (avg.). 1–4 Flurries, cold. 5–11 Showers, mild north; flurries south. 12–17 Sunny, mild north; snowstorm, then flurries, very cold central and south. 18–24 Snow showers, cold. 25–28 Showers and flurries. 29–31 Sunny north, snow south.

FEB. 2018: Temp. 35° (4° above avg. north, 2° below south); precip. 1.5" (avg.). 1–10 Snowstorm, then flurries, cold. 11–17 Sunny, mild north; sunny, then snowstorm, cold south. 18–28 Showers, mild north; flurries south.

MAR. 2018: Temp. 41° (2° below avg.); precip. 0.5" (1" below avg.). 1–6 Rainy periods north; snow, some heavy central and south. 7–15 A few showers, mild. 16–27 A few showers, cool. 28–31 Sunny; mild, then cool.

APR. 2018: Temp. 48° (1° below avg.); precip. 1" (avg.). 1–5 Sunny, mild. 6–13 Rain and snow showers, chilly. 14–21 Sunny, turning warmer. 22–30 Showers north, periods of rain and snow south; cool.

MAY 2018: Temp. 60° (3° above avg.); precip. 0.5" (0.5" below avg.). 1–12 A few showers, warm. 13–21 T-storms, then sunny, cool. 22–28 Scattered t-storms, cool. 29–31 Sunny.

JUNE 2018: Temp. 67° (1° above avg.); precip. 0.3" (0.2" below avg.). 1–4 Sunny, warm. 5–12 T-storms, then sunny, cool. 13–15 Sunny, hot. 16–22 T-storms, then sunny, hot. 23–30 Sunny; cool, then hot.

JULY 2018: Temp. 73.5° (4° above avg. north, 3° below south); precip. 0.3" (0.2" below avg.). 1–5 Sunny, hot. 6–13 Sunny, warm north; t-storms, cool south. 14–18 Sunny, cool. 19–31 Sunny north, a few t-storms south; hot.

AUG. 2018: Temp. 72° (avg.); precip. 0.5" (0.5" below avg.). 1–2 Sunny, hot. 3–8 Isolated t-storms, hot. 9–13 Sunny, cool north; scattered t-storms south. 14–22 Sunny, warm. 23–26 T-storms, then sunny, cool. 27–31 Sunny, hot.

SEPT. 2018: Temp. 60° (2° below avg.); precip. 1.5" (0.5" above avg.). 1–6 T-storms, then sunny, warm. 7–10 Sunny; cool north, warm south. 11–18 Scattered t-storms, cool. 19–23 Sunny, warm. 24–30 Sunny, then showers; cool north, warm south.

OCT. 2018: Temp. 52° (1° above avg.); precip. 1" (avg.). 1–5 A few showers, cool. 6–12 Sunny, warm. 13–20 Showers north, sunny south; warm. 21–26 Rain, then snow north; sunny, mild south. 27–31 Snowstorm.

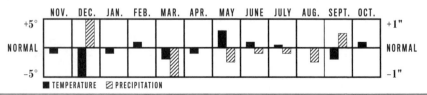

DESERT SOUTHWEST

SUMMARY: Winter will be colder than normal, with above-normal precipitation. The coldest periods will be from late November into early December and in late December and mid-January. Snowfall will be above normal in the east and near to below normal in the west, with the snowiest periods in late December, early and mid-January, and early February. **April** and **May** will be slightly rainier than normal, with temperatures below normal in the east and near normal in the west. **Summer** will be slightly hotter than normal, with the hottest periods in mid- and late June and early August. Rainfall will be below normal in the northwest and above normal in the southeast. **September** and **October** will be cooler and drier than normal.

WEATHER

NOV. 2017: Temp. 53° (3° below avg.); precip. 1.5" (avg. east, 1" above west). 1–3 Sunny, cool. 4–10 Scattered t-storms, cool. 11–25 A few showers east, sunny west; cool. 26–30 Showers, then flurries, turning cold.

DEC. 2017: Temp. 46° (2° below avg.); precip. 0.5" (0.5" above avg. north, 0.5" below south). 1–10 Showers, then sunny, very cold. 11–19 A couple showers east, sunny west; turning mild. 20–31 Rain, then sunny, very cold west; periods of rain and snow, cold east.

JAN. 2018: Temp. 47° (1° below avg.); precip. 0.9" (0.4" above avg.). 1–8 Rain and snow, then sunny, turning milder. 9–18 Showers, then sunny, cold. 19–25 Periods of rain and snow east, sunny west; cold. 26–31 Sunny east, a couple showers west; turning mild.

FEB. 2018: Temp. 48° (3° below avg.); precip. 1" (0.5" above avg.). 1–3 Rain to snow east, sunny west. 4–8 Showers, cool. 9–16 Periods of rain and snow east; sunny, then showers west; cold. 17–20 Sunny, mild. 21–28 A few showers, cool.

MAR. 2018: Temp. 53° (5° below avg.); precip. 1.5" (1" above avg.). 1–5 Rainy periods, cool. 6–12 Snowy periods east, sunny west; cold. 13–21 Rainy periods, cool. 22–31 Snowy periods east, sunny west; cold.

APR. 2018: Temp. 62° (3° below avg.); precip. 0.7" (0.2" above avg.). 1–6 Isolated showers, turning warm. 7–13 Scattered showers, cool. 14–20 Sunny, turning warm. 21–26 T-storms, then sunny, cool. 27–30 Sunny, cool.

MAY 2018: Temp. 74.5° (2° below avg. east, 3° above west); precip. 0.5" (avg.). 1–9 Scattered showers, cool east; sunny, hot west. 10–21 Sunny; cool east, warm west. 22–27 T-storms, then sunny, cool. 28–31 Sunny, hot.

JUNE 2018: Temp. 85° (2° above avg.); precip. 0.4" (0.1" below avg.). 1–3 Sunny, hot. 4–14 T-storms, then sunny, cool. 15–23 Sunny, hot. 24–30 Scattered t-storms east, sunny west; hot.

JULY 2018: Temp. 85° (2° below avg.); precip. 1.8" (0.3" below avg. northwest, 0.9" above southeast). 1–2 Sunny, warm. 3–14 A few t-storms east, sunny west; warm. 15–20 Sunny, warm. 21–26 A few t-storms, cool east; sunny, hot west. 27–31 Sunny east, scattered t-storms west; cool.

AUG. 2018: Temp. 86° (1° above avg.); precip. 1" (0.5" below avg.). 1–8 Scattered t-storms east, sunny west; hot. 9–15 Scattered t-storms, warm. 16–20 Sunny, cool. 21–24 Showers east, sunny west; warm. 25–31 Sunny, cool.

SEPT. 2018: Temp. 78° (1° below avg.); precip. 0.6" (0.4" below avg.). 1–4 Scattered t-storms, cool. 5–11 Sunny, warm. 12–18 Isolated showers, warm east; sunny, cool west. 19–26 Sunny, cool. 27–30 Scattered showers, cool.

OCT. 2018: Temp. 68° (avg.); precip. 0.8" (0.2" below avg.). 1–6 T-storms, then sunny, cool. 7–16 Sunny, warm. 17–22 Sunny, cool. 23–31 Scattered showers east, sunny west; turning cool.

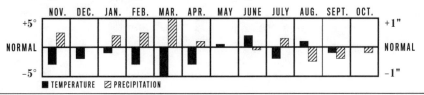

PACIFIC NORTHWEST

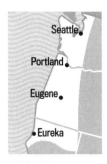

SUMMARY: Winter will be drier and slightly colder than normal, with near- to below-normal snowfall. The coldest periods will occur from late November into early December and in late December, with the snowiest periods in early to mid- and late December. **April** and **May** will be warmer and drier than normal. **Summer** will be warmer and rainier than normal, with the hottest temperatures in mid-June and early and mid- to late July. **September** and **October** will be slightly cooler than normal, with rainfall near normal in the north and above normal in the south.

NOV. 2017: Temp. 46° (1° below avg.); precip. 3.5" (3" below avg.). 1–3 Rainy, mild. 4–10 Showers, turning cool. 11–19 Rainy periods, mild. 20–24 Sunny, cool. 25–30 Rain to snow, then sunny, very cold.

DEC. 2017: Temp. 41° (2° below avg.); precip. 8.5" (2" above avg.). 1–3 Sunny, frigid. 4–7 Snowstorm, then sunny, cold. 8–20 Rain, some heavy, turning mild. 21–26 Showers, mild. 27–31 Snow, then sunny, frigid.

JAN. 2018: Temp. 43° (avg.); precip. 5" (1" below avg.). 1–3 Rain and snow showers. 4–9 Rain, some heavy, turning mild. 10–17 Rainy periods, cool. 18–21 Sunny, cool. 22–31 Rainy periods, cool.

FEB. 2018: Temp. 47° (3° above avg.); precip. 3" (2" below avg.). 1–5 Rainy periods, cool. 6–10 Showers, mild. 11–16 Sunny, mild. 17–25 Rainy periods, mild. 26–28 Misty, mild.

MAR. 2018: Temp. 46° (1° below avg.); precip. 2" (2" below avg.). 1–9 Rainy periods, cool. 10–14 Rain and snow, cool. 15–17 Sunny, mild. 18–25 Rainy periods, cool. 26–31 Sunny, mild.

APR. 2018: Temp. 50° (avg.); precip. 2" (1" below avg.). 1–5 Sunny, warm. 6–11 Rainy periods, cool. 12–14 Sunny, cool. 15–20 Showers, cool. 21–25 Sunny, warm. 26–30 Rainy, cool.

MAY 2018: Temp. 58° (3° above avg.); pre-cip. 1" (1" below avg.). 1–3 Rainy, cool. 4–10 Sunny, very warm. 11–18 Rainy periods, cool. 19–23 Sunny, warm. 24–31 Scattered showers, turning warm.

JUNE 2018: Temp. 61° (1° above avg.); precip. 2" (0.5" above avg.). 1–10 Rainy periods, cool. 11–15 Sunny, turning hot. 16–19 Showers, warm. 20–24 Sunny, cool. 25–30 Scattered showers.

JULY 2018: Temp. 67° (2° above avg.); precip. 0.2" (0.3" below avg.). 1–11 Sunny, turning hot. 12–17 Showers, then sunny, cool. 18–28 Sunny; hot, then cool. 29–31 Showers, cool.

AUG. 2018: Temp. 64° (2° below avg.); precip. 1" (avg.). 1–9 Isolated showers, cool. 10–15 Sunny, cool. 16–21 T-storms, then sunny, cool. 22–28 Showers, then sunny, warm. 29–31 Showers, cool.

SEPT. 2018: Temp. 61° (avg.); precip. 2.5" (1" above avg.). 1–4 Sunny, hot. 5–17 Rainy periods, turning cool. 18–27 Sunny; warm, then cool. 28–30 Rainy, cool.

OCT. 2018: Temp. 53.5° (0.5° below avg.); precip. 3" (1" below avg. north, 1" above south). 1–2 Sunny, cool. 3–8 Rainy periods, cool. 9–11 Sunny, warm. 12–22 Rainy periods, mild. 23–31 Periods of rain and snow, cold.

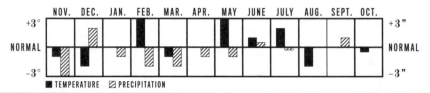

SUMMARY: **Winter** will be cooler than normal, with rainfall above normal in the north and near normal in the south. The coldest periods will occur from late November into early December and in early February. Mountain snows will be above normal, with the stormiest periods in early to mid-November and early and late January. **April** and **May** will be slightly drier than normal. Temperatures will be below normal near the coast and above normal inland. **Summer** will be cooler than normal, with near-normal rainfall. The hottest periods will be from late May into early June and in mid-June and mid-July. **September** and **October** will have near-normal temperatures, with rainfall above normal in the north and below normal in the south.

San Francisco
•Fresno
Los Angeles
San Diego•

WEATHER

NOV. 2017: Temp. 56° (2° below avg.); precip. 4.5" (3" above avg.). 1–5 Rainy periods cool. 6–9 Rain, some heavy. 10–16 Sunny, cool. 17–25 Sprinkles, cool coast; sunny, warm inland. 26–30 Rainy, cold.

DEC. 2017: Temp. 55° (3° above avg. north, 1° below south); precip. 1" (1" below avg.). 1–8 Rain, then sunny, cold. 9–20 Rainy periods, mild north; sunny, warm south. 21–26 Sunny, cool. 27–31 Showers, cool.

JAN. 2018: Temp. 53° (1° below avg.); precip. 4" (3" above avg. north, 1" below south). 1–7 Rain north, some heavy; showers, warm south. 8–14 Rainy periods, cool. 15–17 Sunny, cool. 18–26 Rainy periods, cool. 27–31 Rain, some heavy; mild.

FEB. 2018: Temp. 55° (avg.); precip. 3.5" (2" above avg. north, 1" below south). 1–8 Rainy periods, cool. 9–15 Sunny, turning warm. 16–28 Rainy periods; warm, then cool.

MAR. 2018: Temp. 55° (2° below avg.); precip. 2.5" (avg.). 1–6 Rainy periods, cool. 7–11 Sprinkles, cool. 12–15 Rainy, cool. 16–21 Sunny north, rainy periods south; cool. 22–26 Showers, cool. 27–31 Sunny, warm.

APR. 2018: Temp. 59° (1° below avg.); precip. 0.5" (0.5" below avg.). 1–4 Sunny, warm. 5–11 Scattered showers, cool. 12–21 Sunny; warm, then cool. 22–30 Scattered showers, cool.

MAY 2018: Temp. 65° (avg. coast, 3° above inland); precip. 0.4" (0.1" below avg.). 1–12 Sunny, hot inland; A.M. clouds, P.M. sun

coast. 13–19 Scattered showers, cool. 20–22 Sunny, hot. 23–27 Isolated showers, warm. 28–31 Sunny, turning hot.

JUNE 2018: Temp. 69° (1° above avg.); precip. 0.1" (avg.). 1–2 Sunny, hot. 3–11 Sunny, cool inland; A.M. sprinkles, P.M. sun coast. 12–14 Sunny, hot. 15–17 Sprinkles, cool. 18–22 Sunny; hot inland, cool coast. 23–30 Sunny, cool.

JULY 2018: Temp. 70° (1° below avg.); precip. 0" (avg.). 1–9 Sunny, seasonable. 10–17 Sunny, turning cool inland; A.M. clouds and sprinkles, P.M. sun coast. 18–19 Sunny, hot. 20–31 Sunny, warm.

AUG. 2018: Temp. 69° (2° below avg.); precip. 0.1" (avg.). 1–4 Sunny, cool inland; A.M. sprinkles, P.M. sun coast. 5–10 Isolated showers, cool. 11–15 Sunny, cool north; sprinkles, warm south. 16–21 Sunny inland, A.M. clouds coast; cool. 22–31 Sunny inland; A.M. sprinkles, P.M. sun coast; cool.

SEPT. 2018: Temp. 69° (1° below avg.); precip. 0.5" (0.5" above avg. north, avg. south). 1–4 Sunny, warm. 5–17 Sunny inland; A.M. sprinkles, P.M. sun coast; cool. 18–21 Sunny, hot. 22–28 Sunny, turning cool. 29–30 Rainy north, sprinkles south; cool.

OCT. 2018: Temp. 66° (1° above avg.); precip. 1.5" (2" above avg. north, 0.5" below south). 1–5 Rain then sunny, cool. 6–13 Sunny, turning warm. 14–18 Rain, then sunny, cool. 19–24 Sunny, turning warm. 25–28 Sunny, cool. 29–31 Rain north; sunny, cool south.

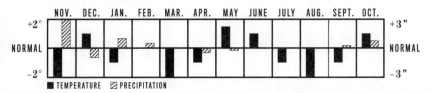

ALASKA

SUMMARY: Winter season temperatures will be milder than normal, with the coldest periods in early to mid-January and early February. Precipitation will be above normal N (see Key below) and near normal S, while snowfall will be above normal C and below normal N and S. The snowiest periods will be in late November, early to mid-December, and late March. **April** and **May** will be warmer than normal, with slightly above normal precipitation. **Summer** will be cooler and a bit rainier than normal, with the hottest periods in early July and mid-August. **September** and **October** will be warmer than normal, with above-normal precipitation N and below-normal S.

KEY: Panhandle (P), Aleutians (A), north (N), central (C), south (S), west-central (WC), east-central (EC), south-central (SC), northwest (NW), southeast (SE), elsewhere (EW).

NOV. 2017: Temp. 17° N, 41° S (15° above avg. N, 5° below S); precip. 0.9" N, 4" S (0.5" above avg. N, 1" below S). 1–4 Snowy periods, mild. 5–10 Flurries, mild. 11–17 Sunny, cold N; snow showers, mild S. 18–22 Snowy periods, mild. 23–30 Snowy periods, mild N; sunny, cold S.

DEC. 2017: Temp. 3° N, 33° S (10° above avg. N, 2° above S); precip. 0.2" N, 5" S (avg.). 1–5 Snow showers, mild. 6–8 Snowstorm P; flurries, cold EW. 9–18 Clear, mild N+C; flurries, cold S. 19–22 Clear; cold N, mild S. 23–31 Snowy periods, turning very mild.

JAN. 2018: Temp. –14° N, 27° S (2° below avg.); precip. 0.2" N, 5" S (avg.). 1–3 Clear, mild. 4–17 Snowy periods S, flurries EW; cold. 18–26 Snowy periods, mild. 27–31 Flurries, mild.

FEB. 2018: Temp. –15° N, 30° S (1° below avg.); precip. 0.7" N, 4.5" S (0.5" above avg.). 1–11 Flurries, cold. 12–15 Snow showers, mild. 16–20 Clear, mild N+C; snow showers, cold S. 21–28 Clear, cold N; snowy periods, mild S.

MAR. 2018: Temp. –9° N, 38° S (4° above avg.); precip. 1" N, 5.5" S (0.5" above avg.). 1–10 Clear, cold N; flurries, turning cold S. 11–20 Clear N, snow showers S; turning mild. 21–31 Snowy periods N, flurries S; mild.

APR. 2018: Temp. 2° N, 41° S (avg.); precip. 0.7" N, 3" S (avg.). 1–4 Snow showers N, showers S. 5–13 Sunny; mild, then cold. 14–22 Snow showers, cold. 23–30 Flurries N, sunny S; mild.

MAY 2018: Temp. 23° N, 49° EW (2° above avg.); precip. 0.9" N, 3.3" S (0.3" above avg.). 1–5 Sunny, cool. 6–12 Flurries north, showers C+S; mild. 13–17 Sunny, mild. 18–23 Scattered showers, cool. 24–31 Snowy periods N, showers C+S; cool.

JUNE 2018: Temp. 33° N, 53° EW (1° below avg.); precip. 0.7" N, 3" S (avg.). 1–10 A few showers, cool. 11–16 Showers, cool N; sunny, warm S. 17–26 Sunny, cool. 27–30 Showers, cool.

JULY 2018: Temp. 40° N, 55° EW (2° below avg.); precip. 1.7" N, 4.5" S (0.5" above avg.). 1–3 Sunny, warm. 4–13 Showers, cool. 14–18 Scattered showers, warm. 19–31 A few showers, turning cool.

AUG. 2018: Temp. 39° N, 55° EW (1° below avg.); precip. 1.7" N, 5.5" S (0.5" above avg.). 1–7 A few showers, cool. 8–16 Scattered showers, warm. 17–23 Showers, cool. 24–31 Showers, mild N+S; sunny, warm C.

SEPT. 2018: Temp. 34° N, 56° EW (2° above avg.); precip. 1.6" N, 6" S (0.5" above avg. N, 1" below S). 1–11 A few showers; cool, then warm. 12–18 Flurries, mild N; snowy periods C; sprinkles, cool S. 19–24 Snowy periods N, rain S. 25–30 Snow showers N+C; showers S; mild.

OCT. 2018: Temp. 18° N, 49° S (6° above avg.); precip. 1" N, 6" S (0.5" above avg. N, 1" below S). 1–10 Snowy periods, turning cold. 11–18 Flurries, mild N; snowy C; sunny, cold S. 19–22 Snowy periods N+C, showers S: mild. 23–25 Sunny, mild. 26–31 Snow showers, mild N; snowy periods C; sunny, cold S.

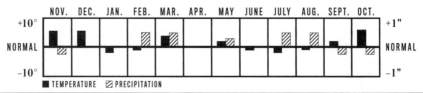

HAWAII

SUMMARY: Winter season temperatures will be below normal, on average, with the coolest periods in early and mid-December, early and mid-January, and mid-February. Rainfall will be below normal, with the stormiest periods in mid-December and early and mid-March. **April** and **May** will be slightly cooler and drier than normal. **Summer** temperatures will be cooler than normal, on average, with slightly below normal rainfall. The warmest period will be in mid-June. **September** and **October** will be cooler and slightly drier than normal.

KEY: east (E), central (C), west (W). Note: Temperature and precipitation are substantially based upon topography. The detailed forecast focuses on the Honolulu–Waikiki area and provides general trends elsewhere.

NOV. 2017: Temp. 76.5° (1° below avg.); precip. 0.5" (2" below avg.). 1–16 Rain and t-storms E, daily showers C and W; seasonable. 17–25 Sunny E, a few showers C and W; cool. 26–30 Sunny, cool.

DEC. 2017: Temp. 73° (2° below avg.); precip. 3.3" (avg.). 1–7 A few showers E, sunny C and W; cool. 8–12 Showers and heavy t-storms, cool. 13–17 Showers, warm. 18–28 A few showers, cool. 29–31 Sunny, warm.

JAN. 2018: Temp. 73° (avg.); precip. 0.5" (2" below avg.). 1–5 Sunny, cool. 6–10 Sunny C, showers E and W; cool. 11–19 Scattered showers; warm E and C, cool W. 20–31 A few showers C, t-storms E and W; warm.

FEB. 2018: Temp. 73° (avg.); precip. 1" (1" below avg.). 1–11 Daily showers C, a few t-storms E and W; warm. 12–17 A few showers, cool. 18–28 Rain and t-storms E, scattered showers C and W; warm.

MAR. 2018: Temp. 75° (1° above avg.); precip. 2" (avg.). 1–10 Showers and heavy t-storms E, scattered showers C and W; warm. 11–26 Showers and heavy t-storms, cool E; daily showers, warm C; scattered showers, cool W. 27–31 Showers, cool E; sunny, warm W.

APR. 2018: Temp. 75.5° (avg.); precip. 0.2" (0.5" below avg.). 1–8 Showers, warm. 9–14 Scattered showers, cool. 15–30 Daily showers, seasonable.

MAY 2018: Temp. 76.5° (0.5° below avg.); precip. 0.7" (avg.). 1–4 Showers, warm. 5–9 Showers E and W, sunny C; cool. 10–20 Rain and t-storms E and W, daily showers C; cool. 21–26 Scattered showers, warm. 27–31 Showers, cool.

JUNE 2018: Temp. 79.5° (avg.); precip. 0.2" (0.2" below avg.). 1–9 A few showers; cool E and W, warm C. 10–15 Scattered showers; cool E and C, hot W. 16–22 A few showers E and W, sunny C; cool. 23–30 A few t-storms E and W, daily showers C; warm.

JULY 2018: Temp. 80.5 (0.5° below avg.); precip. 0.3" (0.2" below avg.). 1–13 Showers and t-storms E and W, daily showers C; cool. 14–21 Scattered showers, warm. 22–31 Showers and a few heavier t-storms E, daily showers C and W; warm, then cool.

AUG. 2018: Temp. 80.5° (1° below avg.); precip. 0.4" (0.2" below avg.). 1–13 A few showers, warm. 14–22 Showers and heavier t-storms E, a few showers C and W; warm. 23–31 Scattered showers, cool.

SEPT. 2018: Temp. 81° (0.5° below avg.); precip. 0.4" (0.4" below avg.). 1–5 Sunny, warm. 6–18 Showers and heavy t-storms E and W, sunny C; warm. 19–27 A few showers; warm E; hot, then cool W. 28–30 Showers, warm.

OCT. 2018: Temp. 79.5° (0.5° below avg.); precip. 2" (avg.). 1–4 A few showers E and W, isolated showers C; warm. 5–15 Showers, cool. 16–22 Rainy E, a few showers C and W; warm. 23–27 Showers, cool. 28–31 Sunny, cool.

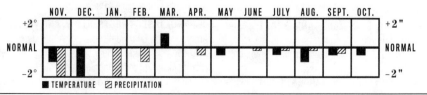

SECRETS OF THE ZODIAC

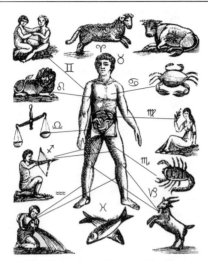

The Man of the Signs

Ancient astrologers believed that each astrological sign influenced a specific part of the body. The first sign of the zodiac—Aries—was attributed to the head, with the rest of the signs moving down the body, ending with Pisces at the feet.

♈ Aries, head	ARI	*Mar. 21–Apr. 20*
♉ Taurus, neck	TAU	*Apr. 21–May 20*
♊ Gemini, arms	GEM	*May 21–June 20*
♋ Cancer, breast	CAN	*June 21–July 22*
♌ Leo, heart	LEO	*July 23–Aug. 22*
♍ Virgo, belly	VIR	*Aug. 23–Sept. 22*
♎ Libra, reins	LIB	*Sept. 23–Oct. 22*
♏ Scorpio, secrets	SCO	*Oct. 23–Nov. 22*
♐ Sagittarius, thighs	SAG	*Nov. 23–Dec. 21*
♑ Capricorn, knees	CAP	*Dec. 22–Jan. 19*
♒ Aquarius, legs	AQU	*Jan. 20–Feb. 19*
♓ Pisces, feet	PSC	*Feb. 20–Mar. 20*

ASTROLOGY VS. ASTRONOMY

Astrology is a tool we use to plan events according to the placements of the Sun, the Moon, and the planets in the 12 signs of the zodiac. In astrology, the planetary movements do not cause events; rather, they explain the path, or "flow," that events tend to follow. The Moon's astrological place is given on **the next page** and in the **Left-Hand Calendar Pages, 140–166.** Astronomy is the study of the actual placement of the known planets and constellations. The Moon's astronomical place is also given in the **Left-Hand Calendar Pages, 140–166.** *(The placement of the planets in the signs of the zodiac is not the same astrologically and astronomically.)*

The dates in the **Best Days** table, **pages 240–241,** are based on the astrological passage of the Moon.

WHEN MERCURY IS RETROGRADE

Sometimes the other planets appear to be traveling backward through the zodiac; this is an illusion. We call this illusion *retrograde motion.*

Mercury's retrograde periods can cause our plans to go awry. However, intuition is high during these periods and coincidences can be extraordinary.

When Mercury is retrograde, remain flexible, allow extra time for travel, and avoid signing contracts. Review projects and plans but wait until Mercury is direct again to make final decisions.

In 2018, Mercury will be retrograde during March 23–April 15, July 26–August 19, and November 17–December 6.

–Celeste Longacre

GARDENING BY THE MOON'S SIGN

USE CHART ON NEXT PAGE TO FIND THE BEST DATES FOR THE FOLLOWING GARDEN TASKS . . .

PLANT, TRANSPLANT, AND GRAFT: Cancer, Scorpio, Pisces, or Taurus.
HARVEST: Aries, Leo, Sagittarius, Gemini, or Aquarius.
BUILD/FIX FENCES OR GARDEN BEDS: Capricorn.

CONTROL INSECT PESTS, PLOW, AND WEED: Aries, Gemini, Leo, Sagittarius, or Aquarius.
PRUNE: Aries, Leo, or Sagittarius. During a waxing Moon, pruning encourages growth; during a waning Moon, it discourages growth.

SETTING EGGS BY THE MOON'S SIGN

Chicks take about 21 days to hatch. Those born under a waxing Moon, in the fruitful signs of Cancer, Scorpio, and Pisces, are healthier and mature faster. To ensure that chicks are born during these times, determine the best days to "set eggs" (to place eggs in an incubator or under a hen). To calculate, find the three fruitful birth signs on the chart below. Use the **Left-Hand Calendar Pages, 140–166,** to find the dates of the new and full Moons. Using only the fruitful dates between the new and full Moons, count back 21 days to find the best days to set eggs.

EXAMPLE:

The Moon is new on April 15 and full on April 29. Between these dates, from April 20 to 22, the Moon is in the sign of Cancer. To have chicks born on April 20, count back 21 days; set eggs on March 30.

The Moon's Astrological Place, 2017–18

	NOV.	DEC.	JAN.	FEB.	MAR.	APR.	MAY	JUNE	JULY	AUG.	SEPT.	OCT.	NOV.	DEC.
1	ARI	TAU	CAN	LEO	VIR	LIB	SAG	CAP	AQU	ARI	TAU	GEM	LEO	LIB
2	ARI	TAU	CAN	VIR	VIR	SCO	SAG	CAP	PSC	ARI	GEM	CAN	VIR	LIB
3	TAU	GEM	LEO	VIR	LIB	SCO	SAG	AQU	PSC	ARI	GEM	CAN	VIR	LIB
4	TAU	GEM	LEO	LIB	LIB	SAG	CAP	AQU	PSC	TAU	CAN	LEO	LIB	SCO
5	GEM	CAN	VIR	LIB	SCO	SAG	CAP	PSC	ARI	TAU	CAN	LEO	LIB	SCO
6	GEM	CAN	VIR	SCO	SCO	SAG	AQU	PSC	ARI	GEM	LEO	VIR	SCO	SAG
7	CAN	LEO	LIB	SCO	SCO	CAP	AQU	PSC	TAU	GEM	LEO	VIR	SCO	SAG
8	CAN	LEO	LIB	SAG	SAG	CAP	AQU	ARI	TAU	CAN	VIR	LIB	SCO	CAP
9	LEO	VIR	LIB	SAG	SAG	AQU	PSC	ARI	GEM	CAN	VIR	LIB	SAG	CAP
10	LEO	VIR	SCO	SAG	CAP	AQU	PSC	TAU	GEM	LEO	LIB	SCO	SAG	CAP
11	VIR	LIB	SCO	CAP	CAP	AQU	ARI	TAU	GEM	LEO	LIB	SCO	CAP	AQU
12	VIR	LIB	SAG	CAP	CAP	PSC	ARI	GEM	CAN	VIR	LIB	SAG	CAP	AQU
13	VIR	SCO	SAG	AQU	AQU	PSC	ARI	GEM	CAN	VIR	SCO	SAG	AQU	PSC
14	LIB	SCO	SAG	AQU	AQU	ARI	TAU	CAN	LEO	LIB	SCO	SAG	AQU	PSC
15	LIB	SCO	CAP	AQU	PSC	ARI	TAU	CAN	LEO	LIB	SAG	CAP	AQU	PSC
16	SCO	SAG	CAP	PSC	PSC	TAU	GEM	LEO	VIR	SCO	SAG	CAP	PSC	ARI
17	SCO	SAG	AQU	PSC	PSC	TAU	GEM	LEO	VIR	SCO	CAP	AQU	PSC	ARI
18	SCO	CAP	AQU	ARI	ARI	GEM	CAN	VIR	LIB	SAG	CAP	AQU	ARI	TAU
19	SAG	CAP	AQU	ARI	ARI	GEM	CAN	VIR	LIB	SAG	CAP	AQU	ARI	TAU
20	SAG	CAP	PSC	ARI	TAU	CAN	LEO	LIB	SCO	SAG	AQU	PSC	ARI	GEM
21	CAP	AQU	PSC	TAU	TAU	CAN	LEO	LIB	SCO	CAP	AQU	PSC	TAU	GEM
22	CAP	AQU	ARI	TAU	GEM	CAN	VIR	LIB	SAG	CAP	PSC	ARI	TAU	CAN
23	CAP	PSC	ARI	GEM	GEM	LEO	VIR	SCO	SAG	AQU	PSC	ARI	GEM	CAN
24	AQU	PSC	TAU	GEM	CAN	LEO	LIB	SCO	SAG	AQU	PSC	TAU	GEM	CAN
25	AQU	PSC	TAU	CAN	CAN	VIR	LIB	SAG	CAP	AQU	ARI	TAU	CAN	LEO
26	PSC	ARI	TAU	CAN	LEO	VIR	SCO	SAG	CAP	PSC	ARI	TAU	CAN	LEO
27	PSC	ARI	GEM	LEO	LEO	LIB	SCO	CAP	AQU	PSC	TAU	GEM	LEO	VIR
28	ARI	TAU	GEM	LEO	VIR	LIB	SCO	CAP	AQU	ARI	TAU	GEM	LEO	VIR
29	ARI	TAU	CAN	–	VIR	SCO	SAG	CAP	AQU	ARI	GEM	CAN	VIR	LIB
30	ARI	GEM	CAN	–	VIR	SCO	SAG	AQU	PSC	ARI	GEM	CAN	VIR	LIB
31	–	GEM	LEO	–	LIB	–	CAP	–	PSC	TAU	–	LEO	–	SCO

BEST DAYS FOR 2018

This chart is based on the Moon's sign and shows the best days each month for certain activities. *–Celeste Longacre*

	JAN.	FEB.	MAR.	APR.	MAY	JUNE	JULY	AUG.	SEPT.	OCT.	NOV.	DEC.
Quit smoking	6, 11	3, 7	7, 16	3, 13	10, 14	7, 11	4, 8, 31	5, 27	1, 28	7, 26	3, 30	5, 28
Bake	1, 2, 29, 30	25, 26	24, 25	20–22	18, 19	14, 15	12, 13	8, 9	4, 5	2, 3, 29, 30	25, 26	22–24
Brew	10, 11	6, 7	5–7	2, 3, 29, 30	26–28	23, 24	20, 21	16, 17	13, 14	10, 11	6–8	4, 5, 31
Dry fruit/vegetables/meat	3, 4, 12, 13	8, 9	8, 9	23, 24	1–3	8, 9	5, 6	1–3, 28–30	6, 7, 26	4, 5, 31	1, 27, 28	6, 25, 26
Make jams/jellies	20, 21	16, 17	15–17	12, 13	9, 10	5–7	2–4, 30, 31	26, 27	22–24	20, 21	16, 17	13–15
Can, pickle, or make sauerkraut	10, 11	6, 7	5–7	2, 3	9, 10	5–7	2–4, 30, 31	8, 9, 27	4, 5	2, 3, 29, 30	6, 25, 26	4, 5, 31
Begin diet to lose weight	6, 11	3, 7	7, 16	3, 13	10, 14	7, 11	4, 8, 31	5, 27	1, 28	7, 26	3, 30	5, 28
Begin diet to gain weight	21, 25	17, 26	21, 25	22, 26	19, 23	19, 24	17, 21	13, 17	14, 24	11, 21	17, 22	15, 19
Cut hair to encourage growth	20, 21, 24–26	21, 22	20, 21, 31	27, 28	24, 25	20–22	18, 19	14, 15	10–12	20, 21	16, 17	13–15
Cut hair to discourage growth	7–9	4, 5	3, 4	1, 12, 13	9, 10	5–7	2–4, 30, 31	4, 5, 27	1, 27, 28	25, 26	4, 5	1–3, 29, 30
Perm hair	17–19	13–15	13, 14	9–11	6–8	3, 4	1, 27–29	23–25	20, 21	17–19	13–15	11, 12
Color hair	24–26	21, 22	20, 21	16, 17	14, 15	10, 11	7, 8	4, 5, 31	1, 27, 28	24–26	21, 22	18, 19
Straighten hair	12–14	8–10	8, 9	4–6	1–3, 29, 30	25, 26	22–24	18–20	15, 16	12–14	9, 10	6, 7
Have dental care	5, 6	2, 3	1, 2, 28–30	25, 26	22, 23	18, 19	16, 17	12, 13	8, 9	6, 7	2, 3, 29, 30	27, 28
Start projects	3	16	18	17	16	14	14	12	10	10	8	8
End projects	1	14	16	15	14	12	12	10	8	8	6	6
Demolish	10, 11	6, 7	5–7	2, 3, 29, 30	26–28	23, 24	20, 21	16, 17	13, 14	10, 11	6–8	4, 5, 31
Lay shingles	3, 4, 31	1, 27, 28	26, 27	23, 24	20, 21	16, 17	14, 15	10, 11	6, 7	4, 5, 31	1, 27, 28	25, 26
Paint	7–9, 24–26	4, 5, 21, 22	3, 4, 20, 21	1, 16, 17, 27, 28	14, 15, 24, 25	10, 11, 20–22	7, 8, 18, 19	4, 5, 14, 15	1, 10–12, 27, 28	8, 9, 24–26	4, 5, 21, 22	1–3, 18, 19, 29, 30
Wash windows	22, 23	18–20	18, 19	14, 15	11–13	8, 9	5, 6	1–3, 28–30	25, 26	22, 23	18–20	16, 17
Wash floors	20, 21	16, 17	15–17	12, 13	9, 10	5–7	2–4, 30, 31	26, 27	22–24	20, 21	16, 17	13–15
Go camping	12–14	8–10	8, 9	4–6	1–3, 29, 30	25, 26	22–24	18–20	15, 16	12–14	9, 10	6, 7

	JAN.	FEB.	MAR.	APR.	MAY	JUNE	JULY	AUG.	SEPT.	OCT.	NOV.	DEC.
Travel for pleasure	3, 4, 31	1, 27, 28	26, 27	23, 24	20, 21	16, 17	14, 15	10, 11	6, 7	4, 5, 31	1, 27, 28	25, 26
Get married	7–9	4, 5	3, 4, 31	1, 27, 28	24, 25	20–22	18, 19	14, 15	10–12	8, 9	4, 5	1–3, 29, 30
Ask for a loan	6, 11	3, 7	2, 7	3, 13	10, 15	7, 11	4, 8	5, 9	1, 9, 28	7, 26	3, 30	5, 26
Buy a home	21, 26	17, 22	21, 30	17, 22	23, 28	19, 24	17, 21	13, 17	14, 24	11, 21	17, 22	15, 19
Move (house/household)	27, 28	23, 24	22, 23	18, 19	16, 17	12, 13	10, 11	6, 7	2, 3, 29, 30	1, 27, 28	23, 24	20, 21
Advertise to sell	24, 25	6, 7	20, 21	17, 29, 30	26–28	23, 24	20, 21	16, 17	14, 24	11, 21	17, 22	15, 19
Mow to increase growth	22, 23	18–20	18, 19	29, 30	26–28	23, 24	20, 21	1–3	13, 14	12–14	9, 10, 18–20	16, 17
Mow to decrease growth	10, 11	6, 7	5–7	14, 15	12, 13	8, 9	5, 6	13, 14	25, 26	6, 7	3, 30	4, 5
Plant aboveground crops	20, 21, 29, 30	16, 17, 25, 26	24, 25	20–22, 29	18, 19, 26–28	14, 15, 23, 24	20, 21	16, 17, 26	13, 14, 22, 23	10, 11, 20, 21	16, 17	8, 14, 15
Plant belowground crops	10, 11	6, 7	5–7, 15, 16	2, 3, 12, 13	9, 10	5–7	2–4, 30, 31	8, 9	4, 5	2, 3, 29, 30	6, 25, 26	4, 5, 31
Destroy pests and weeds	22, 23	18–20	18, 19	14, 15	11–13	8, 9	5, 6	1–3, 29, 30	25, 26	22, 23	18–20	16, 17
Graft or pollinate	1, 2, 29, 30	25, 26	24, 25	20–22	18, 19	14, 15	12, 13	8, 9	4, 5	2, 3, 29, 30	25, 26	22–24
Prune to encourage growth	22, 23	18–20	26, 27	23, 24	20, 21	16, 17	14, 15	18–20	15, 16	12, 13	18–20	16, 17
Prune to discourage growth	3, 4, 12–14	8–10	8, 9	4–6	1–3, 30	8, 9	5, 6	1–3	6, 7, 26	4, 5, 31	27, 28	25, 26
Pick fruit	5, 6	2, 3	1, 2, 28–30	25, 26	22, 23	18, 19	16, 17	12, 13	8, 9	6, 7	2, 3, 29, 30	27, 28
Harvest above-ground crops	24–26	21, 22	20, 21, 28–30	25, 26	22, 23	18, 19	16, 17	12, 13	18, 19	15, 16	11, 12	18, 19
Harvest below-ground crops	5, 6, 15	2, 3, 11, 12	2, 10–12	7, 8	4, 5, 14	10, 11	7, 8	4, 5	8, 27, 28	6, 7, 26	2, 3, 29, 30	27, 28
Cut hay	22, 23	18–20	18, 19	14, 15	11–13	8, 9	5, 6	1–3, 29, 30	25, 26	22, 23	18–20	16, 17
Begin logging	15, 16	11, 12	10–12	7, 8	4, 5, 31	1, 2, 27–29	25, 26	21, 22	17–19	15, 16	11, 12	8–10
Set posts or pour concrete	15, 16	11, 12	10–12	7, 8	4, 5, 31	1, 2, 27–29	25, 26	21, 22	17–19	15, 16	11, 12	8–10
Purchase animals	1, 2, 29, 30	25, 26	24, 25	20–22	18, 19	14, 15	12, 13	8, 9	4, 5	2, 3, 29, 30	25, 26	22–24
Breed animals	10, 11	6, 7	5–7	2, 3, 29, 30	27, 28	23, 24	20, 21	16, 17	13, 14	10, 11	6–8	4, 5, 31
Wean animals or children	6, 11	3, 7	7, 16	3, 13	10, 14	7, 11	4, 8, 31	5, 27	1, 28	7, 26	3, 30	5, 28
Castrate animals	17–19	13–15	13, 14	9–11	6–8	3, 4, 30	1, 27–29	23–25	20, 21	17–19	13–15	11, 12
Slaughter livestock	10, 11	6, 7	5–7	2, 3, 29, 30	27, 28	23, 24	20, 21	16, 17	13, 14	10, 11	6–8	4, 5, 31

BEST FISHING DAYS AND TIMES

The best times to fish are when the fish are naturally most active. The Sun, Moon, tides, and weather all influence fish activity. For example, fish tend to feed more at sunrise and sunset, and also during a full Moon (when tides are higher than average). However, most of us go fishing when we can get the time off, not because it is the best time. But there are best times, according to fishing lore:

■ One hour before and one hour after high tides, and one hour before and one hour after low tides. (Inland, the times for high tides correspond with the times when the Moon is due south. Low tides are halfway between high tides.)

GET HIGH AND LOW TIDE TIMES NEAREST TO YOUR LOCATION AT ALMANAC.COM/TIDES.

■ During the "morning rise" (after sunup for a spell) and the "evening rise" (just before sundown and the hour or so after).

■ During the rise and set of the Moon.

■ When the barometer is steady or on the rise. (But even during stormy periods, the fish aren't going to give up feeding. The smart fisherman will find just the right bait.)

■ When there is a hatch of flies—caddis flies or mayflies, commonly.

■ When the breeze is from a westerly quarter, rather than from the north or east.

■ When the water is still or slightly rippled, rather than during a wind.

THE BEST FISHING DAYS FOR 2018, WHEN THE MOON IS BETWEEN NEW AND FULL

January 1, 16–31
February 15–March 1
March 17–31
April 15–29
May 15–29
June 13–28
July 12–27
August 11–26
September 9–24
October 8–24
November 7–23
December 7–22

Dates based on Eastern Time.

HOW TO ESTIMATE THE WEIGHT OF A FISH

Measure the fish from the tip of its nose to the tip of its tail. Then measure its girth at the thickest portion of its midsection.

The weight of a fat-bodied fish (bass, salmon) = (length x girth x girth)/800

SALMON

The weight of a slender fish (trout, northern pike) = (length x girth x girth)/900

TROUT

EXAMPLE: If a fish is 20 inches long and has a 12-inch girth, its estimated weight is (20 x 12 x 12)/900 = 2,880/900 = 3.2 pounds

CATFISH

Body Restore Method That Tried To Be Blocked For Years

In a year when several health discoveries have already made headlines, this one may be the biggest yet.

Dr. Rand McClain, the Los Angeles based "Doctor to the Stars," released his new technique for what some are calling the Body Restore formula.

His science is based on technology that was actually partially banned by a U.S. Establishment in 2001. However, Dr. McClain and his partners have found a way that allows them to go and take their discovery straight to the American people.

Dr. McClain revealed he's already offering to his celebrity and pro-athlete clients with incredible results.

In the video presentation, he details how some very big name athletes are achieving increased strength, healthier bodies, and even more energy.

But what's really turning heads is that McClain isn't offering this as an injection, surgery, or medical procedure — which is what his health clinic in Los Angeles is famous for.

Instead, the method involves one simple thing: A drink. He has all the clinical trials, the data, he's conducted the test groups...it not only works, it works really well. McClain feels the technique —

which has been shown in clinical trials — works best for people over 40, particularly those who may be experiencing excessive fatigue, weaker bodies, and even foggy thinking.

And when Dr. McClain dropped the final bombshell — video footage of the results he experienced after using the method on himself — it became clear that the discovery is nothing short of groundbreaking, of course your indivitual results will vary, as with any new method.

While surgery is the benchmark and Dr. McClain charges $20,000 and up, he feels he can offer Americans a new method which provides outstanding results.

But the latest development in this story came when the video version of the presentation was made available to the public online. As of this writing, the video has over 3 Million views and is quickly becoming a social media phenomenon.

This is the video that many might not want people to see. But if the link is working, that means the video is still viewable...for now.

Watch the shocking presentation at **www.LCR30.com**

Dr. McClain calls out both the medical industry and certain agencies. One viewer commented: "Why did I not know this before? Rand is telling it like it is... we need more doctors like this!"

See his presentation here **www.LCR30.com**

GESTATION AND MATING TABLES

	PROPER AGE OR WEIGHT FOR FIRST MATING	PERIOD OF FERTILITY (YRS.)	NUMBER OF FEMALES FOR ONE MALE	PERIOD OF GESTATION (DAYS) AVERAGE	RANGE
CATTLE: Cow	15–18 mos.[1]	10–14		283	279–290[2] 262–300[3]
Bull	1 yr., well matured	10–12	50[4] / thousands[5]		
GOAT: Doe	10 mos. or 85–90 lbs.	6		150	145–155
Buck	well matured	5	30		
HORSE: Mare	3 yrs.	10–12		336	310–370
Stallion	3 yrs.	12–15	40–45[4] / record 252[5]		
PIG: Sow	5–6 mos. or 250 lbs.	6		115	110–120
Boar	250–300 lbs.	6	50[6] / 35–40[7]		
RABBIT: Doe	6 mos.	5–6		31	30–32
Buck	6 mos.	5–6	30		
SHEEP: Ewe	1 yr. or 90 lbs.	6		147 / 151[8]	142–154
Ram	12–14 mos., well matured	7	50–75[6] / 35–40[7]		
CAT: Queen	12 mos.	6		63	60–68
Tom	12 mos.	6	6–8		
DOG: Bitch	16–18 mos.	8		63	58–67
Male	12–16 mos.	8	8–10		

[1]Holstein and beef: 750 lbs.; Jersey: 500 lbs. [2]Beef; 8–10 days shorter for Angus. [3]Dairy. [4]Natural. [5]Artificial. [6]Hand-mated. [7]Pasture. [8]For fine wool breeds.

INCUBATION PERIOD OF POULTRY (DAYS)

Chicken	21
Duck	26–32
Goose	30–34
Guinea	26–28
Turkey	28

AVERAGE LIFE SPAN OF ANIMALS IN CAPTIVITY (YEARS)

Cat (domestic)	14	Goose (domestic)	20
Chicken (domestic)	8	Horse	22
Dog (domestic)	13	Pig	12
Duck (domestic)	10	Rabbit	6
Goat (domestic)	14	Turkey (domestic)	10

	ESTRAL/ESTROUS CYCLE (INCLUDING HEAT PERIOD) AVERAGE	RANGE	LENGTH OF ESTRUS (HEAT) AVERAGE	RANGE	USUAL TIME OF OVULATION	WHEN CYCLE RECURS IF NOT BRED
Cow	21 days	18–24 days	18 hours	10–24 hours	10–12 hours after end of estrus	21 days
Doe goat	21 days	18–24 days	2–3 days	1–4 days	Near end of estrus	21 days
Mare	21 days	10–37 days	5–6 days	2–11 days	24–48 hours before end of estrus	21 days
Sow	21 days	18–24 days	2–3 days	1–5 days	30–36 hours after start of estrus	21 days
Ewe	16½ days	14–19 days	30 hours	24–32 hours	12–24 hours before end of estrus	16½ days
Queen cat		15–21 days	3–4 days, if mated	9–10 days, in absence of male	24–56 hours after coitus	Pseudo-pregnancy
Bitch	24 days	16–30 days	7 days	5–9 days	1–3 days after first acceptance	Pseudo-pregnancy

New Pill Can Relieve the Need for Adult Diapers and Padded Underwear

According to Dr. Seipel, Leaking, Squirming, Squeezing, and Night Time Bathroom Trips... Even Accidents Can Now be a Thing of the Past!

NEW YORK, NEW YORK — If life isn't hard enough, now you have to worry about making it to the bathroom in time. The feeling of your bladder bursting and the down right panic of "not making it" in time can be absolutely overwhelming.

Don't even dare to laugh, cough or sneeze at the "wrong" time and when did you start to become scared to take a big sip of tea, coffee or water? You're not alone in your battle to control your bladder. According to The National Institute of Health, as many as 33 million Americans are affected by bladder control issues described above.

The Family Secret Even the Family Doesn't Know

"Most people who have overactive bladders choose to keep their problem a secret," says Dr. Tracey Seipel, a longtime clinician who is one of the world's leading experts in natural urological healthcare.

"They don't even tell their spouse or families about it. It affects their lives in every way, influencing where they go, and even what they will wear in case they have an accident."

A 100% natural, drug-free aid developed by Dr. Seipel is now available in a remarkable, fast-acting natural formula called UriVarx™ featuring urox. This sophisticated patented herbal compound has been shown in clinical studies to help improve UriVarx™ with reductions in bladder frequency, nocturia (having to urinate at night), urgency, and bladder discomfort, sometimes in as little as two weeks.

Dr. Seipel's formula has made a believer out of 45-year-old, mother of three, Brandy W., from Brisbane, Australia. A friend told her about Dr. Seipel's formula. "I was finding that although I felt I needed to urinate, I wasn't as desperate to run to

the toilet. Now, when I get up in the morning," she adds, "I'm able to make the coffee and even have a cup before needing to go, which is a great improvement!"

How Does It Work?

"UriVarx™ helps support bladder health by revitalizing bladder tone and function, and by helping support the kidney. UriVarx™ promotes normal urinary frequency, and reduces urgency, nocturia and those embarrassing, away-from-home bladder accidents," says Dr. Seipel. "The compound invigorates the tone of the bladder wall, assisting a healthy level of firmness by enhancing the bladder's muscular elasticity. This reduces the frequent urge to urinate."

Positive Clinical Trial

This natural, drug-free UriVarx™ formula has performed well in a clinical study. Thirty days later 77% of participants were experiencing benefits. Results like these are not surprising to Dr. Seipel who single-handedly pioneered the bladder care category in the early 2000's, receiving an award from the prestigious US Nutrition Business Journal for her work.

Her patented formula consisting of select, synergistically paired botanicals like Crateva nurvala, Equisetum arvense and Lindera aggregata, was 15 years in the making.

No More Diapers

Insiders in the adult diaper industry are keeping a close eye on Dr. Seipel's bladder support breakthrough because of people like 78-year-old retired teacher, Glenda B. from Gold Coast, Australia.

Glenda wore adult diapers every day to guard against accidents. "My bladder

Finally a clinically proven pill solution to ease all your bladder problems, without a prescription

capacity was good but the leakage and accidents would occur without warning." Since Glenda discovered Dr. Seipel's UriVarx™ formula, you won't find her shopping in the adult diaper section of the store anymore.

Prostate or Bladder? Hard to Tell

Many men confuse the symptoms of overactive bladder syndrome with prostate woes. Dr. Seipel explains, "Prostate enlargement restricts urine flow. The bladder compensates for this by trying harder and harder to push the urine out." As bladder pressure increases, so does instances of urinary frequency and urgency. Long after a man's prostate woes are relieved, he may still experience the same symptoms thanks to his now-overactive bladder.

"It's a his-and-her formula," she smiles. David M., age 46, can attest to this. "I was having to go to the toilet every hour or so and I had to go to the toilet at least four times per night."

How to Get UriVarx™

If you're ready to alleviate your go-now urination urges, and if you are looking for the confidence and security that a healthy bladder can bring to your life, here's your risk-free opportunity.

Experience the life-changing effect UriVarx™ can have, and get a special introductory discount – **Call Toll-Free: 1-800-736-4601.**

PLANTING BY THE MOON'S PHASE

ACCORDING TO THIS AGE-OLD PRACTICE, CYCLES OF THE MOON AFFECT PLANT GROWTH.

Plant annual flowers and vegetables that bear crops above ground during the light, or waxing, of the Moon: from the day the Moon is new to the day it is full.

Plant flowering bulbs, biennial and perennial flowers, and vegetables that bear crops below ground during the dark, or waning, of the Moon: from the day after it is full to the day before it is new again.

The Moon Favorable columns give the best planting days based on the Moon's phases for 2018. (See the **Left-Hand Calendar Pages, 140–166,** for the exact days of the new and full Moons.) The Planting Dates columns give the safe periods for planting in areas that receive frost. See **Frosts and Growing Seasons, page 248,** for first/last frost dates and the average length of the growing season in your area.

GET LOCAL SEED-SOWING DATES AT ALMANAC.COM/PLANTINGTABLE.

Aboveground crops are marked *.
(E) means early; (L) means late.
Map shades correspond to shades of date columns.

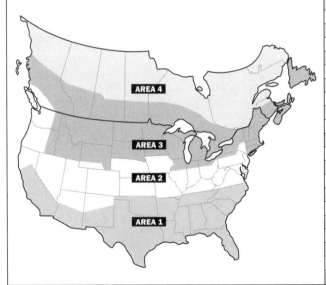

Barley	
* Beans	(E)
	(L)
Beets	(E)
	(L)
* Broccoli plants	(E)
	(L)
* Brussels sprouts	
* Cabbage plants	
Carrots	(E)
	(L)
* Cauliflower plants	(E)
	(L)
* Celery plants	(E)
	(L)
* Collards	(E)
	(L)
* Corn, sweet	(E)
	(L)
* Cucumbers	
* Eggplant plants	
* Endive	(E)
	(L)
* Kale	(E)
	(L)
Leek plants	
* Lettuce	
* Muskmelons	
* Okra	
Onion sets	
* Parsley	
Parsnips	
* Peas	(E)
	(L)
* Pepper plants	
Potatoes	
* Pumpkins	
Radishes	(E)
	(L)
* Spinach	(E)
	(L)
* Squashes	
Sweet potatoes	
* Swiss chard	
* Tomato plants	
Turnips	(E)
	(L)
* Watermelons	
* Wheat, spring	
* Wheat, winter	

PLANTING DATES	MOON FAVORABLE	PLANTING DATES	MOON FAVORABLE	PLANTING DATES	MOON FAVORABLE	PLANTING DATES	MOON FAVORABLE
		AREA 1		AREA 2		AREA 3	AREA 4
15-3/7	2/15-3/1	3/15-4/7	3/17-31	5/15-6/21	5/15-29, 6/13-21	6/1-30	6/13-28
15-4/7	3/17-31	4/15-30	4/15-29	5/7-6/21	5/15-29, 6/13-21	5/30-6/15	6/13-15
/-31	8/11-26	7/1-21	7/12-21	6/15-7/15	6/15-28, 7/12-15	—	—
/-28	2/7-14	3/15-4/3	3/15-16, 4/1-3	5/1-15	5/1-14	5/25-6/10	5/30-6/10
/-30	9/1-8, 9/25-30	8/15-31	8/27-31	7/15-8/15	7/28-8/10	6/15-7/8	6/29-7/8
15-3/15	2/15-3/1	3/7-31	3/17-31	5/15-31	5/15-29	6/1-25	6/13-25
/-30	9/9-24	8/1-20	8/11-20	6/15-7/7	6/15-28	—	—
11-3/20	2/15-3/1, 3/17-20	3/7-4/15	3/17-31, 4/15	5/15-31	5/15-29	6/1-25	6/13-25
11-3/20	2/15-3/1, 3/17-20	3/7-4/15	3/17-31, 4/15	5/15-31	5/15-29	6/1-25	6/13-25
15-3/7	3/2-7	3/7-31	3/7-16	5/15-31	5/30-31	5/25-6/10	5/30-6/10
/-9/7	8/1-10, 8/27-9/7	7/7-31	7/7-11, 7/28-31	6/15-7/21	6/29-7/11	6/15-7/8	6/29-7/8
15-3/7	2/15-3/1	3/15-4/7	3/17-31	5/15-31	5/15-29	6/1-25	6/13-25
/-31	8/11-26	7/1-8/7	7/12-27	6/15-7/21	6/15-28, 7/12-21	—	—
15-28	2/15-28	3/7-31	3/17-31	5/15-6/30	5/15-29, 6/13-28	6/1-30	6/13-28
15-30	9/15-24	8/15-9/7	8/15-26	7/15-8/15	7/15-27, 8/11-15	—	—
11-3/20	2/15-3/1, 3/17-20	3/7-4/7	3/17-31	5/15-31	5/15-29	6/1-25	6/13-25
/-30	9/9-24	8/15-31	8/15-26	7/1-8/7	7/12-27	—	—
15-31	3/17-31	4/1-17	4/15-17	5/10-6/15	5/15-29, 6/13-15	5/30-6/20	6/13-20
/-31	8/11-26	7/7-21	7/12-21	6/15-30	6/15-28	—	—
/-4/15	3/17-31, 4/15	4/7-5/15	4/15-29, 5/15	5/7-6/20	5/15-29, 6/13-20	5/30-6/15	6/13-15
/-4/15	3/17-31, 4/15	4/7-5/15	4/15-29, 5/15	6/1-30	6/13-28	6/15-30	6/15-28
15-3/20	2/15-3/1, 3/17-20	4/7-5/15	4/15-29, 5/15	5/15-31	5/15-29	6/1-25	6/13-25
15-9/7	8/15-26	7/15-8/15	7/15-27, 8/11-15	6/7-30	6/13-28	—	—
11-3/20	2/15-3/1, 3/17-20	3/7-4/7	3/17-31	5/15-31	5/15-29	6/1-15	6/13-15
/-30	9/9-24	8/15-31	8/15-26	7/1-8/7	7/12-27	6/25-7/15	6/25-28, 7/12-15
15-4/15	3/2-16, 4/1-14	3/7-4/7	3/7-16, 4/1-7	5/15-31	5/30-31	6/1-25	6/1-12
15-3/7	2/15-3/1	3/1-31	3/1, 3/17-31	5/15-6/30	5/15-29, 6/13-28	6/1-30	6/13-28
15-4/7	3/17-31	4/15-5/7	4/15-29	5/15-6/30	5/15-29, 6/13-28	6/1-30	6/13-28
15-6/1	4/15-29, 5/15-29	5/25-6/15	5/25-29, 6/13-15	6/15-7/10	6/15-28	6/25-7/7	6/25-28
/-28	2/1-14	3/1-31	3/2-16	5/15-6/7	5/30-6/7	6/1-25	6/1-12
20-3/15	2/20-3/1	3/1-31	3/1, 3/17-31	5/15-31	5/15-29	6/1-15	6/13-15
15-2/4	1/15, 2/1-4	3/7-31	3/7-16	4/1-30	4/1-14, 4/30	5/10-31	5/10-14, 5/30-31
15-2/7	1/16-31	3/7-31	3/17-31	4/15-5/7	4/15-29	5/15-31	5/15-29
15-30	9/15-24	8/7-31	8/11-26	7/15-31	7/15-27	7/10-25	7/12-25
/-20	3/1, 3/17-20	4/1-30	4/15-29	5/15-6/30	5/15-29, 6/13-28	6/1-30	6/13-28
10-28	2/10-14	4/1-30	4/1-14, 4/30	5/1-31	5/1-14, 5/30-31	6/1-25	6/1-12
/-20	3/17-20	4/23-5/15	4/23-29, 5/15	5/15-31	5/15-29	6/1-30	6/13-28
21-3/1	2/1-14	3/7-31	3/7-16	4/15-30	4/30	5/15-6/5	5/30-6/5
/1-21	10/1-7	9/7-30	9/7-8, 9/25-30	8/15-31	8/27-31	7/10-31	7/10-11, 7/28-31
/-3/15	2/15-3/1	3/15-4/20	3/17-31, 4/15-20	5/15-31	5/15-29	6/1-25	6/13-25
/1-21	10/8-21	8/1-9/15	8/11-26, 9/9-15	7/17-9/7	7/17-27, 8/11-26	7/20-8/5	7/20-27
15-4/15	3/17-31, 4/15	4/15-30	4/15-29	5/15-6/15	5/15-29, 6/13-15	6/1-30	6/13-28
23-4/6	4/1-6	4/21-5/9	4/30-5/9	5/15-6/15	5/30-6/12	6/1-30	6/1-12, 6/29-30
/-3/15	2/15-3/1	3/15-4/15	3/15-31, 4/15	5/1-31	5/15-29	5/15-31	5/15-29
/-20	3/17-20	4/7-30	4/15-29	5/15-31	5/15-29	6/1-15	6/13-15
20-2/15	2/1-14	3/15-31	3/15-16	4/7-30	4/7-14, 4/30	5/10-31	5/10-14, 5/30-31
1-10/15	9/1-8, 9/25-10/7	8/1-20	8/1-10	7/1-8/15	7/1-11, 7/28-8/10	—	—
15-4/7	3/17-31	4/15-5/7	4/15-29	5/15-6/30	5/15-29, 6/13-28	6/1-30	6/13-28
15-28	2/15-28	3/1-20	3/1, 3/17-20	4/7-30	4/15-29	5/15-6/10	5/15-29
/15-12/7	10/15-24, 11/7-23, 12/7	9/15-10/20	9/15-24, 10/8-20	8/11-9/15	8/11-26, 9/9-15	8/5-30	8/11-26

FROSTS AND GROWING SEASONS

Dates given are normal averages for a light freeze; local weather and topography may cause considerable variations. The possibility of frost occurring after the spring dates and before the fall dates is 50 percent. The classification of freeze temperatures is usually based on their effect on plants. **Light freeze:** 29° to 32°F—tender plants killed. **Moderate freeze:** 25° to 28°F—widely destructive to most plants. **Severe freeze:** 24°F and colder—heavy damage to most plants. –dates courtesy of National Centers for Environmental Information

STATE	CITY	GROWING SEASON (DAYS)	LAST SPRING FROST	FIRST FALL FROST	STATE	CITY	GROWING SEASON (DAYS)	LAST SPRING FROST	FIRST FALL FROST
AK	Juneau	153	May 3	Oct. 4	ND	Bismarck	134	May 12	Sept. 24
AL	Mobile	272	Mar 2	Nov. 30	NE	Omaha	172	Apr. 21	Oct. 11
AR	Pine Bluff	243	Mar. 17	Nov. 16	NE	North Platte	156	May 2	Oct. 6
AZ	Phoenix	*	*	*	NH	Concord	139	May 13	Sept. 30
AZ	Tucson	291	Feb. 17	Dec. 6	NJ	Newark	220	Apr. 3	Nov. 10
CA	Eureka	301	Feb. 15	Dec. 14	NM	Carlsbad	219	Mar. 31	Nov. 6
CA	Sacramento	280	Feb. 20	Nov. 28	NM	Los Alamos	158	May 4	Oct. 10
CA	San Francisco	*	*	*	NV	Las Vegas	315	Jan. 29	Dec. 11
CO	Denver	155	May 3	Oct. 6	NY	Albany	164	Apr. 28	Oct. 10
CT	Hartford	171	Apr. 24	Oct. 13	NY	Syracuse	167	Apr. 29	Oct. 14
DE	Wilmington	206	Apr. 8	Nov. 1	OH	Akron	177	Apr. 26	Oct. 21
FL	Miami	*	*	*	OH	Cincinnati	187	Apr. 17	Oct. 22
FL	Tallahassee	244	Mar. 19	Nov. 19	OK	Lawton	226	Mar. 26	Nov. 8
GA	Athens	229	Mar. 26	Nov. 11	OK	Tulsa	219	Mar. 30	Nov. 5
GA	Savannah	266	Mar. 6	Nov. 28	OR	Pendleton	162	Apr. 26	Oct. 6
IA	Atlantic	147	May 2	Sept. 27	OR	Portland	245	Mar. 16	Nov. 17
IA	Cedar Rapids	168	Apr. 25	Oct. 11	PA	Franklin	169	May 3	Oct. 20
ID	Boise	167	Apr. 30	Oct. 15	PA	Williamsport	173	Apr. 27	Oct. 18
IL	Chicago	198	Apr. 12	Oct. 28	RI	Kingston	151	May 7	Oct. 6
IL	Springfield	181	Apr. 17	Oct. 16	SC	Charleston	265	Mar. 8	Nov. 29
IN	Indianapolis	183	Apr. 19	Oct. 20	SC	Columbia	223	Mar. 28	Nov. 7
IN	South Bend	174	Apr. 27	Oct. 19	SD	Rapid City	140	May 11	Sept. 29
KS	Topeka	187	Apr. 15	Oct. 20	TN	Memphis	242	Mar. 18	Nov. 16
KY	Lexington	195	Apr. 14	Oct. 27	TN	Nashville	209	Apr. 6	Nov. 2
LA	Monroe	251	Mar. 9	Nov. 16	TX	Amarillo	191	Apr. 15	Oct. 24
LA	New Orleans	329	Jan. 31	Dec. 27	TX	Denton	242	Mar. 19	Nov. 17
MA	Worcester	179	Apr. 22	Oct. 19	TX	San Antonio	274	Mar. 1	Dec. 1
MD	Baltimore	199	Apr. 12	Oct. 29	UT	Cedar City	137	May 19	Oct. 4
ME	Portland	161	May 1	Oct. 10	UT	Spanish Fork	172	Apr. 28	Oct. 18
MI	Lansing	159	May 2	Oct. 9	VA	Norfolk	249	Mar. 20	Nov. 25
MI	Marquette	167	May 4	Oct. 19	VA	Richmond	213	Apr. 4	Nov. 4
MN	Duluth	132	May 17	Sept. 27	VT	Burlington	156	May 4	Oct. 8
MN	Willmar	156	Apr. 30	Oct. 4	WA	Seattle	257	Mar. 8	Nov. 21
MO	Jefferson City	201	Apr. 8	Oct. 27	WA	Spokane	159	Apr. 30	Oct. 7
MS	Columbia	252	Mar. 11	Nov. 19	WI	Green Bay	150	May 5	Oct. 3
MS	Tupelo	224	Mar. 27	Nov. 7	WI	Sparta	148	May 6	Oct. 2
MT	Fort Peck	141	May 9	Sept. 28	WV	Parkersburg	193	Apr. 16	Oct. 27
MT	Helena	134	May 13	Sept. 25	WY	Casper	118	May 25	Sept. 21
NC	Fayetteville	221	Apr. 1	Nov. 9	*Frosts do not occur every year.				

THE OLD
FARMER'S STORE

GIFTS FOR ANY OCCASION!

❧ PURVEYORS OF ❧

ALMANACS ☼ CALENDARS ☼ COOKBOOKS

KITCHEN APRONS • COUNTER STORAGE SOLUTIONS

OUTDOOR THERMOMETERS	GARDEN STAKES	WIND BELLS AND SPINNERS	RAIN GAUGES	GARDEN SIGNAGE

GLASS SUN CATCHERS • HOME GOODS

DECORATIVE OUTDOOR LIGHTING ☼ DOORMATS

WALL DECORATIONS	HAND SOAP	HARVEST BASKETS	NIGHT LIGHTS	COAT RACKS	BALSAM FIR PILLOWS

RAIN CHAINS • DOORSTOPS • READING MAGNIFIERS

CANDLES ☼ ALPACA SOCKS ☼ AND MORE!

Genuine Old Farmer's Almanac–Branded Merchandise

Exclusive Almanac Publications & Offers

❧ CONTINUOUS PROPRIETORSHIP SINCE 1792 ❧

Open Daily | Immense Assortment

WWW.ALMANAC.COM/SHOP • 1-877-717-8924

TABLE OF MEASURES

LINEAR
1 hand = 4 inches
1 link = 7.92 inches
1 span = 9 inches
1 foot = 12 inches
1 yard = 3 feet
1 rod = 5½ yards
1 mile = 320 rods = 1,760 yards = 5,280 feet
1 international nautical mile = 6,076.1155 feet
1 knot = 1 nautical mile per hour
1 fathom = 2 yards = 6 feet
1 furlong = ⅛ mile = 660 feet = 220 yards
1 league = 3 miles = 24 furlongs
1 chain = 100 links = 22 yards

SQUARE
1 square foot = 144 square inches
1 square yard = 9 square feet
1 square rod = 30½ square yards = 272½ square feet = 625 square links

1 square chain = 16 square rods
1 acre = 10 square chains = 160 square rods = 43,560 square feet
1 square mile = 640 acres = 102,400 square rods

CUBIC
1 cubic foot = 1,728 cubic inches
1 cubic yard = 27 cubic feet
1 cord = 128 cubic feet
1 U.S. liquid gallon = 4 quarts = 231 cubic inches
1 imperial gallon = 1.20 U.S. gallons = 0.16 cubic foot
1 board foot = 144 cubic inches

DRY
2 pints = 1 quart
4 quarts = 1 gallon
2 gallons = 1 peck
4 pecks = 1 bushel

LIQUID
4 gills = 1 pint
63 gallons = 1 hogshead
2 hogsheads = 1 pipe or butt
2 pipes = 1 tun

KITCHEN
3 teaspoons = 1 tablespoon
16 tablespoons = 1 cup
1 cup = 8 ounces
2 cups = 1 pint
2 pints = 1 quart
4 quarts = 1 gallon

AVOIRDUPOIS
(for general use)
1 ounce = 16 drams
1 pound = 16 ounces
1 short hundredweight = 100 pounds
1 ton = 2,000 pounds
1 long ton = 2,240 pounds

APOTHECARIES'
(for pharmaceutical use)
1 scruple = 20 grains
1 dram = 3 scruples
1 ounce = 8 drams
1 pound = 12 ounces

METRIC CONVERSIONS

LINEAR
1 inch = 2.54 centimeters
1 centimeter = 0.39 inch
1 meter = 39.37 inches
1 yard = 0.914 meter
1 mile = 1.61 kilometers
1 kilometer = 0.62 mile

SQUARE
1 square inch = 6.45 square centimeters
1 square yard = 0.84 square meter
1 square mile = 2.59 square kilometers

1 square kilometer = 0.386 square mile
1 acre = 0.40 hectare
1 hectare = 2.47 acres

CUBIC
1 cubic yard = 0.76 cubic meter
1 cubic meter = 1.31 cubic yards

HOUSEHOLD
½ teaspoon = 2 mL
1 teaspoon = 5 mL
1 tablespoon = 15 mL
¼ cup = 60 mL

⅓ cup = 75 mL
½ cup = 125 mL
⅔ cup = 150 mL
¾ cup = 175 mL
1 cup = 250 mL
1 liter = 1.057 U.S. liquid quarts
1 U.S. liquid quart = 0.946 liter
1 U.S. liquid gallon = 3.78 liters
1 gram = 0.035 ounce
1 ounce = 28.349 grams
1 kilogram = 2.2 pounds
1 pound = 0.45 kilogram

TO CONVERT CELSIUS AND FAHRENHEIT: $°C = (°F - 32)/1.8$; $°F = (°C \times 1.8) + 32$

TIDAL GLOSSARY

APOGEAN TIDE: A monthly tide of decreased range that occurs when the Moon is at apogee (farthest from Earth).

DIURNAL TIDE: A tide with one high water and one low water in a tidal day of approximately 24 hours.

MEAN LOWER LOW WATER: The arithmetic mean of the lesser of a daily pair of low waters, observed over a specific 19-year cycle called the National Tidal Datum Epoch.

NEAP TIDE: A tide of decreased range that occurs twice a month, when the Moon is in quadrature (during its first and last quarters, when the Sun and the Moon are at right angles to each other relative to Earth).

PERIGEAN TIDE: A monthly tide of increased range that occurs when the Moon is at perigee (closest to Earth).

SEMIDIURNAL TIDE: A tide with one high water and one low water every half day. East Coast tides, for example, are semidiurnal, with two highs and two lows during a tidal day of approximately 24 hours.

SPRING TIDE: A tide of increased range that occurs at times of syzygy each month. Named not for the season of spring but from the German *springen* ("to leap up"), a spring tide also brings a lower low water.

SYZYGY: The nearly straight-line configuration that occurs twice a month, when the Sun and the Moon are in conjunction (on the same side of Earth, at the new Moon) and when they are in opposition (on opposite sides of Earth, at the full Moon). In both cases, the gravitational effects of the Sun and the Moon reinforce each other, and tidal range is increased.

VANISHING TIDE: A mixed tide of considerable inequality in the two highs and two lows, so that the lower high (or higher low) may appear to vanish. ∎

(continued from page 207)
CHIFFON RECIPES

Chocolate Chiffon Cake

The oil in chiffon cake keeps it moist, while the beaten egg whites make it light and fluffy. The oil does not contribute as much flavor as butter, so many recipes include added flavors, such as citrus or cocoa. For a truly elegant dessert, cut the cake into layers, spread with your favorite filling, and stack.

CAKE:
2 eggs, separated
1½ cups sugar, divided
1¾ cups sifted cake flour
¾ teaspoon baking soda
¾ teaspoon salt
⅓ cup vegetable oil
1 cup buttermilk
2 ounces unsweetened chocolate, melted

ICING:
2 cups sifted confectioners' sugar
⅓ cup butter, softened
2 ounces unsweetened chocolate, melted
¼ teaspoon salt

For cake:

1. Preheat oven to 350°F. Grease and flour two round 8-inch cake pans or one 13x9-inch pan.

2. In a bowl, beat egg whites until frothy. Gradually beat in ½ cup sugar. Continue beating until stiff and glossy, then set aside.

3. In another bowl, sift remaining sugar, flour, baking soda, and salt. Add oil and ½ cup buttermilk. Beat for 1 minute at medium speed or by hand for 150 strokes. Scrape sides and bottom of

bowl constantly. Add remaining ½ cup buttermilk, egg yolks, and chocolate. Beat for 1 minute more, scraping bowl constantly. Fold in egg whites mixture.

4. Pour batter into prepared pans. Bake round pans for 30 to 35 minutes or the 13x9-inch pan for 40 to 45 minutes. Cool.

For icing:

1. In a bowl, combine confectioners' sugar, butter, chocolate, and salt. Beat until fluffy and spread over cooled cake. **Makes 8 to 10 servings.**

Strawberry Chiffon Pie

Chiffon pie is a one-crust pie filled with a melt-in-your-mouth flavored filling that contains gelatin and beaten egg whites.

your favorite piecrust
1¾ pounds fresh strawberries
¾ cup plus 1 tablespoon sugar
1 tablespoon lemon juice
¼ cup cranberry juice cocktail
1 tablespoon unflavored gelatin
   (about 2 packets)
2 cups whipping cream, divided
1 teaspoon vanilla extract
6 medium-size strawberries, halved,
   for garnish

1. Preheat oven to 350°F.

2. Prepare crust and bake as directed. Set aside to cool.

3. In a bowl, stir together 1¾ pounds strawberries, ¾ cup sugar, and lemon juice. Using a potato masher or pastry cutter, mash berries. Chill until softened and very juicy, about 30 minutes.

4. Warm cranberry juice in microwave until just steaming. Stir into gelatin and whisk until smooth. Stir gelatin mixture into mashed berries. Chill until partially set, about 20 minutes.

5. Whip 1 cup cream to medium-size peaks and stir into berry mixture. Pour into baked piecrust and chill until firm, about 1 hour.

6. Whip remaining 1 cup cream with remaining 1 tablespoon sugar and vanilla to firm peaks; spread or pipe over top of pie. Garnish with strawberry halves.

Makes 8 servings. ■

(continued from page 60)

PARSLEY RECIPES

Parsley comes into its own when used fresh and in quantity.

Chimichurri

Argentina, famous for its beef, gives us this garlicky green sauce, a perfect condiment for grilled steak.

3 to 5 cloves garlic, or to taste
1 cup packed flat-leaf parsley leaves and stems
⅓ cup packed fresh cilantro leaves
½ cup olive oil
3 tablespoons red-wine vinegar
½ teaspoon salt
¼ teaspoon crushed red pepper flakes, or to taste
¼ teaspoon freshly ground black pepper

1. Place all ingredients in a food processor and process until a smooth sauce is formed. Taste and adjust seasonings. Transfer to a bowl, cover, and let stand at room temperature for 1 hour before serving. Spoon over grilled steak. Any leftovers will keep

at room temperature, covered, for up to 2 days.

Makes about 1 cup.

Persillade

Its name coming from the French word for parsley, persil, *this mixture is sometimes augmented with fresh bread crumbs, lemon zest, and olive oil to make a seasoning or sauce. In French Canada, persillade is often added to cubes of fried potatoes near the end of cooking or to poutine for a punch of flavor.*

Basic Persillade

Add a spoonful to vegetable dishes, soups, and other dishes near the end of cooking.

1½ cups flat-leaf parsley leaves
3 to 4 large cloves garlic

1. In a food processor or by hand, finely chop parsley and garlic together. Leftovers can be stored in the refrigerator in a sealed container for up to 2 weeks.

Makes about 1½ cups.

Variation: Gremolata

This Italian seasoning, sprinkled over vegetables, pork, or lamb, contributes what one food writer called "the cymbals of the food orchestra."

3 tablespoons minced flat-leaf parsley leaves
2 cloves garlic, minced
1 tablespoon grated lemon zest

1. Stir ingredients together in a small bowl. Leftovers can be stored in the refrigerator in a sealed container for 3 to 4 days.

Makes about ¼ cup.

(continued)

Italian Salsa Verde

Not to be confused with Mexican salsa verde, which has a tomatillo base, this uncooked green sauce is delicious as a dip for raw vegetables, cooked shrimp, or crusty bread or served with grilled fish.

2 anchovy fillets
1 large clove garlic, minced
1 teaspoon grated lemon zest
½ teaspoon salt
½ teaspoon freshly ground black pepper
¼ teaspoon crushed red pepper flakes
3 tablespoons fresh lemon juice
¾ cup extra-virgin olive oil
1 cup chopped flat-leaf parsley leaves

1. Using a mortar and pestle, or in a bowl using a fork, combine anchovies, garlic, lemon zest, salt, pepper, and crushed red pepper flakes and mash together to form a paste. Whisk in lemon juice and slowly add olive oil to blend. Stir in parsley and taste for seasonings. Can be made several hours ahead and chilled; return to room temperature before serving and stir well. Leftovers can be stored in the refrigerator in a sealed container for 2 to 3 days.
Makes about 1 cup. ∎

(continued from page 77)
CHICKEN RECIPES

Chicken Potpie

1 chicken (3 pounds), cut into pieces
1 bay leaf
1 teaspoon salt
5 onions, quartered
1½ cups chopped carrots
1 cup fresh or frozen peas
1 cup chopped fresh mushrooms
½ teaspoon poultry seasoning
salt and freshly ground black pepper, to taste
⅓ cup all-purpose flour
½ cup milk
pastry for a single-crust 9-inch pie
1 egg yolk, beaten with 1 tablespoon water

1. Place chicken, bay leaf, salt, and 2 cups of water in a large stockpot. Bring to a boil, then reduce heat to low, cover, and simmer for 1 hour, or until chicken is tender. Strain broth, discard bay leaf, and return to stockpot. Cool chicken, remove meat from bones, and cut into large chunks; set aside.

2. Add onions and carrots to broth and cook, covered, until tender. Drain broth, adding enough water to make 2⅓ cups of liquid, and return to stockpot. Add peas, mushrooms, poultry seasoning, salt and pepper, and chicken.

3. In a bowl, combine flour and milk and mix until smooth. Stir flour mixture into broth and cook over medium heat, stirring constantly, until mixture boils and thickens. Pour hot mixture into a 2-quart casserole.

4. Preheat oven to 400°F.

5. Roll out pastry to fit top of casserole. Place crust over chicken mixture and trim edge, leaving enough to form a ridge. Flute edges and cut slits to vent. Brush with egg wash. Bake for 30 to 35 minutes, or until crust is golden. **Makes 6 servings.**

Chicken, Apple, and Cheese Casserole

5 tablespoons butter, softened, divided
3 apples, cored and sliced
2 onions, thinly sliced
1 teaspoon salt
¼ teaspoon freshly ground black pepper
6 skinless, boneless chicken breast halves
½ cup shredded Swiss cheese
½ cup grated Parmesan cheese
¼ cup dry bread crumbs
½ teaspoon dried thyme
2 tablespoons apple cider or apple juice

1. Preheat oven to 350°F. Coat a 2-quart baking dish with 1 tablespoon of the butter.

2. In a heavy skillet over medium heat, melt the remaining butter. Add apples and onions and cook for 10 minutes, or until apples are tender. Spoon into prepared baking dish.

3. Sprinkle salt and pepper on both sides of chicken, then place on the apple–onion mixture.

4. In a bowl, combine Swiss, Parmesan, bread crumbs, and thyme. Sprinkle over chicken. Drizzle apple cider over the cheese mixture. Bake for 35 minutes, or until cheeses are golden and juices run clear when meat is pierced with a fork. **Makes 6 servings.**

Photo: Becky Luigart-Stayner

Fried Chicken With Cheese

4 skinless, boneless chicken breast halves
4 thick slices Monterey Jack cheese
4 sprigs fresh sage or ½ teaspoon dried sage
2 eggs
1 tablespoon grated Parmesan cheese
1 tablespoon minced fresh parsley
¼ teaspoon salt
¼ teaspoon freshly ground black pepper
1 cup all-purpose flour
¼ cup butter

1. Cut a deep pocket in each chicken breast, being careful not to cut all the way through. In each pocket, place a cheese slice and a sprig of sage. Cover and chill for 2 hours or longer.

2. Preheat oven to 375°F. Spray a baking sheet with nonstick spray.

3. In a bowl, combine eggs, Parmesan, parsley, salt, and pepper.

4. In a separate bowl, place flour. Roll chicken breasts in flour, shake to remove excess, then dip in egg mixture; repeat twice.

5. In a heavy skillet over medium heat, melt the butter. Cook breasts until crisp on both sides, then place on prepared baking sheet. Bake for 10 to 15 minutes, or until juices run clear when meat is pierced with a fork. **Makes 4 servings.**

(continued)

Slow Cooker Chicken Tacos

3 boneless chicken breast halves
1 container (8 ounces) cream cheese
1 packet (1.25 ounces) taco seasoning
1 can (15 ounces) black beans, drained
   and rinsed
1 can (14.5 ounces) fire-roasted tomatoes
   with chiles
hard or soft taco shells
shredded lettuce, for topping
shredded cheese, for topping

1. Place chicken in slow cooker.

2. In a bowl, completely mix together cream cheese and taco seasoning. Add to slow cooker on top of chicken. Add black beans and tomatoes. Cook on low for 6 to 7 hours, or until chicken is very tender.

3. Remove chicken and shred with two forks. Put chicken back into slow cooker and stir.

4. Serve in taco shells with lettuce, cheese, or taco toppings of your choice.
Makes 6 servings. ∎

(continued from page 88)

FORAGE RECIPES

Elder Blow Fritters

Pick flower clusters when they are at their peak, keeping clusters intact.

1 cup all-purpose flour
1 tablespoon sugar, plus more for topping
1 teaspoon baking powder
2 eggs
½ cup milk
12 elder flower clusters
oil for frying

1. In a bowl, mix together flour, sugar, baking powder, eggs, and milk. Dip flower clusters in batter to coat.

2. Heat oil to 375°F. Fry coated flowers until golden brown, about 4 minutes. Drain on paper towels. Sprinkle with sugar. Serve hot.
Makes 4 servings.

Pasta With Cattails

This recipe is from the Wild Vegan Cookbook *(Harvard Common Press, 2010) by Steve Brill.*

1½ pounds peeled young cattail stalks
24 ounces any pasta
½ cup olive oil, divided
4 cloves garlic, finely chopped
½ cup chopped fresh parsley
salt and freshly ground black pepper,
   to taste

1. In a pot of boiling water, cook cattail stalks for 7 to 10 minutes. Drain and cut into 1-inch pieces.

2. In another pot, bring salted water to a boil. Add pasta and 1 tablespoon olive oil. Cook pasta al dente. Drain.

3. In a skillet, heat remaining olive oil, add boiled cattail pieces, and cook for 10 minutes, stirring often. Add garlic and cook for 2 minutes. Add pasta, parsley, and salt and pepper. Heat through and serve.
Makes 6 to 8 servings.

Crustless Quiche With Milkweed Flowers

4 eggs
2 cups milk
¾ teaspoon salt
pinch of ground nutmeg
1 cup grated cheddar or Swiss cheese
8 ounces cooked milkweed flower buds

1. Preheat oven to 425°F. Grease a 9-inch pie pan.

2. In a bowl, combine eggs, milk, salt, and nutmeg and beat with a whisk just until all ingredients are mixed.

3. Arrange cheese and milkweed flower buds in prepared pie plate. Add egg mixture.

4. Bake for 15 minutes. Reduce heat to 300°F and cook for 40 minutes more, or until a knife inserted into the center comes out clean.
Makes 8 servings.

Plaintain Chips

Steve Brill suggests using mature plantain leaves for this recipe and leaves spices and olive oil amounts to taste.

1. Preheat oven to 300°F.

2. Toss torn pieces of plantain leaves with olive oil and your favorite spices.

3. Bake until leaves are dry and crispy, checking them every 5 minutes. ■

(continued from page 79)

SWEET POTATO RECIPE CONTEST WINNERS

FIRST PRIZE: $250
No-Churn Sweet Potato Casserole Ice Cream

1½ tablespoons unsalted butter
¾ cup chopped pecans
1¼ tablespoons dark-brown sugar, packed
1 cup mini marshmallows
scant 2 cups puréed sweet potato
1 can (14 ounces) sweetened condensed milk
1 teaspoon vanilla extract
1 teaspoon ground cinnamon
½ teaspoon ground ginger
pinch grated nutmeg
2 cups heavy whipping cream, chilled

1. Place a 9x5-inch loaf pan in the freezer and allow to chill while preparing ice cream. Line a baking sheet with parchment paper and set aside.

2. In a skillet, melt butter over medium heat. Add pecans and toast lightly, stirring occasionally, for 2 minutes, or until fragrant. Sprinkle brown sugar over pecans and cook, stirring constantly for 2 to 3 minutes, or until sugar caramelizes and makes a glaze. Pour candied pecans onto prepared baking sheet in a single layer. Set aside and allow to cool and harden.

3. On a nonstick baking sheet, spread out marshmallows, making sure that they are not touching. Place baking sheet in oven and broil marshmallows

until lightly browned. Set aside and allow to cool completely.

4. In a bowl, whisk together sweet potato purée, condensed milk, vanilla, cinnamon, ginger, and nutmeg until smooth.

5. In the bowl of a stand mixer, whip heavy cream for 3 to 5 minutes, or until medium peaks form. Using a spatula, very gently fold sweet potato mixture into whipped cream. Add candied pecans and marshmallows and gently fold a few times to fully incorporate.

6. Pour mixture into chilled loaf pan and cover tightly with plastic wrap, making sure that the plastic touches the ice cream to help in preventing crystallization. Place a second layer of plastic wrap over the top, sealing the edges of the pan, and place in freezer for at least 6 hours.

Makes 10 to 12 servings.

–Lindsay Sprunk, Brooklyn, New York

SECOND PRIZE: $150

Sweet Potato Lentil Coconut Curry

2 teaspoons coconut oil
5 cloves garlic, minced
½ medium onion, diced
1 cup diced tomatoes
2 tablespoons minced fresh ginger or
   1 teaspoon ground ginger
1 teaspoon curry powder
½ teaspoon turmeric
½ teaspoon cayenne powder
5 cups peeled and diced sweet potato
1 can (15 ounces) full-fat coconut milk
3 tablespoons red curry paste
1 tablespoon coconut sugar or brown
   sugar

2 cups cooked red lentils
3 tablespoons chopped cilantro,
   plus more for garnish
salt, to taste

1. In a large pan, melt coconut oil over medium heat. Add garlic, onions, tomatoes, and ginger. Cook for 5 to 6 minutes, or until fragrant and translucent.

2. Sprinkle curry powder, turmeric, and cayenne over diced sweet potatoes and toss to coat.

3. Pour coconut milk over tomato mixture and whisk in curry paste and sugar until smooth. Add seasoned sweet potatoes, cover, and simmer for 25 to 30 minutes, or until sweet potatoes are tender. Add lentils, remove from heat, and let stand for 10 minutes to thicken. If too thick, add water, 1 tablespoon at a time, to thin. Add cilantro and salt and adjust seasonings to taste. Garnish with cilantro.

Makes 6 to 8 servings.

–Lucia Qian, Cockeysville, Maryland

THIRD PRIZE: $100

Roasted Garlic Sweet Potato Mac-'n-Cheese

10 cloves garlic, peeled
4 tablespoons extra-virgin olive oil,
   divided
1 pound sweet potatoes, peeled and sliced
   ¼-inch thick
12 ounces macaroni elbows
4 tablespoons (½ stick) butter
4 tablespoons all-purpose flour
½ teaspoon salt
⅛ teaspoon freshly ground black pepper
3 cups half-and-half
2 cups shredded Italian blend cheese,
   divided

¾ cup shredded Asiago cheese, divided
pinch of rosemary
3 cloves garlic, minced
¼ cup Italian panko bread crumbs

1. Preheat oven to 350°F. Butter a
2-quart baking dish.

2. Place peeled garlic on a sheet of
aluminum foil, coat with 2 tablespoons
olive oil, and wrap tightly. Roast for
20 minutes, or until golden. Remove
from foil, mash, and set aside.

3. Place sweet potatoes in a pot of
water and bring to a boil. Cook for
6 minutes, or until fork tender.

4. In a skillet over medium heat, warm
1 tablespoon olive oil. Add sweet
potatoes and cook until caramelized.
Remove from skillet and dice into cubes.

5. Bring a large pot of water to a boil
and add macaroni. Cook for 8 minutes,
stirring often. Drain, then set pasta aside.

6. In the same pot, melt butter
over low heat. Add flour, stirring
constantly for 3 minutes. Add salt
and pepper and whisk in half-and-
half. Increase heat to medium and
allow mixture to boil. Turn off heat
and add 1¾ cups Italian blend cheese
and ½ cup Asiago cheese. Whisk
until smooth, then add mashed garlic,
sweet potatoes, rosemary, minced
garlic, and pasta. Stir to combine,
then pour into prepared baking dish.

7. In a bowl, combine bread crumbs
with remaining cheeses and olive oil.
Sprinkle over macaroni mixture and
bake for 25 to 30 minutes, or until
bubbling and golden brown.
Makes 6 servings.

–Tommy Aquaro, Bumpass, Virginia

Ham and Sweet Potato Hash With Maple Pecan Drizzle

HASH:
1 ham steak (10 ounces), cut into small cubes
3 tablespoons vegetable oil
2 cups peeled and diced sweet potato
½ teaspoon salt
¼ teaspoon freshly ground black pepper
½ teaspoon ground cinnamon

MAPLE PECAN DRIZZLE:
½ cup maple syrup
½ teaspoon ground cinnamon
½ cup chopped toasted pecans

For hash:
1. Spray a skillet with nonstick
cooking spray and warm over
medium heat. Add ham and cook
until browned. Remove ham from
skillet. Add oil and sweet potatoes
to skillet. Cook sweet potatoes for
10 to 12 minutes, or until tender. Add
salt, pepper, and ham. Stir, then add
cinnamon. Cook for 5 minutes more.

For maple pecan drizzle:
1. In a bowl, combine maple syrup and
cinnamon. Heat in microwave for
30 seconds. Stir in pecan pieces.

Spoon hash onto serving plate and
cover with Maple Pecan Drizzle.
Makes 2 servings.

–Amy Freeze, Avon Park, Florida ■

ENTER THE 2018 RECIPE CONTEST: ORANGES
Got a great recipe using oranges
that's loved by family and friends?
It could win! See contest rules on
page 267.

GENERAL STORE CLASSIFIEDS

For advertising information and rates, go to Almanac.com/Advertising
or call RJ Media at 212-986-0016. The 2019 edition closes on May 1, 2018.

CLASSIFIEDS

MADDENING MIND-MANGLERS

Count Me In

In this matching quiz, each question asks you to count something having to do with its words or numbers, possibly including the way they visually appear or characteristics of the words that spell out the digits in the questions. Ignore the word "plus" (+), as well as the sum of any mathematical question (consider only the numbers shown).

EXAMPLES:

A. 14 + 53 has 3 (answer: odd numbers)

B. Understudy has 4 (answer: consecutive letters of the alphabet, r-s-t-u)

C. 49 + 343 has 2 (answer: pairs of digits, 3's and 4's)

QUIZ:

1. Gnome has 1 _____ .

2. Pothole has 2 _____ .

3. 14 + 62 has 3 _____ .

4. 126 + 310 has 4 _____ .

5. 19 + 883 has 5 _____ .

6. Facetiously has 6 _____ .

7. 2 + 4 has 7 _____ .

8. 326 + 741 + 85 has 8 _____ .

9. 22 + 35 + 33 has 9 _____ .

10. Incomprehensible has 10 _____ .

A. circles in its digits

B. letters in its spelled out words

C. separate words that make a whole word when combined

D. consonants

E. vowels

F. different digits

G. silent letter(s)

H. curves in its digits

I. three-letter numbers

J. even numbers

BONUS:
Step + ward has 2 what?

ANSWERS:

1. G; **2.** C (pot, hole); **3.** J; **4.** I (one, two, six, ten); **5.** A (8 = two, 9 = one); **6.** E (in alphabetical order, no less); **7.** B; **8.** F; **9.** H (2 = one, 3 = one, 5 = two); **10.** D; **BONUS:** words that are semordnilaps (Itself a semordnilap of "palindromes," a semordnilap is a word that makes a different word when spelled backward, in this case "pets" and "draw"—as opposed to a palindrome, such as "racecar," which creates the same word when spelled forward and backward.)

–adapted from Morris Bowles

2017 ESSAY CONTEST WINNERS
"The Historical Figure I Would Most Like to Meet and Why"

First Prize: $250

Growing up on a farm in northern Rhode Island surrounded by a long line of German shepherd dogs sparked my soul-self to reach out to Rin Tin Tin. If I could, I would say:

I honor the journey your physical life took on that WWI battlefield where you were found. Bred to be a soldier's comrade, you somehow defied the odds and became a force for good instead of evil. You overcame abandonment, the loss of your sister, a broken leg, and more. You inspired movies, poems, and television and radio shows, then ultimately a bloodline that today provides service dogs for children. To say that everything and everyone in our great universe has a purpose is an understatement when one realizes the people, places, and things that all had to magically cooperate in your achieving what many humans strive to do: become your highest and best self, benefiting life in general. Thank you for the unconditional love you gave to our world.

Signed,
A grateful Human who wishes to remain anonymous

P.S. Thank you for reminding me of all the great German shepherd loves in my life and dogs in general.

–Loribeth Landolfi, South Kingstown, Rhode Island

Second Prize: $150

Whenever I come to babysit, Maddie shouts "Hannah!" and gives me a big hug. We look through her old yearbooks and listen to Taylor Swift. Maddie has Down syndrome. There once was a time when people like Maddie weren't considered worthy of society. But Eunice Kennedy Shriver helped to change that. If I met Eunice, I would ask her about her work in creating the Special Olympics and how it shifted perceptions of mentally disabled people. Her own disabled sister was lobotomized in 1941 and spent the rest of her life in an institution. When mothers called Eunice telling her that their mentally disabled children wouldn't be accepted into a summer camp, her response was "Enough." She immediately started Camp Shriver, created for special needs children.

This developed into the Special Olympics, a place where people with mental disabilities had purpose. When people think of the mentally disabled today, they think of people, individuals like Maddie. I can't imagine a time when someone would look at Maddie and see a burden to society. But some still do. I would ask Eunice where to start after I witness oppression.

She taught us that we must create transformations, we must say "Enough."

–Hannah Reich, Atlanta, Georgia

Third Prize: $100

One day, a young girl moved. On her first day of fourth grade, she walked down the hall to her classroom filled with joy. This was her fourth new school, and every first day was always her favorite.

But, when she walked into the classroom, her excitement disappeared. None of the children looked like her. At recess, she went to play but none of the students would talk to her, and at lunch, she sat alone, hearing the other kids talk about how different she was. "Why is her hair like that?"

It went on for months. Every night she cried, wishing her hair was like the others, and begged her mom to straighten it. One day, her mom took her on a road trip to Tennessee and they went to an MLK museum. The girl walked past the pictures, until she saw one woman with hair just like hers, big, brown, and curly. "Who is that, Mom?"

"Well, that's Angela Davis. She fought for equal rights."

Ever since that day, I have been proud of my hair and all of my other differences because Angela Davis fought for them, and that's why I would love to meet her.

–Sidney Stutzman-Hatchett, Hartland, Wisconsin ■

ANECDOTES & PLEASANTRIES

*A sampling from the thousands of letters, clippings,
articles, and emails sent to us by Almanac readers from all over
the United States and Canada during the past year.*

I Can't Believe It's Butter

....

Oh, yes, you can.

–courtesy of K. B., Sioux City,
Iowa, from washingtonpost.com

....

Irish peat cutter Jack Conway dug up a 22-lb. chunk of 2,000-year-old butter in 2016. It turns out that this find was neither the first nor the largest butter cache yet discovered, a 77-lb. cask of 3,000-year-old spread having been unearthed in 2009.

The coolness and acidity of peat bogs helps them to act as refrigerators, a fact well known to northern settlers throughout the ages. In fact, a 1689 Irish poem refers to "butter to eat with their hog, was seven years buried in a bog." Experts who have tasted the centuries-old spreads have declared them to be like cheese.

SPECIAL DELIVERY?

....

*The mail must go through,
but this is a mystery!*

–courtesy of R. W., Yuba City, California

....

In 1972, I went to work driving a truck in California. My shipping manager was named Fred. We became friends and proceeded to "party on" through the 1970s. Then we parted ways. We never saw each other again until 2005, at which time we renewed our friendship.

Fred passed away in 2014, but my wife and I kept in contact with his wife. In December 2015, Fred's wife mailed a Christmas card from her home in Hickory, North Carolina, to us in Yuba City, California. How it got there, we'll never know: On the envelope was her return address in the top left corner and a cancelled postage stamp in the top right corner—but there was no delivery address! Not my name, my wife's name, our street, our town or state or zip code! The mailman said, after looking it over, "I guess you were supposed to get it."

Bear With Us for Yet Another Way to Forecast the Weather

....

Just when we thought we'd heard them all . . .

–courtesy of M. S., Alamagordo, New Mexico

....

Bear grease weather predicting is legendary in the Southwest. The technique is believed to have originated with the Mescalero Apaches centuries ago, and it was popularized by Gordon "Bear Fat" Wimsatt of Wimsatt, New Mexico, in the 1980s. Wimsatt claimed that he had practiced this "lost art" for more than 50 years, with 90 percent accuracy. Folks in the Southwest still talk about the procedure; one of them told us about it.

Here's how it (supposedly) works: Melt down about a pound of bear fat and pour the grease into a clean jar. (For vessels, the Apaches used animal bladders scraped to be nearly transparent.)

Watch for changes in the grease:
• A few specks on the surface mean a light breeze; many specks mean strong winds.
• If grease builds up, or mounds, in the center or on the side of the jar, expect a storm.
• No change in the grease means no change in the weather.

No advice is given about acquiring the grease.

TRUE TALES OF 9-1-1

"Well, it seemed *like an emergency!"*

–courtesy of R. C., Moose Jaw, Saskatchewan, from theglobeandmail.com

....

As if law enforcement authorities didn't have enough to worry about with real crimes, it turns out that 9-1-1 calls for non-emergency reasons are widespread across the continent. In Newfoundland, a woman reported too little cheese on her pizza. Kentucky cops get asked directions via 9-1-1, while their Las Vegas counterparts get complaints about sore throats and stubbed toes.

In British Columbia, 9-1-1 has been used to report a coffee shop not giving a refill, a roommate using the wrong toothbrush, a kid who wouldn't put his seatbelt on, and a balky vending machine. Perhaps "most creative" goes to the caller to the emergency line who asked for the number of the non-emergency line.

If Bass Makes Beer Taste Bitter, What Makes Beer Taste Better?

....

Background music can affect how people perceive taste.

–courtesy of D. G., Canaan,
New Hampshire, from *Food Quality and Preference* journal

....

A scientist in Belgium decided to see if music affects the taste of beer. Using three different brews with different alcohol percentages, he asked 340 subjects to describe the beers' tastes. Often they would be given the same beer twice in a row, only to describe the second tasting as sweeter if there were a high-pitched soundscape in the background and more bitter if the music consisted mainly of bass and other low pitches. Not only that, but the more bitter beers were also perceived to be more alcoholic, which was not necessarily the case. So, the next time you're in a saloon imbibing a deliciously mellow malt as lilting tunes are playing in the background, you might want to ask yourself if indeed the brew might not be a bit bitter after all.

Valentine Food for Thought

....

A "peachy" poem about "lovage," by Jeanne Losey, former poet laureate of the Indiana State Federation of Poetry Clubs (1925–2013)

–courtesy of and with permission from
Michael Losey, Greenfield, Indiana

....

Cabbage always has a heart;
Green beans string along.
You're such a cute tomato,
Will you peas to me belong?

You've been the apple of my eye,
You know how much I care;
So lettuce get together,
We'd make a perfect pear.

Now, something's sure to turnip
To prove you can't be beet;
So, if you carrot all for me,
Let's let our tulips meet.

Don't squash my hopes and
  dreams now,
Bee my honey, dear;
Or tears will fill potato's eyes,
While sweet corn lends an ear.

I'll cauliflower shop and say,
Your dreams are parsley mine.
I'll work and share my celery,
So be my valentine.

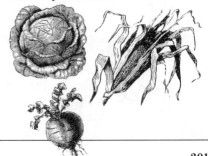

EIGHT THINGS THAT ARE GUARANTEED

Well, maybe nine.

–courtesy of L. K., Tarrytown, New York, from Facebook @TheRiverNEPA

1. You can't wash your eyes with soap.

2. You can't count your hair.

3. You can't breathe through your nose with your tongue out.

4. You just tried #3.

6. When you did #3, you realized that it's possible, but you look like a dog.

7. You're smiling right now because you were fooled.

8. You skipped #5.

9. You just checked to see if there is a #5.

BRIEF SEASON

On the door of *The Old Farmer's Almanac* building, high up in the hills of Dublin, N.H., where snows lie long into the spring, is posted a cartoon showing an elderly native talking to a visitor. The drifts are piled deep and the stormy winds blow. Both characters are well muffled up.

"I understand," the visitor is saying, "that you have a very short summer here . . ."

"Yup," says the old-timer, "sure do. Last year, 'twas on a Thursday."

Advice From an Old Farmer

–courtesy of J. A. R., San Antonio, Texas, from the Internet

• Your fences need to be horse-high, pig-tight, and bull-strong.

• Keep skunks and bankers at a distance.

• Life is simpler when you plow around the stump.

• It don't take a very big person to carry a grudge.

• Good judgment comes from experience, and a lotta that comes from bad judgment.

• The best sermons are lived, not preached.

• Every path has a few puddles.

• The biggest troublemaker you'll probably ever deal with watches you from the mirror every mornin'.

• If you get to thinkin' you're a person of some influence, try orderin' somebody else's dog around.

Send your contribution for *The 2019 Old Farmer's Almanac* by January 26, 2018, to "A & P," The Old Farmer's Almanac, P.O. Box 520, Dublin, NH 03444, or email it to almanac@ypi.com (subject: A & P).

A Reference Compendium

REFERENCE

CALENDAR

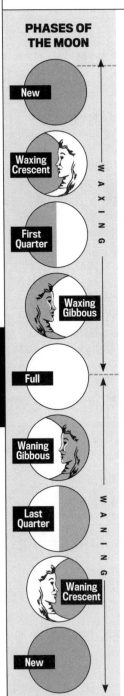

PHASES OF THE MOON

New

Waxing Crescent

WAXING

First Quarter

Waxing Gibbous

Full

Waning Gibbous

Last Quarter

WANING

Waning Crescent

New

REFERENCE

WHEN WILL THE MOON RISE?

A lunar puzzle involves the timing of moonrise. If you enjoy the out-of-doors and the wonders of nature, you may wish to commit to memory the following gem:

The new Moon always rises near sunrise;

The first quarter, near noon;

The full Moon always rises near sunset;

The last quarter, near midnight.

Moonrise occurs about 50 minutes later each day.

FULL MOON NAMES

NAME	MONTH	VARIATIONS
Full Wolf Moon	JANUARY	Full Old Moon
Full Snow Moon	FEBRUARY	Full Hunger Moon
Full Worm Moon	MARCH	Full Crow Moon Full Crust Moon Full Sugar Moon Full Sap Moon
Full Pink Moon	APRIL	Full Sprouting Grass Moon Full Egg Moon Full Fish Moon
Full Flower Moon	MAY	Full Corn Planting Moon Full Milk Moon
Full Strawberry Moon	JUNE	Full Rose Moon Full Hot Moon
Full Buck Moon	JULY	Full Thunder Moon Full Hay Moon
Full Sturgeon Moon	AUGUST	Full Red Moon Full Green Corn Moon
Full Harvest Moon*	SEPTEMBER	Full Corn Moon Full Barley Moon
Full Hunter's Moon	OCTOBER	Full Travel Moon Full Dying Grass Moon
Full Beaver Moon	NOVEMBER	Full Frost Moon
Full Cold Moon	DECEMBER	Full Long Nights Moon

*The Harvest Moon is always the full Moon closest to the autumnal equinox. If the Harvest Moon occurs in October, the September full Moon is usually called the Corn Moon.

THE ORIGIN OF FULL MOON NAMES

Historically, the Native Americans who lived in the area that is now the northern and eastern United States kept track of the seasons by giving a distinctive name to each recurring full Moon. This name was applied to the entire month in which it occurred. These names, and some variations, were used by the Algonquin tribes from New England to Lake Superior.

Meanings of Full Moon Names

JANUARY'S full Moon was called the **Wolf Moon** because it appeared when wolves howled outside Native American villages.

FEBRUARY'S full Moon was called the **Snow Moon** because it was a time of heavy snow. It was also called the **Hunger Moon** because hunting was difficult and hunger often resulted.

MARCH'S full Moon was called the **Worm Moon** because, as the Sun increasingly warmed the soil, earthworms became active and their castings (excrement) began to appear.

APRIL'S full Moon was called the **Pink Moon** because it heralded the appearance of the moss pink, or wild ground phlox—one of the first spring flowers.

MAY'S full Moon was called the **Flower Moon** because blossoms were abundant everywhere at this time.

JUNE'S full Moon was called the **Strawberry Moon** because it appeared when the strawberry harvest took place.

JULY'S full Moon was called the **Buck Moon**; it arrived when a male deer's antlers were in full growth mode.

AUGUST'S full Moon was called the **Sturgeon Moon** because this large fish, which is found in the Great Lakes and Lake Champlain, was caught easily at this time.

SEPTEMBER'S full Moon was called the **Corn Moon** because this was the time to harvest corn.

The **Harvest Moon** is the full Moon that occurs closest to the autumnal equinox. It can occur in either September or October. At this time, crops such as corn, pumpkins, squash, and wild rice were ready for gathering.

OCTOBER'S full Moon was called the **Hunter's Moon** because this was the time to hunt in preparation for winter.

NOVEMBER'S full Moon was called the **Beaver Moon** because it was the time to set beaver traps, before the waters froze over.

DECEMBER'S full Moon was called the **Cold Moon**. It was also called the **Long Nights Moon** because nights at this time of year were the longest.

THE ORIGIN OF MONTH NAMES

JANUARY. For the Roman god Janus, protector of gates and doorways. Janus is depicted with two faces, one looking into the past, the other into the future.

FEBRUARY. From the Latin *februa,* "to cleanse." The Roman Februalia was a festival of purification and atonement that took place during this time of year.

MARCH. For the Roman god of war, Mars. This was the time of year to resume military campaigns that had been interrupted by winter.

APRIL. From the Latin *aperio,* "to open (bud)," because plants begin to grow now.

MAY. For the Roman goddess Maia, who oversaw the growth of plants. Also from the Latin *maiores,* "elders," who were celebrated now.

JUNE. For the Roman goddess Juno, patroness of marriage and the well-being of women. Also from the Latin

juvenis, "young people."

JULY. To honor Roman dictator Julius Caesar (100 B.C.–44 B.C.). In 46 B.C., with the help of Sosigenes, he developed the Julian calendar.

AUGUST. To honor the first Roman emperor (and grandnephew of Julius Caesar), Augustus Caesar (63 B.C.–A.D. 14).

SEPTEMBER. From the Latin *septem,* "seven," because this was the seventh month of the early Roman calendar.

OCTOBER. From the Latin *octo,* "eight," because this was the eighth month of the early Roman calendar.

NOVEMBER. From the Latin *novem,* "nine," because this was the ninth month of the early Roman calendar.

DECEMBER. From the Latin *decem,* "ten," because this was the tenth month of the early Roman calendar.

Easter Dates (2018–21)

Christian churches that follow the Gregorian calendar celebrate Easter on the first Sunday after the paschal full Moon on or just after the vernal equinox.

YEAR	EASTER
2018	April 1
2019	April 21
2020	April 12
2021	April 4

The Julian calendar is used by some churches, including many Eastern Orthodox. The dates below are Julian calendar dates for Easter converted to Gregorian dates.

YEAR	EASTER
2018	April 8
2019	April 28
2020	April 19
2021	May 2

FRIGGATRISKAIDEKAPHOBIA TRIVIA

Here are a few facts about Friday the 13th:

In the 14 possible configurations for the annual calendar (see any perpetual calendar), the occurrence of Friday the 13th is this:

6 of 14 years have one Friday the 13th.
6 of 14 years have two Fridays the 13th.
2 of 14 years have three Fridays the 13th.

No year is without one Friday the 13th, and no year has more than three.

Months that have a Friday the 13th begin on a Sunday.

2018 has a Friday the 13th in April and July.

THE ORIGIN OF DAY NAMES

The days of the week were named by ancient Romans with the Latin words for the Sun, the Moon, and the five known planets. These names have survived in European languages, but English names also reflect Anglo-Saxon and Norse influences.

ENGLISH	LATIN	FRENCH	ITALIAN	SPANISH	ANGLO-SAXON AND NORSE
SUNDAY	dies Solis (Sol's day)	dimanche	domenica	domingo	Sunnandaeg (Sun's day)
		from the Latin for "Lord's day"			
MONDAY	dies Lunae (Luna's day)	lundi	lunedì	lunes	Monandaeg (Moon's day)
TUESDAY	dies Martis (Mars's day)	mardi	martedì	martes	Tiwesdaeg (Tiw's day)
WEDNESDAY	dies Mercurii (Mercury's day)	mercredi	mercoledì	miércoles	Wodnesdaeg (Woden's day)
THURSDAY	dies Jovis (Jupiter's day)	jeudi	giovedì	jueves	Thursdaeg (Thor's day)
FRIDAY	dies Veneris (Venus's day)	vendredi	venerdì	viernes	Frigedaeg (Frigga's day)
SATURDAY	dies Saturni (Saturn's day)	samedi	sabato	sábado	Saeterndaeg (Saturn's day)
		from the Latin for "Sabbath"			

How to Find the Day of the Week for Any Given Date

To compute the day of the week for any given date as far back as the mid–18th century, proceed as follows:

Add the last two digits of the year to one-quarter of the last two digits (discard any remainder), the day of the month, and the month key from the key box below. Divide the sum by 7; the remainder is the day of the week (1 is Sunday, 2 is Monday, and so on). If there is no remainder, the day is Saturday. If you're searching for a weekday prior to 1900, add 2 to the sum before dividing; prior to 1800, add 4. The formula doesn't work for days prior to 1753. From 2000 through 2099, subtract 1 from the sum before dividing.

Example:

THE DAYTON FLOOD WAS ON MARCH 25, 1913.

Last two digits of year: 13
One-quarter of these two digits: 3
Given day of month: 25
Key number for March: 4
                                   ————
                    Sum: 45

45 ÷ 7 = 6, with a remainder of 3. The flood took place on Tuesday, the third day of the week.

KEY

JANUARY	1
LEAP YEAR	0
FEBRUARY	4
LEAP YEAR	3
MARCH	4
APRIL	0
MAY	2
JUNE	5
JULY	0
AUGUST	3
SEPTEMBER	6
OCTOBER	1
NOVEMBER	4
DECEMBER	6

ANIMAL SIGNS OF THE CHINESE ZODIAC

The animal designations of the Chinese zodiac follow a 12-year cycle and are always used in the same sequence. The Chinese year of 354 days begins 3 to 7 weeks into the western 365-day year, so the animal designation changes at that time, rather than on January 1. This year, the Chinese New Year starts on February 16.

RAT

Ambitious and sincere, you can be generous with your money. Compatible with the dragon and the monkey. Your opposite is the horse.

1924	1936	1948
1960	1972	1984
1996	2008	2020

OX OR BUFFALO

A leader, you are bright, patient, and cheerful. Compatible with the snake and the rooster. Your opposite is the sheep.

1925	1937	1949
1961	1973	1985
1997	2009	2021

TIGER

Forthright and sensitive, you possess great courage. Compatible with the horse and the dog. Your opposite is the monkey.

1926	1938	1950
1962	1974	1986
1998	2010	2022

RABBIT OR HARE

Talented and affectionate, you are a seeker of tranquility. Compatible with the sheep and the pig. Your opposite is the rooster.

1927	1939	1951
1963	1975	1987
1999	2011	2023

DRAGON

Robust and passionate, your life is filled with complexity. Compatible with the monkey and the rat. Your opposite is the dog.

1928	1940	1952
1964	1976	1988
2000	2012	2024

SNAKE

Strong-willed and intense, you display great wisdom. Compatible with the rooster and the ox. Your opposite is the pig.

1929	1941	1953
1965	1977	1989
2001	2013	2025

HORSE

Physically attractive and popular, you like the company of others. Compatible with the tiger and the dog. Your opposite is the rat.

1930	1942	1954
1966	1978	1990
2002	2014	2026

SHEEP OR GOAT

Aesthetic and stylish, you enjoy being a private person. Compatible with the pig and the rabbit. Your opposite is the ox.

1931	1943	1955
1967	1979	1991
2003	2015	2027

MONKEY

Persuasive, skillful, and intelligent, you strive to excel. Compatible with the dragon and the rat. Your opposite is the tiger.

1932	1944	1956
1968	1980	1992
2004	2016	2028

ROOSTER OR COCK

Seeking wisdom and truth, you have a pioneering spirit. Compatible with the snake and the ox. Your opposite is the rabbit.

1933	1945	1957
1969	1981	1993
2005	2017	2029

DOG

Generous and loyal, you have the ability to work well with others. Compatible with the horse and the tiger. Your opposite is the dragon.

1934	1946	1958
1970	1982	1994
2006	2018	2030

PIG OR BOAR

Gallant and noble, your friends will remain at your side. Compatible with the rabbit and the sheep. Your opposite is the snake.

1935	1947	1959
1971	1983	1995
2007	2019	2031

REFERENCE

A Table Foretelling the Weather Through All the Lunations of Each Year, or Forever

This table is the result of many years of actual observation and shows what sort of weather will probably follow the Moon's entrance into any of its quarters. For example, the table shows that the week following January 24, 2018, will be fair, because the Moon enters the first quarter on that day at 5:20 P.M. EST. (See the **Left-Hand Calendar Pages, 140–166,** for Moon phases.)

EDITOR'S NOTE: Although the data in this table is taken into consideration in the year-long process of compiling the annual long-range weather forecasts for *The Old Farmer's Almanac,* we rely far more on our projections of solar activity.

TIME OF CHANGE	SUMMER	WINTER
Midnight to 2 A.M.	Fair	Hard frost, unless wind is south or west
2 A.M. to 4 A.M.	Cold, with frequent showers	Snow and stormy
4 A.M. to 6 A.M.	Rain	Rain
6 A.M. to 8 A.M.	Wind and rain	Stormy
8 A.M. to 10 A.M.	Changeable	Cold rain if wind is west; snow, if east
10 A.M. to noon	Frequent showers	Cold with high winds
Noon to 2 P.M.	Very rainy	Snow or rain
2 P.M. to 4 P.M.	Changeable	Fair and mild
4 P.M. to 6 P.M.	Fair	Fair
6 P.M. to 10 P.M.	Fair if wind is northwest; rain if wind is south or southwest	Fair and frosty if wind is north or northeast; rain or snow if wind is south or southwest
10 P.M. to midnight	Fair	Fair and frosty

This table was created more than 180 years ago by Dr. Herschell for the Boston Courier; *it first appeared in* The Old Farmer's Almanac *in 1834.*

SAFE ICE THICKNESS*

ICE THICKNESS	PERMISSIBLE LOAD	ICE THICKNESS	PERMISSIBLE LOAD
3 inches	Single person on foot	12 inches	Heavy truck (8-ton gross)
4 inches	Group in single file	15 inches	10 tons
7½ inches	Passenger car (2-ton gross)	20 inches	25 tons
8 inches	Light truck (2½-ton gross)	30 inches	70 tons
10 inches	Medium truck (3½-ton gross)	36 inches	110 tons

*Solid, clear, blue/black pond and lake ice

The strength value of river ice is 15 percent less. Slush ice has only half the strength of blue ice.

REFERENCE

HEAT INDEX °F (°C)

TEMP. °F (°C)	RELATIVE HUMIDITY (%)								
	40	45	50	55	60	65	70	75	80
100 (38)	109 (43)	114 (46)	118 (48)	124 (51)	129 (54)	136 (58)			
98 (37)	105 (41)	109 (43)	113 (45)	117 (47)	123 (51)	128 (53)	134 (57)		
96 (36)	101 (38)	104 (40)	108 (42)	112 (44)	116 (47)	121 (49)	126 (52)	132 (56)	
94 (34)	97 (36)	100 (38)	103 (39)	106 (41)	110 (43)	114 (46)	119 (48)	124 (51)	129 (54)
92 (33)	94 (34)	96 (36)	99 (37)	101 (38)	105 (41)	108 (42)	112 (44)	116 (47)	121 (49)
90 (32)	91 (33)	93 (34)	95 (35)	97 (36)	100 (38)	103 (39)	106 (41)	109 (43)	113 (45)
88 (31)	88 (31)	89 (32)	91 (33)	93 (34)	95 (35)	98 (37)	100 (38)	103 (39)	106 (41)
86 (30)	85 (29)	87 (31)	88 (31)	89 (32)	91 (33)	93 (34)	95 (35)	97 (36)	100 (38)
84 (29)	83 (28)	84 (29)	85 (29)	86 (30)	88 (31)	89 (32)	90 (32)	92 (33)	94 (34)
82 (28)	81 (27)	82 (28)	83 (28)	84 (29)	84 (29)	85 (29)	86 (30)	88 (31)	89 (32)
80 (27)	80 (27)	80 (27)	81 (27)	81 (27)	82 (28)	82 (28)	83 (28)	84 (29)	84 (29)

EXAMPLE: *When the temperature is 88°F (31°C) and the relative humidity is 60 percent, the heat index, or how hot it feels, is 95°F (35°C).*

THE UV INDEX FOR MEASURING ULTRAVIOLET RADIATION RISK

The U.S. National Weather Service's daily forecasts of ultraviolet levels use these numbers for various exposure levels:

UV INDEX NUMBER	EXPOSURE LEVEL	TIME TO BURN	ACTIONS TO TAKE
0, 1, 2	Minimal	60 minutes	Apply SPF 15 sunscreen
3, 4	Low	45 minutes	Apply SPF 15 sunscreen; wear a hat
5, 6	Moderate	30 minutes	Apply SPF 15 sunscreen; wear a hat
7, 8, 9	High	15–25 minutes	Apply SPF 15 to 30 sunscreen; wear a hat and sunglasses; limit midday exposure
10 or higher	Very high	10 minutes	Apply SPF 30 sunscreen; wear a hat, sunglasses, and protective clothing; limit midday exposure

"Time to Burn" and "Actions to Take" apply to people with fair skin that sometimes tans but usually burns. People with lighter skin need to be more cautious. People with darker skin may be able to tolerate more exposure.

85	90	95	100
135 (57)			
126 (52)	131 (55)		
117 (47)	122 (50)	127 (53)	132 (56)
110 (43)	113 (45)	117 (47)	121 (49)
102 (39)	105 (41)	108 (42)	112 (44)
96 (36)	98 (37)	100 (38)	103 (39)
90 (32)	91 (33)	93 (34)	95 (35)
85 (29)	86 (30)	86 (30)	87 (31)

HOW TO MEASURE HAIL

The **TORRO HAILSTORM INTENSITY SCALE** was introduced by Jonathan Webb of Oxford, England, in 1986 as a means of categorizing hailstorms. The name derives from the private and mostly British research body named the TORnado and storm Research Organisation.

What Are Cooling/Heating Degree Days?

Each degree of a day's average temperature above 65°F is considered one cooling degree day, an attempt to measure the need for air-conditioning. If the average of the day's high and low temperatures is 75°, that's 10 cooling degree days.

Similarly, each degree of a day's average temperature below 65° is considered one heating degree and is an attempt to measure the need for fuel consumption. For example, a day with temperatures ranging from 60° to 40° results in an average of 50°, or 15 degrees less than 65°. Hence, that day would be credited as 15 heating degree days.

INTENSITY/DESCRIPTION OF HAIL DAMAGE

H0 True hail of pea size causes no damage

H1 Leaves and flower petals are punctured and torn

H2 Leaves are stripped from trees and plants

H3 Panes of glass are broken; auto bodies are dented

H4 Some house windows are broken; small tree branches are broken off; birds are killed

H5 Many windows are smashed; small animals are injured; large tree branches are broken off

H6 Shingle roofs are breached; metal roofs are scored; wooden window frames are broken away

H7 Roofs are shattered to expose rafters; autos are seriously damaged

H8 Shingle and tile roofs are destroyed; small tree trunks are split; people are seriously injured

H9 Concrete roofs are broken; large tree trunks are split and knocked down; people are at risk of fatal injuries

H10 Brick houses are damaged; people are at risk of fatal injuries

REFERENCE

WEATHER

HOW TO MEASURE WIND SPEED

The **BEAUFORT WIND FORCE SCALE** is a common way of estimating wind speed. It was developed in 1805 by Admiral Sir Francis Beaufort of the British Navy to measure wind at sea. We can also use it to measure wind on land.

Admiral Beaufort arranged the numbers 0 to 12 to indicate the strength of the wind from calm, force 0, to hurricane, force 12. Here's a scale adapted to land.

"Used Mostly at Sea but of Help to All Who Are Interested in the Weather"

BEAUFORT FORCE	DESCRIPTION	WHEN YOU SEE OR FEEL THIS EFFECT	WIND SPEED (mph)	(km/h)
0	CALM	Smoke goes straight up	less than 1	less than 2
1	LIGHT AIR	Wind direction is shown by smoke drift but not by wind vane	1–3	2–5
2	LIGHT BREEZE	Wind is felt on the face; leaves rustle; wind vanes move	4–7	6–11
3	GENTLE BREEZE	Leaves and small twigs move steadily; wind extends small flags straight out	8–12	12–19
4	MODERATE BREEZE	Wind raises dust and loose paper; small branches move	13–18	20–29
5	FRESH BREEZE	Small trees sway; waves form on lakes	19–24	30–39
6	STRONG BREEZE	Large branches move; wires whistle; umbrellas are difficult to use	25–31	40–50
7	MODERATE GALE	Whole trees are in motion; walking against the wind is difficult	32–38	51–61
8	FRESH GALE	Twigs break from trees; walking against the wind is very difficult	39–46	62–74
9	STRONG GALE	Buildings suffer minimal damage; roof shingles are removed	47–54	75–87
10	WHOLE GALE	Trees are uprooted	55–63	88–101
11	VIOLENT STORM	Widespread damage	64–72	102–116
12	HURRICANE	Widespread destruction	73+	117+

RETIRED ATLANTIC HURRICANE NAMES

These storms have been some of the most destructive and costly.

NAME	YEAR	NAME	YEAR	NAME	YEAR
Katrina	2005	Gustav	2008	Sandy	2012
Rita	2005	Ike	2008	Ingrid	2013
Wilma	2005	Paloma	2008	Erika	2015
Dean	2007	Igor	2010	Joaquin	2015
Felix	2007	Tomas	2010	Matthew	2016
Noel	2007	Irene	2011	Otto	2016

WEATHER

ATLANTIC TROPICAL (AND SUBTROPICAL) STORM NAMES FOR 2018			EASTERN NORTH-PACIFIC TROPICAL (AND SUBTROPICAL) STORM NAMES FOR 2018		
Alberto	Helene	Oscar	Aletta	Ileana	Rosa
Beryl	Isaac	Patty	Bud	John	Sergio
Chris	Joyce	Rafael	Carlotta	Kristy	Tara
Debby	Kirk	Sara	Daniel	Lane	Vicente
Ernesto	Leslie	Tony	Emilia	Miriam	Willa
Florence	Michael	Valerie	Fabio	Norman	Xavier
Gordon	Nadine	William	Gilma	Olivia	Yolanda
			Hector	Paul	Zeke

How to Measure Hurricane Strength

The **SAFFIR-SIMPSON HURRICANE WIND SCALE** assigns a rating from 1 to 5 based on a hurricane's intensity. It is used to give an estimate of the potential property damage from a hurricane landfall. Wind speed is the determining factor in the scale, as storm surge values are highly dependent on the slope of the continental shelf in the landfall region. Wind speeds are measured at a height of 33 feet (10 meters) using a 1-minute average.

CATEGORY ONE. Average wind: 74–95 mph. Significant damage to mobile homes. Some damage to roofing and siding of well-built frame homes. Large tree branches snap and shallow-rooted trees may topple. Power outages may last a few to several days.

CATEGORY TWO. Average wind: 96–110 mph. Mobile homes may be destroyed. Major roof and siding damage to frame homes. Many shallow-rooted trees snap or topple, blocking roads. Widespread power outages could last from several days to weeks. Potable water may be scarce.

CATEGORY THREE. Average wind: 111–129 mph. Most mobile homes destroyed.

Frame homes may sustain major roof damage. Many trees snap or topple, blocking numerous roads. Electricity and water may be unavailable for several days to weeks.

CATEGORY FOUR. Average wind: 130–156 mph. Mobile homes destroyed. Frame homes severely damaged or destroyed. Windborne debris may penetrate protected windows. Most trees snap or topple. Residential areas isolated by fallen trees and power poles. Most of the area uninhabitable for weeks to months.

CATEGORY FIVE. Average wind: 157+ mph. Most homes destroyed. Nearly all windows blown out of high-rises. Most of the area uninhabitable for weeks to months.

REFERENCE

WEATHER

HOW TO MEASURE A TORNADO

The original **FUJITA SCALE** (or F Scale) was developed by Dr. Theodore Fujita to classify tornadoes based on wind damage. All tornadoes, and other severe local windstorms, were assigned a number according to the most intense damage caused by the storm. An enhanced F (EF) scale was implemented in the United States on February 1, 2007. The EF scale uses 3-second gust estimates based on a more detailed system for assessing damage, taking into account different building materials.

F SCALE		EF SCALE (U.S.)
F0 · 40-72 mph (64-116 km/h)	LIGHT DAMAGE	EF0 · 65-85 mph (105-137 km/h)
F1 · 73-112 mph (117-180 km/h)	MODERATE DAMAGE	EF1 · 86-110 mph (138-178 km/h)
F2 · 113-157 mph (181-253 km/h)	CONSIDERABLE DAMAGE	EF2 · 111-135 mph (179-218 km/h)
F3 · 158-207 mph (254-332 km/h)	SEVERE DAMAGE	EF3 · 136-165 mph (219-266 km/h)
F4 · 208-260 mph (333-419 km/h)	DEVASTATING DAMAGE	EF4 · 166-200 mph (267-322 km/h)
F5 · 261-318 mph (420-512 km/h)	INCREDIBLE DAMAGE	EF5 · over 200 mph (over 322 km/h)

Wind/Barometer Table

BAROMETER (REDUCED TO SEA LEVEL)	WIND DIRECTION	CHARACTER OF WEATHER INDICATED
30.00 to 30.20, and steady	WESTERLY	Fair, with slight changes in temperature, for one to two days
30.00 to 30.20, and rising rapidly	WESTERLY	Fair, followed within two days by warmer and rain
30.00 to 30.20, and falling rapidly	SOUTH TO EAST	Warmer, and rain within 24 hours
30.20 or above, and falling rapidly	SOUTH TO EAST	Warmer, and rain within 36 hours
30.20 or above, and falling rapidly	WEST TO NORTH	Cold and clear, quickly followed by warmer and rain
30.20 or above, and steady	VARIABLE	No early change
30.00 or below, and falling slowly	SOUTH TO EAST	Rain within 18 hours that will continue a day or two
30.00 or below, and falling rapidly	SOUTHEAST TO NORTHEAST	Rain, with high wind, followed within two days by clearing, colder
30.00 or below, and rising	SOUTH TO WEST	Clearing and colder within 12 hours
29.80 or below, and falling rapidly	SOUTH TO EAST	Severe storm of wind and rain imminent; in winter, snow or cold wave within 24 hours
29.80 or below, and falling rapidly	EAST TO NORTH	Severe northeast gales and heavy rain or snow, followed in winter by cold wave
29.80 or below, and rising rapidly	GOING TO WEST	Clearing and colder

NOTE: *A barometer should be adjusted to show equivalent sea-level pressure for the altitude at which it is to be used. A change of 100 feet in elevation will cause a decrease of 1/10 inch in the reading.*

WEATHER

WINDCHILL TABLE

As wind speed increases, your body loses heat more rapidly, making the air feel colder than it really is. The combination of cold temperature and high wind can create a cooling effect so severe that exposed flesh can freeze.

	TEMPERATURE (°F)														
Calm	**35**	**30**	**25**	**20**	**15**	**10**	**5**	**0**	**−5**	**−10**	**−15**	**−20**	**−25**	**−30**	**−35**
5	31	25	19	13	7	1	−5	−11	−16	−22	−28	−34	−40	−46	−52
10	27	21	15	9	3	−4	−10	−16	−22	−28	−35	−41	−47	−53	−59
15	25	19	13	6	0	−7	−13	−19	−26	−32	−39	−45	−51	−58	−64
20	24	17	11	4	−2	−9	−15	−22	−29	−35	−42	−48	−55	−61	−68
25	23	16	9	3	−4	−11	−17	−24	−31	−37	−44	−51	−58	−64	−71
30	22	15	8	1	−5	−12	−19	−26	−33	−39	−46	−53	−60	−67	−73
35	21	14	7	0	−7	−14	−21	−27	−34	−41	−48	−55	−62	−69	−76
40	20	13	6	−1	−8	−15	−22	−29	−36	−43	−50	−57	−64	−71	−78
45	19	12	5	−2	−9	−16	−23	−30	−37	−44	−51	−58	−65	−72	−79
50	19	12	4	−3	−10	−17	−24	−31	−38	−45	−52	−60	−67	−74	−81
55	18	11	4	−3	−11	−18	−25	−32	−39	−46	−54	−61	−68	−75	−82
60	17	10	3	−4	−11	−19	−26	−33	−40	−48	−55	−62	−69	−76	−84

WIND SPEED (mph)

FROSTBITE OCCURS IN 30 MINUTES 10 MINUTES 5 MINUTES

EXAMPLE: *When the temperature is 15°F and the wind speed is 30 miles per hour, the windchill, or how cold it feels, is −5°F. For a Celsius version of this table, visit Almanac.com/WindchillCelsius.*
–courtesy of National Weather Service

REFERENCE

HOW TO MEASURE EARTHQUAKES

In 1979, seismologists developed a measurement of earthquake size called **MOMENT MAGNITUDE.** It is more accurate than the previously used Richter scale, which is precise only for earthquakes of a certain size and at a certain distance from a seismometer. All earthquakes can now be compared on the same scale.

MAGNITUDE	EFFECT
LESS THAN 3	MICRO
3–3.9	MINOR
4–4.9	LIGHT
5–5.9	MODERATE
6–6.9	STRONG
7–7.9	MAJOR
8 OR MORE	GREAT

A GARDENER'S WORST PHOBIAS

NAME OF FEAR	OBJECT FEARED
Alliumphobia	Garlic
Anthophobia	Flowers
Apiphobia	Bees
Arachnophobia	Spiders
Batonophobia	Plants
Bufonophobia	Toads
Dendrophobia	Trees
Entomophobia	Insects
Lachanophobia	Vegetables
Melissophobia	Bees
Mottephobia	Moths
Myrmecophobia	Ants
Ornithophobia	Birds
Ranidaphobia	Frogs
Rupophobia	Dirt
Scoleciphobia	Worms
Spheksophobia	Wasps

PLANTS FOR LAWNS

Choose varieties that suit your soil and your climate. All of these can withstand mowing and considerable foot traffic.

Ajuga or bugleweed *(Ajuga reptans)*
Corsican mint *(Mentha requienii)*
Dwarf cinquefoil *(Potentilla tabernaemontani)*
English pennyroyal *(Mentha pulegium)*
Green Irish moss *(Sagina subulata)*
Pearly everlasting *(Anaphalis margaritacea)*
Roman chamomile *(Chamaemelum nobile)*
Rupturewort *(Herniaria glabra)*
Speedwell *(Veronica officinalis)*
Stonecrop *(Sedum ternatum)*
Sweet violets (*Viola odorata* or *V. tricolor*)
Thyme *(Thymus serpyllum)*
White clover *(Trifolium repens)*
Wild strawberries *(Fragaria virginiana)*
Wintergreen or partridgeberry *(Mitchella repens)*

Lawn-Growing Tips

• Test your soil: The pH balance should be 7.0 or more; 6.2 to 6.7 puts your lawn at risk for fungal diseases. If the pH is too low, correct it with liming, best done in the fall.

• The best time to apply fertilizer is just before it rains.

• If you put lime and fertilizer on your lawn, spread half of it as you walk north to south, the other half as you walk east to west to cut down on missed areas.

• Any feeding of lawns in the fall should be done with a low-nitrogen, slow-acting fertilizer.

• In areas of your lawn where tree roots compete with the grass, apply some extra fertilizer to benefit both.

• Moss and sorrel in lawns usually means poor soil, poor aeration or drainage, or excessive acidity.

• Control weeds by promoting healthy lawn growth with natural fertilizers in spring and early fall.

• Raise the level of your lawn-mower blades during the hot summer days. Taller grass resists drought better than short.

• You can reduce mowing time by redesigning your lawn, reducing sharp corners and adding sweeping curves.

• During a drought, let the grass grow longer between mowings and reduce fertilizer.

• Water your lawn early in the morning or in the evening.

Flowers and Herbs That Attract Butterflies

Allium . . . . *Allium*	Mallow . . . . *Malva*
Aster . . . . *Aster*	Mealycup sage . . . .*Salvia farinacea*
Bee balm . . . . *Monarda*	Milkweed . . . . *Asclepias*
Butterfly bush. . . . . *Buddleia*	Mint. . . . . *Mentha*
Catmint . . . .*Nepeta*	Oregano . . . . *Origanum vulgare*
Clove pink . . . . *Dianthus*	Pansy . . . . *Viola*
Cornflower. . . . . *Centaurea*	Parsley . . . . *Petroselinum*
Creeping thyme . . . . . . *Thymus serpyllum*	*crispum*
Daylily. . . . .*Hemerocallis*	Phlox. . . . .*Phlox*
Dill. . . . . *Anethum graveolens*	Privet . . . .*Ligustrum*
False indigo . . . . *Baptisia*	Purple coneflower . . *Echinacea purpurea*
Fleabane. . . . . *Erigeron*	Rock cress . . . . *Arabis*
Floss flower . . . . *Ageratum*	Sea holly. . . . . *Eryngium*
Globe thistle . . . . *Echinops*	Shasta daisy . . . . *Chrysanthemum*
Goldenrod . . . . *Solidago*	Snapdragon. . . . . *Antirrhinum*
Helen's flower . . . . *Helenium*	Stonecrop . . . . *Sedum*
Hollyhock. . . . . *Alcea*	Sweet alyssum . . . . *Lobularia*
Honeysuckle . . . . *Lonicera*	Sweet marjoram. . . . *Origanum majorana*
Lavender . . . . *Lavandula*	Sweet rocket . . . . *Hesperis*
Lilac. . . . . *Syringa*	Tickseed. . . . . *Coreopsis*
Lupine. . . . . *Lupinus*	Verbena . . . . *Verbena*
Lychnis. *Lychnis*	Zinnia . . . . *Zinnia*

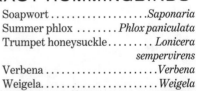

FLOWERS* THAT ATTRACT HUMMINGBIRDS

Beard tongue. . . . . *Penstemon*	Soapwort . . . .*Saponaria*
Bee balm . . . . *Monarda*	Summer phlox . . . . *Phlox paniculata*
Butterfly bush. . . . . *Buddleia*	Trumpet honeysuckle. . . . . *Lonicera*
Catmint . . . .*Nepeta*	*sempervirens*
Clove pink . . . . *Dianthus*	Verbena . . . .*Verbena*
Columbine . . . . *Aquilegia*	Weigela. *Weigela*
Coral bells . . . .*Heuchera*	
Daylily. . . . . *Hemerocallis*	
Desert candle . . . .*Yucca*	
Flag iris . . . . *Iris*	
Flowering tobacco . . . . . . *Nicotiana alata*	
Foxglove. . . . . *Digitalis*	
Larkspur . . . .*Delphinium*	
Lily. . . . . *Lilium*	
Lupine. . . . . *Lupinus*	
Petunia. *Petunia*	
Pincushion flower . . . . *Scabiosa*	
Red-hot poker . . . . *Kniphofia*	
Scarlet sage . . . . *Salvia splendens*	

*NOTE: *Choose varieties in red and orange shades, if available.*

REFERENCE

pH PREFERENCES OF TREES, SHRUBS, FLOWERS, AND VEGETABLES

An accurate soil test will indicate your soil pH and will specify the amount of lime or sulfur that is needed to bring it up or down to the appropriate level. A pH of 6.5 is just about right for most home gardens, since most plants thrive in the 6.0 to 7.0 (slightly acidic to neutral) range. Some plants (azaleas, blueberries) prefer more strongly acidic soil in the 4.0 to 6.0 range, while a few (asparagus, plums) do best in soil that is neutral to slightly alkaline. Acidic, or sour, soil (below 7.0) is counteracted by applying finely ground limestone, and alkaline, or sweet, soil (above 7.0) is treated with ground sulfur.

COMMON NAME	OPTIMUM pH RANGE	COMMON NAME	OPTIMUM pH RANGE	COMMON NAME	OPTIMUM pH RANGE
TREES AND SHRUBS		Bee balm	6.0–7.5	Snapdragon	5.5–7.0
Apple	5.0–6.5	Begonia	5.5–7.0	Sunflower	6.0–7.5
Azalea	4.5–6.0	Black-eyed Susan	5.5–7.0	Tulip	6.0–7.0
Beautybush	6.0–7.5	Bleeding heart	6.0–7.5	Zinnia	5.5–7.0
Birch	5.0–6.5	Canna	6.0–8.0		
Blackberry	5.0–6.0	Carnation	6.0–7.0	**VEGETABLES**	
Blueberry	4.0–5.0	Chrysanthemum	6.0–7.5	Asparagus	6.0–8.0
Boxwood	6.0–7.5	Clematis	5.5–7.0	Bean	6.0–7.5
Cherry, sour	6.0–7.0	Coleus	6.0–7.0	Beet	6.0–7.5
Crab apple	6.0–7.5	Coneflower, purple	5.0–7.5	Broccoli	6.0–7.0
Dogwood	5.0–7.0	Cosmos	5.0–8.0	Brussels sprout	6.0–7.5
Fir, balsam	5.0–6.0	Crocus	6.0–8.0	Cabbage	6.0–7.5
Hemlock	5.0–6.0	Daffodil	6.0–6.5	Carrot	5.5–7.0
Hydrangea, blue-flowered	4.0–5.0	Dahlia	6.0–7.5	Cauliflower	5.5–7.5
Hydrangea, pink-flowered	6.0–7.0	Daisy, Shasta	6.0–8.0	Celery	5.8–7.0
		Daylily	6.0–8.0	Chive	6.0–7.0
Juniper	5.0–6.0	Delphinium	6.0–7.5	Collard	6.5–7.5
Laurel, mountain	4.5–6.0	Foxglove	6.0–7.5	Corn	5.5–7.0
Lemon	6.0–7.5	Geranium	6.0–8.0	Cucumber	5.5–7.0
Lilac	6.0–7.5	Gladiolus	5.0–7.0	Eggplant	6.0–7.0
Maple, sugar	6.0–7.5	Hibiscus	6.0–8.0	Garlic	5.5–8.0
Oak, white	5.0–6.5	Hollyhock	6.0–8.0	Kale	6.0–7.5
Orange	6.0–7.5	Hyacinth	6.5–7.5	Leek	6.0–8.0
Peach	6.0–7.0	Iris, blue flag	5.0–7.5	Lettuce	6.0–7.0
Pear	6.0–7.5	Lily-of-the-valley	4.5–6.0	Okra	6.0–7.0
Pecan	6.4–8.0	Lupine	5.0–6.5	Onion	6.0–7.0
Plum	6.0–8.0	Marigold	5.5–7.5	Pea	6.0–7.5
Raspberry, red	5.5–7.0	Morning glory	6.0–7.5	Pepper, sweet	5.5–7.0
Rhododendron	4.5–6.0	Narcissus, trumpet	5.5–6.5	Potato	4.8–6.5
Willow	6.0–8.0	Nasturtium	5.5–7.5	Pumpkin	5.5–7.5
		Pansy	5.5–6.5	Radish	6.0–7.0
FLOWERS		Peony	6.0–7.5	Spinach	6.0–7.5
Alyssum	6.0–7.5	Petunia	6.0–7.5	Squash, crookneck	6.0–7.5
Aster, New England	6.0–8.0	Phlox, summer	6.0–8.0	Squash, Hubbard	5.5–7.0
Baby's breath	6.0–7.0	Poppy, oriental	6.0–7.5	Swiss chard	6.0–7.0
Bachelor's button	6.0–7.5	Rose, hybrid tea	5.5–7.0	Tomato	5.5–7.5
		Rose, rugosa	6.0–7.0	Watermelon	5.5–6.5

PRODUCE WEIGHTS AND MEASURES

VEGETABLES

ASPARAGUS: 1 pound = 3 cups chopped

BEANS (STRING): 1 pound = 4 cups chopped

BEETS: 1 pound (5 medium) = 2½ cups chopped

BROCCOLI: 1 pound = 6 cups chopped

CABBAGE: 1 pound = 4½ cups shredded

CARROTS: 1 pound = 3½ cups sliced or grated

CELERY: 1 pound = 4 cups chopped

CUCUMBERS: 1 pound (2 medium) = 4 cups sliced

EGGPLANT: 1 pound = 4 cups chopped = 2 cups cooked

GARLIC: 1 clove = 1 teaspoon chopped

LEEKS: 1 pound = 4 cups chopped = 2 cups cooked

MUSHROOMS: 1 pound = 5 to 6 cups sliced = 2 cups cooked

ONIONS: 1 pound = 4 cups sliced = 2 cups cooked

PARSNIPS: 1 pound = 1½ cups cooked, puréed

PEAS: 1 pound whole = 1 to 1½ cups shelled

POTATOES: 1 pound (3 medium) sliced = 2 cups mashed

PUMPKIN: 1 pound = 4 cups chopped = 2 cups cooked and drained

SPINACH: 1 pound = ¾ to 1 cup cooked

SQUASHES (SUMMER): 1 pound = 4 cups grated = 2 cups sliced and cooked

SQUASHES (WINTER): 2 pounds = 2½ cups cooked, puréed

SWEET POTATOES: 1 pound = 4 cups grated = 1 cup cooked, puréed

SWISS CHARD: 1 pound = 5 to 6 cups packed leaves = 1 to 1½ cups cooked

TOMATOES: 1 pound (3 or 4 medium) = 1½ cups seeded pulp

TURNIPS: 1 pound = 4 cups chopped = 2 cups cooked, mashed

FRUIT

APPLES: 1 pound (3 or 4 medium) = 3 cups sliced

BANANAS: 1 pound (3 or 4 medium) = 1¾ cups mashed

BERRIES: 1 quart = 3½ cups

DATES: 1 pound = 2½ cups pitted

LEMON: 1 whole = 1 to 3 tablespoons juice; 1 to 1½ teaspoons grated rind

LIME: 1 whole = 1½ to 2 tablespoons juice

ORANGE: 1 medium = 6 to 8 tablespoons juice; 2 to 3 tablespoons grated rind

PEACHES: 1 pound (4 medium) = 3 cups sliced

PEARS: 1 pound (4 medium) = 2 cups sliced

RHUBARB: 1 pound = 2 cups cooked

REFERENCE

SOWING VEGETABLE SEEDS

SOW OR PLANT IN COOL WEATHER	Beets, broccoli, brussels sprouts, cabbage, lettuce, onions, parsley, peas, radishes, spinach, Swiss chard, turnips
SOW OR PLANT IN WARM WEATHER	Beans, carrots, corn, cucumbers, eggplant, melons, okra, peppers, squashes, tomatoes
SOW OR PLANT FOR ONE CROP PER SEASON	Corn, eggplant, leeks, melons, peppers, potatoes, spinach (New Zealand), squashes, tomatoes
RESOW FOR ADDITIONAL CROPS	Beans, beets, cabbage, carrots, kohlrabi, lettuce, radishes, rutabagas, spinach, turnips

A Beginner's Vegetable Garden

The vegetables suggested below are common, easy-to-grow crops. Make 11 rows, 10 feet long, with at least 18 inches between them. Ideally, the rows should run north and south to take full advantage of the sun. This garden, planted as suggested, can feed a family of four for one summer, with a little extra for canning and freezing or giving away.

ROW	
1	Zucchini (4 plants)
2	Tomatoes (5 plants, staked)
3	Peppers (6 plants)
4	Cabbage

ROW	
5	Bush beans
6	Lettuce
7	Beets
8	Carrots
9	Swiss chard
10	Radishes
11	Marigolds (to discourage rabbits!)

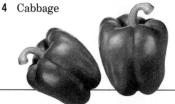

TRADITIONAL PLANTING TIMES

• Plant **CORN** when elm leaves are the size of a squirrel's ear, when oak leaves are the size of a mouse's ear, when apple blossoms begin to fall, or when the dogwoods are in full bloom.

• Plant **LETTUCE, SPINACH, PEAS**, and other cool-weather vegetables when the lilacs show their first leaves or when daffodils begin to bloom.

• Plant **TOMATOES** and **PEPPERS** when dogwoods are in peak bloom or when daylilies start to bloom.

• Plant **CUCUMBERS** and **SQUASHES** when lilac flowers fade.

• Plant **PERENNIALS** when maple leaves begin to unfurl.

• Plant **MORNING GLORIES** when maple trees have full-size leaves.

• Plant **PANSIES, SNAPDRAGONS**, and other hardy annuals after the aspen and chokecherry trees leaf out.

• Plant **BEETS** and **CARROTS** when dandelions are blooming.

REFERENCE

IN THE GARDEN

WHEN TO . . .

	. . . FERTILIZE	. . . WATER
BEANS	After heavy bloom and set of pods	Regularly, from start of pod to set
BEETS	At time of planting	Only during drought conditions
BROCCOLI	3 weeks after transplanting	Only during drought conditions
BRUSSELS SPROUTS	3 weeks after transplanting	At transplanting
CABBAGE	3 weeks after transplanting	2 to 3 weeks before harvest
CARROTS	In the fall for the following spring	Only during drought conditions
CAULIFLOWER	3 weeks after transplanting	Once, 3 weeks before harvest
CELERY	At time of transplanting	Once a week
CORN	When 8 to 10 inches tall, and when first silk appears	When tassels appear and cobs start to swell
CUCUMBERS	1 week after bloom, and 3 weeks later	Frequently, especially when fruits form
LETTUCE	2 to 3 weeks after transplanting	Once a week
MELONS	1 week after bloom, and again 3 weeks later	Once a week
ONION SETS	When bulbs begin to swell, and when plants are 1 foot tall	Only during drought conditions
PARSNIPS	1 year before planting	Only during drought conditions
PEAS	After heavy bloom and set of pods	Regularly, from start of pod to set
PEPPERS	After first fruit-set	Once a week
POTATO TUBERS	At bloom time or time of second hilling	Regularly, when tubers start to form
PUMPKINS	Just before vines start to run, when plants are about 1 foot tall	Only during drought conditions
RADISHES	Before spring planting	Once a week
SPINACH	When plants are one-third grown	Once a week
SQUASHES, SUMMER	Just before vines start to run, when plants are about 1 foot tall	Only during drought conditions
SQUASHES, WINTER	Just before vines start to run, when plants are about 1 foot tall	Only during drought conditions
TOMATOES	2 weeks before, and after first picking	Twice a week

IN THE GARDEN

HOW TO GROW HERBS

HERB	START SEEDS INDOORS (WEEKS BEFORE LAST SPRING FROST)	START SEEDS OUTDOORS (WEEKS BEFORE/AFTER LAST SPRING FROST)	HEIGHT/ SPREAD (INCHES)	SOIL	LIGHT**
BASIL*	6–8	Anytime after	12–24/12	Rich, moist	○
BORAGE*	Not recommended	Anytime after	12–36/12	Rich, well-drained, dry	○
CHERVIL	Not recommended	3–4 before	12–24/8	Rich, moist	◑
CHIVES	8–10	3–4 before	12–18/18	Rich, moist	○
CILANTRO/ CORIANDER	Not recommended	Anytime after	12–36/6	Light	○◑
DILL	Not recommended	4–5 before	36–48/12	Rich	○
FENNEL	4–6	Anytime after	48–80/18	Rich	○
LAVENDER, ENGLISH*	8–12	1–2 before	18–36/24	Moderately fertile, well-drained	○
LAVENDER, FRENCH	Not recommended	Not recommended	18–36/24	Moderately fertile, well-drained	○
LEMON BALM*	6–10	2–3 before	12–24/18	Rich, well-drained	○◑
LOVAGE*	6–8	2–3 before	36–72/36	Fertile, sandy	○◑
MINT	Not recommended	Not recommended	12–24/18	Rich, moist	◑
OREGANO*	6–10	Anytime after	12–24/18	Poor	○
PARSLEY*	10–12	3–4 before	18–24/6–8	Medium-rich	◑
ROSEMARY*	8–10	Anytime after	48–72/48	Not too acid	○
SAGE	6–10	1–2 before	12–48/30	Well-drained	○
SORREL	6–10	2–3 after	20–48/12–14	Rich, organic	○
SUMMER SAVORY	4–6	Anytime after	4–15/6	Medium-rich	○
SWEET CICELY	6–8	2–3 after	36–72/36	Moderately fertile, well-drained	○◑
TARRAGON, FRENCH	Not recommended	Not recommended	24–36/12	Well-drained	○◑
THYME, COMMON*	6–10	2–3 before	2–12/7–12	Fertile, well-drained	○◑

*Recommend minimum soil temperature of 70°F to germinate

** ○ FULL SUN ◑ PARTIAL SHADE

REFERENCE

Annual

Annual, biennial

Annual, biennial

Perennial

Annual

Annual

Annual

Perennial

Tender perennial

Perennial

Perennial

Perennial

Tender perennial

Biennial

Tender perennial

Perennial

Perennial

Annual

Perennial

Perennial

Perennial

DRYING HERBS

Before drying, remove any dead or diseased leaves or stems. Wash under cool water, shake off excess water, and put on a towel to dry completely. Air drying preserves an herb's essential oils; use for sturdy herbs. A microwave dries herbs more quickly, so mold is less likely to develop; use for moist, tender herbs.

HANGING METHOD: Gather four to six stems of fresh herbs in a bunch and tie with string, leaving a loop for hanging. Or, use a rubber band with a paper clip attached to it. Hang the herbs in a warm, well-ventilated area, out of direct sunlight, until dry. For herbs that have full seed heads, such as dill or coriander, use a paper bag. Punch holes in the bag for ventilation, label it, and put the herb bunch into the bag before you tie a string around the top of the bag. The average drying time is 1 to 3 weeks.

MICROWAVE METHOD: This is better for small quantities, such as a cup or two at a time. Arrange a single layer of herbs between two paper towels and put them in the microwave for 1 to 2 minutes on high power. Let the leaves cool. If they are not dry, reheat for 30 seconds and check again. Repeat as needed. Let cool. Do not overcook, or the herbs will lose their flavor.

STORING HERBS AND SPICES

FRESH HERBS: Dill and parsley will keep for about 2 weeks with stems immersed in a glass of water tented with a plastic bag. Most other fresh herbs (and greens) will keep for short periods unwashed and refrigerated in tightly sealed plastic bags with just enough moisture to prevent wilting. For longer storage, use moisture- and gas-permeable paper and cellophane. Plastic cuts off oxygen to the plants and promotes spoilage.

SPICES AND DRIED HERBS: Store in a cool, dry place.

COOKING WITH HERBS

A **BOUQUET GARNI** is usually made with bay leaves, thyme, and parsley tied with string or wrapped in cheesecloth. Use to flavor casseroles and soups. Remove after cooking.

FINES HERBES use equal amounts of fresh parsley, tarragon, chives, and chervil chopped fine. Commonly used in French cooking, they make a fine omelet or add zest to soups and sauces. Add to salads and butter sauces or sprinkle on noodles, soups, and stews.

HOW TO GROW BULBS

COMMON NAME	LATIN NAME	HARDINESS ZONE	SOIL	LIGHT*	SPACING (INCHES)
SPRING-PLANTED BULBS					
ALLIUM	*Allium*	3–10	Well-drained/moist	○	12
BEGONIA, TUBEROUS	*Begonia*	10–11	Well-drained/moist	◑●	12–15
BLAZING STAR/ GAYFEATHER	*Liatris*	7–10	Well-drained	○	6
CALADIUM	*Caladium*	10–11	Well-drained/moist	◑●	8–12
CALLA LILY	*Zantedeschia*	8–10	Well-drained/moist	○◑	8–24
CANNA	*Canna*	8–11	Well-drained/moist	○	12–24
CYCLAMEN	*Cyclamen*	7–9	Well-drained/moist	◑	4
DAHLIA	*Dahlia*	9–11	Well-drained/fertile	○	12–36
DAYLILY	*Hemerocallis*	3–10	Adaptable to most soils	○◑	12–24
FREESIA	*Freesia*	9–11	Well-drained/moist/sandy	○◑	2–4
GARDEN GLOXINIA	*Incarvillea*	4–8	Well-drained/moist	○	12
GLADIOLUS	*Gladiolus*	4–11	Well-drained/fertile	○◑	4–9
IRIS	*Iris*	3–10	Well-drained/sandy	○	3–6
LILY, ASIATIC/ORIENTAL	*Lilium*	3–8	Well-drained	○◑	8–12
PEACOCK FLOWER	*Tigridia*	8–10	Well-drained	○	5–6
SHAMROCK/SORREL	*Oxalis*	5–9	Well-drained	○◑	4–6
WINDFLOWER	*Anemone*	3–9	Well-drained/moist	○◑	3–6
FALL-PLANTED BULBS					
BLUEBELL	*Hyacinthoides*	4–9	Well-drained/fertile	○◑	4
CHRISTMAS ROSE/ HELLEBORE	*Helleborus*	4–8	Neutral–alkaline	○◑	18
CROCUS	*Crocus*	3–8	Well-drained/moist/fertile	○◑	4
DAFFODIL	*Narcissus*	3–10	Well-drained/moist/fertile	○◑	6
FRITILLARY	*Fritillaria*	3–9	Well-drained/sandy	○◑	3
GLORY OF THE SNOW	*Chionodoxa*	3–9	Well-drained/moist	○◑	3
GRAPE HYACINTH	*Muscari*	4–10	Well-drained/moist/fertile	○◑	3–4
IRIS, BEARDED	*Iris*	3–9	Well-drained	○◑	4
IRIS, SIBERIAN	*Iris*	4–9	Well-drained	○◑	4
ORNAMENTAL ONION	*Allium*	3–10	Well-drained/moist/fertile	○	12
SNOWDROP	*Galanthus*	3–9	Well-drained/moist/fertile	○◑	3
SNOWFLAKE	*Leucojum*	5–9	Well-drained/moist/sandy	○◑	4
SPRING STARFLOWER	*Ipheion uniflorum*	6–9	Well-drained loam	○◑	3–6
STAR OF BETHLEHEM	*Ornithogalum*	5–10	Well-drained/moist	○◑	2–5
STRIPED SQUILL	*Puschkinia scilloides*	3–9	Well-drained	○◑	6
TULIP	*Tulipa*	4–8	Well-drained/fertile	○◑	3–6
WINTER ACONITE	*Eranthis*	4–9	Well-drained/moist/fertile	○◑	3

REFERENCE

| | * ○ **full sun** | | ◑ **partial shade** | ● **full shade** |

DEPTH (INCHES)	BLOOMING SEASON	HEIGHT (INCHES)	NOTES
3–4	Spring to summer	6–60	Usually pest-free; a great cut flower
1–2	Summer to fall	8–18	North of Zone 10, lift in fall
4	Summer to fall	8–20	An excellent flower for drying; north of Zone 7, plant in spring, lift in fall
2	Summer	8–24	North of Zone 10, plant in spring, lift in fall
1–4	Summer	24–36	Fragrant; north of Zone 8, plant in spring, lift in fall
Level	Summer	18–60	North of Zone 8, plant in spring, lift in fall
1–2	Spring to fall	3–12	Naturalizes well in warm areas; north of Zone 7, lift in fall
4–6	Late summer	12–60	North of Zone 9, lift in fall
2	Summer	12–36	Mulch in winter in Zones 3 to 6
2	Summer	12–24	Fragrant; can be grown outdoors in warm climates
3–4	Summer	6–20	Does well in woodland settings
3–6	Early summer to early fall	12–80	North of Zone 10, lift in fall
4	Spring to late summer	3–72	Divide and replant rhizomes every two to five years
4–6	Early summer	36	Fragrant; self-sows; requires excellent drainage
4	Summer	18–24	North of Zone 8, lift in fall
2	Summer	2–12	Plant in confined area to control
2	Early summer	3–18	North of Zone 6, lift in fall
3–4	Spring	8–20	Excellent for borders, rock gardens and naturalizing
1–2	Spring	12	Hardy, but requires shelter from strong, cold winds
3	Early spring	5	Naturalizes well in grass
6	Early spring	14–24	Plant under shrubs or in a border
3	Midspring	6–30	Different species can be planted in rock gardens, woodland gardens, or borders
3	Spring	4–10	Self-sows easily; plant in rock gardens, raised beds, or under shrubs
2–3	Late winter to spring	6–12	Use as a border plant or in wildflower and rock gardens; self-sows easily
4	Early spring to early summer	3–48	Naturalizes well; a good cut flower
4	Early spring to midsummer	18–48	An excellent cut flower
3–4	Late spring to early summer	6–60	Usually pest-free; a great cut flower
3	Spring	6–12	Best when clustered and planted in an area that will not dry out in summer
4	Spring	6–18	Naturalizes well
3	Spring	4–6	Fragrant; naturalizes easily
4	Spring to summer	6–24	North of Zone 5, plant in spring, lift in fall
3	Spring	4–6	Naturalizes easily; makes an attractive edging
4–6	Early to late spring	8–30	Excellent for borders, rock gardens, and naturalizing
2–3	Late winter to spring	2–4	Self-sows and naturalizes easily

REFERENCE

SUBSTITUTIONS FOR COMMON INGREDIENTS

ITEM	QUANTITY	SUBSTITUTION
BAKING POWDER	1 teaspoon	¼ teaspoon baking soda plus ¼ teaspoon cornstarch plus ½ teaspoon cream of tartar
BUTTERMILK	1 cup	1 tablespoon lemon juice or vinegar plus milk to equal 1 cup; or 1 cup plain yogurt
CHOCOLATE, UNSWEETENED	1 ounce	3 tablespoons cocoa plus 1 tablespoon unsalted butter, shortening, or vegetable oil
CRACKER CRUMBS	¾ cup	1 cup dry bread crumbs; or 1 tablespoon quick-cooking oats (for thickening)
CREAM, HEAVY	1 cup	¾ cup milk plus ⅓ cup melted unsalted butter (this will not whip)
CREAM, LIGHT	1 cup	⅞ cup milk plus 3 tablespoons melted, unsalted butter
CREAM, SOUR	1 cup	⅞ cup buttermilk or plain yogurt plus 3 tablespoons melted, unsalted butter
CREAM, WHIPPING	1 cup	⅔ cup well-chilled evaporated milk, whipped; or 1 cup nonfat dry milk powder whipped with 1 cup ice water
EGG	1 whole	2 yolks plus 1 tablespoon cold water; or 3 tablespoons vegetable oil plus 1 tablespoon water (for baking); or 2 to 3 tablespoons mayonnaise (for cakes)
EGG WHITE	1 white	2 teaspoons meringue powder plus 3 tablespoons water, combined
FLOUR, ALL-PURPOSE	1 cup	1 cup plus 3 tablespoons cake flour (not advised for cookies or quick breads); or 1 cup self-rising flour (omit baking powder and salt from recipe)
FLOUR, CAKE	1 cup	1 cup minus 3 tablespoons sifted all-purpose flour plus 3 tablespoons cornstarch
FLOUR, SELF-RISING	1 cup	1 cup all-purpose flour plus 1½ teaspoons baking powder plus ¼ teaspoon salt
HERBS, DRIED	1 teaspoon	1 tablespoon fresh, minced and packed
HONEY	1 cup	1¼ cups sugar plus ½ cup liquid called for in recipe (such as water or oil)
KETCHUP	1 cup	1 cup tomato sauce plus ¼ cup sugar plus 3 tablespoons apple-cider vinegar plus ½ teaspoon salt plus pinch of ground cloves combined; or 1 cup chili sauce
LEMON JUICE	1 teaspoon	½ teaspoon vinegar
MAYONNAISE	1 cup	1 cup sour cream or plain yogurt; or 1 cup cottage cheese (puréed)
MILK, SKIM	1 cup	⅓ cup instant nonfat dry milk plus ¾ cup water

REFERENCE

ITEM	QUANTITY	SUBSTITUTION
MILK, TO SOUR	1 cup	1 tablespoon vinegar or lemon juice plus milk to equal 1 cup. Stir and let stand 5 minutes.
MILK, WHOLE	1 cup	½ cup evaporated whole milk plus ½ cup water; or ¾ cup 2 percent milk plus ¼ cup half-and-half
MOLASSES	1 cup	1 cup honey or dark corn syrup
MUSTARD, DRY	1 teaspoon	1 tablespoon prepared mustard less 1 teaspoon liquid from recipe
OAT BRAN	1 cup	1 cup wheat bran or rice bran or wheat germ
OATS, OLD-FASHIONED	1 cup	1 cup steel-cut Irish or Scotch oats
QUINOA	1 cup	1 cup millet or couscous (whole wheat cooks faster) or bulgur
SUGAR, DARK-BROWN	1 cup	1 cup light-brown sugar, packed; or 1 cup granulated sugar plus 2 to 3 tablespoons molasses
SUGAR, GRANULATED	1 cup	1 cup firmly packed brown sugar; or 1¾ cups confectioners' sugar (makes baked goods less crisp); or 1 cup superfine sugar
SUGAR, LIGHT-BROWN	1 cup	1 cup granulated sugar plus 1 to 2 tablespoons molasses; or ½ cup dark-brown sugar plus ½ cup granulated sugar
SWEETENED CONDENSED MILK	1 can (14 oz.)	1 cup evaporated milk plus 1¼ cups granulated sugar. Combine and heat until sugar dissolves.
VANILLA BEAN	1-inch bean	1 teaspoon vanilla extract
VINEGAR, APPLE-CIDER	—	malt, white-wine, or rice vinegar
VINEGAR, BALSAMIC	1 tablespoon	1 tablespoon red- or white-wine vinegar plus ½ teaspoon sugar
VINEGAR, RED-WINE	—	white-wine, sherry, champagne, or balsamic vinegar
VINEGAR, RICE	—	apple-cider, champagne, or white-wine vinegar
VINEGAR, WHITE-WINE	—	apple-cider, champagne, fruit (raspberry), rice, or red-wine vinegar
YEAST	1 cake (⅗ oz.)	1 package (¼ ounce) or 1 scant tablespoon active dried yeast
YOGURT, PLAIN	1 cup	1 cup sour cream (thicker; less tart) or buttermilk (thinner; use in baking, dressings, sauces)

REFERENCE

AROUND THE HOUSE

TYPES OF FAT

One way to minimize your total blood cholesterol is to manage the amount and types of fat in your diet. Aim for monounsaturated and polyunsaturated fats; avoid saturated and trans fats.

MONOUNSATURATED FAT lowers LDL (bad cholesterol) and may raise HDL (good cholesterol) or leave it unchanged; found in almonds, avocados, canola oil, cashews, olive oil, peanut oil, and peanuts.

POLYUNSATURATED FAT lowers LDL and may lower HDL; includes omega-3 and omega-6 fatty acids; found in corn oil, cottonseed oil, fish such as salmon and tuna, safflower oil, sesame seeds, soybeans, and sunflower oil.

SATURATED FAT raises both LDL and HDL; found in chocolate, cocoa butter, coconut oil, dairy products (milk, butter, cheese, ice cream), egg yolks, palm oil, and red meat.

TRANS FAT raises LDL and lowers HDL; a type of fat common in many processed foods, such as most margarines (especially stick), vegetable shortening, partially hydrogenated vegetable oil, many commercial fried foods (doughnuts, french fries), and commercial baked goods (cookies, crackers, cakes).

Calorie-Burning Comparisons

If you hustle through your chores to get to the fitness center, relax. You're getting a great workout already. The left-hand column lists "chore" exercises, the middle column shows the number of calories burned per minute per pound of body weight, and the right-hand column lists comparable "recreational" exercises. For example, a 150-pound person forking straw bales burns 9.45 calories per minute, the same workout he or she would get playing basketball.

Chore	Cal	Recreation
Chopping with an ax, fast	0.135	Skiing, cross country, uphill
Climbing hills, with 44-pound load	0.066	Swimming, crawl, fast
Digging trenches	0.065	Skiing, cross country, steady walk
Forking straw bales	0.063	Basketball
Chopping down trees	0.060	Football
Climbing hills, with 9-pound load	0.058	Swimming, crawl, slow
Sawing by hand	0.055	Skiing, cross country, moderate
Mowing lawns	0.051	Horseback riding, trotting
Scrubbing floors	0.049	Tennis
Shoveling coal	0.049	Aerobic dance, medium
Hoeing	0.041	Weight training, circuit training
Stacking firewood	0.040	Weight lifting, free weights
Shoveling grain	0.038	Golf
Painting houses	0.035	Walking, normal pace, asphalt road
Weeding	0.033	Table tennis
Shopping for food	0.028	Cycling, 5.5 mph
Mopping floors	0.028	Fishing
Washing windows	0.026	Croquet
Raking	0.025	Dancing, ballroom
Driving a tractor	0.016	Drawing, standing position

FREEZER STORAGE TIME

(freezer temperature 0°F or colder)

PRODUCT	MONTHS IN FREEZER
FRESH MEAT	
Beef	6 to 12
Lamb	6 to 9
Veal	6 to 9
Pork	4 to 6
Ground beef, veal, lamb, pork	3 to 4
Frankfurters	1 to 2
Sausage, fresh pork	1 to 2
Ready-to-serve luncheon meats	Not recommended
FRESH POULTRY	
Chicken, turkey (whole)	12
Chicken, turkey (pieces)	6 to 9
Cornish game hen, game birds	6 to 9
Giblets	3 to 4
COOKED POULTRY	
Breaded, fried	4
Pieces, plain	4
Pieces covered with broth, gravy	6
FRESH FRUIT (PREPARED FOR FREEZING)	
All fruit except those listed below	10 to 12
Avocados, bananas, plantains	3
Lemons, limes, oranges	4 to 6
FRESH VEGETABLES (PREPARED FOR FREEZING)	
Beans, beets, bok choy, broccoli, brussels sprouts, cabbage, carrots, cauliflower, celery, corn, greens, kohlrabi, leeks, mushrooms, okra, onions, peas, peppers, soybeans, spinach, summer squashes	10 to 12
Asparagus, rutabagas, turnips	8 to 10
Artichokes, eggplant	6 to 8
Tomatoes (overripe or sliced)	2
Bamboo shoots, cucumbers, endive, lettuce, radishes, watercress	Not recommended
CHEESE (except those listed below)	6
Cottage cheese, cream cheese, feta, goat, fresh mozzarella, Neufchâtel, Parmesan, processed cheese (opened)	Not recommended

PRODUCT	MONTHS IN FREEZER
DAIRY PRODUCTS	
Margarine (not diet)	12
Butter	6 to 9
Cream, half-and-half	4
Milk	3
Ice cream	1 to 2

FREEZING HINTS

FOR MEALS, remember that a quart container holds four servings, and a pint container holds two servings.

TO PREVENT STICKING, spread the food to be frozen (berries, hamburgers, cookies, etc.) on a cookie sheet and freeze until solid. Then place in plastic bags and freeze.

LABEL FOODS for easy identification. Write the name of the food, number of servings, and date of freezing on containers or bags.

FREEZE FOODS as quickly as possible by placing them directly against the sides of the freezer.

ARRANGE FREEZER into sections for each food category.

IF POWER IS INTERRUPTED, or if the freezer is not operating normally, do not open the freezer door. Food in a loaded freezer will usually stay frozen for 2 days if the freezer door remains closed during that time period.

REFERENCE

PLASTICS

In your quest to go green, use this guide to use and sort plastic. The number, usually found with a triangle symbol on a container, indicates the type of resin used to produce the plastic. Visit **EARTH911.COM** for recycling information in your state.

NUMBER 1 · *PETE or PET (polyethylene terephthalate)*
IS USED IN . . . . microwavable food trays; salad dressing, soft drink, water, and juice bottles
STATUS . . . . hard to clean; absorbs bacteria and flavors; avoid reusing
IS RECYCLED TO MAKE. . . carpet, furniture, new containers, Polar fleece

PETE

NUMBER 2 · *HDPE (high-density polyethylene)*
IS USED IN . . . . household cleaner and shampoo bottles, milk jugs, yogurt tubs
STATUS . . . . transmits no known chemicals into food
IS RECYCLED TO MAKE. . . detergent bottles, fencing, floor tiles, pens

HDPE

NUMBER 3 · *V or PVC (vinyl)*
IS USED IN . . . . cooking oil bottles, clear food packaging, mouthwash bottles
STATUS . . . . is believed to contain phalates that interfere with hormonal development; avoid
IS RECYCLED TO MAKE. . . cables, mudflaps, paneling, roadway gutters

V

NUMBER 4 · *LDPE (low-density polyethylene)*
IS USED IN . . . . bread and shopping bags, carpet, clothing, furniture
STATUS . . . . transmits no known chemicals into food
IS RECYCLED TO MAKE. . . envelopes, floor tiles, lumber, trash-can liners

LDPE

NUMBER 5 · *PP (polypropylene)*
IS USED IN . . . . ketchup bottles, medicine and syrup bottles, drinking straws
STATUS . . . . transmits no known chemicals into food
IS RECYCLED TO MAKE. . . battery cables, brooms, ice scrapers, rakes

PP

NUMBER 6 · *PS (polystyrene)*
IS USED IN . . . . disposable cups and plates, egg cartons, take-out containers
STATUS . . . . is believed to leach styrene, a possible human carcinogen, into food; avoid
IS RECYCLED TO MAKE. . . foam packaging, insulation, light switchplates, rulers

PS

NUMBER 7 · *Other (miscellaneous)*
IS USED IN . . . . 3- and 5-gallon water jugs, nylon, some food containers
STATUS . . . . contains bisphenol A, which has been linked to heart disease and obesity; avoid
IS RECYCLED TO MAKE. . . . custom-made products

OTHER

HOW MUCH DO YOU NEED?

WALLPAPER

Before choosing your wallpaper, keep in mind that wallpaper with little or no pattern to match at the seams and the ceiling will be the easiest to apply, thus resulting in the least amount of wasted wallpaper. If you choose a patterned wallpaper, a small repeating pattern will result in less waste than a large repeating pattern. And a pattern that is aligned horizontally (matching on each column of paper) will waste less than one that drops or alternates its pattern (matching on every other column).

TO DETERMINE THE AMOUNT OF WALL SPACE YOU'RE COVERING:

• Measure the length of each wall, add these figures together, and multiply by the height of the walls to get the area (square footage) of the room's walls.

• Calculate the square footage of each door, window, and other opening in the room. Add these figures together and subtract the total from the area of the room's walls.

• Take that figure and multiply by 1.15, to account for a waste rate of about 15 percent in your wallpaper project. You'll end up with a target amount to purchase when you shop.

• Wallpaper is sold in single, double, and triple rolls. Coverage can vary, so be sure to refer to the roll's label for the proper square footage. (The average coverage for a double roll, for example, is 56 square feet.) After choosing a paper, divide the coverage figure (from the label) into the total square footage of the walls of the room you're papering. Round the answer up to the nearest whole number. This is the number of rolls you need to buy.

• Save leftover wallpaper rolls, carefully wrapped to keep clean.

INTERIOR PAINT

Estimate your room size and paint needs before you go to the store. Running out of a custom color halfway through the job could mean disaster. For the sake of the following exercise, assume that you have a 10x15-foot room with an 8-foot ceiling. The room has two doors and two windows.

FOR WALLS

Measure the total distance (perimeter) around the room:

(10 ft. + 15 ft.) x 2 = 50 ft.

Multiply the perimeter by the ceiling height to get the total wall area:

50 ft. x 8 ft. = 400 sq. ft.

Doors are usually 21 square feet (there are two in this exercise):

21 sq. ft. x 2 = 42 sq. ft.

Windows average 15 square feet (there are two in this exercise):

15 sq. ft. x 2 = 30 sq. ft.

Take the total wall area and subtract the area for the doors and windows to get the wall surface to be painted:

400 sq. ft. (wall area)
- 42 sq. ft. (doors)
- 30 sq. ft. (windows)
328 sq. ft.

As a rule of thumb, one gallon of quality paint will usually cover 400 square feet. One quart will cover 100 square feet. Because you need to cover 328 square feet in this example, one gallon will be adequate to give one coat of paint to the walls. (Coverage will be affected by the porosity and texture of the surface. In addition, bright colors may require a minimum of two coats.)

AROUND THE HOUSE

METRIC CONVERSION

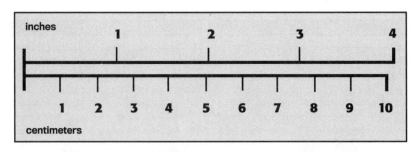

U.S. MEASURE	X THIS = NUMBER	METRIC EQUIVALENT	METRIC MEASURE	X THIS = NUMBER	U.S. EQUIVALENT
inch	2.54	centimeter		0.39	inch
foot	30.48	centimeter		0.033	foot
yard	0.91	meter		1.09	yard
mile	1.61	kilometer		0.62	mile
square inch	6.45	square centimeter		0.15	square inch
square foot	0.09	square meter		10.76	square foot
square yard	0.8	square meter		1.2	square yard
square mile	2.59	square kilometer		0.39	square mile
acre	0.4	hectare		2.47	acre
ounce	28.0	gram		0.035	ounce
pound	0.45	kilogram		2.2	pound
short ton (2,000 pounds)	0.91	metric ton		1.10	short ton
ounce	30.0	milliliter		0.034	ounce
pint	0.47	liter		2.1	pint
quart	0.95	liter		1.06	quart
gallon	3.8	liter		0.26	gallon

If you know the U.S. measurement and want to convert it to metric, multiply it by the number in the left shaded column (example: 1 inch equals 2.54 centimeters). If you know the metric measurement, multiply it by the number in the right shaded column (example: 2 meters equals 2.18 yards).

Where Do You Fit in Your Family Tree?

Technically it's known as consanguinity; that is, the quality or state of being related by blood or descended from a common ancestor. These relationships are shown below for the genealogy of six generations of one family. *–family tree information courtesy of Frederick H. Rohles*

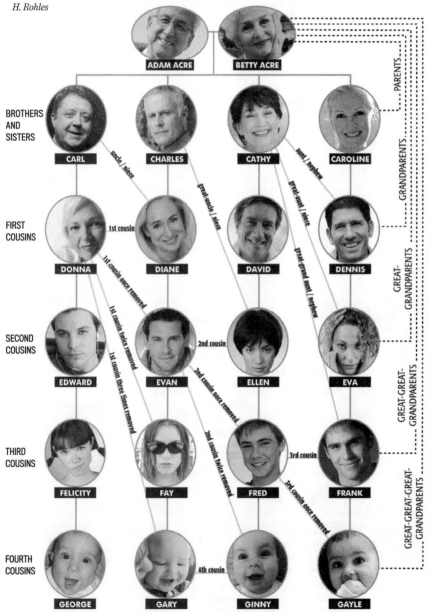

REFERENCE

The Golden Rule
(It's true in all faiths.)

BRAHMANISM:
This is the sum of duty: Do naught unto others which would cause you pain if done to you.
Mahabharata 5:1517

BUDDHISM:
Hurt not others in ways that you yourself would find hurtful.
Udana-Varga 5:18

CHRISTIANITY:
All things whatsoever ye would that men should do to you, do ye even so to them; for this is the law and the prophets.
Matthew 7:12

CONFUCIANISM:
Surely it is the maxim of loving-kindness: Do not unto others what you would not have them do unto you.
Analects 15:23

ISLAM:
No one of you is a believer until he desires for his brother that which he desires for himself.
Sunnah

JUDAISM:
What is hateful to you, do not to your fellow man. That is the entire Law; all the rest is commentary.
Talmud, Shabbat 31a

TAOISM:
Regard your neighbor's gain as your own gain and your neighbor's loss as your own loss.
T'ai Shang Kan Ying P'ien

ZOROASTRIANISM:
That nature alone is good which refrains from doing unto another whatsoever is not good for itself.
Dadistan-i-dinik 94:5
—courtesy of Elizabeth Pool

FAMOUS LAST WORDS

Waiting, are they? Waiting, are they? Well–let 'em wait.
(To an attending doctor who attempted to comfort him by saying, "General, I fear the angels are waiting for you.")
–Ethan Allen, American Revolutionary general, d. February 12, 1789

A dying man can do nothing easy.
–Benjamin Franklin, American statesman, d. April 17, 1790

Now I shall go to sleep. Good night.
–Lord George Byron, English writer, d. April 19, 1824

Is it the Fourth?
–Thomas Jefferson, 3rd U.S. president, d. July 4, 1826

Thomas Jefferson–still survives . . .
(Actually, Jefferson had died earlier that same day.)
–John Adams, 2nd U.S. president, d. July 4, 1826

Friends, applaud. The comedy is finished.
–Ludwig van Beethoven, German-Austrian composer, d. March 26, 1827

Moose . . . Indian . . .
–Henry David Thoreau, American writer, d. May 6, 1862

Go on, get out–last words are for fools who haven't said enough.
(To his housekeeper, who urged him to tell her his last words so she could write them down for posterity.)
–Karl Marx, German political philosopher, d. March 14, 1883

Is it not meningitis?
–Louisa M. Alcott, American writer, d. March 6, 1888

How were the receipts today at Madison Square Garden?
–P. T. Barnum, American entrepreneur, d. April 7, 1891

Turn up the lights, I don't want to go home in the dark.
–O. Henry (William Sidney Porter), American writer, d. June 4, 1910

Get my swan costume ready.
–Anna Pavlova, Russian ballerina, d. January 23, 1931

Is everybody happy? I want everybody to be happy. I know I'm happy.
–Ethel Barrymore, American actress, d. June 18, 1959

I'm bored with it all.
(Before slipping into a coma. He died 9 days later.)
–Winston Churchill, English statesman, d. January 24, 1965

You be good. You'll be in tomorrow. I love you.
–Alex, highly intelligent African Gray parrot, d. September 6, 2007